Spatial 'Christianisation' in Context: Strategic Intramural Building in Rome from the 4th–7th c. AD

Michael Mulryan

Archaeopress Archaeology

Archaeopress
Gordon House
276 Banbury Road
Oxford OX2 7ED

www.archaeopress.com

ISBN 978 1 78491 020 4
ISBN 978 1 78491 021 1 (e-Pdf)

© Archaeopress and M Mulryan 2014

Cover Image: detail of apse mosaic of S. Prassede, Rome. Pope Paschal I holding a model of the church. Detail of author photo.

All rights reserved. No part of this book may be reproduced, stored in retrieval system, or transmitted, in any form or by any means, electronic, mechanical, photocopying or otherwise, without the prior written permission of the copyright owners.

Printed and bound in Great Britain by Marston Book Services Ltd, Oxfordshire

This book is available direct from Archaeopress or from our website www.archaeopress.com

Acknowledgements

This book began its life as a Ph.D thesis at University College London in 2003 on the topic of the sacred (both 'pagan' and Christian) landscape of late antique Rome from Constantine up to the end of the episcopate of Sixtus III (A.D. 440), supervised by Michael Crawford and Benet Salway. Such a project took some time to formulate. A few years earlier, it was working on my MA thesis, also at UCL, with John North, that inspired me to concentrate on the religious history of the Roman world, which in turn led me to the fascinating era now defined as late antiquity. It was Antonio Sennis who suggested I study Rome, and the pieces began to fall into place. However, none of this would have been possible without the encouragement and support of my late father who I owe so much. As important has been the support from my mother and sister. Also, friends, colleagues and staff within the history department at UCL and the Classics departments at KCL and Royal Holloway have provided excellent sounding boards for my ideas. Friends outside the academic bubble have kept me sane, level headed and given me a valuable sense of perspective on this whole process. Their interest as well as bewilderment has been an important tonic. I also need to thank the staff and members of the London Library for helping me pay the rent and introducing me into a wonderful labyrinthine world of bookish delights. This hidden gem was also a valuable library resource. On this note, the staff and resources at the Institute of Classical Studies, the Institute of Historical Research and the Warburg Institute, all in London, were invaluable. It was the UCL Graduate School Research Projects Fund and the University of London Central Research Fund that allowed me to spend some crucial time at the British School at Rome in 2005 and 2006. Particular thanks here must go to Maria Pia Malvezzi for making it possible for me to see much of the archaeology under discussion below. I have also been inspired by the devotion shown towards late antique scholarship by Luke Lavan, whom I met in Leuven in 2005. Working with him since 2008 at Ostia has clarified several thoughts for this book concerning the interpretation of the archaeological evidence. It has also led to the delay in the production and publication of this book, which was no bad thing. My work has moved on quite a bit since the completion of my thesis in 2008, and the decision to cut it in half, to focus solely on Christian buildings, and lengthen the timescale, has led to a tighter and more coherent argument. Ten months spent at the British School at Rome in 2011, working on Ostia, also led to the attendance of several conferences and giving of papers that have helped refine this book. Another important influence has been the work of Simon Malmberg, whom I met at this time. I also need to thank my wonderful girlfriend Ada Nifosi for giving me the final push to finish the book.

I would describe myself as an historian who largely uses archaeology, rather than just texts. I'm interested in the everyday and mundane aspects of the ancient world, the human story of how ordinary people lived their lives, something largely perceptible only through archaeological evidence. The precise phasing and chronology of a building or landscape interests me, but more so when it tells us how the people in it may have thought and acted. Being born and raised in the Roman colonia of Colchester, surrounded by Roman material, makes my interests unsurprising perhaps, but it was the volunteering I did with Colchester Archaeological Trust in the mid to late 1990s that entrenched this passion and taught me the basics of archaeological method and excavation. Other names that deserve a mention and that played a part directly or indirectly in the creation of this book are: Steve Nutt, Dave Huggon, David Nightingale, Christopher Chaffin, Charlotte Roueché, and particularly Richard Alston and Massimiliano Ghilardi for reading through a draft. Abby George helped immensely with the creation of most of the figures in the book, and her professionalism and work was crucial. Final thanks must also go to David Davison at Archaeopress for his patience and assistance. Any remaining errors or infelicities in the text are all, of course, my own.

Table of Contents

Acknowledgements i
0. Introduction 1
    0.1 Problems of Definition 4
    0.2 Historiography 5
1. Building a Titulus-Basilica in Late Antique Rome 8
    1.1 Building in the Republic and Earlier Empire 9
    1.2 Christian Building in the Late Empire 10
    1.3 The Evolution of the State Building Bureaucracy from Diocletian to Sixtus III.......................... 11
    1.4 The System in Practice 14
        1.4.1 An Imperial Building Contract in Late Antiquity: The Reconstruction of the pons Probi and the Rebuilding of the Basilica to St. Paul... 15
        1.4.2 The Titulus Vestinae 17
        1.4.3 Other Christian Building 18
            1.4.3.1 Aristocratic Lay Patronage 18
            1.4.3.2 Clerical Building Managers or Founders 20
            1.4.3.3 Patronage by the Bishop.. 21
            1.4.3.4 Imperial Patronage 23
    1.5 Conclusion 24
2. Christian Basilicas and Baths 25
    2.1 A Water-Filled City. The Balnea. 27
        2.1.1 Case Studies 27
            2.1.1.1 Donated Bath-Baptisteries?... 27
            2.1.1.2 The Balnea-Basilica 28
                2.1.1.2.1 Titulus Pudentis 29
                2.1.1.2.2 Basilica Eudoxia 31
                2.1.1.2.3 Titulus Sanctae Caeciliae... 33
    2.2 Christian Basilicas and Imperial Thermae 34
        2.2.1 Thermae Antoninianae... 35
        2.2.2 Thermae Diocletiani 38
        2.2.3 Thermae Traiani and Suranae... 40
            2.2.3.1 Thermae Traiani 40
            2.2.3.2 Thermae Suranae 41
    2.3 Early Medieval Church Baths 41
    2.4 Conclusion 42
3. Striving for Attention 43
    3.1 The Christian basilica on the Main Road.. 43
    3.2 Clustering off Main Roads 44
        3.2.1 Titulus Iulii trans Tiberim and S. Chrysogoni along the Via Aurelia 44
        3.2.2 Titulus Fasciolae and Basilica Crescentiana off the Via Appia 45
    3.3 Encroachment onto/into Public Spaces 47
        3.3.1 Apsidal Road Encroachment.. 47
            3.3.1.1 Titulus Marci... 48
            3.3.1.2 Titulus Marcelli 50
            3.3.1.3 S. Maria in via Lata... 50
        3.3.2 Encroachment onto Public Spaces/Roads 53
            3.3.2.1 Titulus Sancti Laurentii in Lucina 53
            3.3.2.2 Santa Maria Maggiore 56
            3.3.2.3 Oratory/Arian Basilica of the 'Monte della Giustizia' 57
            3.3.2.4 The Oratory of the Holy Cross at the Lateran 58
    3.4 Entrances on Main Roads 59
        3.4.1 Titulus Gai/S. Susanna 59
        3.4.2 Titulus Pudentis/S. Pudenziana.. 61
        3.4.3 Titulus Mattheus/S. Matteo 62
        3.4.4 Titulus Fasciolae/SS. Nereo ed Achilleo 63
        3.4.5 Titulus Vestinae/S. Vitale.. 63

- 3.5 Reuse of Prestige Public Buildings 63
  - 3.5.1 Basilica sanctorum Cosmae et Damiani/SS. Cosma e Damiano 63
  - 3.5.2 Ecclesia beati Adriani/S. Adriano 64
- 3.6 High Places: Macro Visibility 64
  - 3.6.1 The Christian Basilica on the Hill 64
  - 3.6.2 Basilica Sanctae Mariae on the Cispian Hill 65
  - 3.6.3 Titulus Sabinae/S. Sabina on the Aventine Hill 66
  - 3.6.4 Sanctus Stephanus/Santo Stefano Rotondo on the Caelian Hill 67
  - 3.6.5 The Palatine 68
- 3.7 Conclusion 69

4. The Tituli of Equitius and Sylvester in the Subura 71
- 4.1 What, Where and How Many? 71
  - 4.1.1 The Written Evidence 71
  - 4.1.2 The Archaeology 72
    - 4.1.2.1 The Roman Hall 72
    - 4.1.2.2 Discoveries Elsewhere: the Titulus Silvestri? 74
  - 4.1.3 The Severan Plan Evidence 76
    - 4.1.3.1 The Titulus Silvestri on the Severan Plan? 77
    - 4.1.3.2 The diaconia Sancti Silvestri et Sancti Martini 78
  - 4.1.4 Conclusion 79
- 4.2 The Surrounding Neighbourhood 80
  - 4.2.1 West of the Tituli 80
  - 4.2.2 East of the Tituli 82
- 4.3 Conclusion 84

5. Some Other 4th-7th Century Intramural Christian Basilicas in their Urban Context 86
- 5.1 Damasus and the Circus 86
  - 5.1.1 Titulus Damasi 86
  - 5.1.2 Titulus Anastasiae 89
  - 5.1.3 Conclusion 91
- 5.2 Christian basilicas and Important Cultic Sites 91
  - 5.2.1 Titulus Marci 92
  - 5.2.2 Titulus Anastasiae 93
- 5.3 Centres of Congregation 95
  - 5.3.1 Sacellum Sanctae Agnetis Agonis/S. Agnese in Agone 95
  - 5.3.2 SS. Quirico e Giulitta 96
- 5.4 Conclusion 97

6. Conclusion 98
Bibliography 100
- Ancient Sources 100
- Secondary Sources 101

List of Figures

Figure 1: Rome with location of church-basilicas and *balnea*. Drawn by Abby George from a base map in Reekmans L. 'L'Implantation monumentale chrétienne dans le paysage urbain de Rome de 300 à 850', in *Actes du IXe Congrès internationale d'archéologie chrétienne* (Rome 1989) 861-915. 3

Figure 2a: Photo of the nave of S. Pudenziana during excavations (Soprintendenza ai monumenti del Lazio 4968), in Nash E. *Pictorial Dictionary of Ancient Rome,* vol. 2 (London 1962) 465. 30

Figure 2b: Photo of the nave of S. Pudenziana during excavations: detail of brick-faced water tank (Soprintendenza ai monumenti del Lazio), reproduced in CBCR 3.289. 30

Figure 3: Plan of S. Pudenziana with outline of structures beneath nave in hashed lines. Drawn by Abby George from original plan in CBCR 3. table 14. 31

Figure 4: Plan of S. Pietro in Vincoli with bath and house substructures. Drawn by Abby George from original plan by E. Scoponi in Casti G. B. and Zandri G. *San Pietro in Vincoli* (Rome 1999) 48. 32

Figure 5: Photo of the nave of S. Pietro in Vincoli during excavations showing an apse of the baths (Soprintendenza ai monumenti del Lazio), reproduced in CBCR 3.43 (Italian edn.). 33

Figure 6: Section of the south wall of S. Pietro in Vincoli showing triple arcaded entrance. Drawn by Abby George from original section by E. Scoponi in Casti G. B. and Zandri G. *San Pietro in Vincoli* (Rome 1999) 80. 34

Figure 7: Plan of excavations beneath S. Caecilia. Drawn by Abby George from original plan in Parmegiani N. and Pronti A. 'Complesso archeologico sotto la basilica di S. Cecilia in Trastevere', *BullCom* 93 (1989-90) 107-12. 35

Figure 8: Detail of plate 42 and SS. Nereo ed Achilleo, in Lanciani R. *Forma Urbis Romae* (Milan 1893-1901). 36

Figure 9: SS. Nereo ed Achilleo and the Baths of Caracalla. Author photo. 37

Figure 10: Plan of S. Sisto Vecchio. Drawn by Abby George from original plan in Webb M. *The Churches and Catacombs of Early Christian Rome* (Brighton 2001) 204. 37

Figure 11: Detail of Du Pérac map of Rome from 1577, taken from Frutaz A. P. *Le piante di Roma*, vol. 2 (Rome 1962) CXXVII.7, tav. 254. Reproduced with the kind permission of the Istituto Nazionale di Studi Romani. ... 39

Figure 12: Detail of plate 10 and NE corner of Baths of Diocletian, in Lanciani R. *Forma Urbis Romae* (Milan 1893-1901). 40

Figure 13: Detail of plate 27 and S. Maria in Trastevere and S. Callisto, in Lanciani R. *Forma Urbis Romae* (Milan 1893-1901). 45

Figure 14: Plan of the Palaeo-Christian S. Marco. Drawn by Abby George from a base plan by Lucrezia Spera, in Cecchelli M. 'La basilica di S. Marco a Piazza Venezia (Roma): nuove scoperte e indagni', in *Akten des XII. Internationalen Kongresses für Christliche Archäologie*, edd. E. Dassmann and J. Engemann (Münster 1995) 642, fig.2. 48

Figure 15a: The Palaeo-Christian S. Marco, showing the apse over the road, looking west. Author photo. 49

Figure 15b: The Palaeo-Christian S. Marco, showing the road and the basilica's outer wall, looking east. Author photo. 49

Figure 16: Plan of S. Marcello in Corso showing results of latest excavations. Drawn by Abby George from a base plan in Episcopo S. 'Il battistero della basilica di S. Marcello a Roma fra tarda antichità e medioevo', in *Tardo antico e alto Medioevo. Filologia, storia, archeologia, arte*, ed. M. Rotili (Naples 2009) 235-306.. 51

Figure 17: Detail of plate 15 in Lanciani R. *Forma Urbis Romae* (Milan 1893-1901). S. Marcello al Corso and the via Flaminia, with additions by the author (4th century basilica in black). 51

Figure 18: Plan of porticus west of the via Flaminia with locations of S. Maria in via Lata and the Arcus Novus. Drawn by Abby George from a base plan by Spencer Corbett in CBCR 3.76, fig. 69 (English edn.). 52

Figure 19: Plan of northern Campus Martius with earlier reconstructions of a sundial by Buchner and the location of the obelisk here by Schütz. S. Lorenzo in Lucina and location of probable meridian line also shown. Drawn by Abby George from a base plan in Heslin P. 'Augustus, Domitian and the so-called Horologium Augusti', JRS 97 (2007) 7, fig. I. 54

Figure 20: Plan of area of S. Lorenzo in Lucina showing earlier insula and probable meridian line basin. Drawn by Abby George from a base plan in Rakob F. 'Die Urbanisierung des nördlichen Marsfeldes. Neue Forschungen im Areal des Horologium Augusti', in *L'Urbs: espace urbain et histoire (Ier siècle av. J.-C.- IIIe siècle ap. J.-C.)* (Rome 1987) 699, fig. 5 (687-712). 56

Figure 21: Plan of area of S. Maria Maggiore with possible streets. Drawn by Abby George from a base plan by Spencer Corbett in CBCR 3.12, fig. 2 (English edn.). 57

Figure 22: Detail of plate 17 and Oratory of the Monte della Giustizia (circled), in Lanciani R. *Forma Urbis Romae* (Milan 1893-1901). 58

Figure 23: Plan of Oratory of the Holy Cross and preceding roads and structures. Drawn by Abby George from a a base plan in Johnson M. 'The fifth century oratory of the Holy Cross at the Lateran in Rome', *Architectura* 25.2 (1995) 128-55 (fig. 20)... 59

Figure 24: Phase plan of S. Susanna showing substructures. Drawn by Abby George, with additions by the author, from a base plan by Spencer Corbett and Wolfgang Frankl, in CBCR 4. 243-66 fig. 15 (English edn.)............ 60

Figure 25: Detail of plate 17 showing S. Pudenziana and ancient road, in Lanciani R. *Forma Urbis Romae* (Milan 1893-1901). 61

Figure 26: Detail of plate 30 showing S. Matteo and ancient road, in Lanciani R. *Forma Urbis Romae* (Milan 1893-1901)... 62

Figure 27: Detail of plate 16 showing the titulus Vestinae and road, in Lanciani R. *Forma Urbis Romae* (Milan 1893-1901). 63

Figure 28: Plan of eastern part of city showing S. Maria Maggiore and surrounding hills and roads. Drawn by Abby George from a base plan in Reekmans L. 'L'Implantation monumentale chrétienne dans le paysage urbain de Rome de 300 à 850', in *Actes du IXe Congrès internationale d'archéologie chrétienne* (Rome 1989) 861-915. 65

Figure 29: Detail of plate 33 showing S. Sabina and local topography, in Lanciani R. *Forma Urbis Romae* (Milan 1893-1901). 67

Figure 30: Plan of S. Sabina and surrounding archaeology. Drawn by Abby George from a base plan in Darsy F. M. D. *Recherches archéologiques à Sainte-Sabine sur l'Aventin: géologie, topographie, sanctuaires archaïques, culte isiaque, ensemble architectural paléochrétien* (Vatican City 1968) 52, fig.2. 68

Figure 31: Plan of S. Stefano Rotondo and surrounding ancient structures. Drawn by Abby George from the base plans in plate 36 in Lanciani R. Forma Urbis Romae (Milan 1893-1901) and Brandenburg H. and Pál J. edd. *Santo Stefano Rotondo in Roma: archeologia, storia dell'arte, restauro; atti del convegno internazionale, Roma 10-13 ottobre 1996*, (Wiesbaden 2000) fig. 33, tafel. 13. 69

Figure 32: Plan of the hall next to the current S. Martino ai Monti. Drawn by Abby George from a base plan in Claridge A. *Rome: an Oxford Archaeological Guide* (Oxford 1998) 301, fig. 147. 73

Figure 33: Detail of plate 23 showing S. Martino ai Monti and surrounding archaeology, in Lanciani R. *Forma Urbis Romae* (Milan 1893-1901)... 74

Figure 34: Photo of trench, with finds, just east of apse of S. Martino ai Monti. Courtesy of the British School at Rome: The BSR Photographic Archive, Bulwer Collection, misc.33.. 75

Figure 35: Sections of the Severan Plan west of S. Martino ai Monti. Drawn by Abby George from a base illustration in Rodríguez Almeida A. 'Aggiornamento topografico dei colli Oppio, Cispio e Viminale seconda la *Forma urbis marmorea*', RendPontAcc 48 (1975-76) 263-78. 76

Figure 36: Sections of the Severan Plan around and to the east of S. Martino ai Monti. Drawn by Abby George from a base illustration in Rodríguez Almeida A. 'Aggiornamento topografico dei colli Oppio, Cispio e Viminale seconda la *Forma urbis marmorea*', RendPontAcc 48 (1975-76) 263-78........................... 77

Figure 37: Section of east wall of S. Martino ai Monti showing Roman walls. Drawn by Abby George from a base section by Spencer Corbett (using a survey by Wolfgang Frankl), in CBCR 3...................................... 83

Figure 38: Reconstructed plan of the 4th century S. Lorenzo in Damaso with surrounding structures and roads. Drawn by Abby George from a base illustration by G. Schingo, in Frommel C. L. and Pentiricci M. edd. *L'antica basilica di San Lorenzo in Damaso: indagini archeologiche nel Palazzo della Cancelleria (1988-1993)*, 2 vols. (Rome 2009) 270, fig. 4. 87

Figure 39: Plans of the different phases of the ancient structures on the site of S. Lorenzo in Damaso. Drawn by Abby George from base plans by G. Schingo, in Frommel C. L. and Pentiricci M. edd. *L'antica basilica di San Lorenzo in Damaso: indagini archeologiche nel Palazzo della Cancelleria (1988-1993)*, 2 vols. (Rome 2009) 171, fig. 92 and 207, fig. 4. 88

Figure 40: Outline plan of Capitoline hill showing S. Anastasia and surrounding structures. Drawn by Abby George from base plan in Coarelli F. *Guida archeologica di Roma* (Milan 1974) 136............................... 90

Figure 41: Plan of S. Anastasia with preceding phases and immediately surrounding substructures. Drawn by Abby George from base plans in Cerrito A. 'Contributo allo studio del *titulus Anastasiae*', in *Marmoribus vestita: miscellanea in onore di Federico Guidobaldi*, edd. O. Brandt and P. Pergola (Vatican City 2011) 358, a and b. 91

Figure 42: Plan of area of S. Marco and surrounding archaeology. Drawn by Abby George, with additions by author, from a base plan in Gatti G."Saepta Iulia' e 'Porticus Aemilia' nella 'Forma' Severiana', in *BullCom* 62 (1934) 123-49, fig. 1. 92

Figure 43: Detail of sketch of P. Ugonio of S. Agnese in Agone (Barb. lat. 1994, p.362). Scanned from a reproduction in De Gregori L. *Piazza Navona prima d'Innocenzo X* (Rome 1926) 24. 95

Figure 44: Outline plan of central Rome showing location of SS. Quirico e Giulitta and surrounding ancient structures. Drawn by Abby George from a base plan in Reekmans L. 'L'Implantation monumentale chrétienne dans le paysage urbain de Rome de 300 à 850', in *Actes du IXe Congrès internationale d'archéologie chrétienne* (Rome 1989) 861-915. 96

0. Introduction

"And when you pray, do not be like the hypocrites, for they love to pray standing in the synagogues and on the street corners to be seen by men. I tell you the truth, they have received their reward in full. But when you pray, go into your room, close the door and pray to your Father, who is unseen. Then your Father, who sees what is done in secret, will reward you". (Matthew 6:5-6).[1]

This excerpt from the Bible advises Christians to be humble in prayer and to do so in modest surroundings, away from the public gaze. For three centuries, the followers of Jesus seem to have generally followed this maxim, albeit more through pragmatic necessity than piety, one might suggest.[2] With the imperial acceptance of Christianity by Constantine in A.D. 312, and the money and patronage that accompanied it, prominent Christians and emperors now wished to express their beliefs in the traditional Roman manner: building. The growing Christian congregation did necessitate the construction of purpose-built centres for worship, liturgy and administration, but the practice of building itself gave several elites an avenue and outlet for typical Roman munificence.

This book argues for the idea that several Christian building donors, whether private donors or the Church authorities themselves, sought to advertise their basilica building investments within the city walls of Rome by siting them in prominent places in the city. Several also sought practically useful sites to take advantage of pre-existing water facilities. This is a teleological argument that can never be definitively proven of course, and not every donor thought in these terms it seems, but, as I will set out here, the many examples of prominent and pragmatic site placement seen with early Christian basilicas, coupled with the evidence for a separation between donation and property in Christian patronage in Rome, makes this motivation possible and the most likely scenario. Building in strategically advantageous locations in a city is a long-standing aristocratic Roman tradition as well.

In Rome, imperial spending on Christian building seems to have focused on creating extramural basilicas over or near the graves of Christian martyr heroes, where space for such large structures was available, and where foci for Christian devotion already existed.[3] Recent scholarship has suggested that within the walls of Rome itself, into the 5th century, many Christians still worshipped privately in houses, several elite examples of which were formally converted for Christian use.[4] Certainly the small size and number of 'public' centres of Christian worship/congregation, the so-called *tituli*, up to the early 5th century suggests this may have been the case, if we assume a large Christian population in the city.[5]

What this also implies is that *tituli* were utilised initially for mainly administrative or baptismal purposes perhaps (for more see below), with special celebrations for feast days for important local or popular martyrs taking place in the large extramural 'tomb churches'. Also, *tituli* may have been more manifestations of elite munificence than practical additions to the Roman landscape. Whatever their initial importance however, they were still the first visible manifestation of Christianity in the central and residential areas of Rome.

It is important to note also that these basilicas were the product of the orthodox Nicene, 'catholic', Christianity promoted by the emperor and the bishop. Because these were the only visible sign of Christianity in these centuries we are inevitably focusing on them, but it is crucial to be aware of the fact that many other Christian groups, deemed heretical, existed in the city, particularly in the 4th and 5th centuries, and met in domestic settings within it, so are, so far, archaeologically invisible.[6] Therefore, the first *tituli-*

---

[1] Translation: *New International Version* (1984).
[2] The exception being at least one prominent purpose-built church in the East in Nicomedia, destroyed under Diocletian: Lactant. *De Mort. Pers.* 12.
[3] The long-standing idea that such a pattern was due to the emperor not wanting to offend the majority pagan elite in the city by building such structures in the centre (Von Schöenebeck H. *Beiträge zur Religionspolitik des Maxentius und Constantin* (1962) 88; Krautheimer R. *Rome: Profile of a City, 312-1308* (1980) 3-32; Krautheimer R. *Three Christian Capitals: Topography and Politics* (1983) 28-29 (n.19)), ignores these more positive, pragmatic reasons for the early large extramural basilicas. They also provided spiritually potent places for burial by the faithful, which was their primary purpose.
[4] Bowes K. *Private Worship, Public Values, and Religious Change in Late Antiquity* (2008) 71-75 and passim.
[5] Population: Von Harnack A. *Die Mission und Ausbreitung des Christentums in den ersten drei Jahrhunderten* (1915) 255; Purcell N. 'The populace of Rome in late antiquity: problems of classification and historical description', in *The Transformations of Urbs Roma in Late Antiquity*, ed. W. V. Harris (1999) 135-62; Lo Cascio E. 'Il popolamento', in *Aurea Roma. Dalla città pagana alla città cristiana*, edd. S. Ensoli and E. La Rocca (2000) 52-54; Lo Cascio E. 'La popolazione di Roma prima e dopo il 410', in *The Sack of Rome in 410 AD: the Event, its Context and its Impact: Proceedings of the Conference held at the German Archaeological Institute at Rome, 04-06 November 2010*, edd. J. Lipps, C. Machado and P. von Rummel (2013) 411-22. For the debate concerning tituli, their definition, when they appeared and their function see the classic works: Kirsch J. P. *Die römischen Titelkirchen im Altertum* (1918); Pietri C. 'Recherches sur les domus ecclesiae', *Revue des études augustiniennes* 24 (1978) 3-21; Guidobaldi F. 'L'inserimento delle chiese titolari di Roma nel tessuto urbano preesistente: osservazioni ed implicazioni', in *Quaeritur inventus colitur: miscellanea in onore di padre Umberto Maria Fasola*, edd. P. Pergola and F. Bisconti, vol. 1 (1989) 383-96. The list of works discussing this is exhaustive and too long to list here. However, for a more recent synopsis of the debate see: Bowes K. *Private Worship* (2008) 65-71.
[6] *Libellus precum*: Guenther O. ed. *Epistvlae imperatorvm pontificvm aliorvm inde ab a. CCCLXVII vsqve ad a. DLIII datae Avellana qvae dicitvr collectio (=Coll. Avell.)* (1895) 2.34; Maier H. O. 'The topography

basilicas show us only the development of 'orthodox' Christianity, and as such were also about promoting that orthodoxy in the face of these other groups, as well as promoting the generosity of the donor.

Work looking at early Christian patronage in Rome, since Charles Pietri first put forward the theory, has suggested that the *tituli* were controlled and owned by their private benefactors, whereas the large extramural basilicas and the Lateran were run and owned by the bishop and his administration until the late 5th century when aristocratic patronage shifted elsewhere. However, more nuanced approaches to the patronage of the *tituli* have also come to the fore, with J. Hillner recently arguing that the bishop had more of a role.[7] In her work she attempts to divide the process of foundation and endowment of *tituli*. What I seek to do is subdivide the process of foundation, between the provision of money and the provision of land, which I contend, were not always tied together.

My focus, however, is not patronal or legal problems, for which enough ink has been spilt. My focus is the actual physical impact of a few of these early Christian buildings in the Roman urban landscape up to *ca*. 700. Any questions as to their ownership, status or how they were funded does not preclude any difference in purpose behind Christian basilica construction; that is to say some episcopal or private builders both strove for recognition and a lasting personal legacy with their investment, as befitting any traditional elite Roman munificence. What I will be describing is that with some intramural Christian building, either private or episcopal, this can be perceived in their micro topographical location. Who built and ran them and when is less important for me than knowing that their construction was independent of the state, something all commentators agree on, which would allow for a degree of favourable site choice. Evidence for a separation between donations (towards the building of *tituli*) and the land/property on/in which they were created, alongside their favourable locations, will be used to argue for a degree of strategy in some intramural Christian building in this early period. That is to say, the siting of many of these early Christian foundations in Rome did not rely on the donation of a building, but was more down to a deliberate choice being made by its builders.[8]

The active purchase of small plots of desirable land in the city was more likely after the devastating Gothic Wars, but the favourable siting of many Christian basilicas built before that time suggests deliberate land/property purchase was more common than the donation of a particular plot/building by an aristocratic (lay or episcopal) owner. The epigraphic evidence also points to the former occurring. This goes against the current orthodoxy, explicitly described by F. Guidobaldi, of *tituli* (that is to say early Christian intramural structures) being located in random places determined purely by the donated land given to the Church.[9] Guidobaldi and others, however, have both overlooked the evidence for the separation between donation and property, and only looked at the macro distribution of *tituli* via modern top-down maps (see for example fig. 1), not their micro impact and the buildings immediately around them. When appreciating this, and various macro factors as well, as well as looking at the epigraphic and written evidence again, we begin to notice that several early Christian centres were favourably placed in the urban landscape and that buildings were rarely donated to the Church for conversion.

The favourable siting of several *tituli* involved creating some Christian centres alongside main arteries within the city and on occasion encroaching upon them, and later the building of larger basilicas on the tops of hills within the urban landscape. Such observations are known of course but are only described in passing in discussions of Roman Christian topography, and deserve to be mentioned in the same context as arguments about patronage and urban change, and to be perceived explicitly as deliberate attempts for otherwise modest foundations to attain prominence within the urban fabric, in the same mould as the motives of temple builders in earlier centuries. It is important to stress that these Christian buildings' 'monumentality' rarely bore any comparison in *scale* to the existing temples in the city in this period, but what will be argued is that their monumentality lies in their 'impact' at a street, micro level, not their macro visuality or effect. In other words, in terms of scale and expenditure within the walls, temples and some early *tituli* seem hardly comparable, yet the motivation behind their location and site choice is the same: to make an impression on the urban landscape.

---

of heresy and dissent in late fourth century Rome', *Historia* 44 (1995) 232-49.

[7] Pietri C. *Roma christiana: recherches sur l'Eglise de Rome, son organisation, sa politique, son idéologie de Miltiade à Sixte III (311-440)* (1976) 90-96, 569-73; Pietri C. 'Recherches' (1978) 7; Pietri C. 'Donateurs et pieux etablissements d'après le légendier romain (Ve-VIIe s.)', in *Hagiographie, cultures et sociétés IV-XII siècle. Actes du colloque organisé à Nanterre et à Paris 2-5 mai 1979* (1981) 439 (434-53); Pietri C. 'Régions ecclesiastiques et paroisses romaines', in *Actes du XIe Congrès international d'archéologie chrétienne: Lyon, Vienne, Grenoble, Genève et Aoste, 21-28 septembre 1986*, ed. N. Duval (1989) 1043 (1035-62). This view has been nuanced by, for example, Llewellyn: Llewellyn P. A. B. 'The Roman Church during the Laurentian Schism: priests and senators', *Church History* 45 (1976) 417-27. Greater episcopal role (with a titulus' donations at least): Hillner J. 'Families, patronage and the titular churches of Rome, c.300-c.600', in *Religion, Dynasty and Patronage in Early Christian Rome, 300-900*, edd. K. Cooper and J. Hillner (2007) 225-61. For a recent synopsis of the wider long-running debate concerning how the Church administered the city of Rome, and the role of the bishop and the tituli (and their priests) within this, see: Spera L. 'Il vescovo di Roma e la città: regioni ecclesiastiche, tituli e cimiteri. Ridefinizione di un problema amministrativo e territoriale', in *Atti del XV Congreso Internacional de Arqueologia Cristiana (Toledo, 8-12 septiembre 2008)* (2013) 163-69 (163-98).

[8] Cf. Bowes K. *Private Worship* (2008) 66-67 who defines the term titulus to actually mean donated property. See below for my own view that it is a term defining a particular (still unknown) role and function to the building.

[9] Guidobaldi F. 'L'organizzazione dei tituli nello spazio urbano', in *Christiana loca: lo spazio cristiano nella Roma del primo millennio*, ed. L. Pani Ermini (2000) 125 (123-29). He did admit, however, that with some examples site choice was able to be made by a bishop, something noted by V. Fiocchi Nicolai ('Strutture funerarie ed edifici di culto paleocristiani di Roma dal III al VI secolo', in *Le iscrizioni dei cristiani in Vaticano. Materiali e contributi scientifici per una mostra epigrafica*, ed. I. Di Stefano Manzella (1997) 121-41) but not expanded upon.

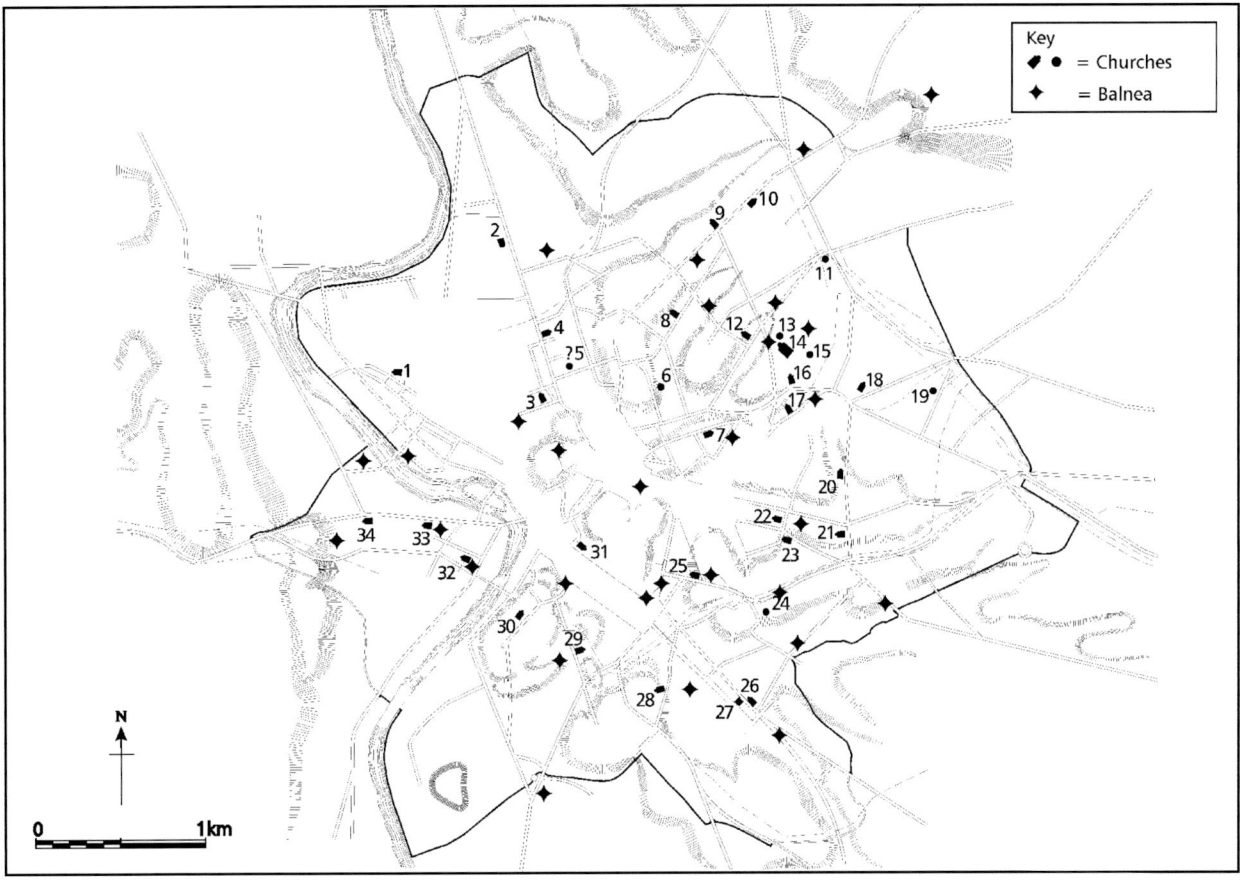

FIGURE 1: ROME WITH LOCATION OF CHURCH-BASILICAS AND *BALNEA*. DRAWN BY ABBY GEORGE FROM A BASE MAP IN REEKMANS L. 'L'IMPLANTATION MONUMENTALE CHRÉTIENNE DANS LE PAYSAGE URBAIN DE ROME DE 300 À 850', IN *ACTES DU IXE CONGRÈS INTERNATIONALE D'ARCHÉOLOGIE CHRÉTIENNE* (ROME 1989) 861-915.

What will also be noted more closely is the symbiotic relationship between several early Christian foundations in Rome and bath buildings. Such foundations were closely related to bathing establishments whether by immediate proximity, by ownership, or by being built within one. What will be explored is why this may be the case and the implications of that for our understanding of early Christian liturgical practice in the city.

Furthermore, to properly understand the impact of spatial 'Christianisation' we need to see the early intramural Christian centres in their contemporary surroundings and to comment on how they affected the use, movement within and perception of the neighbourhood around them. In Rome such detailed topographical information is frustratingly elusive, but there is one exceptional case, with the *tituli* of Equitius and Sylvester, where the ancient sources and archaeology allow for a detailed analysis of the micro topography of the contemporary urban landscape immediately surrounding them. This will reveal a great deal to us about how early Christian worship practically 'worked' in the Subura area where the *tituli* lie, and how that in turn 'reworked' the immediate area and the people who lived and worked in it.

Clearly, not all formal Christian centres up to the 7th century inside the city were favourably placed, some were no doubt purely located based on the site of a donated property, as Guidobaldi suggests, or simply where an empty affordable building was situated. However, many were also strategically situated as has been described: apsidal encroachment onto main roads and the practical liturgical benefits of a bath's water system does suggest selective land purchase by some private donors or churchmen for the benefit of their investment and its conspicuousness. This is something made more apparent in the 5th century with Christian basilicas being constructed on prominent hills, and, from this time, the creation of Christian worship spaces within prestige Roman structures in central locations. There are also two examples of 4th century Christian buildings being constructed in close proximity to major pagan monuments, an indication of a harmonious, rather than antagonistic religious topography, and certainly not one of avoidance.

Therefore, Christian building in the 4th to early 8th century in Rome needs to be seen as any other form of aristocratic munificence in the urban sphere (lay or episcopal), where there was a desire to promote one's investment and for it to be a prominent or important landmark in the city. That is not to say that Rome became an *urbs christiana* overnight, indeed the temples and pagan shrines still vastly outnumbered any Christian buildings within the city until the former's dismantling, destruction or quiet rotting away. However, it can be said that on certain streets and in certain places within the city, Christian buildings were prominent.

Although this book examines urban space and movement, the use of modern urban theoretical models will not be implemented here. These can be favourably employed in ancient urban spaces, but only when we have a complete, or largely complete, street plan available to us, as at Pompeii and Ostia.[10] In Rome we do not have this to any extent, so we are limited in our theoretical scope. In some ways this is a good thing however. Many urban theories are simply ways to scientifically measure something that is often intuitively obvious. We do not need space syntax theory or measures of spatial diversity to tell us a street was private or a building was largely inaccessible, although they can provide valuable insights on a broad city wide scale, or room by room scale within a building, and where surface remains are limited. In this discussion here, however, we are simply observing the spatial relationship between an early Christian building and its immediate contemporary surroundings, and with any material remains beyond this often lacking, the questions are often archaeological rather than theoretical. Terms used by geographers and urban theorists such as 'spatial capital' may be appropriate here with regards the aims of some early Christian builders, just described above, but these terms have not been strictly defined and so have the potential to be misleading.[11]

The incomplete nature of the archaeological evidence of the basilicas in discussion also means some of our conclusions need to be tentative. Their original height and exterior decoration is unknown to us, so I may in fact be underestimating their 'impact'. Equally, in a few cases, a tall structure may have obscured any micro visual prominence such a building may have had, but, where appropriate, this has been noted.

0.1 Problems of Definition

As with all studies of the ancient world our modern definition of an ancient term may be misleading when used to describe a particular ancient group, process, or the function of an object or space. In this study, where the use of such terms is inevitable, we need to set out what we mean before we begin. Particularly problematic is the term 'Christianisation', a monolithic sounding programme seemingly enacted from the top down. Such a process has now been rightly nuanced, with the reality of a very fractured and disparate Christian community in this period being acknowledged (with many 'Christianities'[12]) and, as we will see here, the role of private elite donors being fully appreciated. As such, I will use the term 'Christianisation' here to mean the appearance of defined spaces in Rome for public Christian worship and/or gathering, which may have been originally for non-Catholic use. The clearly delineated nature of public Christian space in the city in this period (marked by the walls of a basilica or later xenodochium and diaconia), and the nebulous nature of so-called 'pagan' or 'secular' space, makes the interaction between all three difficult to judge, but it does allow us to mark out Christian nodes in the cityscape quite easily, and thus the process of spatial 'Christianisation'. This ignores of course the important domestic private sphere of Christian worship, as emphasised recently by K. Bowes,[13] but what is of interest here is how Christians interacted with the urban landscape around them and the tangible manifestation of that is the apsed basilica hall used for public Christian congregation. Meetings and services in houses are private internalising phenomena, and their location cannot be determined in any meaningful way.

Another debatable term is that of *titulus* itself, and what it actually means. It does not appear before A.D. 377 in a Christian context, and has been argued to refer to the legal ownership of the property.[14] Indeed, in the 4th and 5th century Latin literary sources, the term *titulus* is not used at all to denote a Christian place of worship, implying the word acquires that meaning only in the 6th century and was only used in legal or administrative contexts before this.[15] Also, what *tituli* actually were, whether solely places of worship and/or meeting places we cannot say for sure as no archaeological or written source can shine any light on this problem.

Bowes has recently claimed that *titulus* has in fact the meaning of a property gift from a donor and that is why it is sometimes described as distinct from the physical structure of the basilica. Because of the use of the vague 'constituere' for the foundation of the *titulus Vestinae* (described in detail below) she argues for the term being a reference to the donation and property given.[16] Yet it seems to me that this may in fact be a reference to a role or function, in other words a term to describe the building's use, having lost its literal legal meaning in this Christian

---

[10] Most recently: Kaiser A. *Roman Urban Street Networks* (2011); Stöger H. *Rethinking Ostia: a Spatial Enquiry into the Urban Society of Rome's Imperial Port-Town* (2011).
[11] For a definition see: Marcus L. (2007) "Spatial capital and how to measure it: an outline of an analytical theory of the social performativity of urban form", in *Proceedings to the 6th International Space Syntax Symposium, İstanbul, 2007*, edd. A. S. Kubat, Ö. Ertekin, Y. I. Güney and E. Eyüboðlou (2007) 005.1-005.12.
[12] For example Hopkins K. A *World Full of Gods: Pagans, Jews and Christians in the Roman Empire* (1999) and importantly Smith J. Z. *Drudgery Divine. On the Comparison of Early Christianities and the Religions of Late Antiquity* (1990) which reassesses the study of early Christianity in all its multifarious forms. For Rome in particular see: Lampe P. *Christians at Rome in the First Two Centuries: From Paul to Valentinus* (transl. M. Steinhauser, ed. M. D. Johnson) (2003) esp. 358-408.
[13] Bowes K. *Private Worship* (2008).
[14] Inscription of 377: ICUR 1.124 n. 262 and also in a Roman synod attendee list of 499: MGH.AA (=*Monumenta Germaniae historica. Auctores antiquissimi*) 12.410-15. Ownership definition: Pietri C. *Roma christiana* (1976) 90-96, 569-73 and recently: Hillner J. 'Families, patronage' (2007) 232-37 (225-61); Bowes K. *Private Worship* (2008) 66-67.
[15] The terms *ecclesia, basilica* or *dominicum* are generally used for actual places of worship in the 4th century: Guidobaldi F. 'L'organizzazione dei *tituli*' (2000) 123-24 (123-29). *Titulus* in legal contexts in late antiquity: eg. *Cod. Theod.* 1.1.6, 1.4.3, 1.5.12, 13.6.8, 14.3.13, 15.1.2.
[16] Bowes K. *Private Worship* (2008) 66-68.

context.[17] So, Bishop Innocent, in the case of Vestina's foundation, is rather giving the basilica building the role to be assigned to it, 'constituere' also meaning 'organise', and in a legal sense, 'define'.

A contemporary 4th century letter (collated in the so-called *Collectio Avellana*) is very precise in describing Damasus being elected bishop *in Lucinis* in 366, which can only mean the *titulus Lucinae* mentioned in the synod attendee list of 499.[18] In the letter the '*titulus*' term is omitted because the source is describing the building itself, the basilica, and not its function, something that would be appropriate in a list of attendees at a Church meeting and in a description of a basilica's foundation. In the same 4th century letter we hear that bishop Felix set himself up *in iuli trans Tiberim*, again referring to a building, so with no reason to use the title *titulus*.[19] The term 'basilica' is used later with another *basilica iuli* in the same letter, so as to distinguish it from the previous, different structure which lay across the Tiber, and perhaps to deny the places where Felix and Damasus were elected an air of respectability, two events the author of the letter clearly disapproved of.[20] No distinction is made in the 499 synod list between the three presbyters of a *tituli Iuli*, although one Paulinus is described as a *presbyter (tituli) sancti Iuli* in three other manuscripts.[21] Others have thought that '*titulus*' refers to a separate community centre near or inside the basilica,[22] but I think the more nuanced view that it describes the role and function of a particular sort of Christian building (like *diaconia*, *xenodochium*) is more accurate.[23] This meaning changed in later centuries of course, but remained fairly consistent from the 4th to 6th century I believe.

This definition of '*titulus*' may explain the variation in nomenclature which we see, as this variation is based on the type of source in which it is written, that is, what it is telling the reader. This definition, as I have said, is likely to be a largely administrative and community function which also involved, as I will show later, baptisms in owned or nearby baths and where small-scale liturgy also took place by the 4th century, judging by the provision of liturgical type vessels given to several foundations.[24]

To avoid ambiguity then, we shall generally refer to these known Christian centres simply as basilicas (rather than 'churches'), as, as far as we can tell, the form all these early centres took were small basilical structures. These are the buildings that will be the focus for this study. The Lateran complex will not therefore, in itself, be studied, in spite of it being a prominent, large intramural centre.[25]

0.2 Historiography

To put my argument into some sort of context, an overview of the modern scholarship for the archaeology and topography of early Christian Rome is required. Such scholarship began in earnest with Rodolfo Lanciani and his *Pagan and Christian Rome* (1895), a book that is in effect a write-up of the excavations he undertook in the city during the previous years. These excavations were the first thorough and systematic archaeological investigations of Rome's ancient remains, and the first to examine some of its early Christian features. This later period in Rome's ancient history had been largely overlooked by previous scholars, and Lanciani tried to remedy this further with part of his *The Destruction of Ancient Rome* (1899), but especially with *Wanderings Through Ancient Roman Churches* (1925). The latter was the first attempt to look at these early structures in Rome archaeologically and historically, but was quickly followed by the more scholarly *Le Chiese di Roma nel Medio Evo* (1927) by Christian Hülsen. Hülsen's work was in some ways the second part of Samuel Ball Platner's towering contribution to the topography of ancient Rome, completed two years later by Thomas Ashby, *A Topographical Dictionary of Ancient Rome* (1929), the first index to the known monuments of the city, but which ignored the Christian contribution. The fact that this omission has only recently been remedied in the *Lexicon Topographicum Urbis Romae* (1993-2000), and within the *Lexicon Topographicum Urbis Romae: Suburbium* (2001-2008), shows the

---

[17] An early reference to a Roman Christian centre is from a Greek source from about AD 351 (revised after 370), Athanasius (*Apol. c. Ar.* 20). This has been translated as a "place where the presbyter Vito held his congregation" (Schaff P. and Wace H. edd and transl. *A Select Library of the Nicene and Post-Nicene Fathers of the Christian Church: Athanasius: Select Works and Letters* (1892 repr. 1995) 110) with no further detail given. Thus, is this just a meeting place, a place of worship or both? Is this a *titulus*? For the date of the source and its revision see Donker G. J. *The Text of the Apostolos in Athanasius of Alexandria* (2011) 22, with Jones A. H. M. 'The date of the 'Apologia contra Arianos' of Athanasius', JTS 5 (1954) 224-27.
[18] *Coll. Avell.* (ed. Guenther) 1.5; MGH.AA.12.414. Damasus' election was then formalised in the Lateran, the *titulus Lucinae* being unfit for this purpose: De Spirito G. 'Ursino e Damaso - una nota', in *Peregrina curiositas: eine Reise durch den orbis antiquus: zu Ehren von Dirk van Damme*, edd. A. Kessler, T. Ricklin and G.Wurst (1994) 266-68 (263-74).
[19] *Coll. Avell.* (ed. Guenther) 1.3.
[20] This 'basilica iuli' a different structure: Künzle P. 'Zur basilica Liberiana: basilica Sicinini = basilica Liberii', *RömQSchr* 56 (1961) 39-41 (1-61, 129-66); Geertman H. 'Forze centrifughe e centripete nella Roma cristiana: il Laterano, la basilica Iulia e la basilica Liberiana', in *Hic fecit basilicam: studi sul "Liber Pontificalis" e gli edifici ecclesiastici di Roma da Silvestro a Silverio*, ed. S. de Blaauw (2004) 28-31 (17-44) where it is thought to be on the site of the current Sancti Apostoli. The idea that the *Iuli trans Tiberim* and the *basilica Iuli* might in reality have had different statuses based on the former only being regarded as a '*titulus*', has been argued by De Spirito G. 'Ursino e Damaso' (1994) 266. Two separate basilicas of Julius in sources: Liberian catalogue (LP=*Liber Pontificalis*, ed. L. Duchesne, 2 vols. (1886-92) 1.9). Boniface I (418-22) was ordained in *basilica Iuliae* according to the 6th century LP (LP 1.227) but in *ecclesia Marcelli* according to a more reliable contemporary letter (*Coll. Avell.* (ed. Guenther) 14.6). Note the absence of the term *titulus* once more.
[21] *Coll. Avell.* (ed. Guenther) 1.3; MGH.AA. 12.411-2, 414..
[22] For the debate and confusion surrounding one particular example, the tituli of Equitius and Sylvester, see below Chapter 4.
[23] The larger basilicas inside and outside the city (the Lateran, Liberian Basilica, those on or near martyr tombs) are not represented in these synods by their own priests. An explanation may be that these buildings were initially purely for large services on Sundays and feast days and so had no permanent clergy; the priests of *tituli* or the bishop himself presided over services as and when required. An example may well be the presbyters of the *titulus Vestinae* having jurisdiction over S. Agnese fuori le Mura (see chapter 1: n.72).
[24] See for example LP 1.170, 212.
[25] For the most recent research on this structure see Liverani P. 'L'episcopio lateranense dalle origini all'Alto Medioevo', in *Des 'domus ecclesiae' aux palais épiscopaux. Actes du colloque tenu à Autun du 26 au 28 novembre 2009*, edd. S. Balcon-Berry, F. Baratte, J.-P. Caillet and D. Sandron (2012) 119-32.

extent to which the Christian topography of the city had been regarded separately from its non-sacred and pagan buildings. In general, topographers of Rome had largely focused on its pre-Christian structures and their locations, whereas the examination of the first Christian buildings had been confined to archaeologists and architectural historians. The most comprehensive example of the latter approach is Richard Krautheimer's *Corpus Basilicarum Christianarum Romae* (1937-77) which detailed the written and archaeological history of each of Rome's ancient and early medieval Christian buildings. Within this work, the results of the first excavations under them, from the 1920s, were set out. These, aside from providing a valuable chronology to the 4th and 5th century Christian building programme, made obvious the lack of evidence for a visible pre-Constantinian Christian topography in the city, something scholars of the first half of the 20th century had assumed was the template for the later post-Constantinian landscape.[26]

The obvious next step after examining the archaeology and history of the early Christian buildings in Rome, was to look at where they were located within the urban landscape. This, however, has been done only in a cursory fashion, as we have said. The discussion has tended to focus on three subjects: the large imperial structures, the arguments concerning '*domus ecclesiae*' in the city, and brief asides on the general macro spread of the distribution of these early basilicas. The idea that these centres were preceded by *domus ecclesia*, a theory first proposed by Kirsch, is now regarded with a great deal of suspicion, as are the martyr stories that claim a more ancient inheritance and history for many of the first Christian buildings, stories whose reliability has been questioned for some time.[27] Nevertheless, the debate elsewhere on this topic has not moved on very much. It has tended to see the early Christian basilicas in isolation from their contemporary surroundings, preferring to concentrate on broad socio-political motives for their locations. For example, as we have seen, the location of the *tituli* within the city has been explained as simply random, and the lack of imperial foundations in the pagan centre of the city has been argued to be due to that emperor wishing to avoid the ire of the pagan senate.[28] More recently, work has focused on the patronage and ownership of these basilicas and their private nature, as discussed above, and as such their location is taken to depend solely on where the land owned by the donor was situated.

Nonetheless, in the last few years these smaller structures have rightly begun to be seen in the context of the buildings and roads around them at the time in which they were built. Both J. Curran, *Pagan City and Christian Capital* (2000), and H. Brandenburg, *Ancient Churches of Rome from the Fourth to the Seventh Century* (2005) for example, accept the importance of the surrounding buildings, spaces and roads for Christian builders. However, the details of this are not explored, something I wish to do.[29]

The actual location of some of these small basilicas needs to be seen as a feature of the 'Christianisation' of the city. In previous scholarship it is only the actual phenomenon of the appearance of these buildings, rather than where they appeared, that has been regarded as part of this process. Other work on the Christianisation of the city has focused on its social and political dimensions, as well as the progress of the conversion of the Roman aristocracy. One of the most important contributions to this subject is A. Alföldi's *La conversione di Constantino e Roma pagana* (1943), which acknowledged how fundamentally pagan Rome still was, architecturally, socially and politically, long after Constantine's acceptance of Christianity. Equally important is C. Pietri's magisterial *Roma Cristiana* (1976), that looked at the growth of the Roman Church as an organisation, and the physical manifestation of that; that is the appearance of Christian basilicas in the urban landscape. Pietri noted that the building of these structures was a part of the conversion process, but went no further with that train of thought.[30] More recently the debate has moved on, identifying that 'Christianisation' was a more nuanced idea and encompassed all facets of city life, and was in many respects more of a secularisation at first. Nowhere is this approach more clear than in A. Fraschetti's *La conversione: Da Roma pagana a Roma cristiana* (1999). Essentially Fraschetti sees a secularisation of imperial ceremony and a gradual and slow Christianisation of the political, topographical and calendrical spheres. This latter element is also a focus for M. Salzman's work on the Roman calendar in late antiquity.[31] The conversion of the aristocracy, in Rome and elsewhere, has also been looked at in more depth recently, along with the governance of the city in general.[32] Specific case studies looking

---

[26] Eg. Kirsch J. P. *Die römischen Titelkirchen im Altertum* (1918); Vielliard R. *Recherches sur les origines de la Rome chrétienne* (1941).
[27] Domus ecclesiae: Pietri C. 'Recherches' (1978) 3-21; Guidobaldi F. 'L'inserimento delle chiese titolari' (1989) 384-85; Guidobaldi F. 'L'organizzazione dei *tituli*' (2000) 123-24 (123-29). Martyr stories: Delehaye H., 'L'amphithéatre flavien et ses environs dans les textes hagiographiques', *Analecta Bollandiana* 16 (1897) 235-52; Delehaye H., *Étude sur le légendier romain: les saints de novembre et de décembre* (1936) 14-41.
[28] Tituli: see n.9. Lack of central imperial foundations: see n.3. See also Brandt O. 'Constantine, the Lateran, and early church building policy', in *Imperial Art as Christian Art, Christian Art as Imperial Art: Expression and Meaning in Art and Architecture from Constantine to Justinian*, edd. J. Rasmus Brandt and O. Steen (2001) 109-14, where the Lateran is argued to have been a 'private' building and therefore not an appropriate addition to the city centre.

[29] See also Crippa M. A. 'L'urbanistica tardoantica e topografia cristiana, III-VII secolo', in *L'arte paleocristiana. Visione e spazio dalle origini a Bisanzio*, edd. M. A. Crippa and M. Zibawi (1998) 429-42. The most recent example of this more contextual approach is: Spera L. 'Characteristics of the christianisation of space in late antique Rome. New considerations a generation after Charles Pietri's 'Roma Christiana', in *Cities and Gods. Religious Space in Transition*, edd. T. Kaizer, A. Leone, E. Thomas and R. Witcher (2013) 121-42. This focuses on three areas of the city but, however, still only looks at the evidence in general, regional terms, not at the micro street level.
[30] Pietri C. *Roma christiana* (1976) x.
[31] Salzman M. *On Roman Time: The Codex-Calendar of 354 and the Rhythms of Urban Life in Late Antiquity* (1990); Salzman M. 'The christianisation of sacred time and space', in *The Transformations of Urbs Roma* (1999) 123-34.
[32] Cameron A. 'The last pagans of Rome', in *Transformations of Urbs Roma* (1999) 109-21; Salzman M. *The Making of a Christian Aristocracy:*

at early Christian basilicas in the city, based on new archaeological discoveries, or the reassessment of known results, continue to shine more light on the chronology of these structures, often moving their construction into a different era.[33] Topographical studies have also tended to shift more to the previously neglected suburban areas and hinterland of towns and cities.[34] Although they do not impact directly on the study here, their examination of the importance of movement and space to these buildings can be also applied to several Christian intramural structures.

In this way, to view the spatial 'Christianisation' of Rome in terms of a basilica's location and the 'effect' it made is a new approach and one that can give a deeper 'street-level' sense of the changes taking place in the fabric of Rome from the 4th to the 7th century.

Social and Religious Change in the Western Roman Empire (2002); Lizzi Testa R. *Senatori, popolo, papi: il governo di Roma al tempo dei Valentiniani* (2004).

[33] Examples will be cited in later chapters.

[34] For Rome this includes: Bjur H. and Santillo Frizell B. *Via Tiburtina: Space, Movement and Artefacts in the Urban Landscape* (2009); Spera L. and Mineo S. *Via Appia I. Da Roma a Bovillae* (2004) and many of the other books in the 'Antiche Strade. Lazio' series; La Regina A. dir. *Lexicon topographicum urbis Romae: Suburbium*, 5 vols. (2001-2008) is the first comprehensive survey of all of ancient Rome's suburban remains. The bibliography for Rome's Christian extramural tomb churches is, however, already voluminous.

1. Building a Titulus-Basilica in Late Antique Rome

"Suppose one of you wants to build a tower. Will he not first sit down and estimate the cost to see if he has enough money to complete it?" (Luke 14:28).[1]

As has been mentioned above, the sources of the money required to construct the small *tituli* basilicas in 4th and 5th century Rome has been discussed widely, and the current consensus is that this came from private individuals. What has not been looked at, due to the paucity of the evidence, is the process as to how that money was used in order to complete the Christian building project. What evidence there is however, can tell us something and this will be examined closely here for clues. This will I hope help us to understand the more practical considerations the builders had to make and the processes involved in any construction work, which can aid us in getting closer to understanding the decision-making that took place with certain basilicas in certain locations in the city. So, in this chapter we will look briefly at some case-studies from Rome of these types of constructions and how such projects were practically administered. Our evidence here is indeed very fragmentary and relies mainly on the few recorded inscriptions of this period from basilicas, as well as the information from the 6th century records of the *Liber Pontificalis* that look back to this time. We can also get some clues from our knowledge of private patronage in earlier periods for secular or 'pagan' building projects, as well as some insights from state building projects in Rome and references to bishop-led projects elsewhere in late antiquity.

The evidence from Christian inscriptions from the 4th and 5th century Christian buildings in Rome have been largely overlooked in analyses of early Christian patronage in the city, probably because they tell us more about the processes involved *after* any money was donated, but for my purposes they are an ideal source, and the best information we have for answering such a question. These inscriptions, recorded by early medieval copyists, rarely mention any private donor, instead listing state officials, priests, and the bishop himself foremost, and their role in the basilica's construction. As Krautheimer has also argued, this suggests that a bishop-led building committee actually organised and carried out the building of the structure, or the conversion of an existing space, whatever the source of the money given to build it.[2] The implications of this are profound; that is to say, the ecclesiastical authorities or the donor could, in principle, decide where and how to build using the money donated to them with little state interference. According to the inscriptions we have, however, the private donor rarely had any part in the building process once their money was donated. The traditional act of elite munificence, any spiritual benefits and the official name of the structure (identified by a large inscription outside on the façade one must assume) was reward enough it seems. It is strange that this should be commemorated by a personal name rather than a family name, however, but it is something we see with early imperial projects in honour of family members (e.g. Theatre of Marcellus, Porticus of Octavia). So, perhaps with the *tituli*-basilicas we have an ecclesiaistical body building a structure and naming it in honour of the donor who provided the money to build it, or a well-known martyr or a clerical founder if the money came exclusively from Church funds.[3] We can only speculate on that, but the quasi-independence of the Christian building bureaucracy seems apparent and a separation between provision of money and that of land at times can be proven I believe, with site choice flowing from that. Even the ostensibly imperial public construction of the Lateran basilica is more correctly understood as a private donation by the emperor on land chosen and bought by him.[4]

In this way the intramural basilicas, both small and large, at least into the early 5th century, were initially created as appreciably different sorts of spaces to the large basilicas outside the walls, which as we will see, were often large-scale state projects. It may be the case that liturgy and worship took place in these extramural basilicas and continued in private houses/spaces inside the walls until the mid 5th century, whereas the *titulus*/basilica had a more public social/administrative role at first, and were also used for baptism and prayer.[5]

In order to see the Roman practice involved in building projects in the city and how it related to building nomenclature and site choice we will begin by briefly looking at projects undertaken during earlier centuries. In the mid Republic public construction work was administered by an aedile and/or censor under the auspices

---
[1] Translation: *New International Version* (1984).
[2] Krautheimer R. *Corpus Basilicarum Christianarum Romae: the Early Christian Basilicas of Rome (IV-IX cent.)*, 5 vols. (1937-77) (=CBCR) 3. 302; Krautheimer R. *Three Christian Capitals* (1983) 99.
[3] Hillner J. 'Clerics, property and patronage: the case of the Roman titular churches', *Antiquité Tardive* 14 (2006) 59-68 and for a general debate on the names of the *tituli*.
[4] Brandt O. 'Early church building policy' (2001). The unreliable, late 4th/early 5th century *Augustan History* suggests that a group of Christians actually siezed public property in the early 3rd century, presumably for a place of formal congregation or worship: *cum Christiani quendam locum, qui publicus fuerat, occupassent...* (SHA, *Alex. Sev.* 49.6). Notwithstanding the unlikely tolerance of the emperor Alexander Severus in this case, it is perhaps the sheer impossibility of a such a purchase (even in the 4th and 5th century the Church used private land (see below)) that provides the humour the author seems to be looking for.
[5] Bowes K. *Private Worship* (2008) passim. If we are to believe LP 1.164 (Marcellus) the tituli were used for baptisms, repentence and the burial of martyrs in the early years of the 4th century.

of the Senate, in other words a state project but with the resulting building given the family name of the aedile or censor in charge. Occasionally a *praenomen* would be used in the case where initiative and money stemmed from a private individual, for example the *via* and *aqua Appia*.[6] By the late Republic ostensibly state building projects were in fact privately funded building programmes by a small clique of powerful oligarchs, and were given the *cognomen* of their donor and merely rubber stamped by the Senate as a formality. In the earlier Empire, emperors used state money for their own personal quasi-private ventures, which were again given their family names. That is to say, *cognomina* given to a building do not help us to decide whether the programme is private or public, but the use of a *praenomen* does indicate a more personal, or extra-state project. Also, even private projects required official state ratification, even if this was just a formality.

1.1 Building in the Republic and Earlier Empire

The vast majority of building programmes in Republican Rome were state funded, usually by the Senate, and thus with money from taxes and tribute, under the auspices of the censors and aediles, who seem to have had some autonomy, save in respect to the construction of temples where the Senate had to authorise such a programme.[7] Private individuals also sought the cachet of a monument with their family name, funded through the booty acquired from a successful military campaign, although they also required the approval of the Senate, even if they didn't need its money. These private projects took the form of altars and arches for example, and occasionally temples, all to give thanks to or placate the gods and to advertise their *gloria* or *pietas*.[8] The building contract itself was put out to auction, with the magistrate in charge, usually the censor, deciding on the contractor who received it.[9] Therefore, the censor, or later more commonly the aedile, organised the acquisition of land and its clearance. We cannot say whether the senate decided on location or if it was independently chosen by the censor or aedile, who would have their name attached to it. It is likely though, that with their name being directly associated with any project, they did decide on location where possible, which the Senate would then have to approve.

It is only in the later Republic that significant public building projects are funded independently of the Senate and state, as a result of the growing wealth of a few private individuals, itself a consequence of such men dominating the political scene and the military and governmental posts. This change in building patronage began with Sulla in the early 1st century B.C. but was epitomised by Caesar, whose wealth allowed him to buy up private land for 'public' use in the centre of Rome. The land acquired for the Theatre of Marcellus and the Forum of Caesar being examples of the extent to which this could occur.[10]

The Basilica Aemilia is an interesting case study here, a structure built in the mid Republic and restored various times up to the early Empire, at least. The name of the structure and the process involved in its construction and later restoration is indicative of the period. It was first constructed in 179 B.C. in a prominent position in the forum behind some shops, and seems to have been initially named the *Basilica Aemilia et Fulvia*, the *nomina*, or clan names, of the two censors who took charge of the project.[11] By 78 B.C., the ancestor of the former, M. Aemilius Lepidus, in the role of consul, restored the building and decorated it with images of family members, it now being named simply the *Basilica Aemilia*.[12] Soon after this time the building was generally known as the *Basilica Pauli* after the work carried out by the aedile L. Aemilius Paullus, with money from Caesar, and finished by his son L. Aemilius Lepidus Paullus as consul in 55 and 34 B.C.[13] In other words it now acquired the typical *cognomen* of the individual involved, in this case, with its restoration. It is restored again by another of the *Aemilii* clan after a fire under Augustus, and later using the family's own money.[14] This may be why it retained the family nomenclature. The points to note is that the building was only managed by the *Aemilii*, in most cases using the state's money, yet named after them, with their *nomen* then with a more typical family *cognomen*. They also had some freedom as to the decoration of the basilica, but to whom the choice of its location fell, although favourable to the *Aemilii*, cannot be firmly assigned. Under the empire generally the *cognomen*, or family name, of the emperor is used to name buildings built using their money, rather than the usual *nomen*, although this varied, as with the Basilica Ulpia or the Flavian Amphitheatre. Again, the variability in nomenclature lies between the latter two names of the individual, and never the *praenomen*, unless it is a monument dedicated to a particular person rather than simply commemorating the donor.

To get an idea as to land purchase and location choice for public monuments in the Late Republic and early Empire the Forums of Caesar and Augustus are useful test cases. For each we have some knowledge of the process involved in purchasing the land, and that location choice was integral. Caesar's stated aim to connect the Forum Romanum and the Campus Martius explains the site bought for his forum. The huge expense he was willing to

---

[6] Diod. Sic. 20.36.1-2.
[7] Censors in charge of building: Cic., *Leg.* 3.3.7. Senatorial authorisation for temples: Livy, 36.36.4, 40.51-52.
[8] Eg. CIL 6.1301, 1315, 1316.
[9] In the form of a *stipulatio* (formal verbal agreement) or *locatio conductio* (formal written agreement). Censor deciding on contract: Cic. *Verr.* 2.3.16. For a brief discussion of this with references see: Johnston D. *Roman Law in Context* (1999) 98-99. For more detail on temple building in this period see: Orlin E. M. *Temples, Religion and Politics in the Roman Republic* (2002) esp. 140-47.
[10] Theatre of Marcellus: Plin. *HN* 7.121; Dio Cass. 43.49.3; *Mon. Anc.* 4.21 (remainder bought by Octavian). Forum of Caesar: Cic. *Att.* 4.16.9; Plin. *HN* 36.103; Suet. *Iul.* 26.
[11] Livy, 40.51; Varro, *Ling.* 6.4. They may have originally been two different buildings however: Plaut. *Capt.* 815, *Curc.* 472.
[12] Plin. *HN* 35.13; Coin of his son with image of basilica recalling his father's work: RRC 419/3a.
[13] Plut. *Vit. Caes.* 29; App. *B. Civ.* 2.26; Dio Cass. 49.42.
[14] Dio Cass. 54.24; Tac. *Ann.* 3.72

go to so as to get the land is also indicative of this, where he is said to have spent over a hundred million sesterces. The money used was from the spoils of war, so technically state money although in practice his own, and the land purchased was owned by private citizens.[15] The Forum of Augustus follows a slightly different pattern, in that the land on which the forum was built he seems to have already owned, it being described as *privato* in the Latin, implying he inherited it, perhaps from Caesar. The forum itself seems to have been built with monies from military spoils as well.[16] Both involve the purchase of private land for a public building, albeit through private endeavour.

Although the scale and legal power involved these projects are not comparable to the small private donations that the *tituli*-basilicas were in the 4th and 5th centuries A.D., it indicates that within the Roman legal and bureaucratic framework an individual donor could purchase the land he wanted within the city walls and build on it. The sites in question were chosen because of the prominence and importance they gave to their investment and in turn the donor.

This is the practise taken on by the private lay or ecclesiastical (extra-state) donors of the intramural Christian basilicas in the 4th and 5th century A.D. in Rome, albeit without the same spending power, but enough, theoretically, to purchase small plots of land or, in these cases, convert buildings they were donated or they themselves bought. Like the imperial projects (of which we will see an example in late antiquity below) the building work itself was managed by an official body, in the case of imperial programs the state bureaucrats under the Prefect of the City, and with the *tituli*-basilicas, I will argue, ecclesiastical building managers under the bishop or a powerful donor. Both systems are apparent when we examine the written and epigraphic evidence for late antique Rome. The evidence from inscriptions has been strangely overlooked in analyses of early Christian patronage in the city, so both will be examined here.

1.2 Christian Building in the Late Empire

Like with any Late Republican and Imperial private project, location choice in late antique building was determined by how much money there was available and the ambition and power of the donor. Location was also determined, with early Christian patronage, by the nature of the donor's donation, be it either a plot of land or a building, or simply an amount of money. In the latter case more freedom was possible, and in this situation the building managers (the bishop with the clergy) or the donor themselves could have decided the location.

Most of the 4th and 5th century basilicas in the city were built over *domus* but two were built over *insulae* (that is, not single occupancy plots), indeed there may have been more examples of this: the evidence is incomplete.[17] This suggests a different process at work in those cases, that is, not the donation or acquisition of a house easily adaptable for Christian congregation, but the donation or purchase of a large building that required extensive adaptation and demolition. Why would a wealthy Christian donor donate such an unsuitable building? The answer may be that they did not, and in fact our two known cases of *insula* to basilica conversion are more likely active deliberate purchases because of the plots' locations. Both of the Christian basilicas known to have been built over *insulae*, now known as S. Lorenzo in Lucina and S. Anastasia, are situated in very desirable locations, next to a main arterial road by a important imperial monument and right next to the Circus Maximus, respectively. These examples will be explored in later chapters, but this at least suggests that an ecclesiastical building committee, or donor, acquired these desirable pieces of real estate inside the walls of Rome for a small Christian centre to be located.

A glimpse of what might be occurring in Rome can be seen in an account from 5th century Constantinople, which describes the wealthy presbyter Marcian (later Saint Marcian) attempting to purchase a house of an aristocratic widow in the centre of the city to convert into a Christian structure.[18] Although an almost completely private Christian building system existed here,[19] this sort of activity may explain the female names of many basilicas in Rome and repeat the private purchase mechanism Roman presbyters or bishops carried out in order to convert desirably situated houses.

As far as the archaeological evidence allows, the 4th and 5th century basilicas appear to have all been built on private land (*domus, balnea* or *insulae* (which were privately owned) are found beneath them), indeed one could not legally build a private building (like a *titulus*-basilica) on public land without special permission.[20] Roman law clearly stated that private buildings could not extend onto public or state land, although the opposite certainly occurred, as we have seen; compensation was provided for this, however.[21] This would have meant in practice that,

---

[15] Cic. *Att.* 4.17.7; Plin. *HN.* 36.103; Suet. *Iul.* 26.
[16] *Mon. Anc.* 4.21: *In privato solo Martis Vltoris templum forumque Augustum ex manibiis feci*. A late example of aggressive imperial land purchase is Diocletian and his baths: houses, buildings and a quadriga statue of the usurper Piso were moved or destroyed for its construction: SHA, *Tyr. Trig.* 21.6-7; Steinby E. M. ed. *Lexicon topographicum urbis Romae*, 6 vols. (1993-2000) (=LTUR) 5.53.
[17] Guidobaldi F. 'L'inserimento delle chiese titolari' (2000) 386-91.
[18] *Vita Marciani*: Dagron G. *Costantinopoli: nascita di una capitale (330-451)* (1991) 528-29 (Italian transl. of orig. in French: *Naissance d'une capitale: Constantinople et ses institutions de 330 à 451* (1974)).
[19] Bowes K. *Private Worship* (2008) 103-23.
[20] Special permission given by Theodoric to build workshops within the north-west corner of the Roman Forum: Cassiod. *Var.* 4.30 and allowance to purchase public property but only on condition that it is restored: Cassiod. *Var.* 7.44. The question as to the imperial permission given to Sixtus III (432-40) to build a basilica to St. Lawrence—thought to be a reference to S. Lorenzo in Lucina's partial encroachment onto the *ager publicus* of the Augustan horologium monument (now thought to be the site of public gardens rather than a sundial)—is not clear cut: LP 1.234; Geertman H., 'La *Basilica maior* di San Lorenzo fuori le mura', in *Hic fecit baslicam* (2004) 117-26 and see below Chapter 3: Encroachments onto Public Spaces.
[21] Republican law: Livy, 39.44. Late antique laws: *Cod. Theod.* 2.23.1 (AD 423): soldiers are at times exempt from this law; *Cod. Theod.* 15.1.9 (AD 376): public land could be bought in Rome but with caveats.

technically, only private buildings or land could be bought or converted in the 4th and 5th century for intramural (and indeed extramural) Christian basilicas. Yet, there are many examples of private structures encroaching onto public land from the 4th century, and by the 6th and 7th centuries being built within non-private buildings. These activities, in principle, required special permission, which was increasingly granted in late antiquity, although such legal niceties may not always have been observed. This issue and examples of Christian basilicas in Rome that demonstrated this sort of encroachment will be discussed below.[22]

So, it seems the pattern of the sole use of private land for 4th and 5th century Christian centres was at least partly dictated by the law, but this legality was not extended to non-encroachment onto public land, as we will see. The appearance of Christian basilicas within high-profile public buildings by the 6th and 7th centuries, therefore indicates a relaxing of the laws and partial abandonments of these buildings, and thus availability.

For some in the Church hierarchy though, this early pattern of private property use was problematic. In Ambrose we can get some idea as to the orthodox ecclesiastical view towards private property, one that is coloured by religious rhetoric rather than legal reality. Ambrose speaks out against the desire for private property as something that goes against a natural *iustitia*, and describes how God created the earth and everything in it as common property to everyone.[23] He is not against private property in principle however, as long as it is used for the benefit of others, for example in his own use of it to free prisoners of war after Hadrianople in 378.[24] More specifically, he writes about an attempt by the emperor in 385 to seize a church for the Arians in Milan. Ambrose's response is to argue the basilica does not belong to him but to God, and so it is not his to give away.[25] This rhetorical flourish does not hide the fact that the imperial authorities and the Arians saw it as property of the bishop. The bishop's comparison of the church with a private house is also telling.[26] In Rome during the aftermath of the exile of Ursinus, Damasus' rival for the papacy in 366, episcopal ownership of Christian basilicas is also evident. A letter by the emperors sent the following year to the then prefect Praetextatus, asks that the *Basilica Sicinini*, the last stronghold used by the Ursinians, be returned to the authority of Damasus as bishop.[27] Thus, some Christian basilicas in Rome at least were under the direct control of the bishop, which rather assumes their construction also had been, and were independent from the urban prefect's authority and jurisdiction. Praetextatus only had the power to restore the building to the ecclesiastical authorities, because the basilica in question was removed from the bishop's charge by Ursinus.

It is clear that Christian basilicas were generally regarded as private property, and many were under the jurisdiction of the bishop. However, in the East there does appear to have been a differentiation made between public and private examples, whatever that may have meant in practice.[28] It is also clear that by the 6th and 7th centuries such distinctions become blurred or fell away completely with Gothic kings and then bishops of Rome filling the vacuum left by the demise of the Roman administration in the West. In this way, the practice of Christian building could become more ambitious and was no longer tied to the Roman legal proscriptions. This allowed for Christian basilicas to appear on public land and within what were public buildings, as we will see.

In the following section we will look at what the state building bureaucracy looked like in late antiquity and how it evolved, to provide a context for private endeavours, as well as examining two examples of the actual process behind Christian building work in Rome in the late 4th and early 5th century. The first will be a case study of a public imperial Christian project, the other a private foundation of a *titulus*-basilica. Beyond this period up to the 7th century there is a lack of sources that give us this much detail, but the letters of Theodoric, written by Cassiodorus, does make it clear that into the latter 5th and early 6th century restoration and repair continued on public buildings in Rome,[29] but for the provision of Christian buildings we are in the dark as to how such projects were precisely carried out in Rome during that time. As such, we will concentrate for now on this earlier period.

1.3 The Evolution of the State Building Bureaucracy from Diocletian to Sixtus III

To provide a context for our discussion on private Christian patronage of basilicas in late antiquity into the early middle ages, it would be worthwhile examining the changes to the state system in place for carrying out building and restoration in Rome, from the beginning of the 4th century to the middle of the 5th, beyond which any changes cannot be reliably traced. After the middle of the 5th century the evidence for Rome is unclear, but it would be safe to assume that the Church played an even greater

---

Baldini Lippolis I. 'Private space in late antique cities: laws and building procedures', in *Housing in Late Antiquity: from Palaces to Shops*, edd. L. Lavan, L. Özgenel and A. Sarantis (Late Antique Archaeology 3.2) (2007) 195-238 and see Chapter 3: Apsidal Encroachment below. Compensation: Robinson O. F. *Ancient Rome: City Planning and Administration* (1992) 22-23.
[22] See Chapter 3: Encroachments onto Public Spaces.
[23] Amb. *Off*. 1.28, *De Viduis*, 1.5.
[24] Amb. *In Psalmum David CXVIII Expositio* 8.22, *Off*. 2.28; see also Swift L. J. 'Iustitia and Ius Privatum: Ambrose on private property', *AJP* 100 (1979) 176-87 which includes a further bibliography on the issue.
[25] Amb. *Ep*.20, *c. Aux*. 5.35.
[26] Amb. *Ep*.20.19.
[27] *Coll. Avell.*(ed. Guenther) 6.

[28] *Cod. Theod*. 16.5.14.
[29] Cassiod. *Var*. 1.21, 1.28, 2.7, 2.34, 3.29 (conversion of granaries for private use), 3.30-31 (drains, aqueducts and temples restored), 4.51, 7.6. The work undertaken by Theodoric has been argued to be a different sort of restoration and repair than what occurred in earlier centuries. It was now more about preservation, conservation and antiquarianism than practical maintenance and civic pride: Pergoli Campanelli A. 'Nova construere sed amplius vetusta servare. Cassiodoro e la nascita della moderna idea di restauro', *StRom* 59 (2011) 3-40.

role in Christian building or restoration work from that point and began to take a role in other building activities after the Gothic Wars had terminally damaged the Roman civic government.

The period we will focus on, however, begins with the main builder and initiator of projects in the city being the emperor, to a time when the main patron was the bishop of Rome. Financial provision, the founding of Constantinople, and a change in state religion all contributed to this change. This story is one that is comprehensively covered in André Chastagnol's seminal work *La préfecture urbaine sous le bas-empire*. As a result, I will merely summarise the evolution he describes but at the same time be critical of some of the conclusions he makes. Describing this era of change will allow the following discussion on the day-to-day running of the building and restoration bureaucracy to be seen in the right context.

A summary of what we mean by the 'state' regarding the governance of Rome is necessary here, as this unwieldy system involved hundreds of civil officials under the Prefect of the city, the imperial bureaucracy around the emperor himself when he intervened in building projects, as well as the Senate, which continued to have some role well into the 5th century.[30] It is interesting to note that the Senate itself is mentioned far less frequently in inscriptions describing building work than the Prefect and those under him. It may be that the Senate as a body wielded less power than individual senators themselves in certain offices, its members continuing to be held in high esteem into the 5th century, as Sidonius confirms. For our purposes therefore, 'state' building activity can be defined by a project undertaken by an individual in a civic office, working for either the prefect or the emperor; or carried out by the prefect or emperor themselves; or by the Senate as a body. However, the emperor or Senate as a body rarely intervened it seems; it was the Prefect and the civic officials around him that actually ran the city, including the vast majority of building and restoration work, with the Church only taking on these responsibilities in the 6th century.

Our main evidence for what was 'state' building and what was not is the inscriptions that were originally fixed onto newly built or repaired structures, which, ostensibly, describe those involved in the work. To get an idea of the evolution of the bureaucracy therefore, we need to ask how accurate these inscriptions were, and as such, did the appearance or absence of a particular post on these dedications show the demise of that position, as Chastagnol argues, or merely a change in epigraphic conventions? Do they represent a true picture of who was involved, or were they just an official stamp that was bound by praxis? As we will see later, the variety and unconformity of the surviving examples we have for this period in Rome, suggest that they do indeed represent a degree of reality in the city: that is, a centralisation and shrinking of civic governance but not its disappearance.

However, conclusions made concerning minor posts in the administration should be tempered by an acknowledgement of the politics of the time. The disappearance of certain posts from the epigraphic record during this period should be seen alongside the fact that these inscriptions were the only public manifestation of the Prefect's power, and so have a 'propagandistic' and political element. In this way, the omission of minor posts in the record are likely to be a manifestation of the prefect's wish to be seen as solely responsible for the city's upkeep, rather than a true reflection of the civil administration. In spite of this, the evidence inscriptions provide, combined with the legal sources we have, do point to a gradual centralisation of the state bureaucracy during this period. Alongside the epigraphic and legal evidence we have the *Liber Pontificalis*, the ecclesiastical papal source for Christian basilica building, that, unsurprisingly, appears biased in favour of the Roman bishop and his role in the Christian building projects of the period. Nevertheless, the central role it gives him may not be entirely fanciful, as we will see.

In order to understand the system behind the various building projects in the Rome of the 4th to 7th centuries, we need to be aware of the series of offices that were responsible for this aspect of the urban administration. We need to be clear what these posts were and the responsibilities attached to them. Documents, letters and inscriptions give us a basic idea as to what this structure was, and how it operated. Any great detail is, however, elusive. The system in place in late antiquity was first put together by Augustus, more than three hundred years previously.[31] The best evidence for the names of the posts involved in the day-to-day running of the city of Rome in this later period is provided by the early 5th century document known as the *Notitia Dignitatum*. This document lists the governmental and military posts throughout the empire, but it is incomplete and does at times refer back to an earlier, potentially redundant, bureaucracy.[32] Nevertheless, it is a good starting point and framework on which to base our discussion. The *Notitia* does not state the actual function and hierarchical placement of each office, but this can be deduced from the names themselves and their relative placement in the text. The text of the source that is relevant to Rome is laid out as follows:

Sub dispositione viri illustris praefecti urbis habentur
  amministrationes infrascriptae:
  Praefectus annonae.
  Praefectus vigilum.
  Comes formarum.
  Comes riparum et alvei Tiberis et cloacarum.
  Comes portus.
  Magister census.

---

[30] Sid. Apoll. *Carm.* 2, *Epist.* 1.9.

[31] Suet. *Aug.* 37.
[32] Sinnigen W. G. *The Officium of the Urban Prefecture during the Later Roman Empire* (1957) 8.

Rationalis vinorum.
Tribunus forii suarii.
Consularis aquarum.
Curator operum maximorum.
Curator operum publicorum.
Curator statuarum.
Curator horreorum Galbanorum.
Centenarius portus.
Tribunus rerum nitentium.

Officium viri illustris praefecti urbis:
Princeps.
Cornicularius.
Adiutor.
Commentariensis.
Ab actis.
Numerarii.
Primiscrinius.
Subadiuuae.
Cura epistolarum.
Regrendarius.
Exceptores.
Adiutores.
Censuales.
Nomenculatores.
Singularii [33]

We can see from the text the different sub-sections of the urban government under the Urban Prefect that covered the daily running of the city. We could assume from this that the Prefect of the city was merely overseeing and rubber-stamping many of the everyday decisions that needed to be taken, with those listed posts beneath him taking the specific action and making the decisions required. As our focus is building though, we will only be concentrating on the offices of *curator operum maximorum, curator operum publicorum* and *curator statuarum* listed above, and also the *curator aedium sacrarum* which existed earlier, as well as the office of Urban Prefect itself.

Broadly, we can divide the evolution of this system into three parts: the period up to 331; the period 331 to Gratian; and the period after him. This goes along with Chastagnol's assessment. Before 331 most of the *curatores* seem to have been largely independent agents, and it is only after this time that we can say that the Prefect controls this entire element of the administration, as demonstrated by the *Notitia* above.[34] This is implied by the inscriptions we have before this date that list these posts, without the prefect being mentioned, and the minor posts' relative absence after that time, something that is especially evident with the offices that dealt with the buildings of the city.[35] What the inscriptions suggest is a more centralised regime after 331, which also coincides with the disappearance from the epigraphic record of the *curator/consularis aedium sacrarum*.[36] This does not necessarily mean the post also disappeared, and was subsumed by the *curator operum publicorum*, as Chastagnol suggests. Nonetheless, such a reform would go along with the religious mood of the period and a probable simplification of the system following the setting up of a new administration in Constantinople.[37] This meant that the care of the temples was now directly under the tutelage of the prefect, a reality certainly in place by 342, when the emperors write to the Prefect concerning the need to keep intact those temples outside the walls of Rome.[38] Also, there are inscriptions showing prefects restoring pagan structures in the 350s and 360s.[39] After 331 though, his powers do not seem to have extended to Christian monuments.[40] This may be the case because, as we have argued, even state-funded Christian buildings were treated as quasi-private structures. Such a situation is assumed by the evidence from the *LP*, showing imperial donations and interventions for many such foundations, but a lack of epigraphic evidence for such state provision. It is likely that, for the majority of cases, the Church had control of the money as well in these cases.

After the reforms of 331, nothing changed until Gratian, when he banned the use of state property to maintain the pagan cults in 382, and a loophole was closed in 384 when they could not receive legacies either.[41] This effectively cut off all state and other funds for the old religions, and affected the civil administration in Rome by removing all responsibility of the state for pagan temples and shrines. As such, this task was no longer a part of the Prefect's remit, which is reflected in the inscriptions we have, where work on pagan buildings after this time is confined to perhaps two cases, both involving private money.[42]

From then on the prefect had to concentrate purely on Christian and secular buildings, which suggests some new Christian structures became pseudo 'public' projects, if only in legal terms. The first sign of this was with the reconstruction of the Constantinian S. Paolo fuori le Mura in 383/84, after Gratian had died, where the prefect, emperor, bishop and other clergy were all involved.[43] The public baptism and symbolic destruction of Mithraea and pagan statues by the prefect Gracchus in 376/77 could have been another watershed as the initial signal of a change from an apparently religiously neutral prefecture to one where the position could be actively pro-Christian,

---

[33] Seeck O. ed. *Notitia dignitatum: accedunt Notitia urbis Constantinopolitanae et Laterculi provinciarum* (1876) 113-14.
[34] Chastagnol A. *La préfecture urbaine à Rome sous le bas empire* (1960) 43-53.
[35] Chastagnol, *La préfecture* (1960) 45-46 and notes.
[36] It last appears in CIL 14.4449.
[37] Chastagnol, *La préfecture* (1960) 52-53.
[38] *Cod. Theod.* 16.10.3 also 16.1.1 written in 365.
[39] CIL 6.45, 6.102.
[40] Chastagnol, *La préfecture* (1960) 140, 147.
[41] Pronouncements of AD 382 and 384: Symmachus, *Relat.* 3.11-13,16; pronouncement of AD 382: Amb. *Ep.* 17.3-5 and cited in *Cod. Theod.* 16.10.20 (AD 415).
[42] CIL 6.754 (mithraeum); Shackleton Bailey D. R. ed. *Anthologia Latina. 1: Carmina in codicibus scripta* (1982) 22: carmen contra paganos ll.112-14 (Temple of Flora or Venus: for more on this see Mulryan M. 'The Temple of Flora or Venus by the Circus Maximus and the new Christian topography: the 'pagan revival' in action?', in *The Archaeology of Late Antique Paganism*, edd. L. Lavan and M. Mulryan (2011) 209-27.
[43] *Coll. Avell.* (ed. Guenther) 3: see below.

and at times positively anti-pagan.[44] Yet, Gracchus' actions seem rather exceptional, and were probably as much about politics as religion: it is no coincidence that his period in office coincided with Gratian's rise to the purple.

This role in solely Christian and secular building for the prefect continued into the 5th century, but with the decline in population of the city,[45] so the post also declined in importance, along with the removal of some powers. From the inscriptions we have, this did not include the task of building or restoration however, now of course limited to Christian and municipal structures. The list of Urban Prefects becomes intermittent on the eve of the Gothic wars, after which the Church seems to have gradually taken over the entire administration, the future Pope Gregory holding the office in 572/73.[46]

Overall then, we can say the system before 331 was broadly a decentralised one, with specialised *curatores* in charge of certain projects. Between 331 up to the reign of Gratian, we see a centralised bureaucracy with the Prefect overseeing everything and being ultimately in charge of all public building and restoration projects that were pagan or civil in nature. After Gratian, the prefect only tackled Christian and civic programmes, with the pagan work no longer being state-funded. The fate of the *curatores* is unclear, but it is unlikely they disappeared overnight, if at all. We see them occasionally mentioned in inscriptions in Rome, but infrequently after 331 and always beneath the Prefect's name, implying their role was now regarded as more junior.

We could say that epigraphic convention plays a part in the changes we see, something repeated elsewhere in the empire, with governors, for example, appearing more frequently in inscriptions commemorating building/restoration projects. Yet, legal and other documentary evidence does point to a centralisation of the building bureaucracy, with the Prefect and then the bishop into the 6th century, taking on much of the responsibilities in Rome. This does not mean the disappearance of the civic posts described in the *Notitia* however, but they now had less independence and less cachet. The inscriptions reflect that.

1.4 The System in Practice

We now need to look at the evidence there is for the actual day-to-day running of this system, and if the reality bore any comparison to the generalised picture painted by the sources described above. In fact, the written sources of the 4th century portray a more confused situation. In short, they describe a chaotic system where jobs overlap and where the prefect does not know what job is his, or what is the responsibility of his subordinates.

The main focus for our written record of the administrative system surrounding building is the correspondences and letters of Quintus Aurelius Symmachus and his son Lucius. Within these we get a vivid picture of the daily management by the state of the public buildings in Rome in this period. Quintus writes from the point of view of the prefect of the city, the office he held in 384. At this time he wrote his correspondences to the emperor, known as the *relationes*. As we have seen, the post of prefect evolved in its role and power throughout the 4th century, so as such, Symmachus' experience in the office may not be typical of the entire period. Nevertheless, the position was never changed radically thereafter, so represents the situation through to the 5th century and up to the Gothic Wars.

There are three examples in particular of the elder Symmachus' letters to the emperors that illustrate the problems inherent in the system at the time, and the underlying confusion within it. Significantly, this is the period just after Gratian's reforms, which meant the prefect no longer had anything to do with pagan cult buildings. The immediate ramifications of this may have led to much of the confusion Symmachus describes, he himself being a committed polytheist.

Our first example concerns Symmachus' statement that the officials under him in the administration were incompetent and not of sufficient quality:

> "*These prosperous times possess men more worthy of the posts; indeed there is a rich vein of really good men. You will serve the interests of the city better in the future if you appoint men even against their will.*"[47]

Although this cannot be seen as a veiled criticism of the emperor, what with the huge number of people he appointed, it does however show the desperation that Symmachus felt, and an attempt by him, perhaps, to gain the authority to appoint his own officials. With his current staff, he may have felt they would inhibit his ability to do a competent and successful job, which could in turn reflect badly on his career and damage that of his son's. To our modern eyes, this situation highlights the flaw of government appointments being made through familial connections and court favour rather than just ability, yet, this system was integral and fundamental to the mindset of the Roman elite. As such, Symmachus' objections would have lain in who was making these choices, not why. This

---

[44] Prudent. *C. Symm.* 1.5.561-65; Jer. *Ep.* 107.2.
[45] Now proven through recent archaeological projects in Rome focusing on this 'late Roman-early Medieval' period, which shows the steady abandonment of public and some private buildings, but also their active later resuse. The increase in intramural agriculture and burial has also been proven, and indicates a smaller and semi-rural urban area, but one that is still vibrant. For general overviews with further bibliographies, see: Meneghini R. and Santangeli Valenzani R. *Roma nell'altomedioevo: topografia e urbanistica della città dal V al X secolo* (2004); Costambeys M. 'Burial topography and the power of the Church in fifth- and sixth-century Rome', *BSR* 69 (2001) 169-89.
[46] The last known prefect was a Iohannes in 599: Sinnigen, *Urban Prefecture* (1957) 112-14 and notes; Chastagnol A. *Les fastes de la préfecture de Rome au bas-empire* (1962).

[47] Symmachus, *Relat.* 17.2: "*habet temporum felicitas digniores; bonorum virorum vena fecunda est. melius urbi vestrae in posterum consuletis, si legatis invitos.*" (transl. above: Barrow R. H. *Prefect and Emperor: the Relationes of Symmachus, A.D. 384* (1973) 96-97).

is not to say a meritocratic system did not exist, but it did at times play second place. In these situations as Symmachus points out:

"For it is on my shoulders that the burden of the whole administration lies; the rest sink under it..."[48]

All these problems stem from the empire-wide issue of the increasingly burdensome task of office that many of the upper classes were now unwilling to take on.[49] This may explain Symmachus' suggestion to appoint the best men 'even against their will' (*si legatis invitos*). Another useful correspondence suggests the lack of authority the Prefecture had by this stage in fiscal and legal matters.[50] However, for our purposes which concern building and the role of the administration in this, I will focus on two other *relationes*, numbers 25 and 26.

1.4.1 An Imperial Building Contract in Late Antiquity: The Reconstruction of the pons Probi and the Rebuilding of the Basilica to St. Paul

Both these letters describe the situation surrounding the construction, collapse and repair of the *pons Theodosii* which seems to have been a replacement for the *pons Probi*.[51] Along with this project, there was the programme to enlarge the small Constantinian S. Paolo, an imperially funded basilica situated approximately one mile outside the walls on the *Via Ostiensis*. The two, as Symmachus suggests, made up the one contract, of which, significantly, the prefect was now in charge, that is now presiding over the construction of a Christian building.[52] This was an imperially financed building project however, the prefect only leading the work on the ground, so these letters tell us about that process, and the problems and people involved.

In the matter of the bridge, Symmachus describes how the responsibility for the building work was given to a Cyriades and then an Auxentius, the former at least described as a *mechanicae professor*, the best translation for which is a 'specialist engineer'.[53] The fact that the person in charge of a project moved on before it was finished is strange, especially considering his expertise. Symmachus does not give any reason for this and evidently sees the situation as not unusual, so we must assume this commonly occurred. Nevertheless, it was Cyriades and Auxentius who were in charge of the finances, and had access to a central imperial fund on which they could freely draw for the costs of labour and materials.[54] The dispute centred on the amount of money Cyriades took, which was criticised by his successor Auxentius, and the former's alleged poor workmanship, exposed when the bridge collapsed during the winter of 382.[55] Symmachus as prefect set up an enquiry:

"Cyriades was attacked by Auxentius, of the distinguished order of senators, in person on the matter of the excessive cost of the basilica and the bridge; Cyriades, who held the same rank, then thought that Auxentius ought to receive a bite in return, in the form of a counter-charge. It seemed fitting, then, that a trustworthy inspection should appraise the building work for which each of the two were responsible".[56]

Auxentius was then accused of abandoning the work, presumably of the basilica as well as the bridge, which indicates that position's overall control of the project and not just with its finances. Symmachus also makes it clear that such appointments were made by the emperor.[57] He also shows how the prefect at the time had little knowledge and influence with regard the building operations themselves, when he asks about how the costs are calculated. Although personal knowledge of such matters may have varied depending on the prefect involved, it certainly seems that the individual in charge of an imperial project at least, was independent of the prefect's office. This also shows that the control of imperial building operations in Rome, at least at this time, were not managed centrally but rather individually, project by project in a rather ad-hoc fashion. In other words, by the late 4th century, there was a lot of delegation of duties down the line, with the emperor and Prefect of the City purely official figure heads, but with very little actual practical role in the work itself. Thus, with an imperial project, the emperor, using his own money, organised who was doing what independently from the prefect. In the prefect's own work, using his civic funds, it is more likely he had far more control and say on matters. More broadly, all this does tend to indicate that there was no universally agreed system for building and restoration in the city in late antiquity, but rather a series of pragmatic arrangements that were formulated to suit a specific project.

It does seem clear though that Christian building comes under the 'private' sphere, but only in the sense that it is not the emperor or prefect in control.[58] That is, the funding did

---

[48] Symmachus, *Relat.* 17.2: "*meis quippe umeris rerum omnium pondera sustinentur cedentibus reliquis...*" (transl. above: Barrow R. H. *Prefect and Emperor* (1973) 96-97).
[49] The causes and effects of this phenomenon on cities is dealt with in a recent volume, which also summarises the voluminous literature on the issue: Krause J.-U. and Witschel C. edd. *Die Stadt in der Spätantike— Niedergang oder Wandel? Akten des internationalen Kolloquiums in München am 30. und 31. Mai 2003* (2006).
[50] Symmachus, *Relat.* 23 *passim*.
[51] Therefore built or began by the emperor Probus (AD 276-82). This was the bridge which lay south-west of the Circus Maximus and led to the *Transtiberim*, the modern Trastevere region. It is mentioned in the regionary lists: *Not. Rom.* Pontes: Nordh A. ed. *Libellus de regionibus urbis Romae* (1949) 98.13.
[52] Symmachus, *Relat.* 25.2; see also Symmachus, *Ep.* 4.70 & 5.76.
[53] Symmachus, *Relat.* 25.1.
[54] Amm. Marc. 27.3.10; the tax on wine, the *arca vinaria*, paid for mortar: *Cod. Theod.* 14.6.3 (365).
[55] Symmachus, *Relat.* 26.4.
[56] Symmachus, *Relat.* 25.2: "*super basilicae atque pontis immodico sumptu Auxentii v.c. voce perstrictus est, quem Cyriades vir parilis dignitatis mutua accusatione credidit remordendum. Visum est igitur adcommodum, ut utriusque aedificationem fida aestimaret inspectio*" (transl. above: Barrow R. H. *Prefect and Emperor* (1973) 140-41).
[57] Symmachus, *Relat.* 25.2-3.
[58] Being religious buildings this would be unsurprising; temples, shrines and the land on which they stood were always regarded as *rei privatae*.

at times originate from the imperial purse when it came to the larger basilicas. The process by which the Church went about building for itself may not have been that different from the state, in the fiscal and organisational sense, with the individuals in charge also having largely the same roles as those in the public sphere.

As such, the process broadly described by Symmachus over the matter of the bridge, could be a parallel to the Church's own building organisation. Indeed, there is no reason to think they did not use the same state architects and surveyors, the Church being so favoured by the imperial government. The only differences were that projects were initiated by the bishop of Rome, a priest or a private individual rather than the emperor.

If as Symmachus suggests, whoever was in charge of the bridge was also in charge of the basilica, that is S. Paolo, the inscriptions from this period concerning that building show how useful, but also misleading, they can be as compared to the reality. Our knowledge of this structure's enlargement in the late 4th century is uniquely detailed as we have a letter from the emperors to the Prefect of the City concerning its construction, as well as inscriptions commemorating its completion. Within the imperial letter architects are mentioned,[59] and so such individuals were seemingly appointed by the emperors for both civic and Christian buildings in imperial projects, but there is no reason to think that Church-led schemes could not have employed the same people. The inscriptions from S. Paolo show us the people involved, even the administrators (probably the *curatores*) in one instance. The emperors Theodosius I and his son Honorius are mentioned first in one inscription as the initiator and completer of a mosaic respectively. Theodosius' daughter and Honorius' sister Galla Placidia, as well as Pope Leo, are also mentioned in a later example describing the basilica's restoration, but their precise role is not described.[60] Thus, both programs are portrayed as imperial projects. In another inscription, found on a column fragment, Emperor Valentinian II and Neoterius as co-consul are mentioned first followed by the administrator Flavius Phillipus and a Flavius Anastasius.[61] Such details seem more appropriate for an inscription that was not highly visible, but again an imperial program is implied. Inevitably, there is bound to be some simplification in these inscriptions as to those involved of course, so this should be borne in mind when we examine other examples later.

As we have said though, most Christian basilicas were not built through imperial channels, so the letter and inscriptions concerning S. Paolo we have are more informative about secular, imperial schemes of this period rather than Christian builds. However, the fact that this is a Christian construction may give us a clue as to at least what was expected of the various parties in such projects. It had been argued, that the decision to enlarge Saint Paul's was initiated by bishop Damasus (366-84), who influenced the emperors through Ambrose, as part of a policy to counteract the apparent growing pagan influence in the 380s.[62] As we will see though, Damasus was perfectly capable of initiating building projects himself, and, in any case, all the epigraphic and written evidence points towards an imperially-led and initiated building program. The size and nature of the work alone also implies a large amount of imperial involvement.

The letter from the emperor informs us of the chain of authority in this imperial scheme. The emperors write to the Prefect of the city, a Sallust.[63] He was, in turn, ordered to organise the surveying of the chosen site, over the former Constantinian basilica, so they can order the necessary materials:

"*…you have allotted to surveying all matters, as the occasion demanded, and because you have made known to our Serenity's ears by carefulness of suitable language the entire site and aspect of the place, for it has been proper that we, better informed, order what must be ordered*". [64]

and then after:

"*…consultation with the venerable priest*".[65]

which we can assume is the bishop of Rome, in this case Siricius (384-99).[66] This suggests he could have had some impact on the construction process, albeit, in this case, after a site was chosen and the decision to actually build it had been made. The fact that the leading Christian figure in the city should be involved in a project concerning

---

[59] *Coll. Avell.* (ed. Guenther) 3.
[60] ILCV 1.1761a-b (a. Theodosius then Honorius b. Galla Placidia then Leo).
[61] ILCV 1.1857 (Siricius, Valentinian, Neoterius, Phillipus). For the construction of the church and its archaeology in this Theodosian and Leonine phase, see for example: Barkley Lloyd J. 'Krautheimer and S. Paolo fuori le mura. Architectural, urban and liturgical planning in late fourth century Rome', in *Ecclesiae Urbis: atti del congresso internazionale di studi sulle chiese di Roma (IV-X secolo): Roma 4-10 settembre 2000*, edd. F. and A. G. Guidobaldi (2002) 812-16; Liverani P. 'Progetto architettonico e percezione comune in età tardoantica', *BABesch* 78 (2003) 205-19; Docci M. *San Paolo fuori le mura: dalle origini alla basilica delle "origini"* (2006) 29-66. For the inscriptions see Filippi G. and Barbera R. *Il Codice Epigrafico di Cornelio Margarini e le iscrizioni della Basilica di San Paolo fuori le Mura nel XVIII secolo: concordanze e inediti* (2011).
[62] Krautheimer R. *Three Christian Capitals* (1983) 104. The so-called 'pagan revival' is, however, unproven: see most recently: Cameron Al. *The Last Pagans of Rome* (2011).
[63] This is Sallustius Aventius, which dates the letter to 383/84: Chastagnol, *Les Fastes* (1962) 216-17. Cf. PLRE 1. Sallustius 4. He was a pagan, which suggests that in imperial projects religious affiliation was not a factor. This is not surprising; one had to follow the emperor's orders. With Church-led schemes such an issue may have proved a problem though.
[64] *Coll. Avell.* (ed. Guenther) 3.1: "*...ad inspicienda universa, ut res exigebat, detulisti et omnem situm locorumque faciem sermonis congrui diligentia nostrae serenitatis auribus intimasti. Instructiones enim nos iubere decuit, quae iubenda sunt*" (transl. above: Coleman-Norton P. R. *Roman State and Christian Church. A Collection of Legal Documents to A.D. 535*, vol. 2 (1966) 412).
[65] *Coll. Avell.* (ed. Guenther) 3.2: "*...examine cum venerabili sacerdote...*" (transl. above: Coleman-Norton, *Roman State*, vol. 2 (1966) 412).
[66] LP 1. 216.

the enlargement of a Christian place of worship is not surprising. However, this was an imperial project and could show how the bishop now wielded a degree of influence and importance in Rome by this time. It may also indicate the bishop was generally consulted before such projects took place. In this imperially funded example, the bishop was the second rung down in the consultative process, with perhaps only some influence on the layout and design of the basilica. In other more typically ecclesiastical-led ventures, his role seems to have been more senior, at least according to the *Liber Pontificalis* and the inscriptions in Christian buildings describing their completion.

Nevertheless, the significance of the role of the bishop is highlighted by the fact that the senate and the Christian people are only

"...*informed*...[67]

in this process. A referral to the senate may have been typical or necessary for imperial constructions in the city, with the reference to the Christian people having the meaning of priests and their congregations. This implies a consultation process via sermons or an episcopal letter, although a general announcement in the Forum is also likely. Such acts would have emphasised the popular and propagandist value of any imperial work, in this case a Christian basilica. Notwithstanding, this whole process, as described in the letter, clearly delineates where the decision making lay and what the role of each layer of authority had in a Christian construction of this period under imperial patronage.

In the building project of a *titulus*, that is with no emperor at the top overseeing matters, the next layer down and therefore the individual most likely to be in charge, was the bishop and/or the donor. The prefect could still have been involved perhaps, but only as an intermediary, as with the imperial scheme just discussed. The only sources we have for any details behind such private programmes are from the *Liber Pontificalis*, and the various inscriptions associated with the completed basilica. One particularly example of a *titulus* foundation, rich in detail, is the *titulus* of Vestina.

1.4.2 The Titulus Vestinae

Sometime under the episcopate of Innocent I (401/402-17) a building was dedicated in Rome to the Milanese martyrs Gervasius and Protasius using the money from a rich woman named Vestina.[68] This is the best-documented example of lay patronage of a *titulus* in this period. Here, Vestina provides the money for the construction of the *titulus Vestinae*, becoming known as S. Vitale at some point in the 6th century.[69] The donation by Vestina is, unusually, described in detail in the *Liber Pontificalis*, and is the first case of a private donor appearing in this way there. Whether this is then the beginning of a new phase in private Christian building in Rome, as it has been seen, or rather the first time the *Liber Pontificalis'* ad hoc early writers see fit to mention such people, we cannot say. Nevertheless, the detail it provides is of some help to us. The relevant text begins in this way:

> *Then he* [Innocent] *dedicated the basilica of Saints Gervasius and Protasius, from a bequest in the will of a certain illustrious woman Vestina, through the activity of the priests Ursicinus and Leopardus and the deacon Livianus. This woman had directed in the text of her will that a basilica of the holy martyrs should be constructed from her ornaments and pearls by selling what was reckoned to be enough. When the basilica was completely finished blessed Innocentius established in it a Roman titulus, from the assignment of the illustrious woman Vestina...* (transl. R. Davis *The Book of Pontiffs* (2000) 32)[70]

The significant part of this excerpt is that there is no mention of any land or building being donated by Vestina, merely jewellery and 'ornaments' (*ornamenta* also meaning 'furniture' or 'accoutrements') for the Church to sell, to pay for the construction, and to buy the land onto which to build.[71] In this example at least, it seems the Roman Church had control over the resources for the building's construction and where it was constructed.

As described above, it seems most likely that the use of the verb 'constituere' here for the foundation of the Christian centre is actually a reference to a particular role given to it by Innocent, and not related to any donation of a building. The point to be made is that a *titulus* is better understood as a physical space and place, with a specific role. In the case of the *titulus* of Vestina, this was a property that was bought and converted into basilical form by the ecclesiastical authorities, with the money from the sale of Vestina's jewellery and ornaments, for the purpose of giving it the role of a *titulus*.[72]

---

[67] *Coll. Avell.* (ed. Guenther) 3.2: "...*participato*...".
[68] For the importance of these martyrs see: Carlà F. 'Milan, Ravenna, Rome: some reflections on the cult of the saints and on civic politics in late antique Italy', *Rivista di Storia e Letteratura Religiosa* 46.2 (2010) 197-272.
[69] Titulus Vestinae in AD 499: MGH.AA. 12.411-12 and *ca.*600: ICUR 1.1185. Titulus sanctae Vitalis in AD 595: MGH.Ep. (= *Monumenta Germaniae historica.Epistolae*) 1.366-67. An explanation for the change in name can be found in: Thacker A. 'Martyr cult within the walls: saints and relics in the Roman *tituli* of the fourth to seventh centuries', in *Text, Image, Interpretation: Studies in Anglo-Saxon Literature and its Insular Context in Honour of Éamonn Ó Carragáin*, edd. A. Minnis and J. Roberts (2007) 47 (31-70).
[70] LP. I. 220: "*Eadem tempore dedicavit basilicam sanctorum Gervasi et Protasi ex devotione cuiusdam inlustris feminae Vestinae, laborantibus presbiteris Ursicino et Leopardo et diacono Liviano. Quae femina suprascripta testamenti paginam sic ordinavit ut basilica sanctorum martyrum ex ornamentis et margaritis construeretur, venditis iustris extimationibus. Et constructam usque ad perfectum basilicam, in quo loco beatissimus Innocentius ex delegatione inlustris feminae Vestinae titulum Romanum constituit...*".
[71] The church of S. Andrea in Catabarbara may have been founded in the same way (see below).
[72] A funerary inscription found in the pavement of S. Agnese fuori le Mura describes a man named Abundantius as an acolyte of the TT VESTINE. It has been dated to the 4th century (strangely), 414 and by

In other words, in some cases, the ecclesiastical authorities could determine where a basilica was built or created, or the donor themselves could decide, it was not simply a case of private donors always themselves providing a building they already owned to be converted into a *titulus*-basilica. The land could be separate from the donation, allowing for a degree of site choice by the Church or the donor.

1.4.3 Other Christian Building

Other examples of Christian building programs can show us that the donation of a physical structure to be converted into a basilica for Christian use was in fact the exception rather than the rule, based on the evidence we have.

1.4.3.1 Aristocratic Lay Patronage

In the 4th century there is no evidence for any lay donor providing the money for actually building a Christian basilica, but we do have evidence for lay donors decorating a building associated with a basilica, and a woman founding a hospital.[73] There is no detail attached to any of these cases so no more can be said, except the fact that women were prominently involved, which vindicates Jerome's picture of the prominence of aristocratic women and widows in early Christian Rome. The characterisation of Damasus by his enemies as the 'ear-tickler of matrons' (*matronarum auriscalpius*) reinforces this, as does an imperial prescript of 370, addressed to him, not allowing clergy to approach widows and orphans for material benefit, which effectively cut off much private patronage towards the Church.[74] Whether this law reflects the real picture in Rome and elsewhere, or the undue influence of Damasus' critics on the emperors who wrote to the bishop, is open to debate. Our sources tell us there was certainly some female lay patronage directed towards the Church. The model Jerome and others create of this patronage is of interest here.

It has been assumed that the majority of early Christian building was possible because of donors such as these, the female names of the early *tituli* in Rome being evidence of this, it is thought.[75] What is interesting to note, however, is that the lay foundations of the 4th and 5th centuries at least, that we know about from literary or epigraphic sources, rarely show evidence for the lay foundation of Christian basilicas or the providing of money to that end (Vestina being one of the exceptions), merely their decoration, or embellishment in other ways. The vast majority of Christian buildings created by lay donors do seem to have been through aristocratic female patronage, but were in the form of sick or poor-houses, *xenodochia*, nunneries or monasteries.[76] It is strange that so few basilicas appear to have been built through lay donations, as a lack of money cannot have been an obstacle for this group of people. The law of 370 may have been a factor, with Christian private patrons looking for more indirect ways of helping the Church. However, the answer may lie in a letter by Jerome to the widow Demetrias.

In this letter, Jerome states that she should not be building churches and richly decorating them, but rather caring for the poor and hungry and managing the communities of virgins and other Christians.[77] With Jerome being the catalyst for the ascetic movement in Rome from the late 4th century, and the mentor for all the members of it, it is likely such advice meant these rich widows, and the men associated with them, took it to heart. This could explain the lack of patronage of Christian basilicas in Rome by this group, yet the abundant funding of more benevolent projects. In another letter, Jerome also states that monks, nuns, hermits and ascetics should be regarded as a different category from bishops and clergy, who should be in the cities providing for their flocks.[78]

All this tends to suggest that it was rather the clergy's role to provide Christian halls/basilicas for a city, and that other charitable buildings should be created by devout members of the lay community. In any case, the money lay donors gave directly to the Roman Church at least was rarely in the form of property to convert into a Christian basilica, although such money was no doubt used by the Roman bishop and clergy on several occasions for such purchases. Most private lay money was directed elsewhere towards charitable buildings and monasteries and in repairs and embellishment of already existing basilicas. The frequent

---

De Rossi, tentatively, to the late 6th to early 7th century (ICUR 1.1185). This at least shows that the titulus was popularly known by its donor's name, and was a place where some form of liturgy took place requiring an acolyte. It also confirms what the LP says (LP 1.222) that the *titulus* had some sort of administrative attachment to S. Agnese (Carlà F. 'Milan, Ravenna, Rome' (2010) 263). For other evidence for connections between *tituli* and extramural cemeteries and their basilicas, see: Spera L. 'Il vescovo di Roma e la città' (2013) 163-69.

[73] Anastasia and her husband? decorating a building next to S. Pietro in Vaticano (ICUR (NS) 2.4097 (366-84 AD)) and Fabiola establishing a *nosocomion* in the late 4th century in the city: "*Et primo omnium νοσοκομεῖον instituit...*"(Jer. *Ep*. 77.6). An Asella may also have created a hermitage in the centre of Rome, although this may have been more of a metaphorical foundation: Jer. *Ep*. 24.4.

[74] *Coll. Avell.* (ed. Guenther) 1.9-10; Amm. Marc. 27.3.14; *Cod. Theod.* 16.2.20 with Amb. *Ep.* 18.13-14.

[75] Pietri C. *Roma christiana* (1976) 90-96, 569-73 with the bishop as ultimate owner of the property; Llewellyn P. A. B. "The Roman Church during the Laurentian Schism' (1976) 417-27; Llewellyn P. A. B. 'The Roman clergy during the Laurentian Schism (498-506): a preliminary analysis', *Ancient Society* 8 (1977) 245-75, with *collegia* of priests as owners.

[76] See this chapter: n.73 with Jer. *Ep*. 66.11 and 77.10, 108.20, 118.5; Gerontius, *Vita S. Melaniae Junioris*, 20, 22, 41, 48, 49, 57 (Laurence P. ed. and transl. *La vie latine de sainte Mélanie* (2002)); Palladius, *Historia Lausiaca*, 46, 54 (Wellhausen A. *Die lateinische Übersetzung der Historia Lausiaca des Palladius: Textausgabe mit Einleitung* (2003)); Paul. *Ep.* 29.10. However, the Church of the Ascension in Jerusalem was probably constructed in the 380s by a Poemenia: Clark E. A., *The Life of Melania, the Younger: Introduction, Translation, and Commentary* (1984) 115 n.5 for refs. Melania's and her husband Pinian's rich mansion in Rome has been found on the Caelian Hill, but there is no literary or archaeological evidence for it being a public place of Christian worship, something that would surely have been mentioned by Gerontius: Gerontius, *Vita S. Melaniae Junioris*, 14; Clark E. A. *Life of Melania* (1984) 97-99; Hillner J. 'Domus, family, and inheritance: the senatorial family house in late antique Rome', *JRS* 93 (2003) 140-43 (129-45). Examples of domestic churches for private use by elites in Rome is well-attested however: see Bowes K. *Private Worship* (2008) 76-84. Non-elites may also have taken part in more simple Christian rituals in their homes, with Sundays and feast days being the time to visit the basilicas, as has been said.

[77] Jer. *Ep*. 130.14.

[78] Jer. *Ep*. 58.4-5.

female names that appear as the titles of Roman *tituli* in the 499 synod list were only occasionally donors. More often the *tituli* were named after well-known female martyrs by their clerical founder, or after the clerical founders themselves.[79]

The more typical forms of lay patronage in Rome can be seen in the other examples that we have. The prefect Longinianus provides the money for a baptistery at a basilica, possibly S. Anastasia, in 400/402, and is the second recorded example, after S. Paolo, of the Urban Prefect being involved in the building of a Christian structure. This is a further example of the prefect's increasing involvement in Christian building, as he is now not just supervising a Christian project but overseeing it completely, and perhaps initiating it.[80] This is a sign of such patronage being accepted by this time as a legitimate form of public munificence, as well as an acknowledged part of the prefect's job. Further examples of prefectural activity in this sphere throughout the 5th and 6th century reiterate this point.[81] The reason such involvement was not more frequent could be to do with the quasi-private nature of Christian building rather than any disinterest on the prefect's part. The examples we do have of their involvement in Christian construction, may therefore indicate a particular wish to be publicly associated with such a project, and therefore publish their religious affiliation.[82] This implies that for these prefect-led Christian building projects, the full mechanisms of civil government were used in the construction or embellishment process. We must assume therefore that the money to pay for them came out of civic/public funds. Nevertheless, the vast majority of Christian building, of which there was much in the 4th to 5th century period in Rome, did not include the prefect, at least not officially. As the prefect's building role, after 382, was confined to Christian and municipal projects, this suggests once more that most Christian basilica construction or embellishment took place relatively independently from the state and its mechanisms and funds.

The next example we have of a similar lay donation is fifty or so years after Longinianus', by a Gallus. He provided the money for the decoration of part of S. Pietro (in Vaticano). His identification as a former Urban Prefect is uncertain.[83] The other extant examples of private lay donations up to the end of the 5th century, come mainly in the form of embellishment of existing basilicas.[84] The arrangement with S. Stefano in Via Latina, outside the walls, is similar to the *titulus Vestinae*. The private donor, in this case Demetria Anicia, provided the money (but in this case also the land for the basilica-hall), however a cleric, the presbyter Tigrinus, was actually in charge of the construction work, with the building being dedicated by Pope Leo. With the other lay donors it is not clear who is in charge of the actual construction. With these private donations it is doubtful that any specific arrangement or system for construction applied in all cases. Nevertheless, it is highly probable that the Church had some role in all the examples, but it is likely the extent of this varied.

Very occasionally donors did indeed provide land, as with Demetria Anicia, or wished to be more directly involved in the process than others. Another example of land donation occurs under Simplicius (468-83), when the Goth Valila left the Basilica of Junius Bassus in his will to the Church, as well as money to convert it into a Christian centre (S. Andrea in Catabarbara). Once more it was the bishop who was in charge of this conversion process. Importantly, the gift of the building is mentioned in the inscription.[85]

The only other possible example of such a donation we have is with the *titulus Pudentis* (S. Pudenziana), where the scenario of a lay donor and clerical founder could be recurring. Here the evidence is less certain, but it appears the owner of the building on the site before the basilica-hall was built, may have given the structure to be converted into a Christian centre. Brick stamps bearing the name Quintus Servilius Pudens, consul in A.D. 166, were found in the basilica's masonry, suggesting a later ancestor of his could have donated the family's property to the Church, explaining the name of the later ecclesiastical building.[86] An inscription found in the Christian basilica (see below) confirms the role taken by the Church in its construction. The rarity of this sort of patronage in the written and epigraphic record, only serves to indicate how unusual it was to directly donate land or a building in Rome for a Christian centre, both being valuable, and usually consisting of inherited family property.

The only example of an actual lay *founder* (as opposed to donor) of a Christian basilica-hall, is a Pammachius—perhaps the correspondent of Jerome who dies in 409/10[87]—who founded the *titulus Pammachi* sometime before 440. An inscription dating to the pontificate of Leo I (440-61) that was placed at the entrance of the basilica, but

---

[79] Hillner J. 'Clerics, property and patronage' (2006) 59-68, *contra* Guidobaldi F. 'La fondazione delle basiliche titolari di Roma nel IV e V secolo: assenze e presenze nel "Liber Pontificalis"', in *Atti del colloquio internazionale. Il Liber Pontificalis e la storia materiale: Roma, 21-22 febbraio 2002*, ed. H. Geertman (2003) 5-12.
[80] ICUR 2.150 n.19, PLRE 2. Fl. Macrobius Longinianus. The inscription was found near S. Anastasia.
[81] CIL 6. 1666, 1668, 1762.
[82] In the same way as the Urban Prefect Praetextatus in 367/68 put his name in the inscription recording the restoration of the *Porticus Deorum Consentium*: CIL 6.102.
[83] A former *p.u.* if PLRE 2. Gallus 3 is him; ICUR 2.148 n.15.
[84] Flavius Constantius Felix and wife Padusia decorate the apse in S. Giovanni in Laterano in 428/30: ICUR 2.149 n.17; Marinianus (PLRE 2. Marinianus 3) and wife Anastasia decorate the façade of S. Pietro in Vaticano under Leo I (440-61): ICUR 2.55 n.10; Attica wife of Magnus Felix (PLRE 2. Felix 21) builds a chapel next to S. Lorenzo in Damaso in the mid to late 5th century: ICUR 2. 151 n.25; A Severus and his wife Cassia decorate S. Anastasia in 461/68: ICUR 2.24 n.25. Two more substantive donors were Demetria Anicia, who provided the money, and land, for S. Stefano in Via Latina outside the walls between 440-61 (LP 1.238, ILCV 1. 1765), and the *magister militum* Ricimer, who builds S. Agatha dei Goti in 459 or 470 (ICUR 2. 438 n.127).
[85] ICUR 2. 436 n.115; LP 1.249. This reference to a gift by Valila has been questioned though: Cecchelli M. 'Valilae o valide? L'iscrizione di S. Andrea all'Esquilino', *Romano Barbarica* 11 (1991) 61-78. See also: Sapelli M. 'La basilica di Giunio Basso', in *Aurea Roma* (2000) 137-39.
[86] Petrignani A. *La basilica di S. Pudenziana in Roma secondo gli scavi recentemente eseguiti* (1934) 25 with plate I.
[87] If this is he, then after AD. 397 Pammachius became a monk, so technically this may have been a clerical foundation.

is now lost, describes Pammachius as the founder (*condidit aedes*).⁸⁸ This seems like a step further than Vestina, who, as we have described, merely gives jewellery and other material possessions to sell for a basilica building to be created. It's a step further even compared to the donations of Valila and Demetria Anicia, where land or a building was given, but where the official foundation of the basilica was left to the ecclesiastical authorities. This direct foundation by Pammachius may be because he was a monk at the time of the foundation so, as an ecclesiastic, was in a position to take such a step. The entrance inscription lacks the detail we would like, so how the land was acquired for the basilica and precisely when it was built are unknown.⁸⁹

Into the 6th and 7th centuries, evidence for lay patronage disappears, probably the result of the Vandal invasion of North Africa and the Gothic Wars terminally damaging many aristocratic fortunes. In this period, the Christian basilica building that there was, appears to have all originated from ecclesiastical sources.

1.4.3.2 Clerical Building Managers or Founders

With the donors Vestina and Demetria Anicia, we hear of priests being given a leading role in the construction of Christian basilica-halls, which in turn may indicate an interesting arrangement that seems to apply more widely. With the Vestina donation we see the appearance of three clerics being given the role of supervising the construction of the basilica, which shows the Church's intimate involvement in that case. These individuals would be of little interest on their own except for the fact that they appear to be involved in several other Christian basilica constructions of this period. For example, the priest Leopardus appears again, along with a Maximus and an Ilicius, in the inscriptions commemorating the building and decoration of S. Pudenziana in the late 4th or early 5th centuries:

Fund(ata) a Leopardo et Icilio Valent Aug et Eutyciano cos (ILCV 1772A)

Salvo Siricio Episc Eclesiae Sanctae et Ilicio Leopardo et Maximo presbbb (ILCV 1772B)

Maximus fecit cum suis (ILCV 1773A)⁹⁰

Ilicius appears again, building something at a shrine to St. Hippolytus:

Omnia quae videntur a memoria sancti martyris Yppoliti usque huc surgere tecta Ilicius presb sumtu propio fecit (ILCV 1773)⁹¹

And similarly Leopardus, who decorates S. Lorenzo Fuori le Mura:

Succedunt meliora sibi miranda tuenti quae Leopardi labor cura et Vigilantia fec(it)… (ICUR 2.155 n.3)

All this may suggest, as Krautheimer also proposes, that these priests, especially Leopardus and Ilicius, were members of some sort of informal ecclesiastical building committee whose particular job was to lead the building projects of this period, under Siricius, Anastasius and Innocent I.⁹² Indeed it would not be too fanciful to suggest that such a committee had existed for many years, perhaps founded under Damasus, when the first wave of extensive bishop-led Christian building took place. The *LP*, however, suggests that priests were also capable of constructing their own basilicas independently and buying the land around them before 355, with Felix II, when he was still a priest, doing exactly this.⁹³ Indeed, this was probably a common way in which *tituli*-basilicas were created in the 4th and 5th century, most clerics being from wealthy families.⁹⁴

The first definitively known foundation of a Christian basilica by a priest inside the city though is not until the mid 5th century when the presbyter Peter builds S. Sabina under the pontificate of Celestine (422-32).⁹⁵ It seems we have here an established case of a clerical foundation named after a famous female martyr, the pattern suggested by Hillner. Similarly, the *titulus Lucinae* was more likely named after the 3rd century aristocratic woman Lucina—who was believed to have saved the relics of Peter and Paul and laid to rest those of bishop Cornelius—not after a 4th/5th century donor.⁹⁶

There are of course many inscriptions where clerics are absent in reference to a new Christian construction or restoration, but this may not mean they were not involved.

---

⁸⁸ ICUR 2.150 n.20; 2 presbyters in 499: MGH.AA.12.411-12.
⁸⁹ For more on this church see, for the archaeology: CBCR 1. 265-300; LTUR 3.105-106 and for a reinterpretation of the site: Brenk B. 'Microstoria sotto la chiesa dei Ss. Giovanni e Paolo: la cristianizzazione di una casa privata', *RivIstArch* 18 (1995) 169-206.
⁹⁰ For a discussion on the various complexities surrounding the building of the church see: Montini R. U. *Santa Pudenziana* (1958); CBCR 3.299-300; LTUR 4.166-68 and most recently Angelelli C. *La basilica titolare di S. Pudenziana: nuove ricerche* (2010). The church is no longer universally thought to have been a former bathhouse. It is now believed by some to have been installed in the courtyard of a house with fountains: Guidobaldi F. 'Osservazioni sugli edifici romani in cui si insediò l'ecclesia pudentiana', in *Ecclesiae Urbis* (2002) 1057 (1033-71), but this interpretation may relate to an earlier phase. See chapter 2 for more on this church.
⁹¹ Likely to be a reference to his building of a portico at his tomb outside the city: Testini P. 'Nota di topografia romana: gli edifici del prete Ilicio', in *Quaeritur inventus colitur: miscellanea in onore di padre Umberto Maria Fasola*, edd. P. Pergola and F. Bisconti (1989) 779-93.
⁹² CBCR 3. 302.
⁹³ LP. 1.211.
⁹⁴ Hillner J. 'Clerics, property and patronage' (2006) 59-68.
⁹⁵ ILCV 1.1778a: a large mosaic inscription in the church that describes its founder (*…fundavit presbyter urbis Illyrica de gente Petrus…*) and the pontificate. Not completed until the time of Sixtus III? (432-40): LP 1.235.
⁹⁶ LP 1.150-51; Hillner J. 'Clerics, property and patronage' (2006). But see Cooper K. 'The martyr, the *matrona* and the bishop: the matron Lucina and the politics of martyr cult in fifth- and sixth-century Rome', *Early Medieval Europe* 8.3 (1999) 297–317. It is likely that the clerics of tituli-basilicas had a degree of independence from episcopal control though, once the building was complete, even though the bishop and Church nominally owned the building and its endowments: Bowes K. *Private Worship* (2008) 69 nn 55-56.

The appearance of only the bishop in such inscriptions could alone imply the involvement of the building committee described above, he himself likely to have been the head of it. It may have been an epigraphic affectation as to whether the whole committee was mentioned or just the bishop. This informal organisation (no job titles are listed) would specifically manage Christian building programmes, the money for which could have come from a variety of sources. This group would have had a large amount of autonomy and independence from the imperial and state bureaucracy. The recurrence of several clerics' names in building inscriptions in the late 4th-early 5th c. implies a group like this existed at that time, but we cannot say whether this was a long-lasting arrangement.

So, the frequent appearance of the Roman bishop on inscriptions is not a deceit, but rather a reflection of the reality of his own and several priests' central involvement in the construction in question. This clerical involvement could have been within an organising committee or independently. Into the 6th and 7th centuries, the now contemporary *vitae* in the Liber Pontificalis point to several, seemingly solely, episcopal interventions, with clerical intervention disappearing from official records.

1.4.3.3 Patronage by the Bishop

This form of patronage, according to our main source for Christian building in Rome, the *Liber Pontificalis*, was the most common way Christian basilica building was financed in the city. The accuracy of this pro-papal source is questionable of course, especially when it refers to periods before it began to be systematically compiled, in the 6th century. However, the picture the *Liber Pontificalis* (hereafter *LP*) portrays of a Christian building programme initiated largely by the bishop of Rome, is not improbable, such munificence being likely to have been part of the expectations for urban bishops, in the same way as games were for the urban aristocracy. Where the funding itself originally came from is not always obvious though. The terms the *LP* uses after the bishop's name such as *construit* seems to imply they were the Church's own funds, or perhaps from the bishop's personal wealth. There are many basilicas that are claimed to be built by a particular bishop, but for our purposes here we will focus on those examples where we have some written evidence as well as epigraphic proof that backs this up. There are only two of these for the period up to the death of Sixtus III (432-40): the construction of the first S. Lorenzo in Damaso by Damasus in the mid 4th century, and the building of S. Maria Maggiore by Sixtus III himself in the mid 5th.[97]

Damasus' foundation is recorded in the *LP* as to St. Lawrence *iuxta theatrum*, and uses *fecit* when referring to his activity.[98] This could be translated as 'built', but could also mean 'created' or 'made'. Such a differentiation becomes significant when we look at one of the inscriptions that was placed inside this basilica, which survives because it was copied down in the 9th century. It states that Damasus' father, but more likely Damasus himself, rose from *exceptor* to priest here, and may have lived in this place when he was elected bishop. This, combined with the statement that he built an archive on this spot and added some columns, implies a pre-existing building being modified, rather than an entirely new one being 'built':

Hinc pater exceptor, lector, levita, sacerdos,
creverat hinc meritis quoniam melioribus actis,
hinc mihi provecto Christus, cui summa potestas,
sedis apostolicae voluit concedere honorem.
archivis, fateor, volui nova condere tecta,
addere praeterea dextra laevaque columnas,
quae Damasi teneant proprium per saecula nomen
(ICUR II. 135. n.7, 151. n.23)[99]

This rather detailed and informative inscription is at odds with the brief and formalised inscriptions by prefects or emperors, placed on the outside of buildings. The difference probably lies in that the latter are speaking to the whole urban population, whereas Damasus' text, and most other Christian inscriptions it seems, only address the Christian community, them being sited inside Christian basilica-halls. For our purposes, what seems clear is that Damasus does not produce *ex novo* a purpose-built basilica, but rather modifies an already existing structure, for Christian worship. This does not mean it was already a long-standing pre-existing Christian centre, rather such modifications were extremely likely in such a built-up city where open land in prime spots was rare, so the acquisition of houses or *insulae* for modification was necessary. This process was probably the rule for the 4th century bishops, and in this case Damasus seems in charge of the operation and the money used for it.

The other bishop-led project we can examine was certainly an *ex novo* construction, and seems to be a replacement for the so-called Liberian Basilica, built or created in the same area by Liberius more than seventy years previously. This new foundation, now known as S. Maria Maggiore, has structural remains no earlier than the 5th century underneath it, and so does not lie above Liberius' foundation. The *LP* seems confused here then where it suggests the two buildings are the same.[100] Parts of a house still in use in the 4th century have been found under the basilica, where an illustrated calendar was discovered, but there is no evidence to suggest this was ever an earlier Christian centre.[101] This major building project, which seems to have been headed by Sixtus himself, could therefore represent a large step forward in 'papal' building.[102] The two inscriptions from the original

---

[97] The *tituli Marci* and *Iuli*, and *Basilica Liberii*, all named after bishops said to have founded them, can be argued to have been episcopal foundations as well, but lack early surviving/recorded inscriptions: see Hillner J. 'Clerics, property and patronage' (2006).
[98] LP. 1.212.
[99] For more detail on this church see Chapter 5 below.
[100] LP. 1.232.
[101] Magi F. *Il calendario dipinto sotto Santa Maria Maggiore* (1972).
[102] CBCR 3.5 and 53-57, cf. LTUR 3. 217. For more on the church see Chapter 3: High Places. Macro Visibility.

basilica that we have copies of also enlighten us, in that they emphasise the centrality given to the bishop for this project. This is a purely Christian building scheme, and none of the civil administrators are mentioned.[103] Although it is likely some city officials were involved at some level, their absence from the inscriptions, as well as the more unusual omission of Church administrators, may signify a further step away by the Church from city government with regards to building, and the increasing role the bishop took in such projects from this time.

Into the later 5th, 6th and 7th centuries, the *LP* assigns new intramural basilica creation only to various bishops. Simplicius (468-83) '*dedicavit*' basilicas/shrines to St. Stephen (S. Stefano Rotondo: for more on this, see chapter 4 below), St. Bibiana (S. Bibiana) and St. Andrew, where we know a Gothic aristocrat, Flavius Valila, provided the building and the money to convert it (S. Andrea Catabarbara: see n.119).[104] This may suggest that with all these foundations the bishop simply consecrated a building funded by an outside donor, but we cannot be certain. None of these are given the role of a *titulus*; they have no representatives in the lists of titular presbyters present at the Roman synods of 499 and 595 either.

Into the late 5th, 6th and 7th century the *LP* becomes at times a contemporary record.[105] Its *vitae* become more reliable and voluminous as a result, but briefer and less reliable on the subject of Christian basilica construction, with nuances as to the identity of founders, donors and property largely lost. Nevertheless, a useful selection of episcopal foundations for this time include: Felix IV (526-30) who '*fecit*' the basilica of Saints Cosmas and Damian (SS. Cosma e Damiano), which can be translated as 'built', but more accurately in this case would mean 'made' as it was simply the conversion of a pre-existing 4th century hall and vestibule.[106] This hall, whether it was part of the *bibliotheca pacis* or not, was attached to the southwestern part of the Forum of Peace and must have been public property. As such it must have been given to the bishop by Theodoric (or by his daughter Amalasuntha if after 526), which was then converted by Felix, presumably with the Church's own money and at his request, which the apse inscription implies.[107] Pelagius I (556-61) begins the basilica dedicated to the apostles Philip and James (SS. Apostoli), but died soon after the building of it was started (*qui dum initiaretur fabricari*), although again how literally we should take 'building' is open to debate. His successor John III (561-74) completes (*perfecit*) and dedicates it.[108] The famous conversion of the Pantheon to a Christian building dedicated to Mary and the Martyrs is undertaken by Boniface IV (608-15), with the permission of the Byzantine emperor, but this process is better understood as a conversion similar to Felix IV's a century earlier, as the Pantheon was not strictly a temple.[109] The need to ask for the emperor's permission suggests it was his property or under his jurisdiction, much like the Constantinian hall/Library of Peace was under Theodoric's.

The pope's acquirement of two such prestigious properties, and the use of such spaces, by whatever means, indicates the ambition and authority the papacy now possessed and its centrality in prestige Christian building creation by this time. Honorius (625-38) was an even more ambitious builder outside the city, but within the city he *fecit ecclesiam beatorum Quattuor Coronatorum*, however presbyters of this Christian centre existed in 595, so this is just a rebuild.[110] However, it was he who converted the Senate House into a basilica to St. Hadrian (*fecit ecclesiam beati Adriani in Tribus Fatis, quam et dedicavit, et dona multa optulit*), another prestigious acquisition for the Church and a sign of the final collapse of the ancient form of government. The fact that he 'made' it and 'dedicated' it, confirms that the project was completed in his lifetime. With Leo II (682-83) we hear that he 'built/made' (*Hic fecit*) a basilica near to that of Bibiana in the eastern part of the city to deposit the relics of various martyrs, and we know precisely its dedication day of 22 February 683.[111] Bibiana's remains were moved to her basilica at some point.[112]

In a 10th century addition (according to Duchesne) to Leo II's *vita* he is said to have 'ordered' the construction of a 'church' in honour of Saint Sebastian and the martyr George (*...iussu aecclesiam iuxta Velum aureum in honore beati Sebastiani edificata est, necnon in honore martiris Georgii*) now S. Georgio in Velabro, between the Arch of Janus and the *Arcus Argentarii* (Arch of the Silversmiths).[113] It has been noted that the phraseology is significant. The verb *(a)edificare* is used, implying new building work rather than modification or conversion of an existing structure, and the pope makes an order (*iussu*), suggesting this was a private self-funded papal project where he had control of the permits for construction.[114] Permissions are no longer

---

[103] ICUR 2. 435 n. 111 and 2. 71 n. 42, 2. 98 n.6, 2. 139 n.28.
[104] LP 1. 249.
[105] For a brief summary of the manuscript tradition of the LP see Davis R. ed. and transl. *The Book of Pontiffs (Liber Pontificalis): the Ancient Biographies of the First Ninety Roman Bishops to AD 715* (2000) xlvi-xlviii.
[106] See Chapter 3: Reuse of Prestige Public Buildings.
[107] Apse inscription: ICUR 2.71, 134, 152, 353, 439. Pronouncement of Theodoric allowing private ownership of public property, but with the condition that the building needs to be restored (as with this basilica): Cassiod. *Var.* 7.44.
[108] LP 1. 303, 305.
[109] LP 1. 317. The use of the term *templum* in the text here may be a reference to this structure having been just a sacred area, its literal meaning, rather than an *aedes* (the pagan religious building housing the deity confined to priests, or 'temple'). However, such etymological nuances were probably lost by this time, and its identity as a temple was probably just an assumption by the compiler based on the existence of statues of deities within it or their recent removal.
[110] LP 1. 324; MGH.Ep. 1.367.
[111] LP 1. 360. The church no longer survives: Coates-Stephens R. 'Dark-age architecture in Rome', *BSR* 65 (1997) 187 (177-232).
[112] LP 1. 249.
[113] LP 1.360, 439 n.51. An inscription from the Catacombs of Callixtus from 482 mentions an Augustus, who was '*lectoris de belabru*' (ICUR 1.388 n.871) which could suggest an older church on the site. This may also be a reference to an earlier diaconia there (LP 1.434 and see CBCR 1.246-63; LTUR 2.370-71), S. Anastasia or possibly another Christian foundation in the area: Cerrito A. 'Contributo allo studio del *titulus Anastasiae*', in *Marmoribus vestita: miscellanea in onore di Federico Guidobaldi*, edd. O. Brandt and P. Pergola (2011) 352 n.28 (345-71).
[114] Frutaz A. P. 'La diaconia di S. Giorgio in Velabro', in *Collegium cultorum martyrum, primo exeunte saeculo* (1980) 159-87.

required by this time. However, Leo may in fact have been using a pre-existing structure, in spite of the LP's rhetoric. There was said to be a *diaconia*, or welfare centre, here before this.[115] Evidence for a Roman building also exist on the site, and 7th century walls are apparent. The most recent investigations confirm that Leo's foundation was a small single naved hall that incorporated a 6th-7th century structure and part of 2nd-3rd century building.[116] So this is not an *ex novo* build, but the project did enlarge on pre-existing structures, one of which may have already been Christian, as part of a private papal venture.

1.4.3.4 Imperial Patronage

The large and expensive imperial Christian projects were mainly restricted to funerary or later conventional basilicas over or near the graves of various Roman martyrs outside the city, but a word on their frequency and organisation is appropriate here. Surprisingly there are only three periods when imperial activity took place: the Constantinian period or just after, the late 4th century, and the middle of the 5th century. We cannot easily say why this should be, but it emphasises the relative independence of Christian building from the imperial bureaucracy, as well as from the civil administration. That is, the Church usually initiated building projects with, as we have seen, some sort of clerical building management, using a mixture of aristocratic donations at first, but increasingly its own money. In this way the emperor rarely felt it necessary to fund such programs, aside from large prestige foundations outside the walls. Beyond the mid 5th century, the emperor's power and interest was focused on either Constantinople or Ravenna, so a lack of imperial intervention is not surprising.

The organisation of an imperial Christian building project has already been examined through our discussion of the second S. Paolo Fuori le Mura above, in fact the only imperial new build that we have evidence for such a system. As such, we cannot assume this case can be applied to the seven schemes that Constantine or his sons began.[117] The inscriptions marking their completion are lost and were not copied down,[118] but it is likely that the organisation apparent in the imperial prescript for the rebuilding of S. Paolo was not very different to that first implemented under Constantine or soon after. However, we do have more information with two cases of imperial money going towards improving already existing basilicas, when Valentinian III and his mother Galla Placidia were involved as donors.

When the empress, around 440/50, repaired the damaged mosaic of S. Paolo, she acknowledges the other reconstruction work of Leo I. In the inscription describing his restoration, the role played by two priests, named Felix and Adeodatus, is acknowledged. This again implies these two individuals actually organised the day-to-day running of the project, with the pope being the initiator and official donor.[119] It is interesting to note that with the imperial inscription no other people are mentioned as being involved in the mosaic's repair, yet with the papal work others are referred to. This is likely to have been more a reflection of how imperial work was portrayed, that is as a personal gift from the emperor, rather than an accurate picture of the bureaucratic reality behind the programme. Yet, as we have seen, when the second S. Paolo was built, the ecclesiastical authorities were informed and questioned, but do not seem to have been directly involved in the building work. The emperors employed their own separate architects and planners, shown by the discussion of the Theodosian Bridge project, which was part of the same programme.

The imperial family members Galla Placidia, Valentinian III and his sister Honoria also repaired the mosaics in S. Croce in 425/44, but again no detail is given of who else took part in the project.[120] This is characteristic of many imperial building programmes as we have said, where the dedicatory inscription marking its completion is used as a way of promoting their munificence and generosity, rather than providing an accurate record of who was involved in the work. Such acknowledgements are more of a priority where imperial money is not involved. As such, our knowledge of imperial Christian projects is limited, with the construction of the second S. Paolo being our only, albeit detailed, template for any speculation.

The evidence for the foundation of *Sancti Apostolorum in Eudoxia* (S. Pietro in Vincoli) by the empress Eudoxia in the mid 5th century is interesting in this respect. The inscriptions describing the completion of the project are suggestive of a joint imperial-ecclesiastical intervention as well as a solely imperial one.[121] This may mark a watershed between the independent, sporadic, imperially funded programs and the increasingly common self-funded papal/clerical projects. Any reference to the foundation is strangely absent from the *LP*.

---

[115] See this chapter: n.113 above.

[116] It was thought that Leo's 7th century structure had been largely lost in the reconstruction of the basilica by Gregory IV (827-44), but a nearby car bomb in 1993 exposed the brickwork of the façade showing it to be largely 7th century: Turco M. G. 'Analisi delle apparecchiature murarie. Conferme e nuovi apporti', in *La chiesa di San Giorgio in Velabro a Roma. Storia, documenti, testimonianze del restauro dopo l'attentato del luglio 1993* (2002) 89-128.

[117] These being the ambulatory basilicas of S. Agnese fuori le Mura, S. Lorenzo fuori le Mura, SS. Marcellino e Pietro and the churches of S. Pietro in Vaticano, S. Croce in Gerusalemme, the first S. Paolo fuori le Mura and S. Giovanni in Laterano. For the idea that the Lateran should be regarded more as a 'private' building project see Brandt O., 'Early church building policy' (2001).

[118] The only exceptions are some fragmentary copies made from old St. Peter's which seem to confirm Constantine's primary involvement, but do not enlighten us as to any other individuals' role: ICUR 2. 345 nn.1-2. However, there was an inscription on the gold cross above the apostle's tomb mentioning Constantine and his mother Helena: ICUR 2.199 n.1, 346 n.3.

[119] Empress' repair: ICUR 2. 81 n.17, 98 n.5, 68 nn.82-83/ ILCV 1. 1761 a-c. Leo I's repair: ICUR (NS) 2. 4783.

[120] ICUR 2. 435 n.107.

[121] CBCR 3.221; LTUR 4.82-3; Bartolozzi Casti G. and Zandri G. *San Pietro in Vincoli* (1999) 41-58; work by the presbyter Phillipus and dedicated by Sixtus III: ICUR 2.110 n.67/134 n.3, 134 n.2; Eudoxia: ICUR 2.110 n.66.

1.5 Conclusion

In general, intramural Christian building can be characterised as independent from the rest of the construction and restoration activity in Rome, until the Church itself began to run the city administration. A law of 364 prohibited new building in Rome by the prefect in favour of just restoration.[122] This still allowed for new Christian building though (and imperial projects), which, as we have seen, did not require the attention of the prefect. With the collapse of the civil administration in the wake of the mid 6th century Gothic Wars, the Pope and the Church filled the gap, which led to examples of Christian centres being created within suitable prestige structures in the centre of the city that were, by this time, unused. Even from the 4th century, the evidence we have points to a system where the bishop led, or had a senior role in, the construction of many of the Christian buildings in the city, notable exceptions being the imperial projects where he seems to have been used only in an advisory capacity. The actual daily running of individual Christian basilica building projects, at least for a time, appears to have been headed by priests, who were part of some sort of informal building committee.

In this way, the Church could in principle buy property within the city with the money they received from rents from property gifts, exhaustively listed in the 4th and 5th century *vitae* of the LP, or from private donations. It is assumed that such donations also included the building into which the basilica was to be created, but there are actually very few attested cases of such property gifts. The donation was usually separate from the building used. Lay aristocratic donors could also have deliberately acquired sites in favourable places as well of course, similar motivations to the bishop also being apparent.

In the examples of Christian foundations described in the following chapters, the favourable location and pre-existing archaeology on the site point to the deliberate purchase of a building that would enhance the visibility of an otherwise small structure, and/or allow the utilisation of a space suited to liturgical needs. Many of the Christian buildings of the period up to the 7th century inside the walls are either: small basilicas next to main roads, sometimes encroaching onto them; larger basilicas on hills or high points in the city; basilicas constructed within prestige central structures; and others within or near bath buildings for the use of convenient pre-existing bathing facilities for baptismal and liturgical uses.

This suggests that at times, the bishop, a clerical building committee, or an individual cleric or private lay donor, chose to locate a new basilica in a prominent part of the city landscape to enhance the prestige and prominence of the foundation and in turn their own cachet. As members of the aristocratic elite, such a motivation should not surprise us.[123] Their own sizeable wealth and their access to significant private donations, and the revenues from imperial land and property grants, made this possible.

As for the position of the bishop in particular: the holy man as a *patronus*, first described by Peter Brown, was a natural evolution in role for those from leading families entering the episcopate.[124] It was the combination of this money and spiritual authority that meant a bishop quickly become a very powerful individual within their sphere of influence. Their building role could be described therefore as a curious mix of Christian evangelism and local civic expectation.[125] Men with private wealth already seem to have had a greater chance of rising to the episcopate; the many reported cases of simony may explain this.[126] We can also see the degree to which the bishopric of Rome was coveted, by the violent pursuit of the position in 366 between Damasus and Ursinus.[127] The famous sarcastic statement said to have been made by the well-known aristocratic pagan senator Praetextatus, concerning the position, is equally revealing.[128]

Outside Rome, the importance of Christian basilica location, and the role of a bishop in this, is apparent in the building activity of the bishop of Nola, Paulinus, in the early 5th century. It is obvious from one of Paulinus' letters to his friend Sulpicius Severus in 403/404, that a bishop was capable of having direct control over the location and design of a new basilica. Paulinus describes the building of a structure dedicated to the local saint, Felix, just to the north of Nola, that was deliberately located and designed so as to have a strong relationship with the nearby Church of the Apostles. This was in order to increase the prestige of Felix, and to increase the popularity of his cult.[129] Also, at Gaza, an account of the construction of a Christian basilica, probably in 402, shows not only the central role the bishop played, but also the influence he had on the precise positioning of the structure and the funds required to build it.[130] The acquisition of buildings in Rome may have been a more complex business, particularly at first in the 4th and 5th centuries, negotiating lay and imperial fiscal donations and property ownership. Yet, the motivations shown by the bishops of Nola and Gaza were no less apparent at Rome.

---

[122] *Cod. Theod.* 15.1.11; an urban prefect trying to circumvent this: Amm. Marc. 27.3.7.

[123] For the role and importance of the bishop in late antiquity see: Klauser T. *Der Ursprung der bischöflichen Insignien und Ehrenrechte* (1949); Brown P. L. R. *Power and Persuasion in Late Antiquity: Towards a Christian Empire* (1992). More recent scholarship has also emphasised the continued independence the role enjoyed from the Roman state: Chadwick H. 'Bishops and monks', *Studia Patristica* 24 (1993) 45-61; Sterk A. *Renouncing the World Yet Leading the Church: The Monk-Bishop in Late Antiquity* (2004).
[124] Brown P. L. R. 'The rise and function of the holy man in late antiquity', *JRS* 61 (1971) 80-101.
[125] Rapp C. *Holy Bishops in Late Antiquity: the Nature of Christian Leadership in an Age of Transition* (2005) 223.
[126] Rapp C. *Holy Bishops* (2005) 199-203, 211-12 with notes.
[127] Amm. Marc. 27.3.12-13.
[128] Jer. *c. Joh. Hierosol.* 8: "*Miserabilis ille Praetextatus, qui designatus consul est mortuus, homo sacrilegus et idolorum cultor, solebat ludens beato papae Damaso dicere: 'Facite me Romanae urbis episcopum, et ero protinus Christianus.'*"
[129] Paul. *Ep.* 32.13-15, *Carm.* 27.370-1; Goldschmidt R. C. *Paulinus' Churches at Nola* (1940) 17, 19-20.
[130] Mark the Deacon, *Life of Porphyry*, 43, 45, 53 (Hill G. F. transl. *The Life of Porphyry, Bishop of Gaza* (1913)).

2. Christian Basilicas and Baths

"Then the angel showed me the river of the water of life, as clear as crystal, flowing from the throne of God and of the Lamb down the middle of the great street of the city" (Revelations 22:1-2).[1]

A pragmatic and utilitarian building program emerges when we discuss the relationship between some of the intramural Christian buildings of the 4th to 7th centuries in the city and the pre-existing baths, and those baths that were newly created in this period. Our evidence becomes much clearer for some kind of relationship between the two after the Gothic Wars when the aqueducts were greatly damaged and the Church began to take a leading role in water maintenance and provision, so baths appear more frequently in our main source, the *LP*. However, before this, the proximity of several Christian buildings to the fully functioning large *thermae*, the ownership of many baths by *tituli*, and with some actually built within former bathing establishments, there is good reason to think a pragmatic, practical relationship existed earlier.[2]

There were eleven *thermae* and eight or nine hundred *balnea* in Rome in the mid to late 4th century,[3] and with water being such an important symbolic and liturgical element for Christianity, it seems unlikely that the newly enfranchised Church would not use such plentiful facilities, especially before purpose-built baptisteries widely appeared inside the walls from the mid 5th century.[4] In fact, it is in this period that the baptismal rite was especially important, it still being at this time an initiation rite and formal act of conversion from a catechumen to a fully-fledged Christian.[5]

Several early *tituli* are given in their endowments, recorded in the *LP*, small *balnea*, but this seems to have been to provide an income for the *titulus* in question through renting it out to a third party, rather than it being a practical addition, as the revenues they will provide are also listed. Indeed, the frequency of the association between bath houses and basilicas seems to have led to certain later hagiographies mentioning baths as frequent meeting places for the early Christian communities.[6] It has not been possible yet to uncover enough definitively Christian baths to be able to establish any way archaeologically of distinguishing those that had a Christian function and those without.[7] Nevertheless, early medieval baths for pilgrims and clergy and baptisteries from the mid 5th century should be regarded as purpose-built manifestations of facilities that were just as necessary in the 4th and early 5th centuries, but which at that time the still functioning *thermae* and *balnea* throughout the city could only provide for. The Constantinian Lateran baptistery, the only purpose-built baptistery in the city in this earlier period, could not have catered for an increasingly Christian city as a whole and is likely to have been reserved for the Roman elite.

The nature of the relationship between the Christian basilica and the baths in Rome is a somewhat ambiguous one however, as well as being pragmatic and functional. This is reflected in contemporary western Christian thought on the subject of bathing, that is to say a distaste for bath houses, but an approval of the act of bathing itself for hygienic reasons. This generally positive attitude western ecclesiastical elites had towards baths and bathing would not have discouraged such a practical relationship. Pope Gregory I in a letter or sermon to the Roman people in September 603 says that bathing must not be an activity that we derive pleasure from, of whatever sort, but is rather a purely utilitarian activity to clean the body for hygienic reasons.[8] Even in the Rome of the early 7th century then, bathing was still popular, for the 'wrong' reasons perhaps, but was still widely occurring in establishments throughout the city. This was in spite of the cutting of the aqueducts nearly sixty years earlier, during the siege of Vitiges the Goth, which is said to have put the large imperial baths permanently out of use. From Gregory though, it would seem the smaller *balnea* were still patronised and kept running by the now ecclesiastical administration, and that the larger imperial *thermae* may have continued to be used in some form. Augustine, also writing in the western tradition, recognises the positive hygienic and health factors, but at the same time warns

---

[1] Translation: *New International Version* (1984).
[2] In spite of this evidence any sort of relationship between the two is often rejected: Stasolla F. R. *Pro labandis curis: il balneum tra tarda antichità e medioevo* (2002) 68.
[3] *Not. Rom.* Breviarium: Nordh ed. *Libellus* (1949) 105.6 and see here nn.187-88 below.
[4] Cecchelli M. 'Dati da scavi recenti di monumenti cristiani. Sintesi relativa a diverse indagini in corso', *MÉFRM* 111.1 (1999) 227-51. The exception was the Lateran baptistry built by Constantine: LP 1.174.
[5] Infant baptisms are not unknown, however: eg. Cyprian, *Ep.* 58.
[6] Within the Acts of St. Justin, he meets his followers in the 'Baths of Timothy' in Rome, which may be the 'Baths of Novatus', themselves only known through the Acts of Saints Pudentiana and Praxedis (Cabrol F. ed., *Dictionnaire d'archéologie chrétienne et de liturgie* (1907-53) vol. 2.1: 111-12 and refs. ('Bains'); LTUR 1.165-66 and refs. There is also the legendary foundation of S. Pudenziana in the 2nd century (see below): Bollandists edd. *Acta Sanctorum*, 67 vols. (1902-70, repr. of orig. 1643-1883) (=*AA.SS.*) Mai IV.300. Christians are said to have met informally in baths in Constantinople and Carthage as well: Cabrol F. ed., *Dictionnaire* (1907-53) vol.2.1: 115 and refs.
[7] See Cosentino A. 'Il battesimo a Roma: edifici e liturgia', in *Ecclesiae Urbis* (2002) 109-42 and Stasolla F. R. 'Balnea ed edifici di culto: relazioni e trasformazioni tra tarda antichità e alto medioevo', in *Ecclesiae Urbis* (2002) 143-51 with discussion (157-58).
[8] Gregory, *Ep.* 13.3.

against their over frequent use.⁹ A 5th century inscription reused in the medieval floor of S. Martino ai Monti argues the same,¹⁰ and it is not unlikely that the original location of this inscription was at the entrance of a bath house in the city as a reminder to its Christian customers. Examples of Christian buildings created outside large *thermae*, which we will examine below, may have had a similar effect. B. Ward-Perkins nicely summarises the situation as a move away from ideas of luxury to those of necessity, which is mirrored in other forms of Christian patronage.¹¹ The close association of baths and basilicas was also helped by the essential absence of 'pagan' cultic activity in them, unlike many other parts of the city up to the 5th century.¹² Martial, our only source for what went on in the smaller *balnea*, only refers to them as having a social function. We can be fairly safe therefore in assuming that the gods' place was outside of the *balnea*, in which human activity took priority.

However, we do have some evidence, from the 2nd century A.D., that private baths were used by the cult of Isis. Apuleius writes that as part of the initiation into the cult, he underwent a ceremony, very much like a Christian baptism, in the *balneas*.¹³ Even though such pagan religious behaviour in a *balnea* appears to be unusual, the case for saying that early Christian groups utilised the same buildings for the same ritual purpose is not unlikely, especially in the post-Constantinian era, but it is of course currently unprovable. The only small hint that this may have occurred, can be seen in a brief statement in the life of bishop Liberius (352-66) in the *LP*. It appears in the context of the events surrounding the interventions of the Arian emperor Constantius II and the exile of the orthodox, Catholic, bishop Felix at Rome, with particular reference to Arian rebaptism by 'heretic' clergy and the persecutions that took place of Catholics in Rome at that time. The passage mentions how members of the orthodox clergy and *sacerdotes*:

" ...*could gain no entry into church or baths.*"¹⁴

This clearly connects the two structures in a Christian context, and implies priests of various grades may have used them for purposes linked with Christian activity, in this context, baptisms. No archaeological evidence in bath houses, or any other literary reference refers to such activity however, so we must remain cautious.

Yet, in practical terms, the baths gave access to clean flowing water, and were thus ideal spaces to adapt for Christian use or for a *titulus* to own or be located next to. Up to the mid 5th century Christian centres did not have formal baptisteries or purpose-built 'Christian baths', so such facilities had to be found elsewhere. The use of simple wells or fountains would have provided a short term solution, but the Church was now a respectable organisation endowed by the emperor. Thus, a more formal setting for baptisms, for example—that most crucial of Christian ceremonies, particularly in this early period—was now appropriate and desirable. The common practice of full immersion baptisms, to replicate Christ's own baptism by John the Baptist in the River Jordan, also necessitated a significant pool of water.¹⁵ Possible evidence for the use of a Roman bath house in Kent for Christian baptism shows this could have occurred throughout the empire.¹⁶ Although the early Church states a preference for baptisms at Easter and Pentecost, the existence of eighteen formal baptisteries inside the city, including the Vatican, by the Early Middle Ages (most of which were next to small local basilicas), suggests such ceremonies were taking place more frequently than this, and throughout the city, if such numerous formal provision was later required.¹⁷

Aside from the baptismal rite itself, water was also needed for the washing of hands by the priest when using the oil of exorcism (*oleum exorcidiatum*) and the oil of chrism (*oleum chrismae*) during the baptismal ceremony.¹⁸ Equally, washing in general was encouraged for ritual reasons connected with a Feast Day or before entering a Christian basilica.¹⁹ In the urban environment, it is likely the private house baths of a wealthy Christian provided for this in the pre-Constantinian era. The appearance, as we will see, of private baths associated with new Christian basilicas after Constantine, may simply be a continuation of this practice. This ritual washing or cleansing was also part of the service provided by the *diaconia* that appeared later in the city. Baths for pilgrims were also a feature from the mid 5th century outside the city. With the advent of purpose-built Christian facilities, the need to utilise pre-existing 'secular' facilities gradually disappears, so the examples in this chapter will be confined mainly to the 4th and 5th centuries. Later bathing and water-

---

⁹ August., *Ep.* 211.13. For a general picture of Rome in the late 6th to early 7th century, with extensive bibliography, see Ghilardi M. 'Iam vacua ardet Roma: la città di Roma al tempo di Gregorio Magno', in *Il tempo di natale nella Roma di Gregorio Magno* (2010) 1-105.
¹⁰ Silvagni A. 'La basilica di S. Martino ai Monti: l'oratorio di S. Silvestro e il titolo costantiniano di Equizio', *Archivio della Reale Società romana di storia patria* 35 (1912) 408-10 (329-437).
¹¹ Ward-Perkins B. *From Classical Antiquity to the Middle Ages: Urban Public Building in Northern and Central Italy, AD 300-850* (1984) 152.
¹² The large Mithraeum below the north exedra of the Baths of Caracalla complex is a notable exception, but its presence may have been unknown to non-adherents of the cult: LTUR 3.267-68.
¹³ Apul., *Met.* 11.23.1.
¹⁴ LP 1.208: "...*neque in ecclesia neque in balnea haberent introitum*" (transl. R. Davis (2000) 29).

¹⁵ Mark 1:9-10.
¹⁶ Pitts M. 'Roman pool may be for early Christian baptism', *British Archaeology* 91 (Nov.-Dec. 2006) 8.
¹⁷ Tert. *De bapt.* 19, which may in fact be saying that the period from Easter to Pentecost is preferable, but also states that any day is suitable. Cosentino A. 'Il battesimo a Roma', in *Ecclesiae Urbis* (2002) 116-41; Coates-Stephens R. 'The water-supply of Rome from late antiquity to the early middle ages', in *Rome AD 300-800: Power and Symbol, Image and Reality*, edd. J. Rasmus Brandt *at al* (2003) 178-79 (165-86).
¹⁸ LP. 1.171 and Cabrol F. ed. *Dictionnaire* (1907-53) vol. 6.2: 2778-82 ('Huile'); Pietri C. *Roma christiana* (1976) 106-11. There was indeed a large baptismal ceremony that was held on Holy Saturday every year up to the 6th century at least. This does not exclude the possibility of smaller individual ceremonies being held in other churches throughout the year, however.
¹⁹ Ward-Perkins B. *From Classical Antiquity* (1984) 127, 141. An elaborate fountain was provided at S. Pietro in Vaticano for washing: Paul., *Ep.* 13.13.

supply developments up to the 7th century will be briefly discussed, however.[20]

Away from purely practical considerations, it is worth noting that with the large imperial *thermae* in the city still in good working order until the 6th century, at least, those Christian foundations created next to them up to that time would have benefited in other ways. The public imperial baths were places where a sizeable portion of the population of the city frequently visited, and such movements of people would have benefited the popularity of a basilica situated nearby. In this way, those centres that were built close to such complexes may have had a dual motive for being built there, that is to utilise the baths and to be the place of worship for its customers.

2.1 A Water-Filled City. The Balnea.

Places where there was water, such as springs or wells, dotted the city. There were ten thousand three hundred and fifty two in the 4th century.[21] These were no doubt mainly used for washing and drinking, and are unlikely to have served a formal religious function in connection with a nearby shrine or temple, purpose-built facilities would have been provided for that. The smaller private baths in Rome, the *balnea*, were also a very frequent feature of the Roman landscape, and seem to have been the haunts of the middle and upper-classes as social clubs. This was certainly the case in Martial's day when the only large baths were those of Agrippa, Nero and Titus. Even the addition of three enormous imperial establishments by the 4th century does not seem to have affected this situation.[22] The impression is that these smaller privately-owned bath houses were frequented by the educated classes and had perhaps a 'members only' policy, whereas the large imperial baths were for everyone else. This may explain the practice of these *balnea* being given as property to *tituli* in the 4th and 5th centuries to provide rental income from a prospective middle or upper class tenant to use for this social purpose.

Balnea is a plainer, less sophisticated term than *thermae*, itself a word which was not used until the imperial period, and which tended, at that time, to signify the large, public, more luxurious bathing establishments. The personalised names of the *balnea* further suggests their private nature and/or ownership as well as their modest size. From the mid 4th century lists of the contents of the city, the *Notitia* and *Curiosum*, there seems to have been eight hundred and fifty six such establishments or more in Rome at that time.[23] We know by name as many as fifty-one from various sources, although this may be less if some entries in the *Notitia* or *Curiosum* are taken as only one building. Only twenty-nine of these can be located approximately and only three have been found.[24] (see fig.1) From the, albeit uncertain, numbers we have for each area of the city, region 14 across the Tiber is described as having on average a *balneum* every 17 m^2, in region 12 approximately the same, but only one every 40 m^2 or so in region 5 in the east of the city. Nevertheless, their frequency is startling, which apart from emphasising their private use, also indicates that wherever one built in the city one of these bath houses would be nearby. As such, to argue for an association between a small bath house and a Christian building explicit evidence is required, proximity alone is not enough. That evidence does exist for a few examples. With the larger *thermae*, the close proximity of a Christian structure to a functioning establishment alone provides a compelling argument for an intended relationship of some description.[25]

2.1.1 Case Studies

2.1.1.1 Donated Bath-Baptisteries?

In the life of bishop Marcellus (305/06-309?), the *LP* informs us that he:

> "...organised the twenty-five tituli within Rome as dioceses for the baptism and repentance of many converts from paganism, and for the burial of martyrs."[26]

The *tituli* had a baptismal role therefore, and the nature of the donations given to them in the 4th and 5th century may reflect this. Whatever the origin of these donations given to the newly created *tituli* in the 4th and 5th century, listed in some detail in the *LP*, many of them included bath buildings, or houses with baths. We see this with the *titulus Equitii* (S. Martino ai Monti), which in itself is not far from Domitian's baths, but received a house with its own bath house in a nearby *regione*; the *titulus Damasi* (S. Lorenzo in Damaso) owned baths near to it; and the *titulus Vestinae* (S. Vitale) gained two baths and a house with a bath.[27] These gifts are clearly to provide revenue for the basilica

---

[20] For this period and beyond, the authority for the Roman water supply is Robert Coates-Stephens, for which see: Coates Stephens R. 'The walls and aqueducts of Rome in the early Middle Ages', *JRS* 88 (1998) 166-78; Coates Stephens R. 'Gli acquedotti in epoca tardoantica nel suburbio', in *Suburbium. Il suburbio di Roma dalla crisi del sistema delle ville a Gregorio Magno*, edd. P. Pergola, R. Santangeli Valenzani and R. Volpe (2003) 415-36.
[21] *Not. Rom.* Breviarum: Nordh ed. *Libellus* (1949) 105.7-8.
[22] For these baths as pre-dinner meeting places: Mart., *Epigram* 9.19, 11.52.1-4; in the 4th century: Amm. Marc. 28.4.10.
[23] For the problems and issues with the names, the ownership, clientele and with their numbers see Fagan G. G. *Bathing in Public in the Roman World* (1999) 123-26, 189-222, 357 respectively. For the latter see also Yegül F. K. *Baths and Bathing in Classical Antiquity* (1992) 74. What is not in doubt is that there were very many.
[24] For ambiguity in the *Notitia* and *Curiosum* see for example *Not. Rom.* I: Nordh ed. *Libellus* (1949) 73.15, 74.1; XIIII: Nordh ed. *Libellus* (1949) 95.17-18. See also Fagan G. G. *Bathing* (1999) 359-66 for a list of the baths. The *Balnea Caenidianum, Gratiarum* and *Cerealis* have been found : LTUR. 1.160-61, 2.79, *Caenidianum* only in Richardson. L. *A New Topographical Dictionary of Ancient Rome* (1992) 48.
[25] For a more detailed discussion of *balnea*, including their form, clientele and management into the medieval period, see: Stasolla F. R. *Pro labandis curis* (2002) esp. 43-53, 69-81.
[26] LP 1.164: *...XXV titulos in urbe Roma constituit, quasi diocesis, propter baptismum et paenitentiam multorum qui convertebantur ex paganis et propter sepulturas martyrum.* (transl. R. Davis (2000) 13).
[27] LP. 1. 170-71, 213, 220-21. For the debate as to the origin of these endowments see Hillner J. 'Families, patronage' (2007) and refs.

in question so that it is self-supporting, as it mentions the revenue expected from each. Interestingly though, with the *titulus Equitii* and *Vestinae*, also part of the donations are liturgical vessels used for baptismal rites, those for the latter being quite extensive.[28] The presbyters of the newly founded establishment were therefore expected to carry out baptisms, but with no formal baptistery provided for either of these foundations at this time—or any other in this period in the city, aside from the Lateran—it suggests that the presbyters had to use a bath house for this ritual function, most likely the ones they were donated. The most probable scenario is of a normally functioning private bath house, independently run with a rent paid to the *titulus* in question, but with its presbyters using it on certain occasions, as owners, for baptisms. Their use as simply bathing facilities for the clergy and monks is also likely. This multiplicity of function is typical of what we see elsewhere in Italy in this period and later with Church-owned baths.[29]

These donated baths in Rome are all described as near their respective *tituli*, allowing for convenient use. Sixtus III's (432-40) foundation of the *basilica sanctae Mariae* (S. Maria Maggiore) also included in its donations Palmatus' house inside the city:

> "...almost next to the basilica, with bath and bakery...a silver stag at the font, pouring water...all the sacred vessels for baptism...".[30]

It does not say where this *fontem* (meaning an immersion basin here) is, and the word is a later addition, not appearing in the manuscript Duchesne uses, but Davis (the *LP*'s most recent translator) does not acknowledge this, clearly believing it is reliable. Its appearance in the text implies this basin was either at the bath at Palmatus' house right next to the new basilica, or within Sixtus' basilica to the Virgin. Only further excavation could ever confirm that, however.

It is interesting to note that the earliest known possible case of a *titulus* with a purpose-built baptistery was funded by an Urban Prefect at the most central and prestigiously located example in the city at the time: the *titulus Anastasiae* next to the Circus Maximus at the foot of the Palatine in 400/402.[31]

In any case, these basilicas just described were not deliberately constructed in places so as to be near to *balnea* they could use; as we have described such proximity was difficult to avoid. What they do instead show is that the local *titulus* was also a property owner who, before formal baptisteries were widely built, used that property for its own purposes. In this way the *titulus* became quite quickly an integral part of the immediate urban social and physical landscape. This was a subtle spatial Christianisation at the micro level.

2.1.1.2 The Balnea-Basilica

Another more intimate spatial association between the Christian basilica and the bath house can be shown with the three examples of basilicas created in this period actually within or on top of bath buildings. These are the *titulus Pudentis* (S. Pudenziana), *the titulus sanctae Caeciliae* (S. Caecilia) and the *basilica Eudoxiae/Sancti Apostolorum in Eudoxia* (S. Pietro in Vincoli). They provide physical evidence for the practical use by early Christian builders of pre-existing bathing facilities and the water that provided. In these cases a basilica was physically on the same site as a source of water, rather than within an owned property nearby. We should not overestimate this phenomenon however, we have only three certain examples after all. Yet, the conversion of a small bath building—probably using the long apsidal room that was a common feature—into a Christian hall seems like a natural evolution of the space. This room of the bath was an open apsed space that had easy, direct access to a source of water, ideal for liturgical and baptismal rites. The topos seen in many of the martyr legends of the pre-Constantinian bishops is of the domestic baptism, as part of the conversion process of the owner and their household. This event may be a way of emphasising the authority of the bishop in relation to the laity at the time they were written, in the late 5th to early 6th century.[32] It may also reflect the reality of former domestic bathing spaces now being baptismal ones, as exemplified by the case studies below.

It has been argued that the descriptions of baptisms in these legendary narratives implies that most baptismal rites in the *tituli* during the period they were written took place in places without access to water, it being described as being blessed and being brought in from elsewhere.[33] This may be a reference to the bringing in of water from a nearby bath house to a *titulus*, which tallies with the image described above. It could also be a description of a two basin arrangement, where blessed water from a small one with running water is poured over the person being baptised in a larger one next to it, as may have been the case at San Lorenzo in Lucina.[34] In any case, the ideal model bap-

---

[28] A chrism-paten for the *titulus Equitius*, and two chrism-patens, two vessels for the oil of exorcism and chrism, and a pouring jug for the *titulus Vestinae*.
[29] Stasolla F. R. 'Balnea ed edifici di culto', in *Ecclesiae Urbis* (2002) 148.
[30] LP. 1.233: "...*iuxta inibi basilicae, cum balneum et pistrinum, praest. sol. CLIIII, siliquas III; domus Claudi, in Sicininum, praest. sol. CIIII; cervum <in fontem> argenteum fundentem aquam, pens. lib. XX; omnia uasa baptismi sacrata argentea, pens. lib. XV...*" (transl. R. Davis (2000) 37).
[31] The urban prefect was a Longinianus: ICUR 2.150 n.19. It may be referring to the example at S. Pietro in Vaticano (LTUR 1.38), but the inscription was found near S. Anastasia.
[32] Sessa K. 'Domestic conversions: households and bishops in late antique 'papal legends'", in *Religion, Dynasty and Patronage in Early Christian Rome, 300-900*, edd. K. Cooper and J. Hillner (2007) 79-114, esp.106-14.
[33] Nestori A. 'L'acqua nel fonte battesimale', in *Studi in memoria di Giuseppe Bovini*, vol. 2 (1989) 419-27; Brandt O. 'Passiones e battisteri', in *Domum tuam dilexi. Miscellanea in onore di Aldo Nestori* (1998) 109-12.
[34] Most recently: Brandt O. 'The excavations in the baptistery of San Lorenzo in Lucina in 1993, 1995 and 1998', in *San Lorenzo in Lucina. The Transformations of a Roman Quarter*, ed. O. Brandt (2012) 49-77. I thank Prof. Brandt for sending this article to me.

tistery, seen in the Constantinian Lateran centre, had running water, possible, in part, by its construction over earlier working bath buildings.[35] Such direct access to water would be therefore the most desirable option, the 'bringing in' of water being hard work and time-consuming. The examples of close relationships between baths and basilicas, which we will examine below, are early attempts to negate such a problem.

2.1.1.2.1 Titulus Pudentis

With our first example, the *titulus Pudentis* (S. Pudenziana), it is difficult to say whether this was a deliberately acquired site or a practical donation. Like many of the Christian basilicas of this period it has an early history that is difficult to prove and that is shrouded in myth. If the *Liber Pontificalis* and martyr acts are to be believed this is one of the oldest sites for a Christian centre in Rome. They describe the bishop Pius I (*ca.*145-64?) dedicating a basilica at the *thermae Novati* which were on the *Vicus Patricius*, at the request of a Praxedis, to be named after her sister Pudentiana. The LP also says Pius built a font for baptism there.[36] However, this whole story in the LP is a later interpolation, probably from the 11th century, and seems to rely heavily on the legendary martyr acts of the two women in question, which are 6th or 7th century. In these, Praxedis asks Pius to create the 'church' in the Baths of Novatus—the name of the recently deceased brother of Timothy, who were both fellow Christians—as they are now out of use and are also large and spacious.[37]

The kernel of truth around which this legend was formed is the real presence of water tank structures under S. Pudenziana, excavated in 1894 and 1960, and seemingly interpreted as such in the early Middle Ages when these stories were written, perhaps uncovered during a restoration at that time. The archaeology has revealed evidence for a Hadrianic house which was completed in 129, to which was attached a pre-existing courtyard structure. About ten years later this courtyard was filled with vaults in order to support a terrace that was made level with the roof of the 2nd century house, which therefore changed in use. This has been argued to have been built in order to support a bath building with an apsidal room, into which the 'church' was later installed. This theory rests on the discovery of decoratively shaped recesses in the floor of the Roman building on the basilica site. A mosaic of marine subjects was built over them later. (Figs. 2a, 2b and 3) It is the 2nd century date of this conversion that may have given rise to the confusion and story surrounding the Christian basilica's very early creation.

Within the structure of S. Pudenziana were found bricks bearing stamps of Quintus Servilius Pudens, consul in A.D. 166. As such, it seems, after the 2nd century conversion, he was the owner of the baths or house. A Pudens is also mentioned in the 6th/7th century Acts of Pudentiana and Praxedis as providing his house for a *titulus*, where a baptistery was also built. In this case then, judging from its 5th century name, it would seem the same family owned the building in the 4th century, and either donated the water-filled hall to the Church or it was bought off them by a bishop or the series of priests involved in its construction (see Chapter 1 above). The Church's need for a space where the water for a baptistery could be provided is clear, whatever the means by which they acquired it. The oratory formerly dedicated to Saint Pastor (another figure featuring in the acts) located in the basilica, and now the 'Capella Caetani', could have been the baptistery in question. Both are said to be of likely 4th century origin.[38] The first reliable evidence for S. Pudenziana's existence comes from a series of inscriptions found in the basilica mentioning a Maximus, one of the priests who built or rebuilt and decorated it, and whose work began in 390.[39]

It is believed by some that the nature of the architecture of the building in which the Christian basilica was constructed does not allow it to be a bath complex. It has been argued to have been a courtyard with fountains for example.[40] It is the lack of other bath features that has led to this conclusion. Yet the space where the later basilica inhabited need only be one room in a larger bath building—perhaps the *frigidarium*, with the recesses found under the nave being plunge pools—with any bath features being removed in the conversion, the courtyard features relating to the earlier phase. A reference is made in a fragmentary inscription on a decorated architrave to a Maximus, the name of a priest involved in the construction of the *titulus Pudentis* (see chapter 1 above) building on the site of what had formerly been baths. The inscription is likely to date from the early or late 4th century. However, it is of uncertain provenance, so it does not help to clear up the ambiguity of the material evidence.[41]

---

[35] Pelliccioni G. *Le nuove scoperte sulle origini del Battistero Lateranense* (1973).
[36] LP 1.132; the current church is indeed alongside this ancient street on the (Augustan) RegioVI side.
[37] LP. 1.132 (n.8); see this chapter: n.6. The legend itself is first recorded in the 8th century: LTUR. 1.165-6; AA.SS. Mai IV.300. For a propogandal use for this story see Llewellyn P.A.B. 'The Roman Church during the Laurentian schism' *Church History* 45 (1976) 418-27.
[38] Indeed the church was known as the *titulus Pudentis* in 499 and 595: MGH.AA.12.411, MGH.Ep. 1.367. Baptistery: Cecchelli M. 'Il sacello di S. Pietro e l'oratorio di S. Pastore in S. Pudenziana: una messa a punto', *Romano Barbarica* 9 (1986-87) 47-64. S. Prassede, situated about 350m to the south, off the *clivus Suburanus*, is associated with the *titulus Praxedis* or *Praxidae*, which is probably 5th century: MGH. AA.12.410,414; LP 2.54.
[39] See Chapter 1: Clerical Builders and Managers above. The other priests were Ilicius and Leopardus; the project was finally finished under Innocent I (401-17): ILCV 1.1772A/B, 1773A. A lost epitaph from 384 suggests congregation and clergy by that time though: ICUR 1.347.
[40] CBCR. 3.279, 287-93; LTUR. 4.166-68, 2.166-67. Courtyard with fountains: Guidobaldi F. 'Osservazioni sugli edifici romani in cui si insediò l'ecclesia pudentiana', in *Ecclesiae Urbis* (2002) 1057 (1033-71); Brandenburg H. *Ancient Churches of Rome from the Fourth to the Seventh Century: the Dawn of Christian Architecture in the West* (2005) 138.
[41] CIL 6. 29769: *Maximus has olim therm(as).../ divinae mentis ductu cum...* ; De Rossi G. 'Dei musaici e d'altri monumenti fatti da Massimo prete', *BACrist* 1.5.4 (1867) 55, 57. See this chapter: n.39. It is now seen as referring to M. Gavius Maximus, the 2nd century A.D. builder of the Forum Baths in Ostia: Meiggs R. *Roman Ostia* (1973) 415, 475; Cicerchia P. and Marinucci A. *Le Terme del Foro o di Gavio Massimo* (Scavi di Ostia 11) (1992) C107bis (tav.XIII).

FIGURE 2A: PHOTO OF THE NAVE OF S. PUDENZIANA DURING EXCAVATIONS (SOPRINTENDENZA AI MONUMENTI DEL LAZIO 4968), IN NASH E. *PICTORIAL DICTIONARY OF ANCIENT ROME,* VOL. 2 (LONDON 1962) 465.

FIGURE 2B: PHOTO OF THE NAVE OF S. PUDENZIANA DURING EXCAVATIONS: DETAIL OF BRICK-FACED WATER TANK (SOPRINTENDENZA AI MONUMENTI DEL LAZIO), REPRODUCED IN CBCR 3.289.

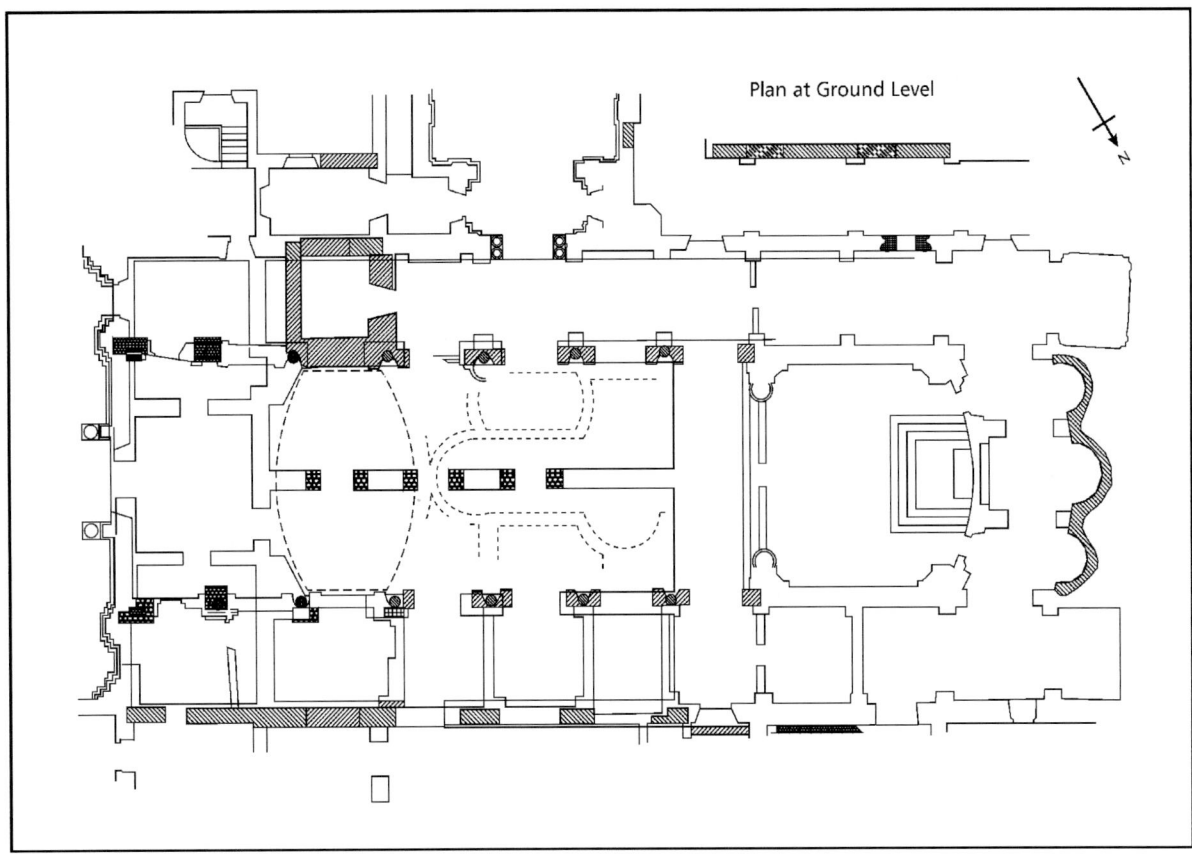

FIGURE 3: PLAN OF S. PUDENZIANA WITH OUTLINE OF STRUCTURES BENEATH NAVE IN HASHED LINES. DRAWN BY ABBY GEORGE FROM ORIGINAL PLAN IN CBCR 3. TABLE 14.

In any case, whatever the nature of the structure here prior to its Christian conversion, there was certainly a pre-existing sophisticated water supply system in place, whether for nymphaea or for plunge pools, for the later basilica to use.

2.1.1.2.2 Basilica Eudoxia

A similar example to S. Pudenziana is the *basilica Eudoxiae/titulus Apostolorum/Sancti Apostolorum in Eudoxia* (S. Pietro in Vincoli), just to the west of the Baths of Trajan. Its early name refers to the daughter of Emperor Theodosius II and Eudocia, who provided the money for the basilica. This was done under Sixtus III (432-40) who rededicated an earlier ecclesiastical structure on this site of uncertain date. The work was carried out by a presbyter named Phillipus.[42] The remains of a rich *domus* and an apsidal hall have been discovered under the current church. (fig.4) These finds, combined with inscriptions from the basilica that mention Sixtus and Eudoxia separately, has meant there is a theory that originally two Christian buildings existed here in the 5th century. One became a *titulus* and was dedicated to Peter and Paul by Sixtus III, the other was the imperial foundation by Eudoxia built probably between 450-55.[43] Around the apse of the current S. Pietro there has been found a 2nd century building that encloses some tanks and a hypocaust, suggesting baths. (figs.4 and 5) The lower part of the north transept wall, and the wall parallel to it under the north wing of the existing church, are 4th century in date. This is either a different building or a later addition to the bath house. It is this brickwork that means that a Christian basilica cannot have been built here before the first quarter of the 4th century.[44]

Recent renovations have allowed for some new observations to be made in the south wall of the current basilica. Evidence for a grand triple-arched side entrance into the building has been discovered, belonging to the second phase in the basilica's history (fig.6). This is a unique feature in Roman Christian basilicas, and the only close parallels are in the first S. Clemente and at the 5th century S. Lorenzo in Lucina, both of which led through to a baptismal area.[45] This suggests that a basin for baptisms existed here at least by a second phase (mid 5th-6th century?), which implies the utilisation of the pre-existing infrastruc-

---

[42] See chapter 1: n.121.
[43] CBCR 3.221; LTUR. 4.82-3. Cf. Bartolozzi Casti G. and Zandri G. *San Pietro in Vincoli* (1999) 41-58; Bartolozzi Casti G. 'Nuove osservazioni sulle basilche di San Pietro in Vincoli e dei Santi Giovanni e Paolo. Relazioni strutturali, proposte di cronologia', in *Ecclesiae Urbis* (2002) 953-56 (953-77).
[44] CBCR 3.192-3, 221, 223, 228; Bartolozzi Casti G. 'Le trasformazioni di un complesso edilizio urbano: San Pietro in Vincoli', in *Roma dall'antichità al medioevo*, vol. 2: *Contesti tardoantichi e altomedievali*, edd. L. Paroli and L. Vendittelli (2004) 380-89.
[45] Bartolozzi Casti G. 'Battisteri presbiteriali in Roma: un nuovo intervento di Sisto III?', in *Studi Romani* 47.3-4 (1999) 270-88; Bartolozzi Casti G. 'Nuove osservazioni', in *Ecclesiae Urbis* (2002) 958-61.

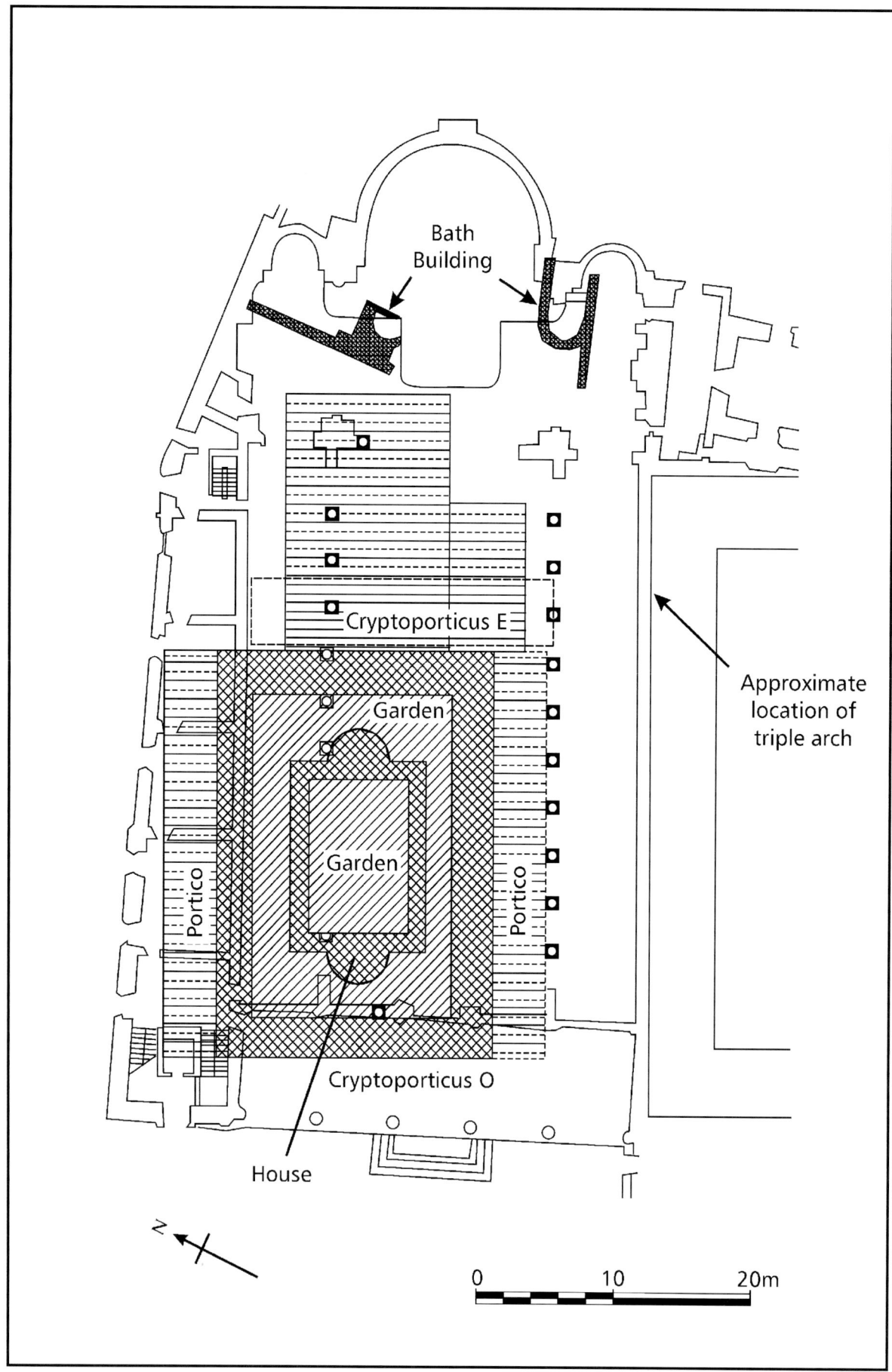

FIGURE 4: PLAN OF S. PIETRO IN VINCOLI WITH BATH AND HOUSE SUBSTRUCTURES. DRAWN BY ABBY GEORGE FROM ORIGINAL PLAN BY E. SCOPONI IN CASTI G. B. AND ZANDRI G. *SAN PIETRO IN VINCOLI* (ROME 1999) 48.

FIGURE 5: PHOTO OF THE NAVE OF S. PIETRO IN VINCOLI DURING EXCAVATIONS SHOWING AN APSE OF THE BATHS (SOPRINTENDENZA AI MONUMENTI DEL LAZIO), REPRODUCED IN CBCR 3.43 (ITALIAN EDN.).

ture of the 2nd century bath house, and may be the reason the basilica was constructed on this site.

As with the *titulus Pudentis*, we may be seeing a pragmatic adaptation of a bath building for Christian liturgical and baptismal purposes, as well as for worship. In this case a deliberate acquisition with imperial or episcopal money seems like the most likely scenario.

2.1.1.2.3 Titulus Sanctae Caeciliae

The situation with the *titulus Sanctae Caeciliae* (S. Caecilia) is similar to the *Basilica Eudoxiae*. This structure, according to a damaged inscription, may date from 379-464. Another inscription of 5th century date is said to refer to the centre, and the priests of the *titulus* attended the synods of 499 and 595 in the city.[46] A 5th century martyrology, initially attributed to Jerome, rather confusingly names Caecilia on three separate days, but the 6th century *LP* comes down on the 22nd November for her feast day, the day when pope Vigilius (537-55) was arrested in her *ecclesia*.[47] The story of Caecilia's life, originating from the late 5th century, involves her repeatedly failing to die in her bathhouse after being condemned, eventually succumbing elsewhere in her house, said to be where the *titulus* was built.[48] This legend seems to have been certainly believed and accepted by the 9th century, when the current basilica was built by Pascal I (817-24). He returned the body of the saint to the basilica along with the remains of Valerian, Tibertius and Maximus, who appear as other martyrs in the account of her life and death.[49] An inscription within the apse also records the fact that Pascal's basilica replaced a much older structure, which was famous in his day, presumably because of the story that surrounded it.[50]

The remains found underneath this 9th century structure are therefore of interest. They date from the 2nd century B.C. to the 9th century A.D., none of which can be confidently identified with a *titulus* or basilica on this site preceding the current building. (see fig.7) The *insula* found here, lying below the existing church, dates to the first half of the 2nd century A.D. The first Christian structure on this site is likely to have been constructed within it. The remains of an early Christian baptistery have been found just beyond the north wall of the current church, that date from the 4th or 5th centuries, so perhaps contemporary with the founding of the *titulus*. This baptistery was essentially a small hall with a hexagonal baptismal pool in the centre,

---

[46] ICUR 1.816, 116; MGH.AA. 12.411,414; MGH.Ep. 1.367. For a more detailed analysis for the foundation of the titulus see: Parmegiani N. and Pronti A. *S. Cecilia in Trastevere: nuovi scavi e ricerche* (2004) 3-9.
[47] *Martyrologium Hieronymianum* in *AA.SS.* Nov. II.1.121, 144, 146; LP 1. 297.
[48] Delehaye H. *Étude sur le légendier romain* (1936) 77-96, 219-20.
[49] LP 2.56; Goodson C. J. 'Material memory: rebuilding the basilica of S. Cecilia in Trastevere, Rome', *Early Medieval Europe* 15.1 (2007) 2–34.
[50] ICUR 2.151, 156, 444.

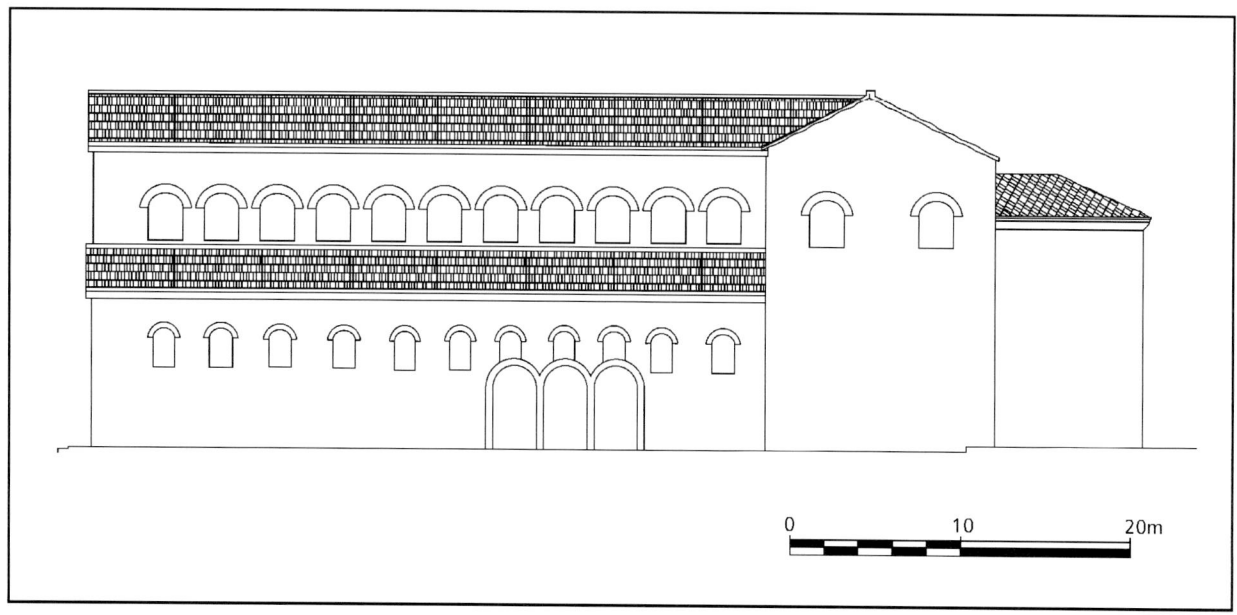

FIGURE 6: SECTION OF THE SOUTH WALL OF S. PIETRO IN VINCOLI SHOWING TRIPLE ARCADED ENTRANCE. DRAWN BY ABBY GEORGE FROM ORIGINAL SECTION BY E. SCOPONI IN CASTI G. B. AND ZANDRI G. *SAN PIETRO IN VINCOLI* (ROME 1999) 80.

the last phase of which was 9th century as part of Pascal's reconstruction of the site. To the east of this was found a small bathhouse that is the traditional place assigned for Caecilia's attempted martyrdom, and dates from the 3rd to the early 4th century. The presence of baths here seems to have provided a detail for her martyrdom story. The baths and the later baptistery were at different levels so a staircase probably joined the two arcas.[51]

Therefore, beneath the level of the current 9th century basilica and just to its north—and so beyond the right aisle—lies a 4th or 5th century baptistery and a 3rd or early 4th century bath house, this presumably feeding the baptistery and explaining its location. (fig.7) The fact that a 4th or 5th century Christian centre was located right next to this, should not surprise us therefore. The three spaces worked together. On a micro level the location of these baths made it an ideal site for the later Christian *titulus* and the baptismal and liturgical rites that took place next to it that required access to water. With the martyrdom legend the baptistery and the bath house were also linked liturgically as well as practically, with an annex of the baptistery perhaps housing Caecilia's relics from the 9th century.[52]

The baptistery, and by implication the earlier bath house, seem to have been fed by the aqueduct feeding the Trastevere region, the *Aqua Traiana*, as an inscription on the pipe feeding it mentions the basilicas of S. Caeciliae and S. Crysogono. Only an aqueduct could supply two buildings over 200m apart.[53] This is unlikely to have classified as private use from an aqueduct, a common, yet illegal, practice in Rome it seems, that required imperial censure in 389.[54]

2.2 Christian Basilicas and Imperial Thermae

The next and last examples of Christian basilicas with an intimate association with baths are those that were topographically linked, through sheer proximity, to the large imperial *thermae*. The above examples showed that several Christian foundations converted former bathing spaces for their own practical purposes before formal purpose-built baptisteries appeared more widely in the city from the mid 5th century. This final set of case studies show the remarkable pattern of several early Christian basilicas being located right next to, or even within, large imperial bath complexes. For there to be a case of Christian use any foundation must date to before the cutting of the aqueducts (the mid 6th century) that is said to have ended the life of these large baths, or at least diminished their use considerably.

There were three monumental examples of these imperial structures by the 4th century: the *Thermae Traiani*, *Antoninianae* and *Diocletiani*, the latter being the largest and most recently constructed.[55] There are four Christian foundations that can claim an association with them, and another with the more modest *Thermae Decianae* on the Aventine.

The imperial *thermae* themselves were seen by all the emperors as a propaganda tool to promote their name and to garner public support as part of justifying their rise to the purple. Indeed, there appears to be a pattern with the con-

---

[51] LTUR 1.206-207; Parmegiani N. and Pronti A. *S. Cecilia in Trastevere* (2004) 67-73, 87-96.
[52] Parmegiani N. and Pronti A. *S. Cecilia in Trastevere* (2004) 104-108 where also the ideal location for this Christian centre and baptistry is acknowledged, and where it is also argued that all *tituli* must have had baptistries very early on.
[53] Cited in Coates-Stephens R.'The water-supply of Rome' (2003) 180.
[54] *Cod. Theod.* 15.2.5.
[55] Completed *ca.*AD 110, 216 and 305/6 respectively.

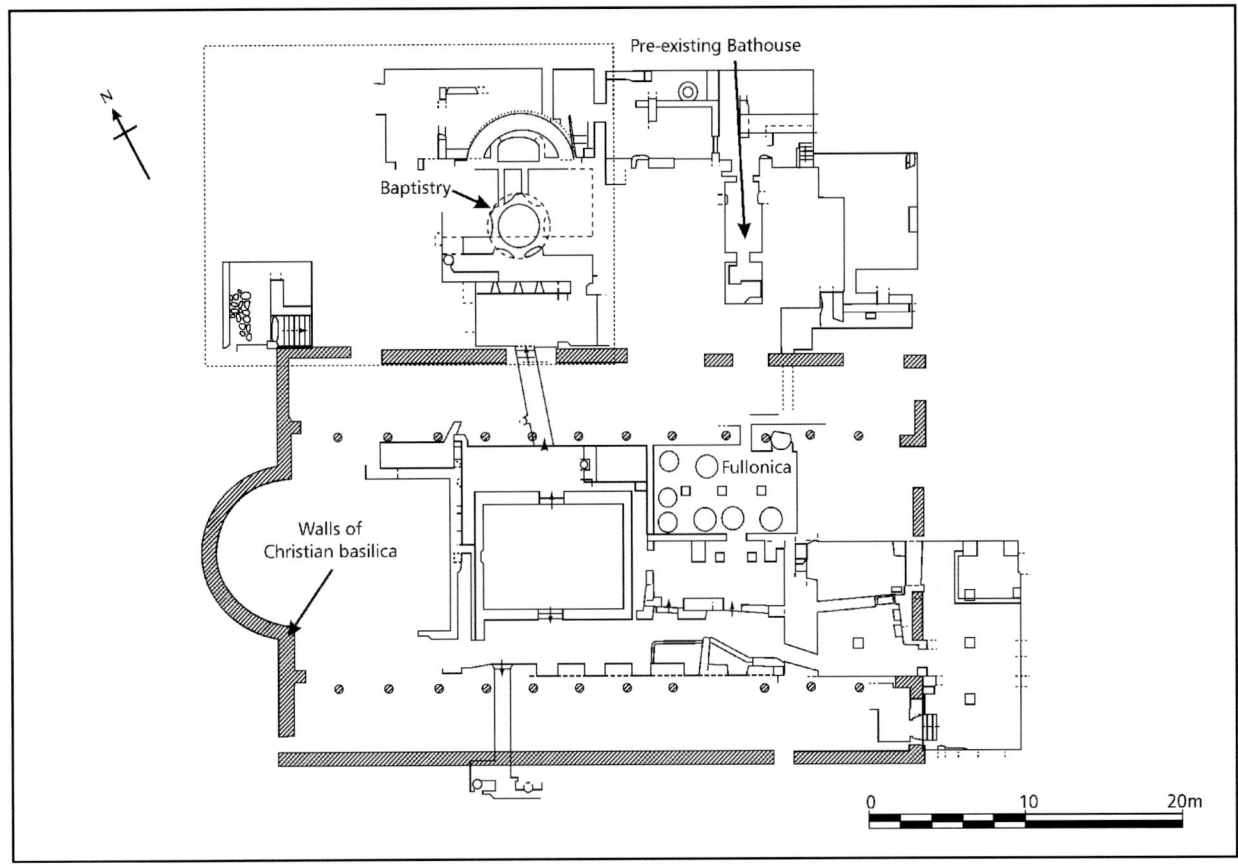

FIGURE 7: PLAN OF EXCAVATIONS BENEATH S. CAECILIA. DRAWN BY ABBY GEORGE FROM ORIGINAL PLAN IN PARMEGIANI N. AND PRONTI A. 'COMPLESSO ARCHEOLOGICO SOTTO LA BASILICA DI S. CECILIA IN TRASTEVERE', *BULLCOM* 93 (1989-90) 107-12.

struction of these buildings coinciding with the arrival of a new regime or the end of a civil war.[56] Their creation did not stop with the advent of a Christian administration from Constantine. He built baths in Rome on the Quirinal and in his new capital Constantinople, for example.[57] The imperial baths at Rome were certainly still in working order until the siege by the Goth Vitiges in 537-38 when the aqueducts were cut along with their water supply.[58] In this way, Christian foundations originating before this time can be argued to have utilised these baths in some form or another for their own purposes. Indeed, it may be too simplistic to say these baths no longer worked or were used after the 6th century; there is evidence to suggest there were problems with the water supply to the Baths of Caracalla before this, and yet they continued to function. Furthermore, finds within the same baths imply that they remained in use in some form into the early middle ages, as we will see. In any case, the Gothic damage would have been easy to repair. This was indeed carried out under the post-war Byzantine administration, and in the 8th-9th century, with the aqueducts continued use being apparent in the 10th and 11th centuries.[59] As such, a long continuity of use by the Church of these bath buildings seems likely and desirable.

2.2.1 Thermae Antoninianae

The first possible example of a relationship between imperial *thermae* and a Christian building is an interesting concentration of two early foundations built next to each other on the via Appia in the late 4th to early 5th century. The first is the *titulus Fasciolae*, founded around 377 or earlier, as such it may be another Damasian foundation. It was renamed after the martyrs Nereus and Achilleus by the late 6th century.[60] The existing Carolingian construction to SS. Nereo ed Achilleo is not thought to be on the same site as the 4th century basilica. There is no archaeological evidence for the earlier structure under the present basilica, and the *LP* states that the rebuilding under Leo III (795-816) was on a more elevated site than the original basilica. The Leonine structure seems to have been built on a podium to protect it from flooding, a problem therefore for

---

[56] Fagan G. G. *Bathing* (1999) 123.
[57] He enlarged the Baths of Zeuxippus near the hippodrome in Constantinople: Malalas 13.8.
[58] Procop., *Goth.* 1.19. For a review of Procopius' account of Rome during the Gothic Wars see: Ghilardi M. '"Com'essa sia fatta io, che l'ho vista, vengo a riferire". La città di Roma nel De Bello Gothico di Procopio di Cesarea', *Romanobarbarica* 19 (2006-2009) 109-35.
[59] DeLaine J. 'Recent research on Roman baths', *JRA* 1 (1988) 21-22 (11-32); Coates-Stephens R. 'The water-supply of Rome' (2003) 168-69.
[60] Inscription of 377: ICUR 1.124 n. 262. Archaeology: CBCR 3. 135, 147-48; Pietri C. *Roma christiana* (1976) 466-67; Curran J. R. *Pagan City and Christian capital: Rome in the Fourth Century* (2000) 145. Synod of 499, three priests of *titulus Fasciolae*: MGH.AA. 12.413, 414. Synod of 595, one priest of the *Titulus SS. Nerei e Achillei*: MGH. Ep. 1.367.

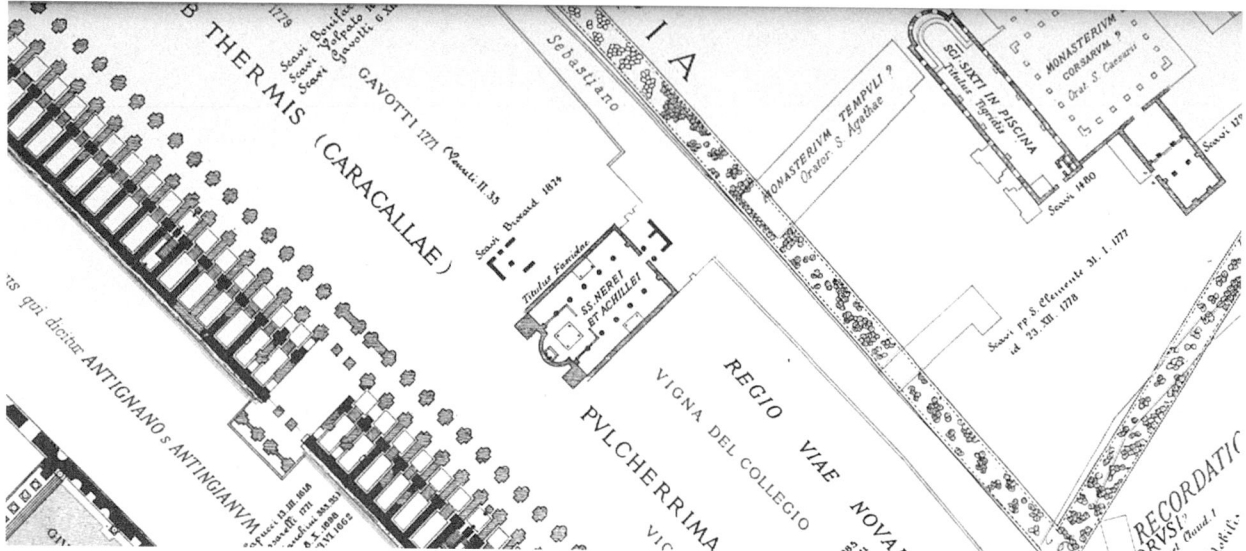

FIGURE 8: DETAIL OF PLATE 42 AND SS. NEREO ED ACHILLEO, IN LANCIANI R. *FORMA URBIS ROMAE* (MILAN 1893-1901).

the original basilica perhaps, which seems to have been in ruins by this time.[61]

The more elevated site mentioned could, therefore, just be a reference to this podium under the new basilica, rather than elevated land. Some excavation work immediately around the current church in the late 19th to early 20th century discovered ancient walls just to the north (fig. 8) and, more interestingly, an east facing apse and fragments of a marble transenna behind the existing apse to the west.[62] This seems like the best candidate for the site of the earlier Christian basilica here (and therefore nearer the bath's entrance) but the vague description of these discoveries and others nearby at that time means this must be just a best-guess. We do know that the *titulus Fasciolae* does not lie under the existing 9th century building, however. More recent excavations there discovered one or more mid imperial *insulae* with some late antique modifications. Yet, the area seems to have been abandoned in the 5th century and there is no sign of any activity between then and the Carolingian period and the construction of the current church.[63] The written sources do make it clear that the *titulus* lay near the current church but it still remains elusive.

Wherever it lies, though, the whole area is clearly one not ideal for such a building with this tendency to flood. Why such a location was chosen seems strange therefore, but the Carolingian construction lies almost directly opposite the entrance to the large Baths of Caracalla; they are only around thirty metres away. (figs.8 and 9) By that period the baths were partly ruined and were being looted, some of which for the church.[64] If of course the 4th century building was only even in the approximate area, the case for it having an intimate association with these baths, is virtually certain. The extent to which this was a practical relationship is more difficult to ascertain. Any Christian misgivings towards bath houses does not seem to have applied here, and the longevity of use of the Caracallan baths indicates a Christian building at the entrance did not affect their popularity either.[65]

Just opposite the 9th century SS. Nereo ed Achilleo, to its north on the other side of the *via Appia*, is the *Basilica Crescentiana* (S. Sisto Vecchio), founded by Pope Anastasius I (399-401). (see fig.10) It was reconstructed under Sixtus III (432-40), from whom it gained its name *titulus sancti Sixti* by the 6th century.[66] To have founded this establishment so near to the *titulus Fasciolae*, and so soon after that basilica was created, may suggest an intentional relationship between the two. Importantly, neither has or had a baptismal *fons*.

The question is whether these two foundations were built here to utilise the water supply or a room, or rooms, of the Caracallan baths for baptismal and other liturgical purposes or whether this occurred in later centuries, by virtue of their location, where evidence for adaptations in the baths is apparent. The discovery of Constantinian and Theodosian brick stamps in the Caracallan complex show a continuity of use into the early 6th century. Perhaps the addition of small pools to various rooms in a late phase was more about a new baptismal use, rather than a sign of a degrada-

---

[61] CBCR. 3.148; Pietri C. *Roma christiana* (1976) 466-67; LP. 2.33; LTUR 2.241.
[62] Lais G. *Memorie del titolo di Fasciola e discussione sul valore storico degli atti de' ss. mm. Flavia, Domitilla, Nereo, Achilleo* (1880) 13; Lanciani R. *Forma Urbis Romae* (1893-1901) pl. 42; Marucchi O. 'Resoconto delle adunanze', *NuovB* 11 (1905) 274-75 (273-98).
[63] Pavolini C. 'I resti romani sotto la chiesa dei SS. Nereo e Achilleo a Roma. Una rilettura archeologica', *MEFRA* 111.1 (1999) 405-48.

[64] CBCR. 3.143.
[65] Procop., *Goth*. 1.20.5; late restoration of baths: CIL 15.1665.3-4, 1669.7; CIL 6.1750.
[66] LP 1.218; CBCR. 4. 163-77; LTUR 1.325, 4.330; its current name is after the 3rd century martyred pope Sixtus II, whose relics were moved here in the 9th century. For the problems with the name and dating see CBCR. 4. 174-75.

FIGURE 9: SS. NEREO ED ACHILLEO AND THE BATHS OF CARACALLA. AUTHOR PHOTO.

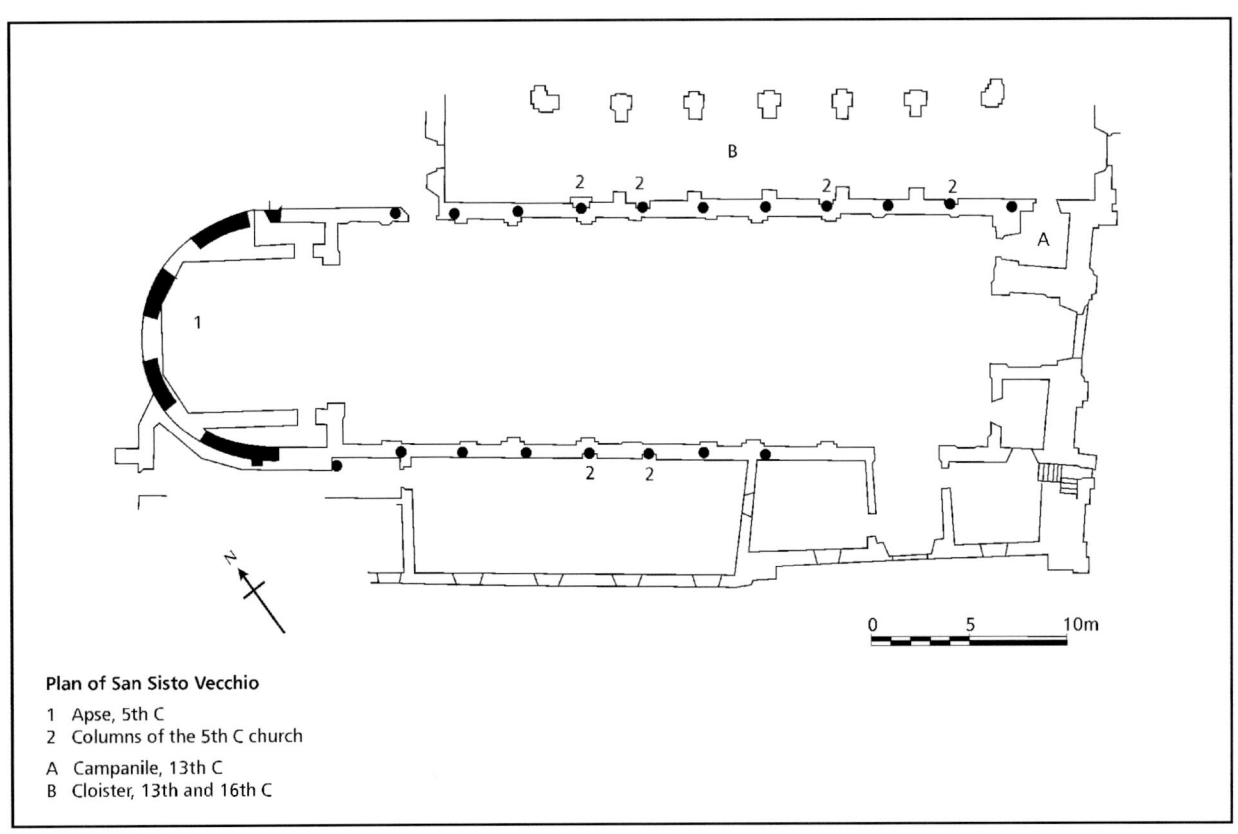

FIGURE 10: PLAN OF S. SISTO VECCHIO. DRAWN BY ABBY GEORGE FROM ORIGINAL PLAN IN WEBB M. *THE CHURCHES AND CATACOMBS OF EARLY CHRISTIAN ROME* (BRIGHTON 2001) 204.

tion in the water-supply, as has been argued.[67] Indeed, 8th-9th century repairs can be said to have been made on the *Aqua Antoniana*, the aqueduct branch that fed the baths.[68]

Alternative explanations for the two basilicas' locations do not explain why they were both situated in such proximity to each other and directly opposite the Baths. They were indeed on the main thoroughfare on entering Rome from the south, the *via Appia*, and so could have been the Christian centres for visitors to the city from that direction, with two being required on such a busy road.[69] The *titulus Fasciolae* has been said to be located here because it lay on the spot where the *fasciola*, or small bandage, fell from St. Peter's wounds during his escape from prison, and so the place where, presumably, the relic was kept. This story, however, is a later invention, elaborating the late 2nd/early 3rd century legend of the apostle's escape along the *Appia*, and confusing the name of the basilica (after a martyr, donor or region) with the Latin for bandage.[70] None of the other more plausible theories explain why it was built in front of the baths and not elsewhere on the road either.

The importance of the *via Appia* as a road is clear, but to pick this site outside the entrance to the Caracallan baths for not one, but two, Christian basilicas requires another explanation. Clearly there was some association between the baths and the basilicas, and the nature of this is not easily apparent, but a utilitarian reason should not be dismissed. Perhaps these two foundations were intended to be baptismal centres in this early period.

By the 6th and 7th centuries any liturgical use for the baths seems to have evolved into a more philanthropic arrangement. The 6th and 7th century burials found in the outer precinct of the Caracallan baths have been argued to be associated with SS. Nereo ed Achilleo, which became a *diaconia*, a place for the care of the poor, certainly by the early 9th century and probably from the 7th.[71] Perhaps it used a part of the baths for the bathing of the poor, in the same way that it had, or still, utilised these facilities for liturgical purposes.[72] This suggests a continuity of use for these baths by Christian groups in some form or another, from the 4th to the 7th century at least. The reference to a *xenodochium*, a Christian hostel, in the area in 591 may also be connected to this complex,[73] this whole area being utilised by that time as a place of refuge for the poor, sick and pilgrims because of its location on a main busy thoroughfare into the city and its position next to the remaining facilities of the Caracallan baths. In this way, the two basilicas potential initial use of part of the baths as full immersion baptismal areas became, therefore, by the early middle ages, a place where the baths were likely utilised for Christian benevolence and as a stopping-off point for pilgrims. Whatever the case, the *titulus Fasciolae* and *basilica Crescentiana* likely used at some point, and were intimately connected with, the large imperial baths located just yards from their doors.

2.2.2 Thermae Diocletiani

Another, even more intimate, correlation between a Christian basilica and an imperial bath complex is between the *titulus Cyriaci* (S. Ciriaco in Thermis), and the Baths of Diocletian. It was constructed before 499, shown by its presence on the signatures of presbyters for the Roman synod of that year.[74] Beyond this nothing is known of its foundation. The basilica no longer survives, but the best evidence for its position shows it within what was the baths' precinct between the main bath building itself and the north-east corner of the outer boundary wall. Later medieval descriptions of the basilica, the discovery of the remains of an apse, walls and four arches in this area, coupled with 16th century sketches and maps of the same place showing an apse—likely a small chapel that was part of a larger basilica—all point to a Christian building within the boundary wall of the baths (fig.11).

In 1309 the door of the basilica is described as next to the *medius modiolus* (middle terminating nave?) by the baths in the vineyard that then surrounded the ruins of the main bath block, and in 1010 the *monasterium Sante Quiriace* is 'inside the baths of Diocletian'. Another theory, that the basilica in fact lies outside the walls of the baths, just to the north, relies on the discovery of a mosaic pavement, columns and Christian inscriptions on the corner of the modern Via Pastrengo and Via 20 Settembre in the early 20th century.[75] (see fig.12) This is unlikely to be the *monasterium* seen in the medieval texts, however, as this is explicitly described as within the baths (see above). It may be a much older Christian structure though, that had disappeared by the Renaissance, as it does not appear on drawings or maps of that time.

---

[67] DeLaine J. 'Recent Research' (1988) 22; Delaine J. *The Baths of Caracalla: a Study in the Design, Construction, and Economics of Large-Scale Building Projects in Imperial Rome* (1997) 37-41.
[68] Coates-Stephens R. 'The water-supply of Rome' (2003) 172.
[69] The same argument has been put forward for the positioning of the Caracallan baths to get such custom: Fagan G. G. *Bathing* (1999) 118-19. See Chapter 3 below.
[70] Late 2nd/early 3rd century story: the apocryphal Acts of St. Peter: *Acta Vercellenses* 35, in Lipsius R. A. ed. *Acta Apostolorum Apocrypha*, vol.1 (1891) 7-8, 171, 233. Later legend: account, which is 5th or 6th century, describes Peter's bandage dropping "...*apud sepem in via nova: cumque venisset ad portam Appiam...*": *AA.SS*.Julii I.304. Neither the *via Nova* nor the *Porta Appia* existed in the 1st century AD. In any case, even if such an important relic did reside in the church it would hardly have been superseded by the remains of two local martyrs. Regio Fasciolae: Valentini R. and Zucchetti G. edd. *Codice topografico della città di Roma*, 4 vols. (1940-53) (=Val. Zucc.) 3.23 (Mirabilia (12th century)).
[71] LP 2. 9, 21, 33; Geertman H. *More veterum. Il Liber pontificalis e gli edifici ecclesiastici di Roma nella tarda antichità e nell'alto Medioevo* (1975) 106, 111-12.
[72] Cecchini M.G. 'Terme di Caracalla. Campagna di scavo 1982/83 lungo il lato orientale', in *Roma: archeologia nel centro*, vol. 2, edd. A. M. Bietti Sestieri *et al*, (1985) 592-93 (583-93); Cecchini M. G. 'Contributi sulla topografia della regione *duodecima piscina publica ubi dicitur Sancto Gregorio* in periodo altomedievale', *RACrist* 64 (1988) 89-107.
[73] Greg., *Ep.* 1.44; LTUR 5.43. For the various theories on the location of the *xenodochium* see LTUR 5.217-18.
[74] MGH.AA. 12.412.
[75] Hülsen C. *Le chiese di Roma nel medio evo: cataloghi ed appunti* (1927) 245-46 with refs; Rava A. 'San Ciriaco in thermis', *Roma* 6 (1928) 160-68; CBCR. 1.114-16; LTUR. 1.338-39. Renaissance sketches and drawings show a small apsed chapel inside the baths' walls in the

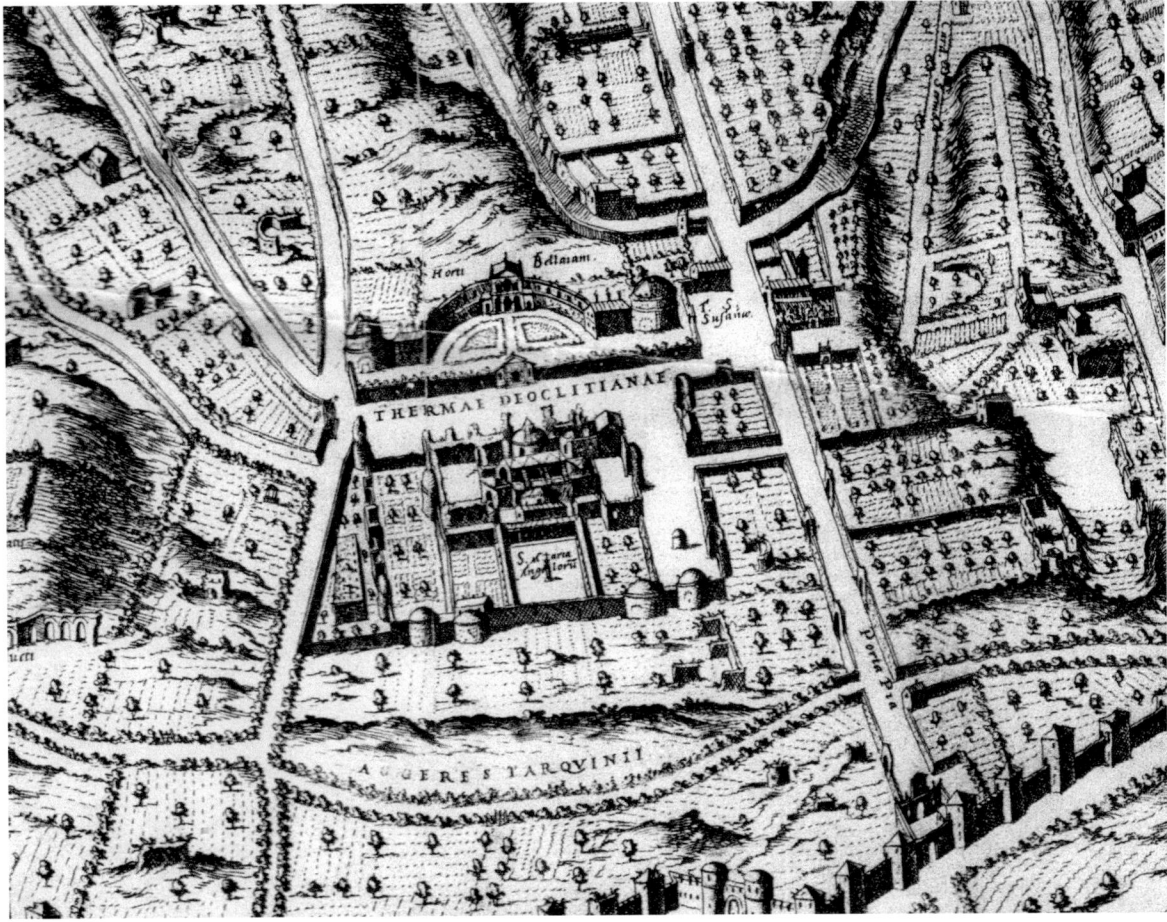

FIGURE 11: DETAIL OF DU PÉRAC MAP OF ROME FROM 1577, TAKEN FROM FRUTAZ A. P. *LE PIANTE DI ROMA*, VOL. 2 (ROME 1962) CXXVII.7, TAV. 254. REPRODUCED WITH THE KIND PERMISSION OF THE ISTITUTO NAZIONALE DI STUDI ROMANI.

In any case, the small simple apsed building within the baths on these drawings and the commensurate finds, all point to an early basilical *ecclesia-titulus*. The monastery 'inside the baths' seems most likely to be an adaptation around this building, with the ancillary structures being torn down. The idea that the finds further north outside the boundary wall represent the *titulus* and the structure inside the baths is the monastery (or vice versa), would be an unusual arrangement, with the basilica and monastery being separate. Further, a mosaic floor would suggest a domestic or bathing establishment. Neither structure has been convincingly dated so further clarification is impossible.

The evidence does stack up more favourably though for an early Christian foundation within the walls of the bath precinct. We should not find this an unusual arrangement because, as Krautheimer points out, religious structures do occur within *thermae*, such as the *mithraeum* within the Baths of Caracalla, and by the 5th century a Christian structure here would not have raised any objections amongst the urban elite.[76] Its location within what was the gardens of the baths means that the *titulus* had to have been built *ex novo*, so was not an adaptation of an existing building, and was on public imperial land. There seems to be no record of the imperial permission required—as with the similar example of the *titulus Lucinae* or the *basilica sancti Laurentii* outside the walls—which may have given rise to an unlikely foundation myth for this *titulus*.[77] The *terminus ante quem* for its construction, 499, suggests a close connection between the basilica and the fully working baths for at least thirty-eight years, but it was probably much longer.[78]

Its appearance here, only accessible to bathers and so close to working baths, indicates a clear relationship. This was intended to be the bather's place of worship and the use of the bathing facilities for baptisms would work with that

---

north-east corner, eg.: Du Perac map of Rome of 1577: Frutaz A. P. *Le piante di Roma*, vol. 2 (1962) tav. 254 (see fig. 11); Antonio di Sangallo the Elder plan of Baths of Diocletian produced before 1534: Bartoli A. *I monumenti antichi di Roma nei disegni degli Uffizi di Firenze*, vol. 1 (1914-22) fig.176.
[76] CBCR I.114.
[77] This describes a Cyriacus miraculously curing the emperor Diocletian's daughter who is then given a house *iuxta thermas Diocletianas* as a reward, which becomes a meeting place for Christians: *AA.SS*. Mai II. 619. Imperial permission for extension of S. Lorenzo in Lucina onto *horologium Augusti*, or perhaps S. Lorenzo fuori la mura, under Sixtus III: LP I.234 (see Chapter 3: Encroachments onto Public Spaces below). For the legal issues here see Hillner J. 'Le chiese paleocristiane di Roma e l'occupazione degli spazi pubblici', in *Ecclesiae Urbis* (2002) 321-29.
[78] A later baptistry and well were found in this area, which indicates a need for such water facilities, and the provision of these once the Baths of Diocletian were ruinous and perhaps inaccessible: Coates-Stephens R. 'The water-supply of Rome' (2003) 179; Hubert E. *Espace urbain et habitat à Rome du Xe siècle à la fin du XIIIe siècle* (1990) 79.

FIGURE 12: DETAIL OF PLATE 10 AND NE CORNER OF BATHS OF DIOCLETIAN, IN LANCIANI R. *FORMA URBIS ROMAE* (MILAN 1893-1901).

function. What better baptistery than the palatial baths built by the last great persecutor of Christians. This is very much Christianity becoming part of the social fabric of the city and part of the urban landscape. Even if the *titulus* itself was small its intentions were much larger. It Christianised the bathing experience and marked a step towards Christianising the city in a more fundamental way. This was the Roman Church not rejecting the contemporary world and the bathing that was a major feature of it, but embracing it and making Christian devotion an adjunct of a regular daily activity. The addition of a monastery in the Middle Ages suggests it retained some cachet, even if the baths now no longer functioned in the same way.

2.2.3 Thermae Traiani and Suranae

Our two final examples are far more tentative cases; they lack the written or archaeological evidence seen above linking them to a bathing establishment, but their sheer proximity to bath buildings means they deserve a brief mention.

2.2.3.1 Thermae Traiani

The first may date from the post Gothic War period. Remains of a small oratory, named S. Felicita in Thermis, or more accurately *in Domus Aurea*, were found in the early 19th century below the large southern semi-circular exedra of Trajan's baths, built into a room of the *Domus Aurea* beneath it. The Baths of Titus lay above just to the west. It has been attributed to Saint Felicity, based on the frescoes seen at its discovery, which are thought to date from somewhere between the 4th to 8th century. There was no documentary evidence of its existence. The oratory consists of a small barrel vaulted rectangular room with a niche with an altar below. The frescoes, which were mainly in the niche, have now disappeared.[79] Its location here could mean it was founded just before the aqueducts were cut and the baths above put largely out of use from 537/38. Similarly, it may provide evidence for the baths continued use, in some form or another, into the early middle ages, or certainly that some sort of activity continued here in that period. These rooms were converted into living areas at some point, but it is not clear how this relates to the creation of this Christian space.

Atop the reservoirs of Trajan's baths (the so-called Sette Sale) in the 4th century, a series of rooms was converted into a sumptuously decorated *domus*, a room of which included an apsidal hall and an elaborate fountain.[80] In other words, a building attached to working baths, most likely formerly for the baths' personnel, was adapted for the

---

[79] De Rossi G. B. 'Pittura ritraente S. Felicita ed i sette figliuoli in un antico oratorio presso le terme di Tito', *BACrist* 4.3 (1884-85) 157-66; Armellini M. *Le chiese di Roma dal secolo IV al XIX* (1891) 136-38; CBCR 1.218; LTUR 2.246; Cerrito A. 'Sull'oratorio di S. Felicita presso di Terme di Traiano a Roma', in *Domum tuam dilexi: miscellanea in onore di Aldo Nestori* (1998) 155-84 with refs.

[80] Cozza L. 'I recenti scavi delle Sette Sale', *RendPontAcc* 47 (1974-75) 79-101; Volpe R. 'La domus delle Sette Sale', in *Aurea Roma* (2000) 159-60.

partial purpose of utilising its water supply. The Christian structure's use as a small oratory may mean it was not connected to the baths in such a utilitarian way, but it is hard to see why it was constructed here, in such an unusual place, and between two large imperial *thermae*.

It is likely people were living here, judging by the later modifications to the area, but there is nothing in Felicity's *passio* to suggest any connection to baths, although Trajan's baths were perhaps favoured by women, so that may have encouraged the construction of this female cult place.[81] It has also been thought this was where Felicity and her sons were imprisoned before their trial and deaths, but there is no evidence for that.[82] Perhaps the oratory dates to as late as the 8th century and this ruinous district was now home to residents reusing the spaces for safety or simple expediency? Perhaps the oratory was a private domestic arrangement? We cannot be certain of any practical relationship as the dating is unclear and no water pipes have been found leading from the oratory to the baths, but it does repeat the pattern of Christian spaces being created within bathing environments, in this case below large imperial ones that may have continued to be used into the medieval period. Trajan's baths were embellished with statues in the 4th or 5th century by Iulius Felix Campanianus, a prefect of the city, and the continuing repair of the aqueducts in the early middle ages may have prolonged the baths' life further.[83]

2.2.3.2 Thermae Suranae

Our second example lies on the Aventine hill. As with the Baths of Caracalla, the *Thermae Surae/Suranae* (a Trajanic foundation which may or may not have been built with imperial money[84]) includes a Mithraeum very close to them, in this case just to the south. Above this, or at least in the approximate area, the late 4th/early 5th century *titulus Priscae* (S. Prisca) was created.[85] This mithraeum-*titulus* correlation is likely to be coincidental, as elsewhere, but as with the cult foundation in the Caracallan baths, the mithraeum's location may be a pragmatic decision in order to use the same water supply as the baths. In turn the *titulus* above may have done the same for its own liturgical rites. If the belief that Prisca was baptised by the apostle Peter is this early—the story is medieval at least due to the legend surrounding the font in the current church—then a symbolic need for a water supply and a nearby baptistery for the first Christian building here existed.

An inscription found in this area records the restoration of a *cella tepidaria* in 414, so the baths were still in use not long after *the titulus priscae* was created, probably around 400. The Severan Marble Plan shows baths of modest size here, so they should perhaps be interpreted as private *balnea*.[86] The much larger imperial Baths of Decius lay just across the road to the west, however, enjoying a commanding position and view of the Murcian valley and Circus below. The close proximity of two bath complexes, one minor the other major, and the apparent lack of an early baptistery at the Christian centre, allows us to imagine the possibility at least that they were used by the presbyters of the *titulus Priscae* for baptismal ceremonies.

2.3 Early Medieval Church Baths

More definitive examples of early medieval Christian use of water facilities, can inform us to some extent as to the arrangement in earlier centuries. The apparent need for later purpose-built baptisteries to be supplied, strangely, from aqueducts, may be a vestige of an earlier system that relied on the aqueducts that fed into both large and small bathing establishments in the 4th and early 5th centuries in the city. In the late 8th century, we hear that the *Aqua Traiana* (by this time known as the *Forma Sabbatina*) and *Aqua Claudia* fed the baptisteries of the Vatican and Lateran respectively, the latter also feeding many others.[87] The same can be said of the *Traiana*, which also fed the baptisteries at S. Caecilia and S. Crisogono, as we have seen.

Aside from baptisteries, other explicitly Christian bathing establishments begin to appear in the written sources annexed to Christian basilicas outside the city housing martyr's relics, so presumably for the use of pilgrims and resident clergy and monks. It has been argued that such Church-owned baths may have been set up to rival the other *balnea* in the city, which were regarded as potential dens of immorality. They could have been seen as 'safer' for clergy, and possibly the general Christian population as well.[88] However, the often practical and close spatial relationship between Christian centres and existing *thermae* and *balnea* inside the city, as seen above, suggests that such qualms did not exist. These new pilgrim baths were merely practical additions to the landscape.

---

[81] *AA.SS.* Iul. 3.12-13; *Chronicle of the City of Rome* (in *The Chronography of 354*): MGH.AA. 9.146; Cerrito 'S. Felicitia' (1998) 183-84.
[82] Lanciani R. *The Ruins and Excavations of Ancient Rome: a Companion Book for Students and Travellers* (1897) 364; Armellini M. (and Cecchelli C. ed.) *Le chiese di Roma dal secolo IV al XIX* (new edn. 1942) 1.178; LTUR 2.246.
[83] Campanianus: CIL 6.1670; PLRE 2. Iulius Felix Campanianus 4. He may have been prefect as late as A.D. 467: Scharf R. 'Der Stadtprafekt Iulius Felix Campanianus', *ZPE* 94 (1992) 274–78. Aqueducts: Coates-Stephens R. 'The water-supply of Rome' (2003) 168-73. The existence of a cemetery in the area, in use from the 5th to 7th century (Carboni F. "Scavi all'esedra nord-orientale delle Terme di Traiano, *BullCom* 104 (2003) 65-80) suggests a self-contained community existed here at that time, and may have encouraged the continued maintenance of the baths.
[84] Dio Cass. 68.15.3; Aur. Vict., *Caes.* 13.8; *Epitome de Caesaribus* 13.6 (authorship disputed).
[85] The current structure dates to *ca.*1100 but the ancient *titulus* must be very close to or on the same site. The exact site is still unknown, but possible paleochristian walls have been seen under and to the right of the current basilica: Cecchelli M. 'Dati da scavi recenti' (1999) 240-41. The date of the destruction of the mithraeum (via the pottery fill) has been used to date the early *titulus*. The first documentary evidence for it is late 5th century however: ICUR. 2. 5153, 5160; MGH.AA.12.413. For more details see: Platner S. B. and Ashby T. *A Topographical Dictionary of Ancient Rome* (1929) 532-33; CBCR 3.274-75, 263; Vermaseren M. J. and Van Essen C. C. *The Excavations in the Mithraeum of the Church of Santa Prisca in Rome* (1965); LTUR 4.162-63, 3.268-69.
[86] Marble Plan: Lanciani R. *Forma* (1893-1901) pl.35. Tepidarium restoration: CIL 6.1703.
[87] LP 1.504-505; Coates-Stephens R. 'The water-supply of Rome' (2003) 178-80.
[88] Ward-Perkins B. *From Classical Antiquity* (1984) 135.

Bishop Hilarus (461-68) built two baths, one of which was open-air, at the *Basilica Sancti Laurentii* (S. Lorenzo fuori le Mura), Symmachus (498-514) built *balnea* at the *basilica Sancti Pancrati* (S. Pancrazio) and the *basilica beati Pauli* (S. Paolo fuori le Mura) and Leo III (795-816) constructed baths explicitly for the poor and pilgrims at S. Pietro (in Vaticano).[89] Inside the city, in the mid 7th century, the eastern emperor Constans II bathed at the Basilica of Vigilius at the Lateran.[90]

Baths were also an important part of the facilities at *diaconia*, in these cases expressly for the poor, but often used in this way as part of devotional activity on a feast day. The example of S. Angelo in Pescheria, built into the Portico of Octavia by the Theatre of Marcellus, is interesting. In this area, purpose-built baths were built at about the same time as the *diaconia*-basilica complex, in the mid to late 8th century, which have therefore been interpreted as baths for the poor within that.[91] This arrangement at a *diaconia* should be seen as a mirror of what was occurring at the *diaconia* of Nereus and Achilleus on the via Appia, by the Baths of Caracalla, at the same time. With this example the remaining facilities at those baths provided the facilities required.

2.4 Conclusion

The bathing establishments of Rome were solely places of leisure and hygiene prior to the 4th century. After this, several Christian basilicas were built within and near them. It seems likely this was for practical purposes in order to use their facilities for liturgical ceremonies such as baptism, before purpose-built baptisteries were created for many of the Christian basilicas in the city from the 5th century. The use of wells or springs for such ceremonies would no longer have been appropriate for a now imperially sanctioned religion. In the case of the imperial *thermae*, it may also have been a hope that the use of a formal, if not luxurious, setting for a key Christian ceremony like baptism would legitimise the newly enfranchised religion and encourage more people to be interested in converting, so as to see it as less of a persecuted minority cult favoured only by society's outsiders.

The creation of baptisteries from the 5th century was the natural evolution of this process, the use of pre-existing *balnea* and *thermae* being the immediate short-term solution. It seems that once these baptisteries appeared, the ancient baths and newly built examples began to be used for the poor, pilgrims, and the clergy.

The reservations of Christian writers towards bathing did not, it appear, impact on the location choices made by the Christian builders of Rome. The practical advantages provided by the baths overrode any moral concerns. Equally, the popularity of the large imperial *thermae* was something that would benefit a Christian basilica built nearby. These were basilicas that used the facilities of baths, and those next to the large imperial establishments were religious foci for the Christian bathers going there. These latter examples were a sign perhaps that the Roman ecclesiastical authorities recognised the habits of the populace of the city, and could use those habits in order to further Christianise the social life of Rome and its population.

---

[89] LP 1.245, 262, 2.27-28.
[90] LP 1. 343. The Lateran baths seem to have been quite luxurious by the 8th century, with a portico and stairs leading down into them (LP 1. 470-71, 502-503). Their precise use is still unclear. For other examples of the changing role of baths beyond Rome in northern and central Italy into later centuries see Ward-Perkins B. *From Classical Antiquity* (1984) 135-146 with refs.
[91] Stasolla F. R. 'Balnea ed edifici di culto', in *Ecclesiae Urbis* (2002) 149; Meneghini R. 'Edilizia pubblica e privata nella Roma altomedievale. Due episodi di riuso', *MEFRM* 111 (1999) 175-82 (172-82). Foundation of diaconia in A.D. 755 or 770: LP 1. 514 n.2; Hülsen C. *Le chiese di Roma* (1927) 196.

3. Striving for Attention

"You are the light of the world. A city on a hill cannot be hidden." (Matthew 5:14).[1]

3.1 The Christian basilica on the Main Road

A particular phenomenon of 4th-7th century Christian basilica location is their frequent appearance along the main arteries within (as well as beyond) the walls of Rome.[2] From our modern top-down plan perspective of the ancient city this may look a neat pattern, but what did this actually mean for the contemporary Roman walking on that road? It is only when we look a little closer that we can get a more accurate view as to what impact these new structures had on the urban landscape and the ancient viewer.

The first question we need to ask is why this pattern might be occurring. This question has never really been answered in any thorough way by scholars, probably because nothing definitive can be said; there are no contemporary sources that describe any reasoning behind the pattern. Yet the pattern is clear, and coincidence is not an adequate explanation. The most obvious motive is an age-old one: for your foundation to be seen and admired by everyone. Whether a *titulus*, *diaconia* or *xenodochium* was a lay, episcopal or imperial foundation, the motive would be the same. Only by seeing these early Christian foundations as the traditional aristocratic donations they were, can we understand their physical position in the city. Their generally modest size only emphasises more the need for their patron to advertise their investment.

We need to be careful here though, as there are several examples which, on the usual macro modern plans of the city in late antiquity or the early middle ages, appear to be next to the main road. On closer inspection many are in fact on side roads off it, the *titulus Lucinae* (S. Lorenzo in Lucina) being a good example of such, just off the *via Lata-Flaminia*. These examples will therefore be eschewed, unless there is obvious clustering.

More significant than Christian foundations just off or on main roads are those which actually encroach onto a road with their apse. There are a few examples of this we know from the archaeology, meaning the basilica entrance was accessed from a side street. Anyone moving down the road in question would have seen and noticed such a partial blocking of the road, with this acting as a clear marker of the building's existence as well as a visual signpost for finding it. It could be argued that this encroachment may just be a side-effect of the need by the builders to have the basilica entrance off the main noisy street in a pre-existing structure that lay perpendicular to that road, and not a deliberate attention seeking act. However, this does not explain the same structures' expensive reversal of orientation in later centuries (why did such apparent noise avoidance not apply then?) and that such an encroachment onto a public space like a road technically required special permission, so was not done thoughtlessly.[3] It also fails to explain the few examples from this period whose entrances did face onto the main road.

Several small basilicas inside Rome, therefore, sought to and succeeded in impacting on public spaces, although not the imperial fora or squares, which were still the preserve of the temples, until the 6th century. As the majority of Christian centres in Rome were small and architecturally modest basilicas, they needed to be made distinguishable from other buildings in the city so they could be found by worshippers—the basilical hall was a common building type—but we have no evidence how this was done, and the earliest images of the exterior of these structures are from early medieval apse mosaics, by which time their façade may have altered considerably. We cannot assume the brick structures of the first Christian basilicas that do survive were unclad or had no other architectural ornament. Any evidence for what that may have been is archaeologically undetectable, and no surviving source describes the early façades. As such, we have no good idea to what extent these smaller basilicas attempted to impose themselves in other ways visually on the landscape, only that they must have been an identifiable Christian building in some way. With this absence of evidence we can only say that some attempted to do this by, for example, lying next to an important busy road with their apse protruding onto it.

This is not say all the *tituli* on main arterial roads looked away from them. Several seem to have had entrances that directly led onto these busy thoroughfares, indicating a willingness again by Christian builders to embrace and be a part of the urban landscape and secular life of Rome.

We will also examine the phenomenon of clustering of basilicas on or just off main roads. It is often suggested that this pattern is the result of a high density of Christians in the area at the time they were built.[4] This is likely to have

---

[1] Translation: *New International Version* (1984).
[2] The phenomenon has recently been examined by B. Brenk who focuses on a few examples. The prominence and importance this would have given these foundations is described: Brenk B. 'Kirche und Strasse im frühchristlichen Rom', in *Rom in der Spätantike*, edd. R. Behrwald and C. Witschel (2012) 171-91. I thank Prof. Brenk for providing me with an offprint of this article.
[3] Cassiod. *Var.* 4.30 and see below.
[4] Eg. Lampe P. *Christians at Rome* (2003) 41-47. See also Christie N. *From Constantine to Charlemagne: An Archaeology of Italy AD. 300-800*

been the case, but does not explain why some examples were situated on the main arteries, and not within the dense housing further off them. This speaks of a need for the foundation to be noticed and for it to be easily locatable for non-locals and outside visitors to the city.

These main arteries of course often led out to the suburbs where several burial catacombs along them there were long-standing foci for Christian devotion (from the 3rd century at least), with the burial of several important local martyrs within them. Several of these were embellished from the 4th century with Christian buildings to formalise this devotional activity and provide purpose-built places for the devout to be buried near to such Christian heroes, and to benefit from their sanctity. The appearance of a significant number of early intramural tituli along these same routes should be seen in this context as well.[5]

3.2 Clustering off Main Roads

3.2.1 Titulus Iulii trans Tiberim and S. Chrysogoni along the Via Aurelia

Our first example, thought to be on the site of the current S. Maria in Trastevere, has a complicated and unclear history. It has been related to a *titulus Iulii et Callisti*, which from the sources seems to have originally been two separate foundations that were later joined together by the 6th century, or at least given only one presbyter between them. The *titulus Iuli(i)* implies by its name that it was founded by Bishop Julius (337-52), and other sources also attribute it to him.[6] One source implies that a *Callistum* already existed at that time near the *titulus*, which the *LP* doubtfully attributes to bishop Callistus (218-22) himself.[7] Archaeology has confirmed the date of the current church of S. Maria in Trastevere to the 12th century, but a *titulus sancte Marie* is mentioned in 587, but its presbyter is not referred to in the synod list eight years later. The reference to a *basilica Iuli(i)* as *trans Tiberim*, the connection to that of Callistus, and some 8th century references describing a basilica to the virgin in this region *quae vocatur Calisti*, all link Julius' foundation to that of S. Maria in Trastevere.[8]

Excavations under the church have revealed the existence of an earlier basilica on the site with the same orientation but much smaller. What may be a late antique *domus*, with frescoes, was found beneath this first basilica, with the palaeo-Christian apse built not long after its abandonment. More precise dating has not been possible so far, but the archaeology combined with the written evidence suggests a 4th or 5th century date for the first Christian building here.[9]

Either way, the *titulus Iuli(i)* was connected to, or an enlargement of, a centre dedicated to Callistus. A church by this name, San Callisto, still exists, and is less than fifty metres from S. Maria, and both are alongside the line of the ancient *via Aurelia*, the main road into Rome from the west. S. Maria is also at the junction of the modern Via della Lungara/Scala road that passes through the Porta Settimiana, coming into this area from the north. (fig.13) These are all Renaissance features, but appear to have followed ancient precedents, as the gate seems likely to have been Severan. With the construction of S. Pietro in Vaticano, this road would have become a major route taken by Christians from that basilica into Rome and vice versa.[10] In this way, a Christian basilica or basilicas situated at the confluence of two such important roads into the city would have provided visitors and Romans with an ideal place to worship and rest. A kind of devotional route was thus created, with the *titulus Iulii* and *Callistum* being the markers of its beginning perhaps.

Also along the *via Aurelia* we find S. Crisogoni, or Chrysogoni, a *titulus* first mentioned in 499.[11] Remains of a hall, which was probably attached to a rich *domus* dating to the late 3rd or early 4th century found underneath the current church, may have been the first Christian centre here. Adaptations to it to create an apse and a narthex do not occur until the second half of the 5th century, but that does not rule out its use as a place of Christian worship before this. The discovery of several basins of Roman date and the unusual plan of the first basilica, has caused some to think that it was converted from a *fullonica* building.[12] It is located further east along the road on the same side as S. Maria. They are only about three hundred metres apart. In some ways then, one could say they complemented each other, providing two places of worship for Christians coming into the city from the west. Coming or leaving from that direction they would have been difficult to avoid or ignore. We cannot say how much they stood out from surrounding buildings in this period, but they must have had some exterior feature that marked them out as a Christian building, so that the faithful would know where to go. They were also a sign, therefore, of the increasing Christianisation of Rome for the human or wheeled traffic along it. This stretch of the road inside the walls could have been regarded as a Christian zone once these foundations were constructed.

The *via Aurelia* itself began at the *pons Aemilius*, a bridge that may have been constructed at the same as the road,

---

(2006) 207.
[5] For more on this idea and devotional connections see: Mulryan M. 'The establishment of urban movement networks: devotional pathways in late antique and early medieval Rome', in *TRAC 2011: Proceedings of the Twenty-First Annual Theoretical Roman Archaeology Conference*, edd. M. Duggan, F. McIntosh and D. J. Rohl (2012) 123-34.
[6] LP 1.206, 230; MGH.AA. 12.411; MGH.Ep. 1.367.
[7] LP 1.9 (Liberian Catalogue), 141. It may not be that outlandish a suggestion however. We know that there was a funerary memorial to Peter outside the walls by about A.D. 250, and that the *Transtiberim* region was also outside the city walls during most of the 3rd century, before Aurelian's new fortifications. The *Callistum* may therefore have simply been a small shrine, like Peter's, only later embellished to become a *titulus*.
[8] *Coll. Avell.* (ed. Guenther) 1 passim; LTUR 3.119-20, 219-20; LP 1.509, 2.16, 19, 26.
[9] Coccia S. *et al.* 'Santa Maria in Trastevere: nuovi elementi sulla basilica paleocristiana e altomedievale', *Meded* 59 (2000) 161-74.
[10] LTUR 3.311-12.
[11] MGH.AA. 12.411.
[12] Luciani R. and Settecasi S. *San Crisogono* (1996); LTUR 1.266-67; CBCR 1.144-64.

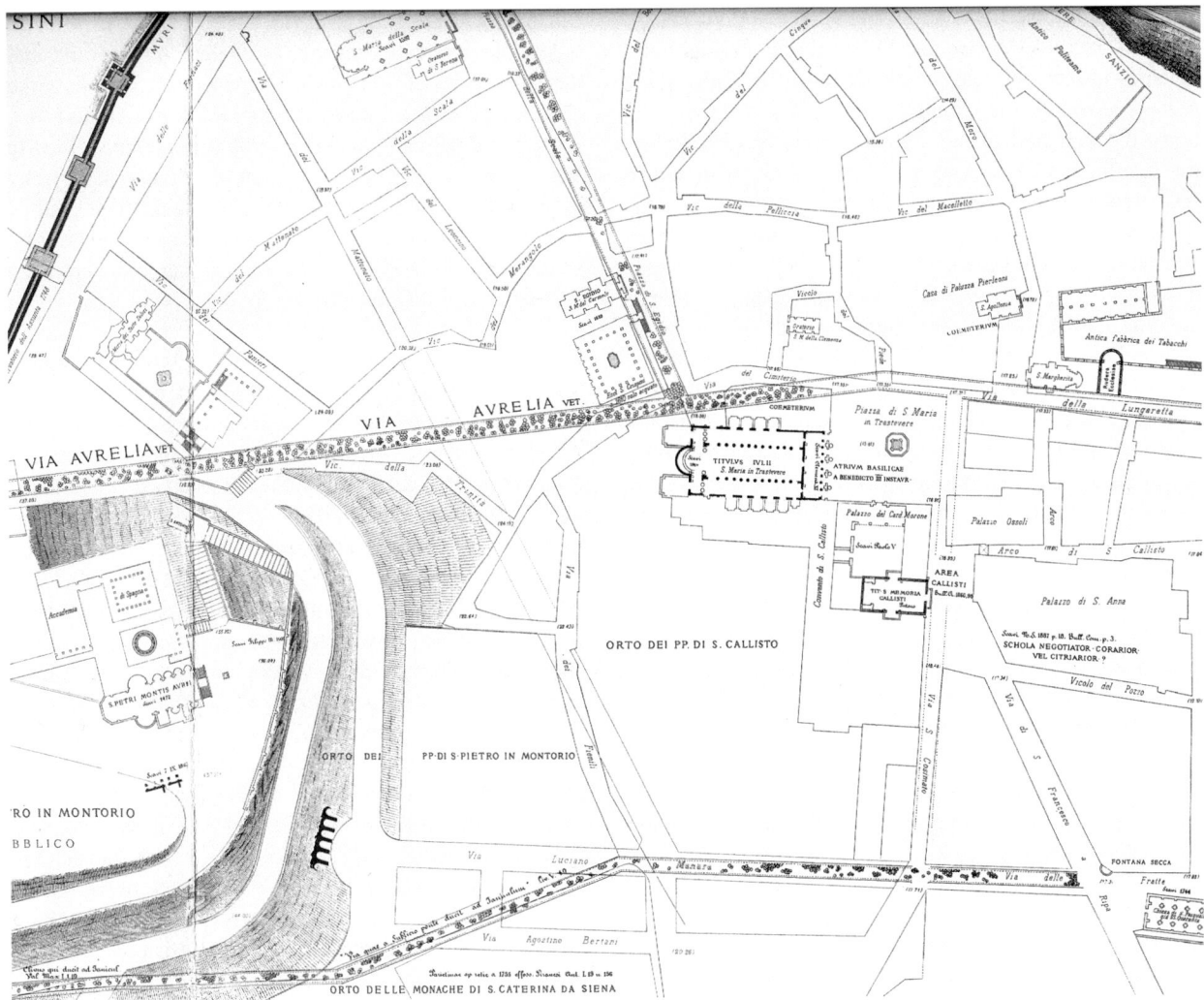

FIGURE 13: DETAIL OF PLATE 27 AND S. MARIA IN TRASTEVERE AND S. CALLISTO, IN LANCIANI R. *FORMA URBIS ROMAE* (MILAN 1893-1901).

that is about the mid 3rd century B.C.[13] The road led into the heart of the ancient city and was a very important and well-used thoroughfare as a result. The significance then of the construction of two or three Christian centres alongside it should not be underestimated. Also, from the mid 4th century, Julius, and from the 3rd century, martyr-bishop Callixtus, were buried in the Catacombs of Calepodius just off the *Aurelia* at the 3rd mile, and in the late 5th or early 6th century a basilica to St. Pancras, containing his relics, also existed alongside the *Aurelia* just outside the city walls.[14] From that time therefore, this road would have become even more popular, and these intramural centres would have been at the junction of two Christian devotional routes. Indeed, this was the case before the martyr's basilica was constructed. The catacombs, over which the tomb basilica to St. Pancras was built and where Callixtus and Julius were buried, were already a long-standing popular focus for Christian martyr devotion. That is, all these Christian foundations built alongside the *via Aurelia* were likely built in acknowledgement of this road being an existing Christian avenue of some importance.[15] A formal procession between S. Pancrazio and S. Pietro in Vaticano took place in the 6th century at least.[16]

3.2.2 Titulus Fasciolae and Basilica Crescentiana off the Via Appia

These two basilicas provide us with another strong case for arguing for a strategy by some Christian builders in the 4th and 5th century to build Christian centres where human traffic was greatest and where they would be noticed. Both are late 4th or early 5th century, and lay a matter of yards from each other. These two centres, apart from being located next to the ancient *via Appia*, were also situated in front of the entrance to the Baths of Caracalla, as discussed above, thus their placement is interesting in two ways. (fig.8) The significance of the latter has already been described above, so here we will concentrate on the two basilicas' relationship with the *via Appia* and the importance of this.

---

[13] Its final destination is also a matter of debate: LTUR 5.134.
[14] LP 1.141, 205, 262;
[15] Mulryan M. 'The establishment of urban movement networks' (2012) 128-30.
[16] LP 1. 303.

The *via Appia* itself was began in 312 B.C. by the censor Appius Claudius Caecus, and linked Rome with its Latin colonies in the south-east corner of Italy.[17] It began at the *porta Capena* by the Circus Maximus. From Republican times the first part of the road was used as a showpiece for familial and later imperial propaganda, with tombs and arches being common features. The fact that the *Appia* was the route by which returning armies or foreign delegations entered the city from the south-east explains this, as well as its frequent use by the general public.[18] Severus' *Septizodium* was placed just inside the *porta Capena* so as to be visible by all who took this road into Rome.[19] Many religious buildings were also built along it, often in association with the many tombs and burials that characterised the initial stretch of the road. These temples no doubt benefited from the road's frequent use. By the imperial period this first part of the road became more built up, with burials decreasing. With the construction of the Aurelianic wall this practice ceased completely.[20] There seems to have been a proliferation of bath buildings along the road as well, dominated by those of Caracalla of course from the 3rd century, but also smaller *balnea* and the larger complexes built by Severus and Commodus.[21] These baths assumed appearance along the road, the majority probably by the *porta Capena* itself, suggests their placement was to take advantage of the consistent flow of people here and the easy access to water supplies from the springs and aqueducts in the area.

As such, all the builders of the major structures along the *Appia* were, in one way or another, utilising the road and its common usage by the people of Rome, as well as visitors from the south and returning armies, for their own advantage. That is, for their monuments to be widely noticed and/or used. It is in this context that we need to appreciate the construction of the two Christian centres in the late 4th and early 5th century on this same stretch of the *Appia*.

The history of the *titulus Fasciolae* has been discussed in detail in the previous chapter, but it is worth noting again that it is mentioned initially in an inscription dated to 377, and is thought to have lain near, but not on the site of, the existing church of SS. Nereo ed Achilleo. Archaeological evidence suggests it may lie to the north or north-west of the current church, but it is certainly not under the current church; the literary evidence confirms it is not far away from it, and thus still next to the *Appia*.[22] Its title, in the 5th or 6th century, was erroneously thought to refer to a *fasciola* or small bandage, in connection with the 2nd century legend of St. Peter's escape from Rome along the *Appia*. The original structure was built in a flood-prone area, a replacement having to be built in the late 8th/early 9th century on higher ground or a podium nearby, by which time it was also a hostel for the poor.[23] The basilica was built between the *via Appia* and the new road built by Caracalla in front of his baths that lead up to the entrance of the Circus Maximus, the *via Nova*.[24]

The *Basilica Crescentiana* (S. Sisto Vecchio) was founded under Anastasius I (399-401) and had representatives at the Roman synod of 499.[25] There is some debate as to its location, as the *LP* mentions that it was *in regione II, via Mamurtini*. It is unclear whether region two refers to an ecclesiastical region or an Augustan one, and the location of the *via Mamurtini* is also uncertain. The *titulus* has been argued to have been on the Quirinal, on the basis of a *vicus Mamuri* or *Mamurtini* existing there near to S. Susanna.[26] It is more likely, however, to be on or very near to the site of the current S. Sisto Vecchio in the *via Appia/Nova* area, as there is a *balneum* or *templum Mamurtini/Mamuri* between the *via Appia* and *Latina*, and this is also in the second ecclesiastical region. The bath or temple is thought to have been named after the road on which it lay. Other theories also put the road cited in the *LP* in this area and thus the basilica as well.[27] It is also clear from this that the early basilica was not directly on the *Appia* itself, but on the *via Mamurtini* road just off it. A Christian foundation of the late 4th-early 5th century has been confirmed by archaeology on the site of the existing S. Sisto Vecchio of the same orientation, with its entrance on what is now the Via Druso.[28] (figs.8 and 10) A basilica dedicated to St. Sixtus first appears in 595, where a presbyter attached to it attended the Roman synod of that year. The name may be as a result of a reconstruction by Sixtus III in the mid 5th century, or a rededication to the martyred 3rd century bishop Sixtus II. Whatever its original name, a late 4th-early 5th century Christian basilica lay alongside and parallel to the *Appia*.

Even if this foundation was to complement and eventually replace the damaged *titulus Fasciolae* across the road, it still shows the importance the Christian authorities gave to endeavouring to ensure that a Christian basilica

---

[17] Livy, 9.29.5-6; Diod. Sic. 20.36.1-2; CIL 11.1827.
[18] The existence of the *area Carruces*, the place where travellers left their carriages, and the *area Radicaria*, a vegetable market and/or customs post, in the area attests to the road's frequent public use. The existence of the *Mutatorium Caesaris*, where emperors changed from military to civilian clothes after returning from campaign, opposite the Caracallan baths, confirms its common use as the military route into the city from the south: *Not. Rom.* I: Nordh ed. *Libellus* (1949) 73.14, 16; XII: Nordh ed. *Libellus* (1949) 92.10.
[19] SHA, *Sev.* 24.3.
[20] LTUR 5.130-33.
[21] *Not. Rom.* I: Nordh ed. *Libellus* (1949) 73-74. The precise locations of the *balnea* and the Severan and Commodian baths are unknown.
[22] See chapter 2: nn.60-63 above. The current church is an 8th/9th century rebuild on a different site nearby: LP 2.33.
[23] See chapter 2: nn.70-71.
[24] SHA, *M. Ant.* 9.9; Aur. Vict. *Caes.* 21.4; LTUR 5.142.
[25] LP 1. 218; MGH.AA. 12. 412, 414.
[26] AA.SS.. Aug II. 632; Cecchelli M. 'Note sui 'titoli' romani', *ArchCl* 37 (1985) 293-305.
[27] The *balneum mamurtini*: *Not. Rom.* I: Nordh ed. *Libellus* (1949) 73.15; LP 1.221 for a *templum mamuri* and a *clivus mamuri*, perhaps a reference to the baths; LTUR 1.338, 5.177-78; Geertman H. 'Titulus sancti Sixti', in *Hic fecit basilicam* (2004) 127-32. For the configuration of the second ecclesiastical region, and the other ecclesiastical regions of the city see: Spera L. 'Il vescovo di Roma e la città' (2013) 169-82 esp. 171-72.
[28] CBCR 4.157-70; LTUR 4.330; Geertman H. 'Ricerche sopra la prima fase di S. Sisto Vecchio in Roma', *RendPontAcc* 41 (1968-69) 219-28; Geertman H. 'Titulus sancti Sixti', in *Hic fecit basilicam* (2004) 127-32.

was situated by the *via Appia*. The provision of two such centres emphasises this further of course.

It appears the *Appia* also marked the border between the first and second ecclesiastical regions in the city and so it marked a divide in clerical authority as well. In this way, their proximity may be a reflection of internal Church competition and ambition, with their location on or just off a main road and at their respective limits of jurisdiction. Whatever the situation, the existence of two Christian basilicas, certainly the case at some point in the 5th century, either side of this main artery into Rome, is significant. The many 2nd and 3rd century catacombs and Christian cemeteries alongside the *via Appia* beyond the city walls, now formally embellished, meant this road had long been a popular Christian devotional route. In this way, these basilicas can also be argued to have been built to provide for this devotional traffic (as with the *titulus Iulii* and *Chrysogoni* on the *via Aurelia*), which in turn would give prominence to the foundation itself and its donor. From the 6th century, with the appearance of a *xenodochium* in the area, it seems provision was starting to be made here for an influx of pilgrims from beyond the city.

3.3 Encroachment onto/into Public Spaces

The legal and archaeological evidence for the late antique city suggests there was a persistent problem with private buildings encroaching onto public spaces.[29] Repeated laws trying to curb the activities of private individuals building within and next to public spaces and buildings, suggests the authorities were fighting a losing battle.[30] This section deals with a specific aspect of this problem, that is the encroachment of Christian basilicas onto public spaces. The laws rarely describe the situation relating to ecclesiastical property specifically, and when doing so it is nearly always in reference to a basilica's seizure by 'heretics' or the abuse of its power of refuge. The exception is a law of 423 where it is stated Christian buildings are no longer obliged to pay to maintain or build the roads and bridges in the area where they are situated.[31] This is to say, before this Christian basilicas had to pay for the upkeep of the road outside, so any encroachment onto it would have had serious financial consequences for its clergy, a decision in other words not to be taken lightly, and one where it does occur before 423, needs to be seen as a calculated choice.

The Church might have been exempt from most other property laws, but there are many examples of other private property, that didn't enjoy such exemptions, encroaching onto roads throughout the East. Indeed, encroachment onto public space has been seen as officially sanctioned there.[32] In the West, in Rome, the late 4th/early 5th century reconstruction of the *Domus Gaudentius* on the Caelian obstructed a road.[33] Perhaps the financial and legal implications of such encroachment were not a sufficient deterrent for an aristocratic builder, or desperate shopkeeper needing a prime space to sell their wares, or perhaps it was indeed officially sanctioned? Yet, to partly or completely block a public highway or build onto public land is a deliberate attempt to impose one's own structure onto the urban landscape in an aggressive way.

This cannot just be seen as a need for extra space on the part of the *titulus* builders. The financial and legal implications meant this was not a thoughtless act taken lightly. Examples of Christian encroachment onto public highways, and in one example onto an open public space, in Rome, indicate a keen interest on the part of several aristocratic *titulus* builders to increase the prominence and impact their modestly sized donations made on the urban landscape, and in turn the people who lived in the immediate area. This can be seen elsewhere in the Roman empire as well, so this practice by Christian builders was not confined to the western capital.[34]

As well as encroachment we also see the physical creation of Christian spaces within former public buildings. This process, up to the end of the 7th century, was largely carried out within centrally located prestige structures. This in itself indicates an increasing confidence amongst aristocratic builders, now confined to the papacy. This seems to have been all part of a more overt strategy in imposing their munificence on the urban landscape, something that required a more subtle approach in earlier centuries.

3.3.1 Apsidal Road Encroachment

There is one confirmed case of apsidal road encroachment with early ecclesiastical property in Rome,[35] and two other basilicas whose apses deliberately face away from the

---

[29] Baldini Lippolis I. 'Private space in late antique cities' (2007) 195-238.
[30] Eg. *Cod. Theod.* 14.14.1, 15.1.4, 15.1.25, 15.1.46 and 47.
[31] *Cod. Theod.* 15.3.6.
[32] Baldini Lippolis I. 'Private space in late antique cities' (2007) 201-202 with refs.; Saliou C. 'Identité culturelle et paysage urbain: remarques sur les processus de transformation des rues à portiques dans l'antiquité tardive', *Syria* 82 (2005) 207-24. For the legal issues of early churches in Rome and encroachment onto public spaces see Hillner J. 'Le chiese paleocristiane di Roma' (2002) 321-29.
[33] Pavolini C. 'Le *domus* del Celio' and Spinola G. 'La *domus* di Gaudentius', in *Aurea Roma* (2000) 147-48, 152-55. See also Gauthiez B. 'La transformation des rues à la fin de l'Antiquité romaine: contextes, processus', in *La rue dans l'Antiquité. Définition, aménagement et devenir de l'Orient méditerranéen à la Gaule: actes du colloque de Poitiers, 7-9 septembre 2006*, edd. P. Ballet, N. Dieudonné-Glad and C. Saliou (2008) 141-48. For the issues surrounding the legal definitions of roads and the implications of that see: Saliou C. 'La rue dans le droit romain classique', in *La rue dans l'Antiquité* (2008) 63-68. For an interesting example of a (private) Donatist basilica in North Africa being converted into a (public) food bar in the early 4th century see *Passio SS. Donati et Advocati* 4 (Tilley M. A. ed. and transl. *Donatist Martyr Stories: the Church in Conflict in Roman North Africa* (Translated Texts for Historians 24) (1996) 55).
[34] Churches or baptisteries encroaching onto fora: Lincoln, Valencia, Aix, Herdonia, Diana Veteranorum, Lepcis Magna, Phaselis, Elaussia Sebaste, Iasos, Xanthos, Cherson (Crimea), Philippi, Pergamon, Knidos, Ariassos, Seleucia/Lyrbe and Rhodes. Churches encroaching onto streets: Timgad (with apse), Lepcis Magna (with apse), Philippi and Philippopolis. For references and more details see: Lavan L. *Visualising the Late Antique City: Secular Urban Space* (forthcoming 2014) appendices 1.A2, 6.V1-V3.
[35] The only other example of a potential Christian apsidal road encroachment may exist with the 4th century *titulus fasciolae*, but this

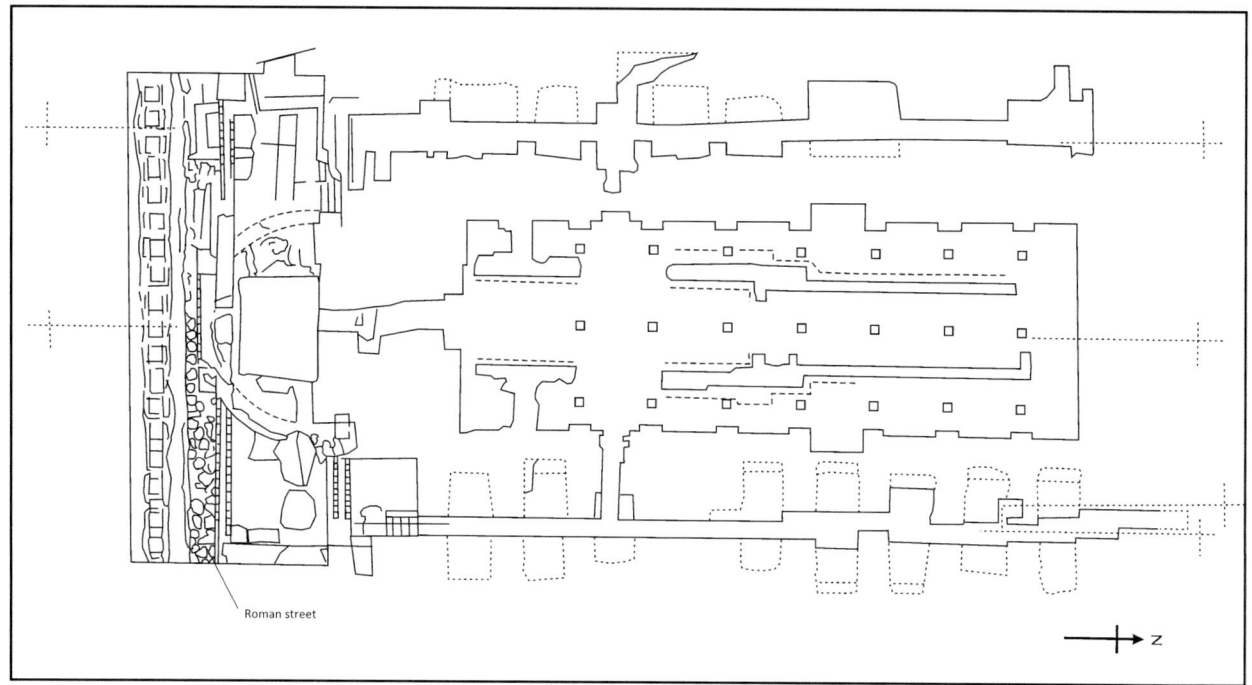

FIGURE 14: PLAN OF THE PALAEO-CHRISTIAN S. MARCO. DRAWN BY ABBY GEORGE FROM A BASE PLAN BY LUCREZIA SPERA, IN CECCHELLI M. 'LA BASILICA DI S. MARCO A PIAZZA VENEZIA (ROMA): NUOVE SCOPERTE E INDAGNI', IN *AKTEN DES XII. INTERNATIONALEN KONGRESSES FÜR CHRISTLICHE ARCHÄOLOGIE*, EDD. E. DASSMANN AND J. ENGEMANN (MÜNSTER 1995) 642, FIG.2.

main road, the implications of which will be discussed. All three examples went through expensive reversals of orientation in later phases, suggestive of a modified road network, rising ground levels and a later desire to be accessible straight off a major highway.

3.3.1.1 Titulus Marci

This basilica is said to have been founded by bishop Marcus in 336, the sole year of his episcopate, *iuxta pallacinis*, an area perhaps at the end of the *via Lata* behind the Capitoline. An inscription dated to around 348 describing an Antius *lector de pallacine* may be a reference to the foundation. It was totally rebuilt in the 9th century by Gregory IV.[36] We have no reason to doubt its early 4th century existence, and the precise description of its land grants by the *LP* implies the compiler had access to a genuine document.[37] Excavations that finished in 1990 brought to light more of the pre-Gregorian, Marcian remains, and showed definitively that the first Christian building on the site was a single naved hall structure, and also discovered that the 4th century apse of Marcus' foundation lay perpendicular to and over a basalt paved street, argued to be the *vicus Pallacinae*. (Figs.14 and 42) This apse lay to the south, a reversal of the 9th century and existing structure. There was a baptistery, and probably a sacristy, either side of the apse, the former perhaps 5th or 6th century. Remains of a pre-existing structure were found also, argued by some to be the house of the Turcii on the basis of two inscriptions found to the south.[38] This seems rather doubtful, however, as the family are likely to have still been pagans into the late 4th century.[39]

More interestingly for us is that this pre-existing structure did not include the apse and the shoulder walls off it, which were later connected to the walls of the pre-existing building. These new Christian additions meant that an apse now encroached onto this street, (figs. 15a and 15b) more likely to be an unknown but important road that led to the *via Lata* rather than the *vicus Pallacinae*, which probably lay outside the entrance to the north (fig. 42). The exact width of this unknown street in antiquity is unclear due to modern intervention just south of the apse, so we don't

---

is very hypothetical: Pavolini C. 'I resti romani sotto la chiesa dei SS. Nereo e Achilleo a Roma', in *MEFRA* 111.1. (1999) 438 n.88 (405-48).
[36] LP 1.202; ICUR 1.62 no.97; LP 2.74. The area was mentioned for the first time in the 1st century B.C.: Cic. *Rosc. Am.* 18, 132.
[37] CBCR 3.217.
[38] LTUR 3.212-13; Cecchelli M. 'S. Marco a Piazza Venezia: una basilica romana del periodo constantiniano', in *Costantino il Grande: dall' antichità all'umanesimo: colloquio sul Cristianesimo nel mondo antico: Macerata 18-20 Dicembre 1990*, 2 vols., edd. G. Bonamente and F. Fusco (1992-93) 299-310; Cecchelli M. 'La basilica di S. Marco a Piazza Venezia (Roma): nuove scoperte e indagni', in *Akten des XII. Internationalen Kongresses für Christliche Archäologie*, edd. E. Dassmann and J. Engemann (1995) 640-44; Cecchelli M. 'S. Marco', in *Roma dall'antichità al medioevo*, vol. 1: *Archeologia e storia nel Museo Nazionale Romano Crypta*, edd. M. S. Arena et al. (2001) 635 (635-36); CIL 6.1772, 1773.
[39] Turcius Secundus, alive in the late 4th century, was the first Christian in the family: PLRE 1. Secundus 4. An attractive theory would be that the Esquiline Treasure, which may refer to this individual, shows him marrying a Christian and perhaps converting and giving his house here to the Church. However, the date of Marcus' foundation is too early for the treasure, there is no reason to think Turcius converted, and the location of his house is likely to have been further to the south, where the inscriptions were found.

FIGURE 15A: THE PALAEO-CHRISTIAN S. MARCO, SHOWING THE APSE OVER THE ROAD, LOOKING WEST. AUTHOR PHOTO.

FIGURE 15B: THE PALAEO-CHRISTIAN S. MARCO, SHOWING THE ROAD AND THE BASILICA'S OUTER WALL, LOOKING EAST. AUTHOR PHOTO.

know to what extent this apse would have blocked the road. In spite of this we can be sure it made some impact on the use of this street from the mid 4th century.

As described above, such encroachment is a purposeful act that disregarded any financial implications, and if not breaking the law it certainly required legal permission. Such an encroachment could have been avoided in the case of this *titulus*, as the apse was not pre-existing and was constructed *ex novo* over the road by the Christian builders. The apse could just as easily have been built to avoid the road, only making the hall marginally smaller. So, although not an uncommon practice in late antiquity, this encroachment can be seen as an attempt to get an otherwise small, largely anonymous foundation to become a feature in the urban landscape. Those using this road—which must have had some importance as it was a conduit between the Capitoline/Fora area and the central Campus Martius (fig. 42)—would now have noticed this new apse feature over it.

An important factor here may be the fact that this was one of the earliest purpose-built Christian centres within the city walls, if not *the* earliest. Much of the sudden influx of imperial patronage in the first half of the 4th century for the Roman Church focused on the construction of extramural structures within or around the tombs of the Christian hero-martyrs, with provision for formal worship within the city, in this case at least, being provided by the bishop's own money. This explains the foundation's modest size, but also the desire for this aristocratic donor to make his building, named after him, to be as prominent as possible. We can only speculate as to the form and appearance of the hall's original façade, but this apse encroachment and its central location would have made it a noticeable addition to the urban environment to those using this important road.[40]

What is also characteristic of this foundation is that Marcus did not decide to create the entrance on this main artery, but rather to the north away from it. We don't know the nature of the road that went by the basilica door, but perhaps the bishop wanted a quieter entrance for his foundation. We can see two other Christian foundations which continue this practice of facing away from main roads, in these examples from the very important *via Flaminia/Lata*, now the modern Via del Corso.

3.3.1.2 Titulus Marcelli

The basilica of St. Marcellus was built off the *via Lata* and is first mentioned in 418, when Boniface I was consecrated pope here. The priests of the basilica attended the Roman synods of 499 and 595.[41] Remains of a north-south wall which could date from 380-450 were observed by Krautheimer in the mid 20th century under the north wall of the current church on the site (S. Marcello al Corso), and are thought to belong to the original *titulus*. A 4th or 5th century baptistery has also been found just to the north-east of these remains, which seems to backup this claim. The 8th century structure that replaced it had its apse facing the ancient *via Lata* road, the reverse of the surviving church today, which is 16th century.[42] (fig.16)

This baptistery and the immediate area were examined more closely in a series of investigations from 1990-2000, which also brought to light the apse of an early 4th century building, which was reused when it was later transformed into a Christian basilica.[43] It is clear that the apse is a good distance away from the ancient via Lata, it lying under what is now the entrance to the current church.[44] (fig.17) Thus, the orientation and location of the *titulus* was pre-determined and not a decision made by Christian builders.[45] The acquisition of a site right by the important *via Lata* is significant, but its entrance was from a side street off it, with there likely being another building between its apse and the road. It was thus an easily accessible foundation, but one that was largely hidden. This 'turning away' from the main road, although in this case predetermined, repeats what we see with Marcus' Christian hall.[46] Their small size is an indication of the limited budget available for intramural *tituli* in the 4th century, but their location shows a desire to create a centre that was at least easily locatable and accessible for a congregation.

3.3.1.3 S. Maria in via Lata

The Christian nature of the *via Lata* is further emphasised by the existence of a probably 6th to early 7th century *diaconia* almost opposite S. Marcello on the other side of the road, just to the south. The two indeed may have been originally connected in some practical way. This

---

[40] Interestingly, the sources and several archaeological discoveries point to the presence of the large and ancient Altar of Mars and one of his temples in the area just to the north of the *titulus*. For more on this see chapter 5 below.
[41] *Coll. Avell.* (ed. Guenther) 14; MGH.AA. 12.413; MGH.Ep. 1.367.
[42] LTUR 3.211-2; CBCR 2.211-4; LP 1. 509. The name of the church and its apparent location near to the *Catabulum* (the stables for the public post) gave rise to an elaborate legend surrounding its foundation by the 6th century: LP 1.164; *AA.SS.* Ian. 2. 9, 11-12. An inscription attests to a mid 5th century repair of the *Catabulum* (Orlandi S., Panciera S., Virgili P. 'Attività edilizia monumentale nel centro di Roma nel V sec. d.c. A proposito di una nuova iscrizione del prefetto urbano Rufius Valerius Messala', in *Les cités de l'Italie tardo-antique (IVe–VIe siècle)*, edd. M. Ghilardi, C. J. Goddard and P. Porena (2006) 123-36), a building which was still in use under Theodoric (Cassiod. *Var.* 3.10, 4.47).
[43] Episcopo S. 'La basilica di S. Marcello al Corso a Roma. Nuove scoperte', in *Akten des XII. Internationalen Kongresses für Christliche Archäologie* (1995) 734-740; Episcopo S. *Il Titulus Marcelli sulla via Lata: nuovi studi e ricerche archeologiche (1990-2000)* (2003) esp. 81-92.
[44] See Lanciani R. *Forma* (1893-1901) pl.15, which makes this distance clear.
[45] In spite of its east-west alignment with the altar at the east end, of which only a few early Christian basilicas in Rome in fact comply with (see fig. 1). The clearest example of this orientation was the original S. Pietro in Vaticano, and this may have provided the Christian model for what seems to have been a later universal practice, although largely outside Italy: Hoare P. G. and Sweet C. S. 'The orientation of early medieval churches in England', *Journal of Historical Geography* 26.2 (2000) 162-73. See also Brandt O. 'The archaeology of Roman ecclesial architecture and the study of early Christian liturgy', *Studia Patristica* 71 (2014) 30-33 (21-52) for the most recent discussion with references.
[46] This pattern is noted by G. De Spirito in LTUR 5.140, with other later examples.

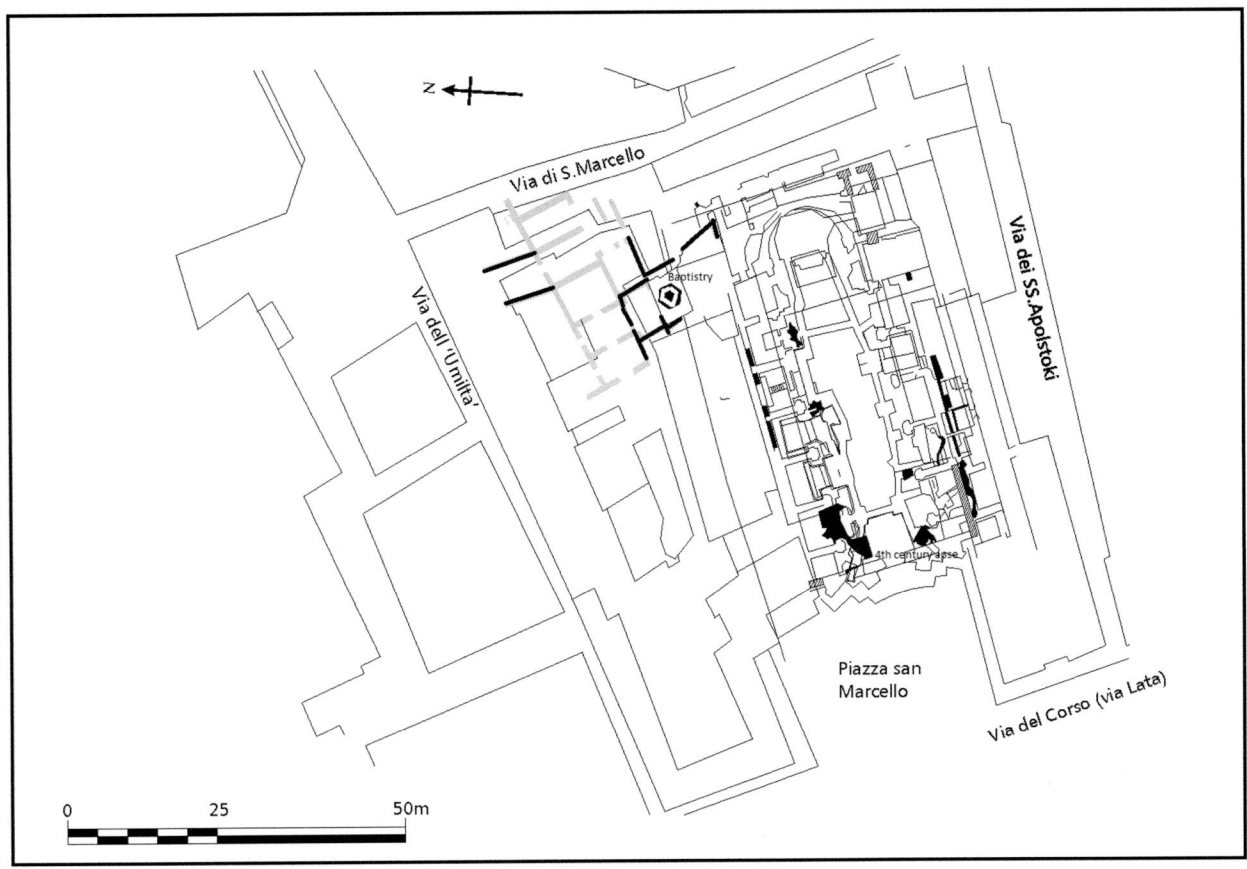

FIGURE 16: PLAN OF S. MARCELLO IN CORSO SHOWING RESULTS OF LATEST EXCAVATIONS. DRAWN BY ABBY GEORGE FROM A BASE PLAN IN EPISCOPO S. 'Il BATTISTERO DELLA BASILICA DI S. MARCELLO A ROMA FRA TARDA ANTICHITÀ E MEDIOEVO', IN *TARDO ANTICO E ALTO MEDIOEVO. FILOLOGIA, STORIA, ARCHEOLOGIA, ARTE,* ED. M. ROTILI (NAPLES 2009) 235-306.

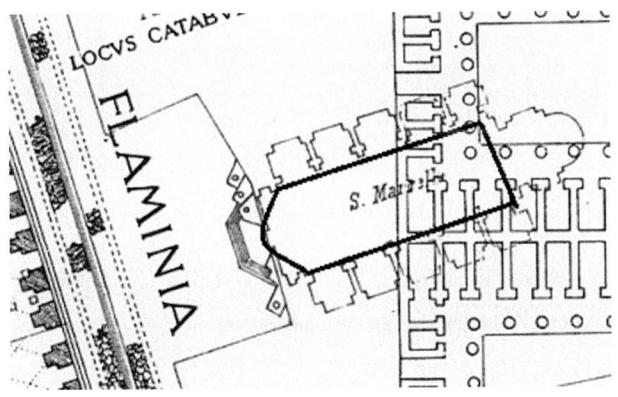

FIGURE 17: DETAIL OF PLATE 15 IN LANCIANI R. *FORMA URBIS ROMAE* (MILAN 1893-1901). S. MARCELLO AL CORSO AND THE VIA FLAMINIA, WITH ADDITIONS BY THE AUTHOR (4TH CENTURY BASILICA IN BLACK).

west. Part of this conversion process involved the creation of an apse in the central of the surviving rooms, which was the oratory, that turned it away from the ancient *via Lata* road, with its entrance most likely being from the west.[47] This apse's apex lay about seven metres from a large Roman arch—probably the *arcum novum* mentioned in the Regionary Catalogues—which spanned the *via Lata*/Via del Corso until the 15th century, and which may have been built by Diocletian. The rebuilding of this Christian centre from 1491 necessitated the destruction of the arch, so the two elements must have been intimate.[48]

Once more then we have an early Christian building turning away from a main road, preferring an entrance from a quieter side street. This orientation in this case required an awkward squeeze against a triumphal arch, so it was clearly a deliberate preference on the part of the

Christian building was created within a 1st century A.D. *porticus* that existed between the modern Via Lata and Vicolo Doria streets. In the 3rd century this structure was converted into an *horrea*, or warehouse, the northern *cellae* of which became parts of the diaconia. (fig.18) The elements of the diaconia that survive are its oratory and the immediate rooms off it; the storage, accommodation and other utilitarian rooms probably lying to the south and

---

[47] Sjöqvist E. 'Studi archeologici e topografici intorno alla Piazza del Collegio Romano', *OpArch* 4 (1946) 47-98; CBCR 3.72-81; Bertelli C. and Galassi Paluzzi C., *Santa Maria in via Lata* (1971); LTUR 5.140; LTUR 3.221-23; Pardi R. *La diaconia di Santa Maria in Via Lata, Roma* (2006). First mentioned in the written record under Leo III (795-816): LP 2. 12, 19.

[48] *Not. Rom.* VII: Nordh ed. *Libellus* (1949) 82.16; *Chronicle of the City of Rome* (in *The Chronography of 354*): MGH.AA. 9.148; Lanciani R. *Storia degli scavi di Roma e notizie intorno le collezioni romane di antichità*, vol. 1 (1902) 88; Laubscher H. P. *Arcus Novus und Arcus Claudii, zwei Triumphbögen an der Vita Lata in Rom* (1976); LTUR 1.101-102.

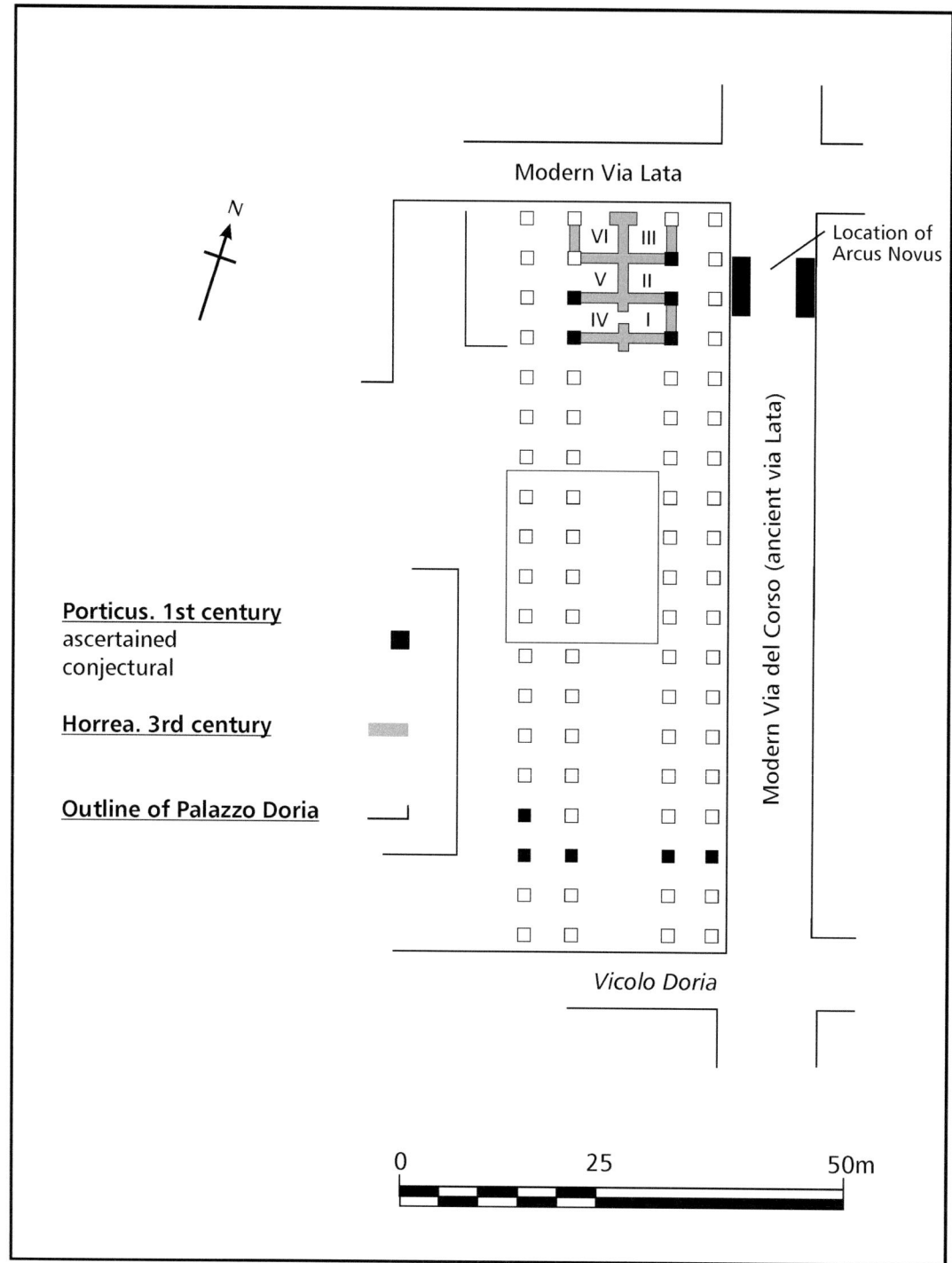

FIGURE 18: PLAN OF PORTICUS WEST OF THE VIA FLAMINIA WITH LOCATIONS OF S. MARIA IN VIA LATA AND THE ARCUS NOVUS. DRAWN BY ABBY GEORGE FROM A BASE PLAN BY SPENCER CORBETT IN CBCR 3.76, FIG. 69 (ENGLISH EDN.).

donor. The building of a *diaconia* within a public building already equipped with food storage facilities indicates its location was a pragmatic practical decision, but why was the oratory wedged in next to the arch? We don't know the exact layout of the rest of the *diaconia*, or the condition of the rest of the *horrea* in the 6th-early 7th century, although three piers still exist within the structure of the Palazzo Doria to the south. But, the positioning of a new Christian building next to a major landmark would make it easy to find in the city, this arch also having the *titulus Marcelli* just to its north on the other side of the road. Perhaps the arch was a useful marker for what were largely invisible buildings from the main artery road, and which turned away from it, the *diaconia* deliberately so. Even if this was not the intention of the builder, it would certainly have provided the visitor to either with a clear landmark to find them, and it is likely it provided both structures with a location designation of *iuxta arcus*.

3.3.2 Encroachment onto Public Spaces/Roads

There are a few examples of Christian buildings encroaching onto public spaces in a more significant way. Perhaps we should regard this as normal practice in late antique building, judging by the frequency with which we see such a phenomenon throughout the empire at this time. There is a general change in the morphology of the late antique city, that is clearly occurring here, where public land is no longer regarded as sacrosanct and is part of the general 'privatisation' of the urban milieu in the late Roman period. This is characterised most obviously by the increase in large private *domus* in cities and towns, and small-scale retail outlets encroaching onto intra-urban roads.[49] How should we see this encroachment then? A natural evolution of the environment? An increasing disuse of once busy roads and spaces? Or an internalisation of the social and living environment amongst elite builders with larger and more elaborate housing and cantonments? What is clear is that such encroachment was a deliberate choice by builders that impacted on the working of the city with regards movement and the use of public spaces.

The construction of a religious building within such a space is a smaller-scale reflection of the practice seen in the Republic and earlier empire, where temples were often to be found within public squares, and were a consistent feature of fora in Rome and elsewhere. The appearance of small Christian centres should perhaps be seen in this light and within this tradition, but this more ad-hoc late antique approach was more like an imposition than a planned architectural marriage. This is clearly a micro-monumentality versus an earlier macro one, yet the street-level effect from such Christian building meant that structure became immediately noticeable as a result, as it required an awkward visual readjustment by those using and passing the space.

A simple desire for a larger area on which to build, as with the *domus Gaudentius* mentioned above, may be the central reasoning behind such a move, but there was clearly a tacit awareness that such a program would alter and make prominent the building in question. Was this a desired side-effect for Christian donors trying to make an impact in what was still a city largely devoid of Christian landmarks within the walls? Nothing can be definitively proven here, but it is worthwhile to examine several examples of this to analyse their effect on the immediate urban environment.

Before discussing this, however, the legal issues surrounding such a move should be mentioned. J. Hillner has briefly analysed this problem and has demonstrated that not only did the Church request 'state land'—one and the same as imperially owned property (or private property) from the time of Constantine—on which to build, apparent from 6th century sources,[50] but went about it in different ways depending on the type of state owned land they wanted. For 'public property' the civil official responsible was the person to approach, but with state land, the emperor was the only person capable of granting such permission. On the ground in Rome, for public property, this was carried out by the Urban Prefect and the *curator operum publicorum*, and *curator operum maximorum* under him. It is likely, however, that the permissions for building projects of the bishop were imperially favoured and were addressed directly to the emperor, whatever the legal status of the land, with the bishop being able to carry out projects, such as the blocking of a road, that the civil authorities may have refused. Imperial, or land owned by the fisc, would have been under the jurisdiction of the *comes rei privatae* on behalf of the emperor himself. Any planning decision in favour of the Roman bishop would have been in part to further propagate the Christian faith but also to encourage the embellishment of the city with aristocratic money, the civic coffers being less able to sustain such a program in Rome by this time.[51] Hillner also suggests that the same motive may have lay behind the permission Theodoric gave to Felix IV to create a basilica, SS. Cosma e Damiano, within the building to the south of the *templum pacis*, an example we will discuss below.[52]

It is interesting to note that, according to a law of A.D. 405, private buildings on public land were liable to a rent which went into a public fund to help maintain the city as a whole.[53] In other words such a construction decision after this time had a serious financial consequence, and so would not have been taken lightly.

The reference, in the life of Sixtus III (432-40) in the *LP*, to the imperial concession of land to the Church for the construction of a *basilicam* to St. Lawrence, ties in with the situation around that of S. Lorenzo in Lucina, which is our first case-study.

3.3.2.1 Titulus Sancti Laurentii in Lucina

It has been convincingly argued that this basilica was not in fact built over a part of the so-called *horologium* of Augustus; in fact a large paved sundial area here cannot be substantiated in any way. More likely, a solar meridian—a narrow paved strip showing the position at noon of the sun throughout the year on a marked north-south line—existed about 30 metres east of today's Via del Campo Marzio, and nearly 100 metres due west of the existing church of S. Lorenzo in Lucina (fig. 19). This was Domitianic, and a likely restoration of an Augustan original.[54] Nevertheless, even if there was not a large paved square/*horologium*

---

[49] For an overview of the late antique city see Lavan L. ed. *Recent Research in Late-Antique Urbanism* (JRS Supplementary Series 42) (2001) passim.

[50] Damasus formerly asking for a *hortus*, on which to build a church to St. Lawrence, from, anachronistically, Valentinian III (*AA.SS*. Nov. 1.128); the LP describing Sixtus III building a Laurentian church built with the same emperor's permission (LP 1.234).
[51] Hillner J. 'Le chiese paleocristiane di Roma' (2002) 324-26.
[52] Hillner J. 'Le chiese paleocristiane di Roma' (2002) 326.
[53] *Cod. Theod*. 15.1.43
[54] Heslin P. 'Augustus, Domitian and the so-called Horologium Augusti', *JRS* 97 (2007) 1-20.

Spatial 'Christianisation' in Context

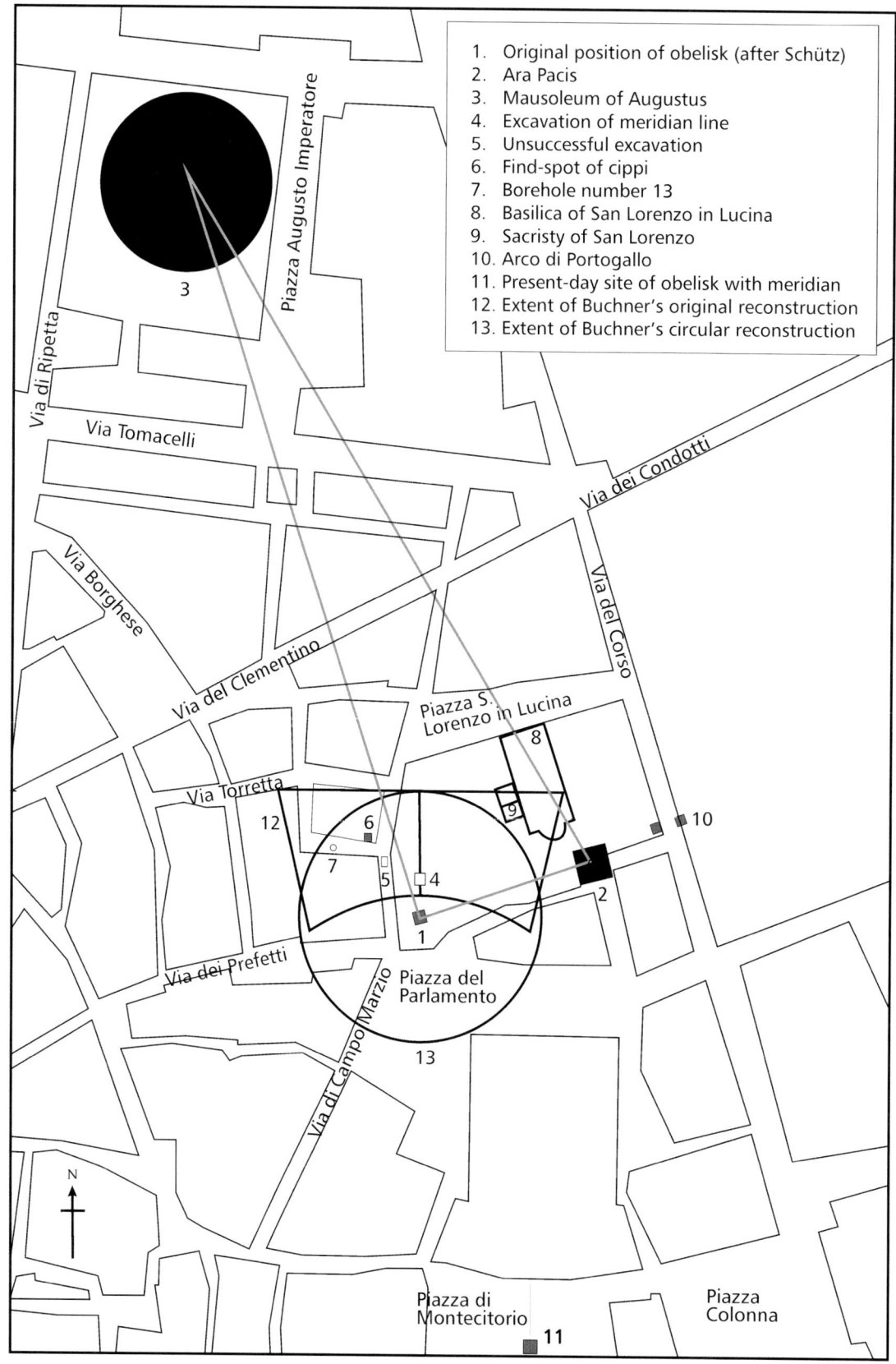

FIGURE 19: PLAN OF NORTHERN CAMPUS MARTIUS WITH EARLIER RECONSTRUCTIONS OF A SUNDIAL BY BUCHNER AND THE LOCATION OF THE OBELISK HERE BY SCHÜTZ. S. LORENZO IN LUCINA AND LOCATION OF PROBABLE MERIDIAN LINE ALSO SHOWN. DRAWN BY ABBY GEORGE FROM A BASE PLAN IN HESLIN P. 'AUGUSTUS, DOMITIAN AND THE SO-CALLED HOROLOGIUM AUGUSTI', JRS 97 (2007) 7, FIG. I.

on which this basilica was extended or built onto, there is good reason to think there were gardens of some description here. Much of this relies on this basilica being identified with the cult centre to Lawrence described in the *LP* as *fecit* by Sixtus III, with the agreement of the emperor Valentinian III (425-55).[55]

Much ink has been spilt in trying to identify which Laurentian basilica this refers to; either the ambulatory basilica in the area of his tomb outside the walls or the *titulus Sancti Laurentii in Lucina* inside the walls. In spite of arguments in favour of the former,[56] the evidence in favour of it being the latter is more convincing. Ambulatory basilicas are a distinctively Constantinian type and the inscriptions found within the extramural structure are also of that date, furthermore the law that forbade the moving of the dead for a building, a move therefore requiring imperial permission, was not needed in the case of martyria over or near their graves, from 386.[57] A middle position may be that the reference to Sixtus III was in fact a description of a rebuild of the extra-mural Constantinian basilica, but the archaeology cannot sustain that.[58] Indeed, no imperial agreement would be needed for such a project either. The intramural basilica seems the most likely candidate therefore, for requiring an imperial building sanction.

The written reference, and the archaeological data at San Lorenzo in Lucina, are somewhat ambiguous, however. The term *fecit*, seen in the *LP* to describe Sixtus' activity, is used as often for rebuilds as well as *ex novo* projects, so we cannot be sure as to the process involved in creating this cult centre.

Equally, the archaeology at San Lorenzo in Lucina is rather unclear, at the current time, as to the date of the first Christian building on the site. We know that a 2nd century building with a mosaic floor and painted walls lay on the site of the later basilica. This was replaced by an *insula* in the 3rd century, which was partly commercial and partly residential, with a pillared projecting porch with separate rooms behind. However, this *insula* was abandoned and partially destroyed in the early 4th century, which therefore puts in doubt the feasibility of a Christian centre *in lucinis* being on this site in 366, where Damasus was said to be elected bishop. However some mid 4th century pottery has been found within the *insula* remains, so the space continued to be partly in use, but perhaps for workshops of some description. (fig.20)

The surviving walls of the palaeo-Christian edifice here could be 4th or 5th century and partly reuse the walls of the *insula*, so the evidence does allow for the building of some sort of structure for Christian use before 366 within, and reusing, the ruins on this site. That is to say, the remains originally identified as the Sixtian basilica may well be a mid 4th century Christian building.[59] Certainly the appellation *Lucina* continued to be used for the basilica during the synod of 499, so it is likely that there was a building used by Christians here of the same name in 366. A 5th century baptistery has also been found just to the west of the basilica.[60]

Equally, the 4th century finds found sealed below the '5th century basilica' make it possible that this is all that remains of the place designated as *lucinis*, and perhaps embellished by Damasus once he was secure in his episcopate. This could all be suggestive of a 4th century structure (a small apsed hall or converted space?) that was largely demolished by a 5th century rebuild: a demolition within a partly demolished building would be very difficult to perceive archaeologically. This would tie in with our written sources, and may also explain the reference in the 6th century to a Damasian construction of a Laurentian cult centre (see above n. 296), but under a mid 5th century emperor, the result of a confusion with records of Damasian and Sixtian projects here, perhaps.[61]

In the same source we hear that Damasus wanted to build over a *hortus*, and gardens are described as surrounding the Mausoleum of Augustus in the 1st century B.C., which were opened up to the public by that emperor.[62] These were then imperial property, and as such were likely to have been respected until the 4th and 5th centuries. Furthermore, as Hillner notes, the use of the technical legal term *concessit* in the *LP* implies genuine access by the author of Sixtus III's *vita* to a papal archive where the original legal document lay; we see the same legal terminology suggesting a 'request' or a 'demand' of land in the 6th century legend.[63] This indicates that this project was a deliberate purchase attempt by Sixtus III to build anew, or extend the *titulus*/basilica *Lucinis* mentioned in 366, onto a *hortus* that existed here in late antiquity as part of the imperial gardens that surrounded Augustus' mausoleum. It was not a donation of land.

The size and nature of the partly abandoned *insula* on the site is unclear, but it may well have been imperial

---

[55] LP 1.234.
[56] Geertman H. 'La *Basilica maior* di San Lorenzo fuori le mura', in *Hic fecit basilicam* (2004) 117-26.
[57] *Cod. Theod.* 9.17.7; Hillner J. 'Le chiese paleocristiane di Roma' (2002) 321-22.
[58] La Regina A. dir. *Suburbium* (2001-2008) 3.205-206.
[59] Archaeology: CBCR 2.182-83; Bertoldi M. E. 'L'area archeologica di San Lorenzo in Lucina a Roma', *Bollettino di Archeologia* 13-15 (1992) 127-34; Bertoldi M. E. *S. Lorenzo in Lucina* (1994); LTUR 3.183-85; Brandt O. 'Jews and Christians in late antique Rome and Ostia', *Opuscula Romana* 29 (2004) 20-22 (7-27); Brandt O. 'The early Christian basilica of San Lorenzo in Lucina', in *San Lorenzo in Lucina. The Transformations of a Roman Quarter*, ed. O. Brandt (2012) 123-154. I thank Prof. Brandt for sending this article to me. Damasus election: *Coll. Avell.* (ed. Guenther) 1.5.
[60] Synod of 499: MGH.AA. 12.410. Baptistry: Brandt O., 'Sul battistero paleocristiano di S. Lorenzo in Lucina', *Archeologia Laziale* 12.1 (1995) 145-50; Brandt O., 'La seconda campagna di scavo nel battisterio di S. Lorenzo in Lucina a Roma: rapporto preliminare', *OpRom* 20 (1996) 271-74; Brandt O. 'The excavations in the baptistery of San Lorenzo in Lucina in 1993, 1995 and 1998', in *San Lorenzo in Lucina. The Transformations of a Roman Quarter*, ed. O. Brandt (2012) 49-77.
[61] Dufourcq A. Étude sur les g*esta martyrum romains* (1900) 140.
[62] Suet. *Aug.*100.4.
[63] Hillner J. 'Le chiese paleocristiane di Roma' (2002) 323, 328-29.

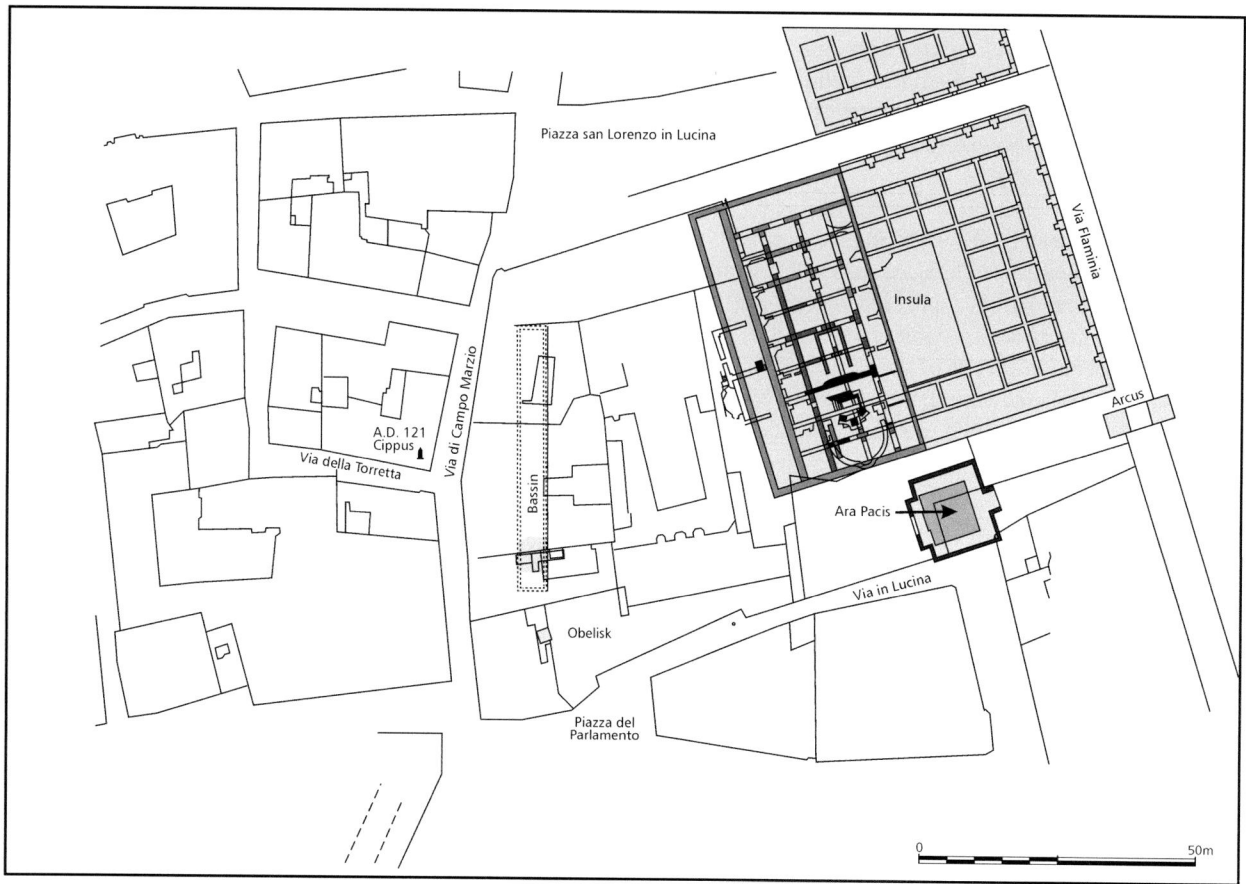

FIGURE 20: PLAN OF AREA OF S. LORENZO IN LUCINA SHOWING EARLIER INSULA AND PROBABLE MERIDIAN LINE BASIN. DRAWN BY ABBY GEORGE FROM A BASE PLAN IN RAKOB F. 'DIE URBANISIERUNG DES NÖRDLICHEN MARSFELDES. NEUE FORSCHUNGEN IM AREAL DES HOROLOGIUM AUGUSTI', IN *L'URBS: ESPACE URBAIN ET HISTOIRE (IER SIÈCLE AV. J.-C.- IIIE SIÈCLE AP. J.-C.)* (ROME 1987) 699, FIG. 5 (687-712).

property,[64] built onto or at the edge of imperial gardens, where, whatever its legal status, the replacement of it with a privately funded religious building, now encroaching further onto those gardens perhaps, required imperial permission. No mention is made of any such permission granted to Damasus, implying *in Lucinis* was a designated space owned by a Lucina within the partially demolished *insula* which Damasus may have then embellished, with Sixtus demolishing the whole edifice to create a purpose-built basilica dedicated to Lawrence.

In any case, to build a Christian centre on imperial land, or to extend onto it, around which still lay imperial gardens—presumably still open to the public in this monumental area—suggests an ambitious prominence was given to this foundation, something that would be typical of the Sixtian programme (see S. Maria Maggiore below) and a manifestation of the increasing confidence shown by the episcopate by the mid 5th century. An, albeit small, Christian building in the same compass as Augustan monuments (the Ara Pacis was just to the south as well) within imperial gardens, gave this foundation a cachet and prominence desired by Sixtus, and more humbly demonstrated by Damasus a century earlier, another bishop

with an eye for the importance of building, something typical of any Roman aristocrat.

3.3.2.2 Santa Maria Maggiore

This foundation will be tackled in more detail below, in reference to its position at the summit of the Cispian hill in Rome, but we will briefly mention here that the basilica may also have been built over a road that then must have gone out of use as a result of this Christian intervention. Basalt stones were found under the current basilica beneath the middle of the west aisle and also beneath the sacristy, which is in the east aisle by the church entrance. This was thought to be the remains of a single road, running, therefore, due east-west below the basilica.[65] Both Magi and Krautheimer took this idea on in their plans of the basilica (see fig.21). Yet more recent excavations found no such evidence for this thoroughfare, and on the same alignment there was found no basalt stones at all, which are not definitive evidence for a road in any case.[66] As

---

[64] Hillner J. 'Le chiese paleocristiane di Roma' (2002) 329 n.31.

[65] Gerardi F. 'Note sulla topografia dell'Esquilino settentrionale nell'alto medioevo', in *Archeologia del medioevo a Roma: edilizia storica e territorio*, edd. L. Pani Ermini and E. de Minicis (1988) 130 (127-37).

[66] Liverani P. 'L'ambiente nell'antichità', in *Santa Maria Maggiore a Roma*, ed. C. Pietrangeli (1988) 45-53.

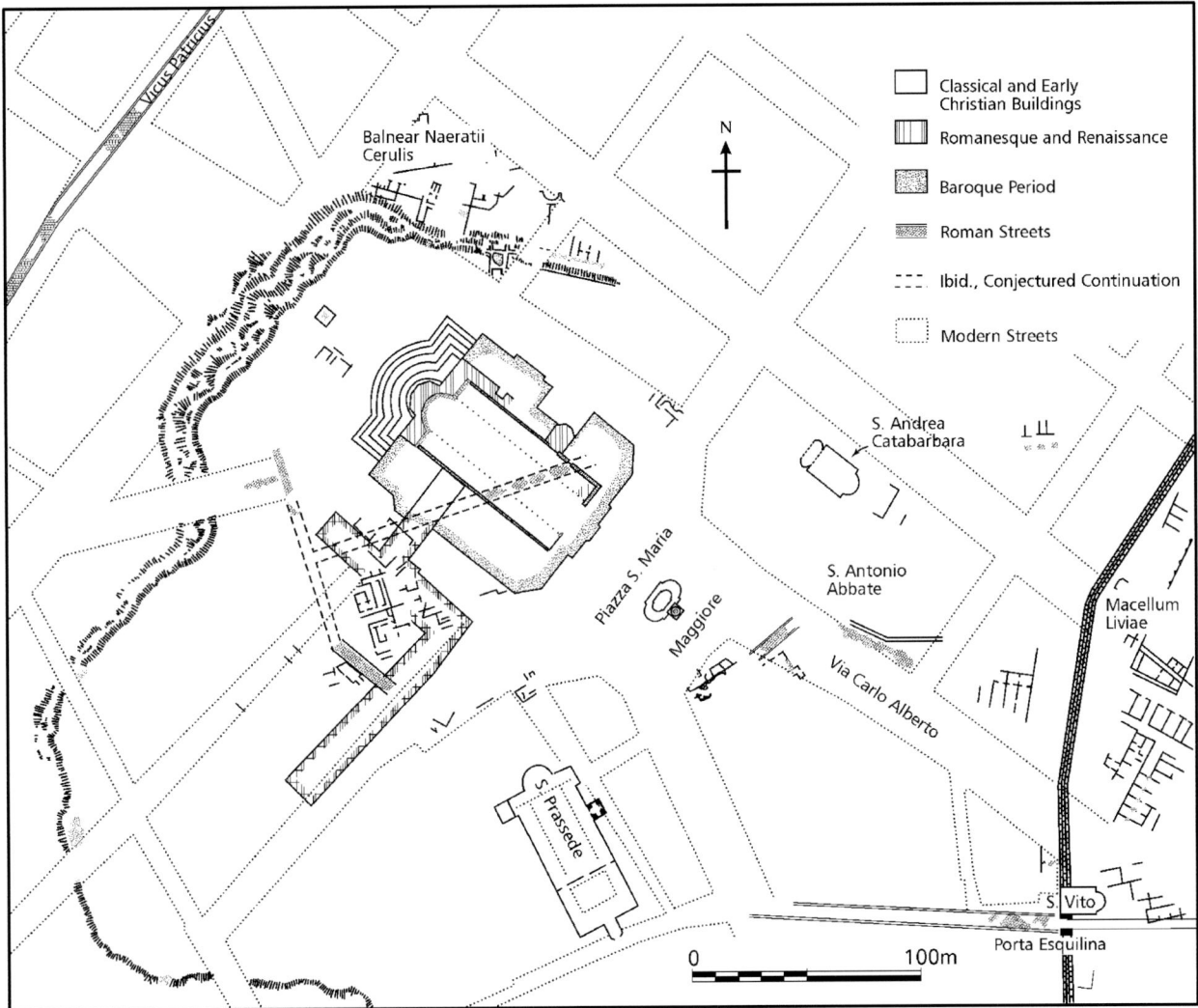

FIGURE 21: PLAN OF AREA OF S. MARIA MAGGIORE WITH POSSIBLE STREETS. DRAWN BY ABBY GEORGE FROM A BASE PLAN BY SPENCER CORBETT IN CBCR 3.12, FIG. 2 (ENGLISH EDN.).

such, we need to be sceptical about a road lying beneath the basilica, but the presence of basalt slabs do at least allow this as a possibility that cannot be completely dismissed. Any road that did exist even bordering the new basilica would certainly have gone out of use. The fact that this was a sole project of the ambitious builder Sixtus III (see above) means that such a dramatic alteration to the road network should not be ruled out, but the evidence for such a road(s) is not sufficient for us to be able to say that this is what occurred here.[67]

There are two other Christian structures that more convincingly block streets in the city, however.

3.3.2.3 Oratory/Arian Basilica of the 'Monte della Giustizia'

This oratory, or small Arian basilica, has been dated to the second half of the 4th to the early 5th century and was built within a space between a public building and a *domus*, with Christian decoration added in the apse. This space seems to have been occupied by a narrow street, and if so the Christian building put it completely out of use as a through route. Unfortunately the remains were found during the construction of Termini railway station, and so were destroyed for its completion, so our records are limited to some sketches and a single report.[68] From this though, it seems it was an apsidal hall, 3 metres in width, with a room on the north side and two recesses either side of the apse (fig. 22). The quality and classicising nature of the apse decoration suggests a private oratory built by a Christian aristocrat as an extension to their house, or as a part of a Christian virgin's private *cubicula*, rather than a publicly accessible basilica/oratory, but we cannot be certain. A 'public' Christian basilica built over a road could

---

[67] B. Brenk argues that the neighbourhood must have been largely depopulated for such a large church building project and road reorientation to have taken place (Brenk B. 'Kirche und Strasse' (2012) 184), but the wider archaeological evidence does not support this supposition either.

[68] De Rossi G. B. 'Oratorio privato del secolo quarto scoperto nel Monte della Giustizia presso le Terme Diocleziane', *BACrist* 3.1 (1876) 37-58, and looked at again more recently by Testini: Testini P. 'L'oratorio scoperto al "Monte della Giustizia" presso la porta Viminale a Roma', in *Pasquale Testini: scritti di archeologia cristiana. Le immagini, i luoghi, i contesti*, vol.2, edd. F. Bisconti, P. Pergola, L. Ungaro (2009) 887-928 (orig. publ. in *RAC* 44 (1968) 219-60).

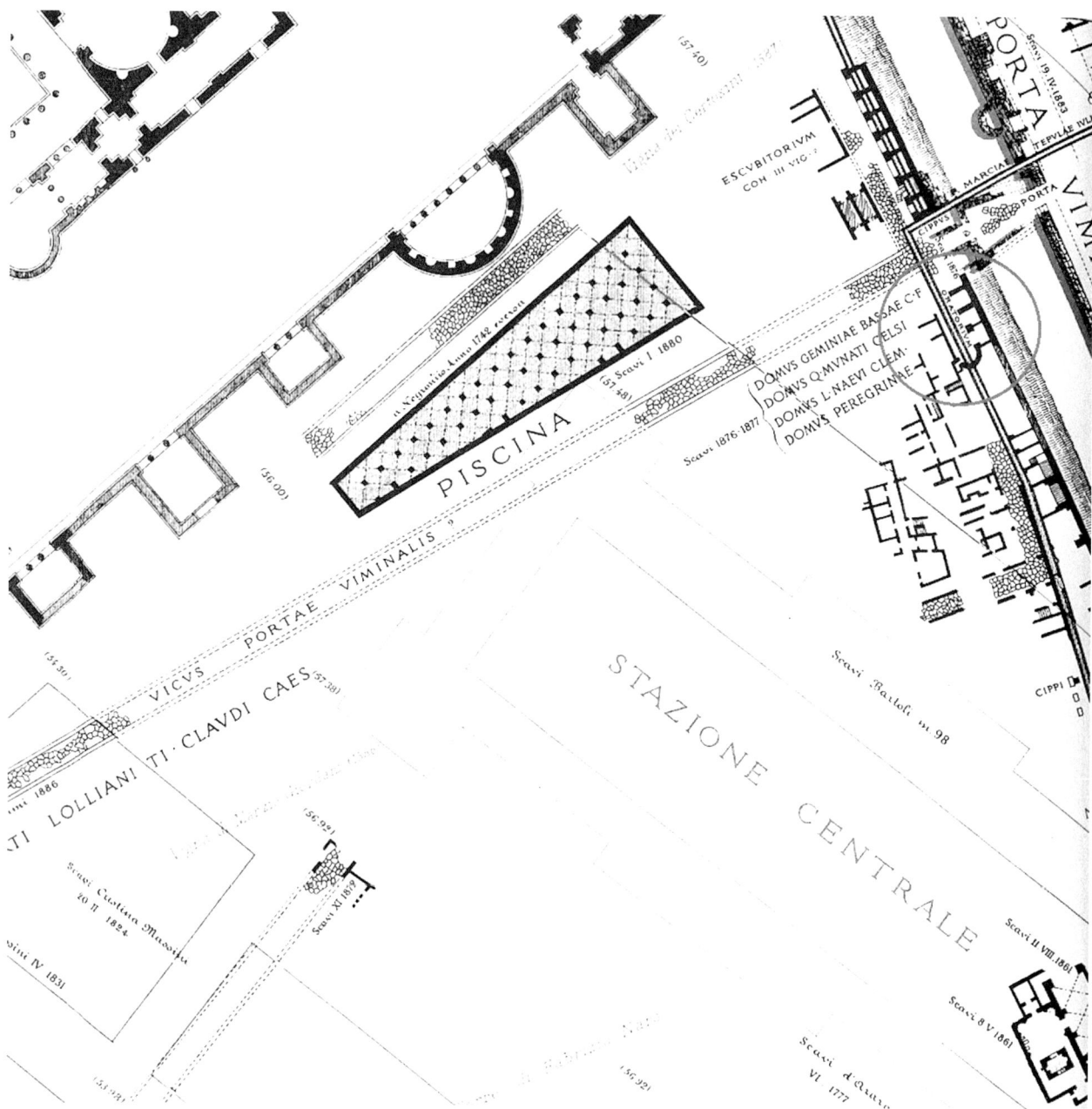

FIGURE 22: DETAIL OF PLATE 17 AND ORATORY OF THE MONTE DELLA GIUSTIZIA (CIRCLED), IN LANCIANI R. *FORMA URBIS ROMAE* (MILAN 1893-1901).

be seen as a sign of a degrading road network but also an odd site to choose, sandwiched between two pre-existing buildings. However, this may have been an ideal site for a minority 'heretical' wing of Christianity who sought a low profile, although its appearance in the landscape would have made a significant impact at the local level.

It is not clear from the plans and drawings that we have where the entrance is, so the relationship between the Christian building and the road is unclear. If this was a private chapel over a road it would be another example of the type of private encroachment onto public space we see with the *domus* of Gaudentius (see above) in Rome and throughout the empire at this time. This does not necessarily imply a decline in the urban road network, but perhaps an alteration or evolution of it to the detriment of minor roads in favour of main arteries.[69] Whatever the legal definition and precise function of this Christian structure, it's another clear indication of the Christian presence imposing itself on the urban landscape at the micro local level.

3.3.2.4 The Oratory of the Holy Cross at the Lateran

In the 460s, under Bishop Hilarus, a cruciform structure, approximately 13 metres wide, was newly built next to the Lateran to house the remains believed to be of the True

---

[69] As seen, for example, in late antique Ostia: Gering A. 'Plätze und Staßensperren an Promenaden. Zum Funktionswandel Ostias in der Spätantike', *RömMitt* 111 (2004) 299-382; Lavan L. 'Public space in late antique Ostia: excavation and survey in 2008-2011', *AJA* 116 (2012) 649-91.

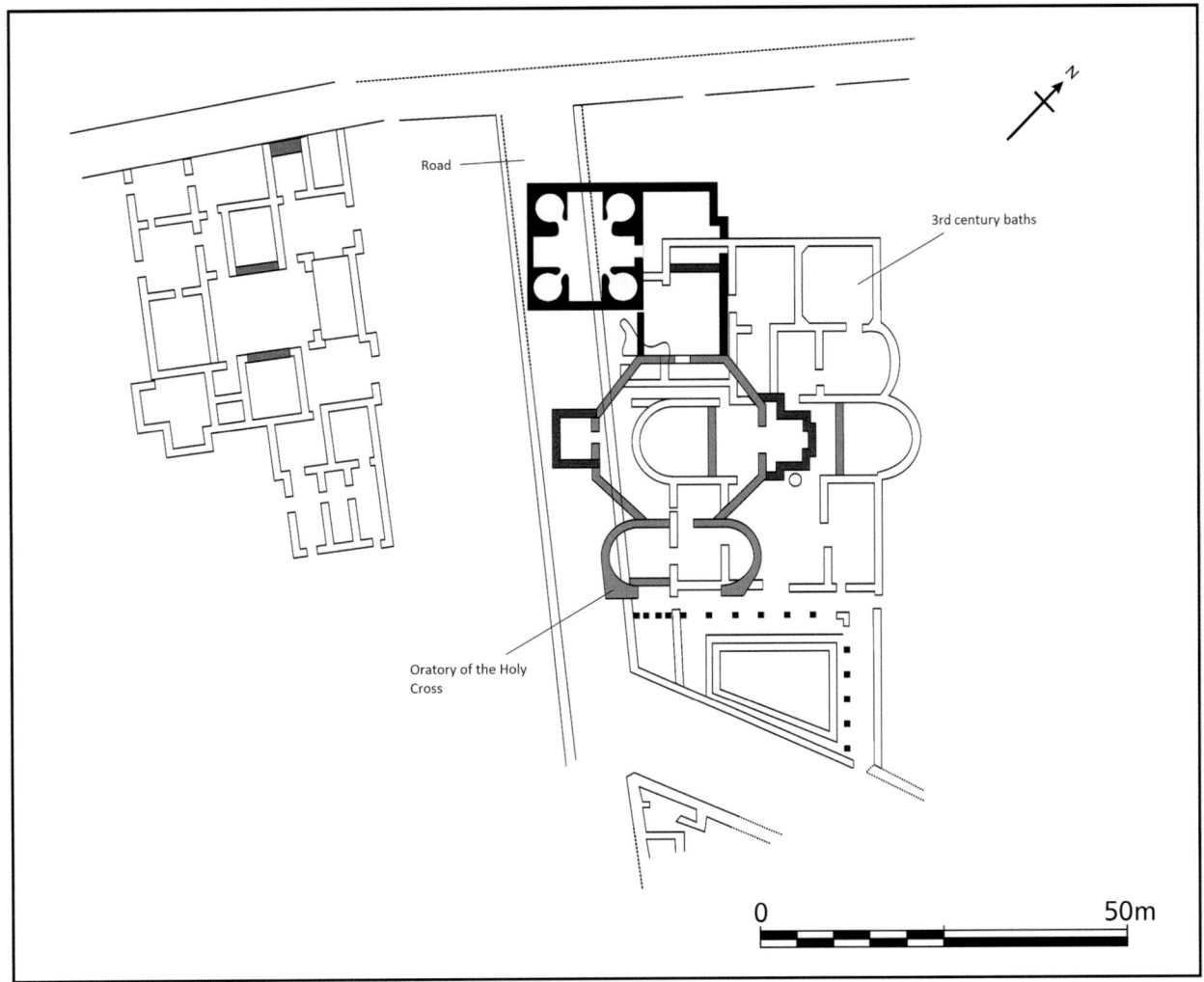

FIGURE 23: PLAN OF ORATORY OF THE HOLY CROSS AND PRECEDING ROADS AND STRUCTURES. DRAWN BY ABBY GEORGE FROM A A BASE PLAN IN JOHNSON M. 'THE FIFTH CENTURY ORATORY OF THE HOLY CROSS AT THE LATERAN IN ROME', *ARCHITECTURA* 25.2 (1995) 128-55 (FIG. 20).

Cross. It was constructed above the remains of 3rd century baths and next to the Lateran baptistery. We can reconstruct the appearance of the oratory from Renaissance drawings and plans, drawn before its demolition in the 16th century. From these plans, and the results of the bath excavations, it seems the oratory encroached and largely blocked a road running NW-SE that had run alongside the earlier baths. Strangely, this road had given access to the baptistery, which was much earlier in date than the oratory.[70] (see fig.23)

So, by all accounts the construction of the oratory suggests a realignment of the access to the area, and the deliberate closing off of an important road as part of this. Was this part of a general reordering or evolution of the urban landscape in this part of the city in the mid 5th century, or was it more about the need to site an important reliquary at a prominent spot next to the bishops' palace. An inscription, which is said to have been situated in the courtyard in front of the oratory, describes the area just before its construction as covered in rubble of a great height,[71] which suggests the latter. In other words, the road here was already out of use, and the inscription shows the enormous commitment it was to build the oratory on this site.

3.4 Entrances on Main Roads

3.4.1 Titulus Gai/S. Susanna

This foundation poses us with a problem. Krautheimer's detailed study of the archaeology within and beneath the current S. Susanna points to two *domus*, of late 1st and early 3rd century A.D. date, aligned with the major *Alta Semita* road, below the nave of a large late 3rd-early 4th century secular basilica, with its entrance directly onto the *Alta Semita*. The basilica was, unusually, galleried above the aisles and he believed it was rebuilt, rather than built anew, around 800 by Leo III (795-816).[72] This basilica was no longer secular by 499, when a *titulus Gai* has two

---

[70] LP 1.242-43; Johnson M. 'The fifth century oratory of the Holy Cross at the Lateran in Rome', *Architectura* 25.2 (1995) 128-55 esp. 147-52 and fig.20.

[71] ICUR 2.147.
[72] LP 2.3; CBCR 4. 254-78.

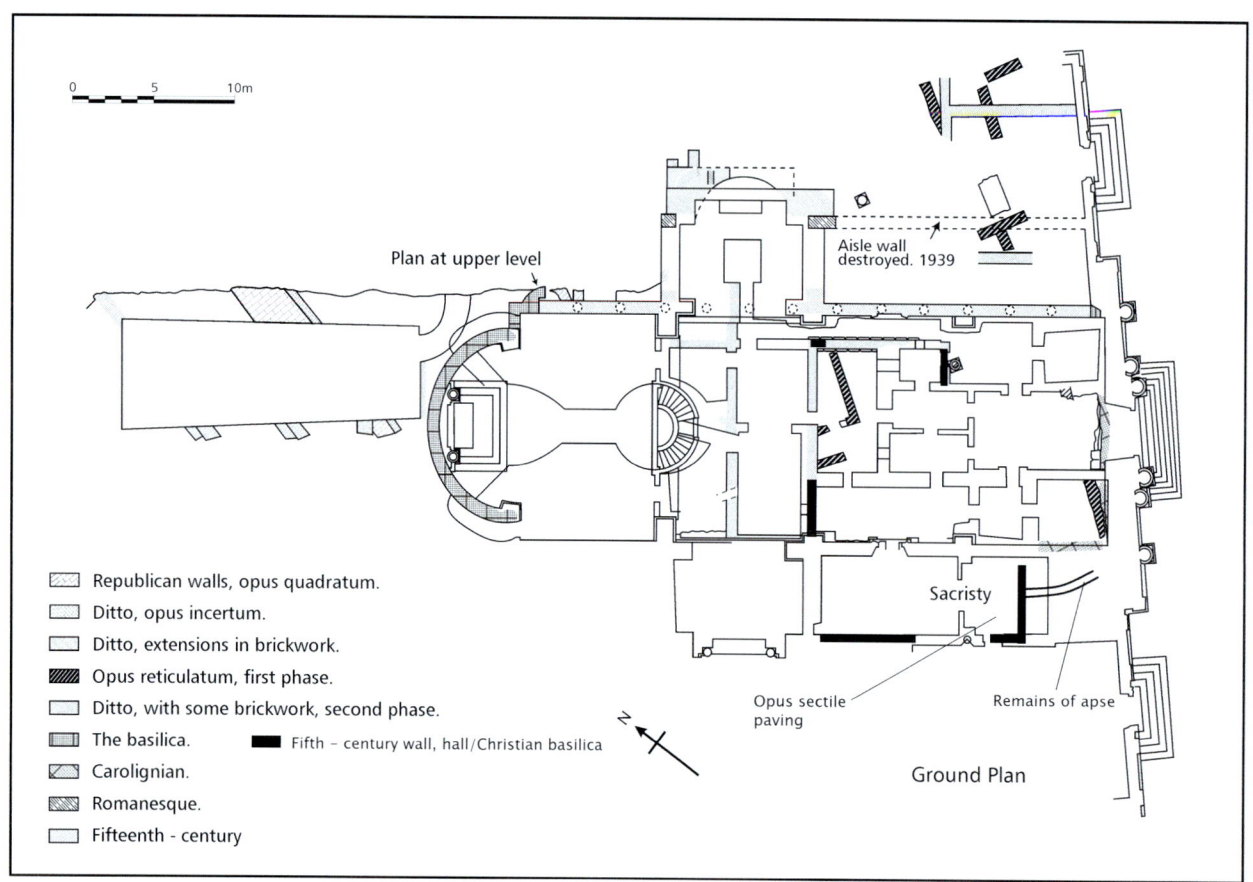

FIGURE 24: PHASE PLAN OF S. SUSANNA SHOWING SUBSTRUCTURES. DRAWN BY ABBY GEORGE, WITH ADDITIONS BY THE AUTHOR, FROM A BASE PLAN BY SPENCER CORBETT AND WOLFGANG FRANKL, IN CBCR 4. 243-66 FIG. 15 (ENGLISH EDN.).

priests in the Roman synod of that year.[73] Yet, in a 5th century version of the *Martyrologium Hieronymianum*, and in the 6th century legend of Susanna, it still describes two houses here, which, Krautheimer remarks, makes this first basilica most likely a secular addition to a *domus* with an oratory to the saint within it.[74] In this way it might be similar to the 'Monte della Giustizia' structure described above, perhaps. It seems to have been rededicated to Susanna by the late 6th century,[75] possibly as a result of the appearance of her written *passio*.

More recent excavations, however, have concluded that the first basilica on this site was not 4th century but was in fact a new build by Leo III, as the foundations of the left/south wall are of that date, as well as the façade. Yet, at the same time the remains of what are likely to be early 5th century walls and an opus sectile floor, were found below the current church. An apse was also found that was added later, at some point between the 5th and 8th century, that seems to face south-westward (and so parallel with the road) that partly reused an earlier wall. Within and just outside this structure several burials were also found, including a reused 2nd century A.D. sarcophagus with the remains of an early medieval fresco showing John the Baptist. The area within these walls has been interpreted as a small hall, which was then dedicated to Susanna sometime in the 6th century.[76] (fig. 24)

Our problem lies in whether this small hall was the *titulus Gai* before this, or whether the Leonine basilica, that makes up the core of the current church, was the first significant Christian building on this site, with the *titulus* elsewhere.[77] In other words, was the orientation of this earlier apsed hall, perhaps parallel with a major road, a Christian project, or simply a secular aristocratic one to enlarge a house or to provide it with a private oratory? Until we can answer this question definitively, we cannot say whether we have a Christian *titulus* being newly built deliberately placed alongside a major arterial road, in the 5th century or being built first around 800 directly facing onto it. The 5th and 6th century descriptions of two houses on this site do not

---

[73] MGH.AA. 12.413.
[74] *AA.SS*. Nov. 2.1.104, 2.2.434-35; LP 1.161: the passage about S. Susanna is a later interpolation, see LP.1.xcix; *AA.SS*. Feb. 3.61-64, Aug. 2.632.
[75] MGH. Ep.1.367.
[76] LTUR 4.387-88; Bonanni A. 'La basilica di S. Susanna a Roma: indagni topografiche e nuove scoperte archeologiche', in *Akten des XII. Internationalen Kongresses für Christliche Archäologie* (1995) 586-89; Bonanni A. 'Scavi e ricerche in S. Susanna a Roma. Le fasi paleocristiane e altomedievali', in *Atti del VII Congresso Nazionale di Archeologia Cristiana, Cassino, 20-24 settembre 1993*, vol. 1 (2003) 359-76; Cecchelli M. 'Santa Susanna', in *Roma dall'antichità al medioevo* (2004) 328-43.
[77] Cecchelli believes this hall was only an oratory at best: Cecchelli M. 'Dati da scavi recenti' (1999) 239. This *titulus* had a wooden then marble canopy above the altar in the late 7th century: LP 1.375.

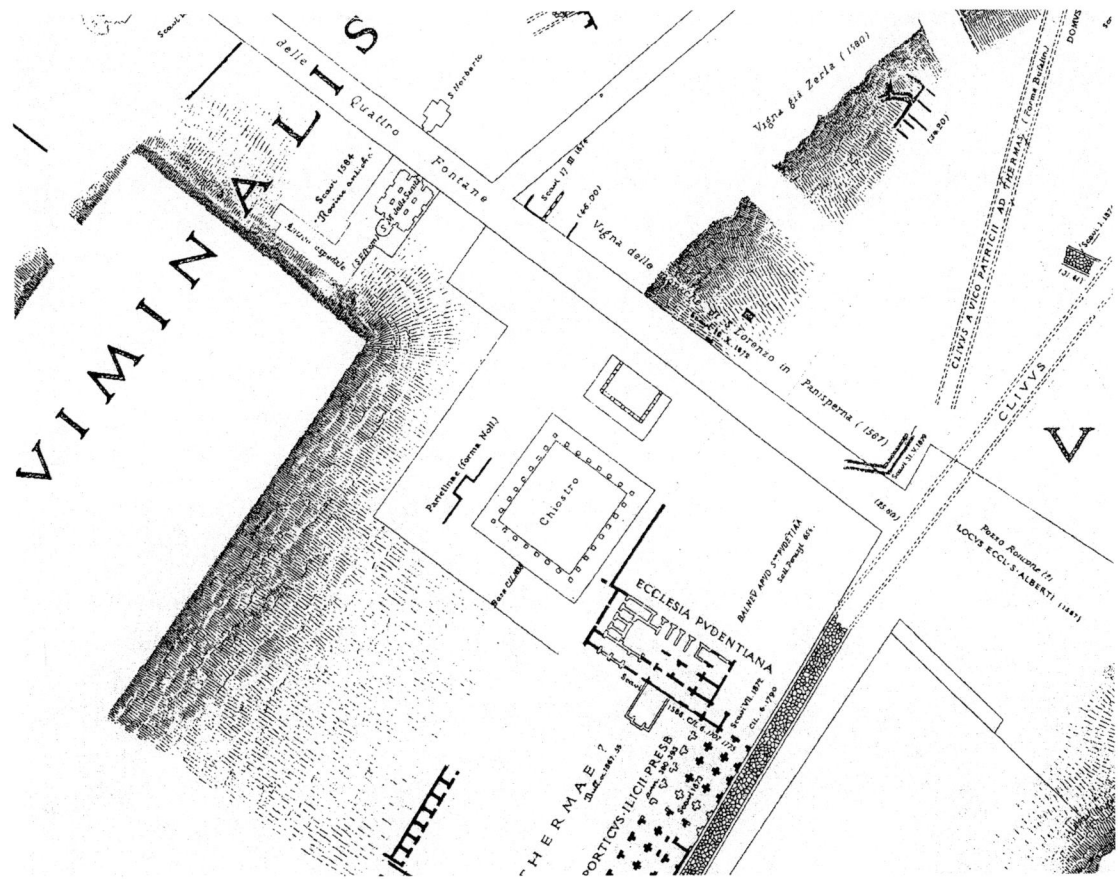

FIGURE 25: DETAIL OF PLATE 17 SHOWING S. PUDENZIANA AND ANCIENT ROAD, IN LANCIANI R. *FORMA URBIS ROMAE* (MILAN 1893-1901).

rule out the possibility of a small Christian basilica here, but they may instead refer to remains of Roman buildings found opposite the current church near the 17th century S. Caio.[78] Perhaps this was the site of the first *titulus Gai*, with Leo III building his new basilica across the road at the turn of the 9th century? The name of the baroque church may show that four hundred years ago, at least, the *titulus* and S. Susanna were thought to be on different sites.

A close examination of the Roman houses below the nave of S. Susanna would help clarify the situation, but this early 5th century hall is most likely a domestic/private structure reusing and adapting the houses here. When this hall had a Christian use is still conjectural, but the early medieval burials give us an approximate *terminus ante quem*.

Our evidence, both archaeological and literary, is too ambiguous and unreliable to be able to say much for sure, but the deliberate insertion of a Christian place of worship alongside the *Alta Semita* in the 5th century is an interesting possibility, and would once more refute the suggestion that somehow Christian buildings were largely invisible in the late antique Roman landscape. For now, we can say such a move certainly took place around 800 by Leo III, and so seems part of a wider pattern at that time of placing the entrances to Christian places of worship on main roads in the city, something we see elsewhere with the reversal of the orientations of S. Marco and S. Marcello (see above).

3.4.2 Titulus Pudentis/S. Pudenziana

This foundation is notable for the unusual basin-like features underneath the nave and a likely connection with the water provision that supplied the space before the Christian basilica was created, which we have discussed above. It is also worth noting briefly that the entrance of the first *titulus* here also lay next to and was accessed directly from the important *vicus Patricius* road in the city, possibly via a portico (fig. 25). The *titulus* was installed within a pre-existing structure as already mentioned, whose entrance faced onto the road, so its orientation was not deliberately chosen by the Christian builders. The building was donated to or bought by the Church in the late 4th century, and although not an *ex novo* creation, the significance of an early Christian basilica directly accessible off the important *vicus Patricius* road should not be underestimated.[79] If the building was bought by the ecclesiastical authorities it is also suggestive of a desire for a prominent, easily accessible Christian place of worship in the city landscape, as well as one with water provision.

---

[78] CBCR 4.275 n.2 with refs. The houses described may instead be a reference to those of the Ceionii and the Nummii, which lay in the region: LTUR 2. 217.

[79] For references see chapter 2: nn.36-41 above.

Spatial 'Christianisation' in Context

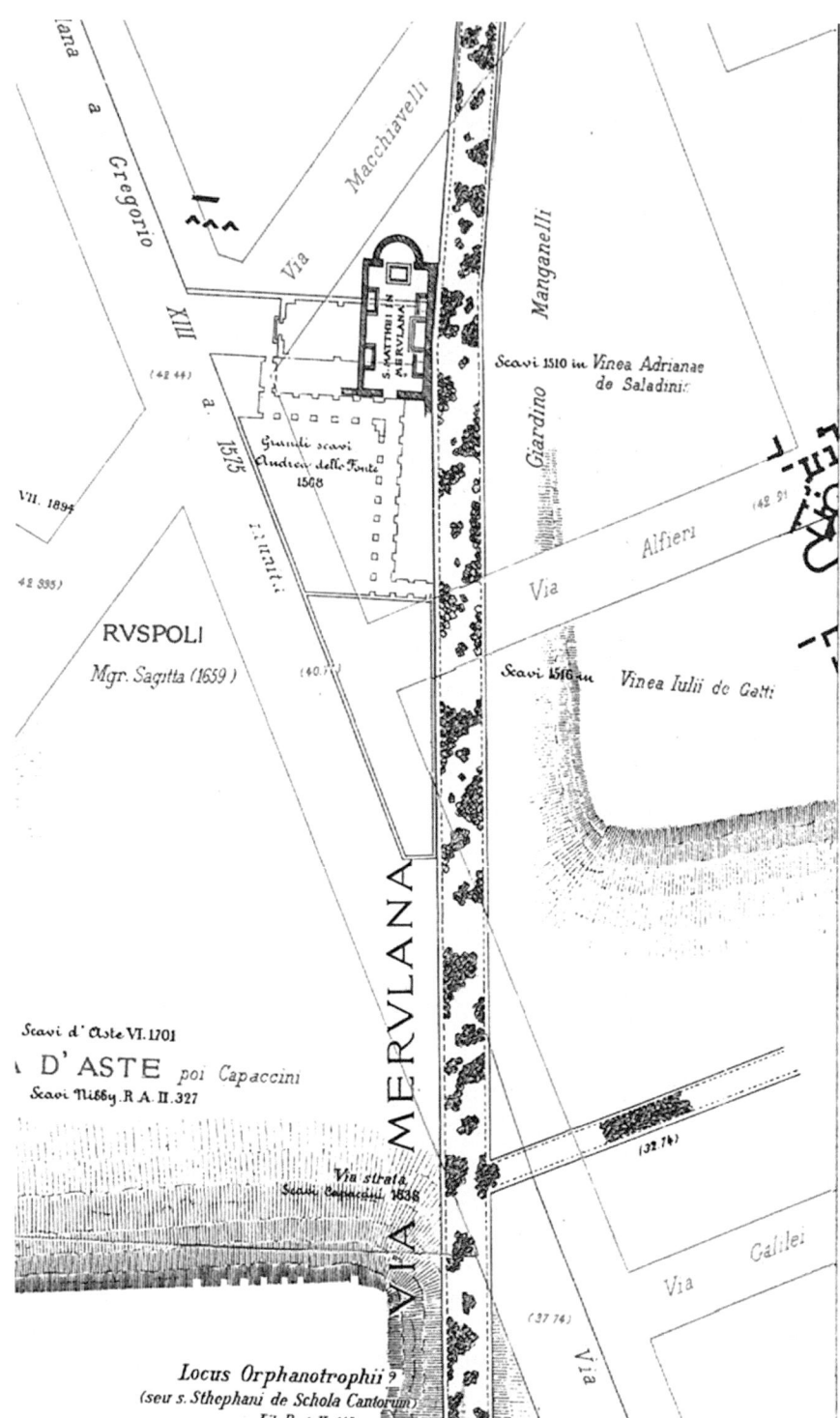

FIGURE 26: DETAIL OF PLATE 30 SHOWING S. MATTEO AND ANCIENT ROAD, IN LANCIANI R. *FORMA URBIS ROMAE* (MILAN 1893-1901).

3.4.3 Titulus Mattheus/S. Matteo

This foundation, demolished in the early 1800s, lay parallel with and next to the ancient via Merulana. The ancient road had a north-south alignment compared to the north-west to south-east 16th century, and current road, of the same name. The basilica lay at the point of the junction with the modern Via Alfieri. (fig.26) Its entrance is said to have faced the ancient road and been accessible via a portico from it.[80] This road was a very important one throughout antiquity as it joined the Esquiline with the Caelian. The basilica certainly existed by the late 5th century.[81] As far as I am aware no excavations of the site have been published, so any more detail is elusive relating

---

[80] Armellini M. *Le chiese di Roma* (1891) 244-46; Henze C. 'San Matteo in Merulana', in *Miscellanea Francesco Ehrle*, vol. 2: *Per la storia di Roma e dei papi* (1924) 404-14; LTUR 3.234.
[81] MGH.AA. 12. 412.

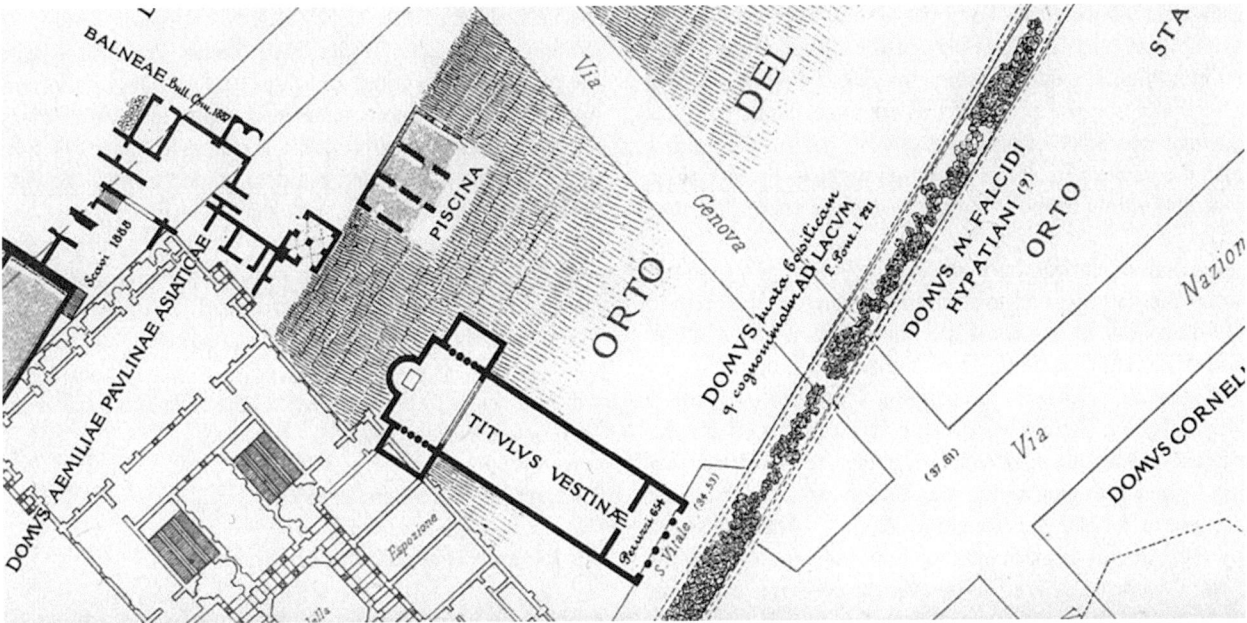

FIGURE 27: DETAIL OF PLATE 16 SHOWING THE TITULUS VESTINAE AND ROAD, IN LANCIANI R. *FORMA URBIS ROMAE* (MILAN 1893-1901).

to the palaeo-Christian building and its relationship with the road.

3.4.4 Titulus Fasciolae/SS. Nereo ed Achilleo

The 4th century Christian building on this site, discussed earlier concerning its relationship to the Caracallan Baths and the *Basilica Crescentiana* across the road, is now lost, but was located in the vicinity of the current church, which is another foundation of Leo III facing directly onto a main road, in this case the *via Appia* (see above). Its date means it is again beyond the scope of this book, but it is clear the original 4th century *titulus* lay nearby, which the remains of an apse and walls just to the west and north may testify to. The remains of a road behind the existing church were also found.[82] In other words, the *titulus fasciolae* lay next to the *via Appia* as well, but we cannot say whether it was directly accessible from it, as is the case with the Leonine church today. Yet, this is a possibility and should not surprise us.

3.4.5 Titulus Vestinae/S. Vitale

This early 5th century creation, described above in relation to the detailed information we have regarding its foundation,[83] was also built with its entrance facing onto a main road, the *vicus Longus*, which is now the Via di San Vitale. The basilica was accessed from the road via an arcaded portico with granite columns, which was an entirely 5th century creation as part of the construction of the Christian basilica.[84] This would thus have created a deliberately impressive façade along an important road in the city. As seen above, this was not a donated site, Vestina merely providing the money, so this was an intentional acquisition by the Church precisely because it lay along this main urban artery, and was provided with an impressive entrance façade in order to accentuate its presence there (fig.27).[85]

3.5 Reuse of Prestige Public Buildings

3.5.1 Basilica sanctorum Cosmae et Damiani/SS. Cosma e Damiano

This 6th century foundation was the first Christian intervention in the Roman Forum area, and as such marks a watershed in Christian building. For the first time, Christian builders felt able to intervene in a major public space of the city. According to the *LP*, Pope Felix IV (526-30) dedicated a basilica to these doctor saints in the *via Sacra* area near to the *templum urbis Romae*, thought to be a reference to the building now known as the Basilica of Maxentius.[86] This required the slight modification of a Roman apsed hall—which may have been a library, the *biblioteca Pacis* perhaps, or an archive building in its final secular phase—attached to the south-west corner of the Forum of Peace.[87] This building was accessed from the *via*

---

[82] For references see chapter 2: nn.60-63 above.
[83] See chapter 1: nn.69-70.
[84] Junyent E. 'Le recenti scoperte nella chiesa titolare di S.Vitale', *RACrist* 16 (1939) 129-34; Matthiae G. 'Basiliche paleocristiane con ingresso a polifora', *BdA* 42 (1957) esp. 107-10 (107-20); CBCR 4.299-316; LTUR 2.371.
[85] Although not mentioning the façade, B. Brenk also makes this point, but describes Vestina as the builder: Brenk B. 'Kirche und Strasse' (2012) 179.
[86] LP 1.279.
[87] Whitehead P. B. 'The church of SS. Cosma e Damiano in Rome', *AJA* 31.1 (1927) 1-18; CBCR 1.137-43; LTUR 1.324-25; Pazzelli R. *La Basilica dei Santi Cosma e Damiano in via Sacra* (2001); Fiore P. 'Fortuna di un modello architettonico tardoantico: la chiesa dei santi Cosma e Damiano nel Foro Romano', *Quaderni dell'Istituto di storia dell'architettura* 39 (2002) 145-54; Tucci P. L. 'Nuove acquisizioni sulla basilica dei Santi Cosma e Damiano', *StRom* 49 (2001) 275-93; Tucci P. L. 'Nuove osservazioni sull'architettura del Templum Pacis', in *Divus*

Sacra via a 4th century vestibule, erroneously labelled the 'Temple of Romulus', as part of the remodelling of the building that stood here, which involved providing it with a roof and an apse opposite this entrance. Thus, the later basilica was also accessed directly off the *via Sacra*, but also the basilica itself was installed within a prestigiously placed building in the still monumental centre of the city.

As described earlier, permission must have been required from the Gothic administration to convert this public building, but this was a permission that the Church actively sought, judging from the pope's prominence in the apse mosaic and the building's prestige location.[88] An intriguing theory has recently been proposed for the basilica's particular placement. It has been argued that the former presence in the area of the treasures from the Temple of Jerusalem, brought to Rome by Titus and stole by the Vandals in 455, was an important motivation for Felix IV's project here.[89] Whatever the case, it is clear that the use of a prestige Roman public building in the centre of Rome was now possible and desirable, and gave this foundation an extra cachet that would reflect well on Felix and the papacy as a whole.

3.5.2 Ecclesia beati Adriani/S. Adriano

This practice of utilising prestige Roman buildings continued in the 7th century under Honorius I (625-38), when the Senate House itself, rebuilt by Diocletian, was converted into a 'church' dedicated to Saint Hadrian.[90] It is noticeable that few modifications were made to the ancient structure by Honorius, and so the foundation in its early phases, until the 13th century, still closely resembled the *Curia Senatus*.[91] I would argue that this was a deliberate ploy by the pope to retain the aura of the original building so as to give his foundation an added prestige of its own and to imbue the church with a sense of Christian continuity with the glorious Roman past. Its location in the city would also have made it an important focal foundation.

Other, less prestigious, public buildings were also converted into Christian buildings in this period, such as the Basilica of Junius Bassus which became S. Andrea in Catabarbara, a structure now demolished.[92] During the time of Theodoric, the conversion of no longer utilised public buildings for other uses was officially sanctioned.[93] So a practice, that was perhaps beginning to occur anyway, would have accelerated, as part of a policy of preservation, as far as Theodoric was concerned. For the donors involved in such schemes the cachet attached to using important Roman monuments for their investments would have been the primary motivation, and those utilising less important buildings would have benefitted from the lower costs involved coupled with a still impressive space. Before the 5th century, Christian builders tended to reuse private buildings (*domus, insulae*) or demolish them to use the site. The increasing reuse of public buildings in all projects from the 6th century onwards implies decreasing funds but increasing ambition, and an urban landscape in flux. The utilisation of prestige central structures by the Church suggests the same, but also an increasing confidence within the papacy and a desire to gain reflected glory from such potent monuments.[94]

3.6 High Places: Macro Visibility

3.6.1 The Christian Basilica on the Hill

From the mid 5th century we begin to see a new building strategy by the Christian authorities. We start to see Christian basilicas appearing on the top of prominent hills, challenging the thousand year old macro visual dominance of the pagan temples within the city. The previous Christian buildings we have been discussing were largely invisible from other neighbourhoods, but now Christian basilicas began to loom above the still dense urban sprawl. Even with the extensive abandonment of parts of the city from after the Gothic Wars of the 6th century, a Christian building on a hill still spoke of prominent visuality and a metaphysical pre-eminence. This would in turn reflect well on the builder, and the creation of Christian places of worship on high points in the city were intended, in the 5th to 7th centuries, to challenge the common sight of a pagan sanctuary and its temple atop many of the intramural hills.

The intentional visuality of temples was written into ancient architectural textbooks,[95] and it should not surprise us that Christian builders sought the same thing. The Palatine and Capitoline temples were the obvious templates and inspiration for such a tactic, but several cult centres also lay on the Aventine and on other minor hills, and were often the most ancient foundations.

It is interesting to note that most of these Christian hill-top foundations are mid 5th century, which is also the time when the stational liturgy begins to be formalised within the city.[96] We could say that this period represents

---

Vespasianus. Il Bimillenario dei Flavi, ed. F. Coarelli (2009) 158-67. See also chapter 1: n.107
[88] ICUR 2.71, 134, 152, 353, 439 and see Chapter 1: Patronage by the Bishop.
[89] Osborne J. 'The Jerusalem Temple treasure and the church of Santi Cosma e Damiano in Rome', *BSR* 76 (2008) 173-81. See also Brenk B. 'Kirche und Strasse' (2012) 172-78.
[90] LP 1. 324.
[91] CBCR 1.1; Bartoli A. *Curia senatus: lo scavo e il restauro* (1963); Mancini A. 'La chiesa medioevale di S. Adriano nel Foro Romano', *RendPontAcc* 40 (1967-68) 191-245; LTUR 3.8-9.
[92] See chapter 1: n.85.
[93] Cassiod. *Var.* 3.29, 4.30, 7.44.
[94] This practice continued into the 8th century with the diaconia of S. Lucia *in VII vias*, which was located either next to the Septizodium or within the curved end of the Circus Maximus (Augenti A. *Il palatino nel Medioevo: archeologia e topografia (secoli VI-XIII)* (1996) 68-70; LTUR 3.192), and the diaconia of SS. Sergius and Bacchus (which might be earlier), which was next to the Arch of Septimius Severus in the forum (Bonfioli M. 'La diaconia dei Ss. Sergio e Bacco nel Foro Romano. Fonti e problemi', *RACrist* 50 (1974) 55-85; LTUR 4.303-304).
[95] Vitr. *De arch.* 1.7.1-2, 4.5.2. The temples still dominated the landscape in AD 404: Claudian, *de VI cos. Hon.* 39-52 (Loeb edn. (1922)).
[96] An established permanent stational calendar did not appear until Pope Hilarius (461-68), in all likelihood: Baldovin J. F. *The Urban Character of Christian Worship: the Origins, Development, and Meaning of Stational Liturgy* (1987) 147-53; LP 1. 244. The stational liturgy in

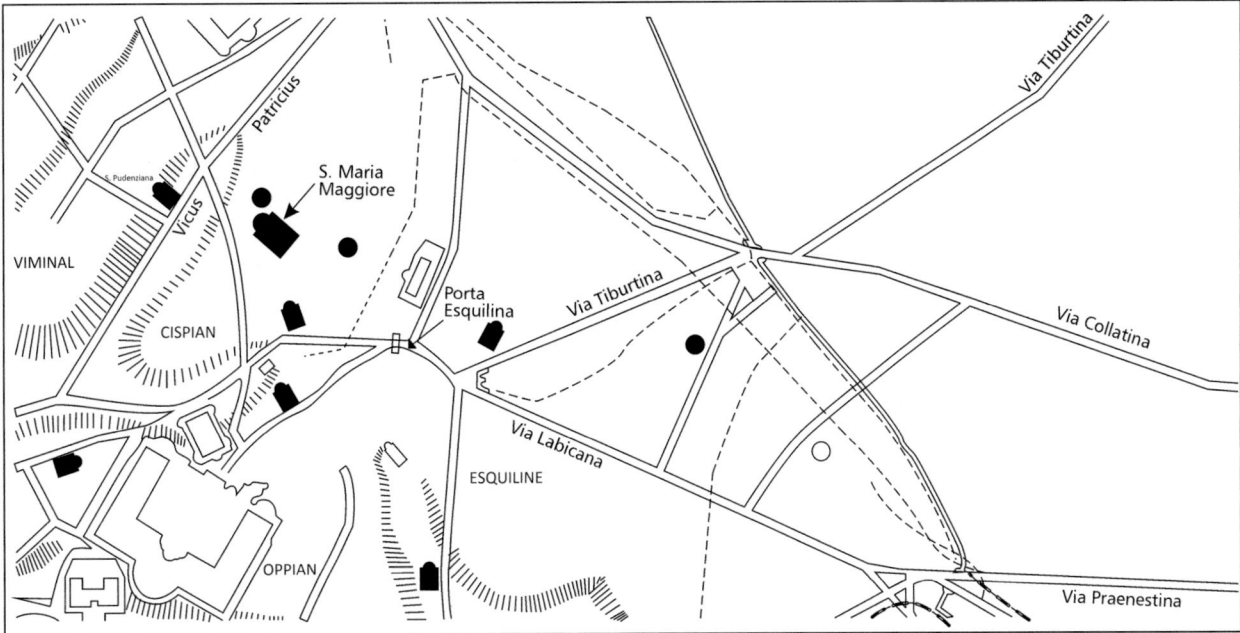

FIGURE 28: PLAN OF EASTERN PART OF CITY SHOWING S. MARIA MAGGIORE AND SURROUNDING HILLS AND ROADS. DRAWN BY ABBY GEORGE FROM A BASE PLAN IN REEKMANS L. 'L'IMPLANTATION MONUMENTALE CHRÉTIENNE DANS LE PAYSAGE URBAIN DE ROME DE 300 À 850', IN *ACTES DU IXE CONGRÈS INTERNATIONALE D'ARCHÉOLOGIE CHRÉTIENNE* (ROME 1989) 861-915.

a time when the Roman (Catholic) Church is actively promoting itself and Rome as an overtly *visibly* Christian centre, to tie in with the bishopric asserting its authority and stating its pre-eminence more forcefully. This was perhaps in the light of the Council of Chalcedon's (A.D. 451) pronouncement concerning the status of the See of Constantinople and the various liturgical and theological disputes that were occurring at the time, that were a threat to Nicene Christianity.[97]

The first example of Christian building on a hill begins in the 420s or 430s, and is possibly the most impressive and ambitious example of this in our period, before declining funds and urban decay and abandonment reduces the motivation for such bold statements.

3.6.2 Basilica Sanctae Mariae on the Cispian Hill

The site and the size of this foundation is, I believe, a watershed in the physical Christianisation of the city of Rome, at least for its contemporary inhabitants. This foundation has already been discussed with regards its entirely episcopal patronage and its relationship with a possible road it was built over. Yet its distinguishing features are its size (86 x 35 metres) and location. It was constructed or completed *ex novo* by Sixtus III (432-40) on the summit of the Cispian hill, a spur of the Esquiline, and soon became a major Christian centre within the city, only equalled in size within the walls by the Lateran basilica. (fig.28) In the *LP* it is associated with the Liberian basilica, and it is implied that it replaced that structure.[98] The archaeological evidence goes against this however, with no Christian remains before the early to mid 5th century surviving on the site.[99] In fact, below the basilica was found an Augustan structure, which was still in use in the 4th century, and contained remains of a fresco of an illustrated calendar. It is variously argued to be the *macellum liviae* (described as next to both the Liberian basilica and Sixtus' construction by the *LP*), or a house. It is now widely believed, however, that Liberius' foundation lies elsewhere in the area, perhaps represented by the existing S. Vito or S. Bibiana. The precise location of the Markets of Livia is also uncertain.[100]

This foundation in many ways marked the beginning of a new phase of intramural building, both in scale and

---

Rome can be defined as the process of the pope (or his representative) saying mass in differing churches throughout the city; the church, or shrine, being chosen based on the feast, fast or commemoration being celebrated: Baldovin J. F. *Urban Character* (1987) 36-37. For the stational liturgy's earlier, informal, origins see Baldovin J. F. *Urban Character* (1987) 145-47.
[97] Council of Chalcedon: canon 28 (stating that the See of Constantinople was now second in prestige below Rome, but with equal privileges, perhaps confirming a similar ruling of the Council of Constantinople (in 381)): Price R. and Gaddis M. edd. and transl. *The Acts of the Council of Chalcedon*, vol. 3 (2005) 67-91, with McLynn N. ''Two Romes, beacons of the whole world': canonizing Constantinople', in *Two Romes: Rome and Constantinople in Late Antiquity*, edd. L. Grig and G. Kelly (2012) 345-63. The dedication of one of these hill top foundations to the Virgin may be the result of the increased status given to her by another council, that of Ephesus (431), that is the title of *Theotokos*: Cormack R. 'The visual arts', in *CAH* 14, edd. Av. Cameron et al (2000) 894 (884-916).

[98] LP 1.232.
[99] Cecchelli argues for the Liberian Basilica being under the nave, however: Cecchelli M. 'Dalla Basilica Liberiana al complesso paleocristiano e altomedievale', in *Santa Maria Maggiore a Roma*, ed. C. Pietrangeli (1988) 71-84.
[100] CBCR 3.1-60 (esp.13-14, 53-57); Magi F. *Il calendario dipinto sotto Santa Maria Maggiore* (1972); Geertman H. 'The builders of the *Basilica Maior* in Rome', in *Hic fecit basilicam* (2004) 1-16; Liverani P. 'L'ambiente nell'antichità', in *Santa Maria Maggiore a Roma* (1988) 45-53; LTUR 1. 181, 2. 68-69, 3. 217.

prominence. This basilica not only marked a hinge point in western architectural design, incorporating classical and what were to become standard medieval church features, it was also the largest non-imperial Christian foundation inside the walls thus far. Recently, the basilica was the focus for a study trying to recreate the interior of important ancient Roman buildings, and from this it is clear that internally, as well as externally through its topographical location, it was designed to impress.[101] This overtly large and prominently placed basilica, on the crest of a hill, is doubly significant as Sixtus himself seems to have been the donor as well as the initiator of the project,[102] and as such is an enormous statement of intent by him and a sign of growing episcopal confidence.

Such a move also seems in line with Sixtus as an individual, someone who embellished, enlarged or founded many Christian basilicas. It almost goes without saying that this example was certainly the most widely visible within the city at that time, and its location does not appear coincidental as a result. It is clear from Sixtus' other projects that he wanted to make a material impact on the city, and to be a second Damasus in that sense. This was no doubt motivated by personal ambition and a quest for prestige, but also to show to others, and to the inhabitants of Rome, that their city was no longer a pagan stronghold but was now a fully fledged Christian capital.

It was not just the hill and the basilica's height that made it the first real macro Christian landmark within the city; it was also its position in relation to major roads that ensured it was a prominent mental signpost for the population of the city and its visitors.[103] This area is at the intersection of three main roads at what may have been the *Forum Esquilinum*, just to the south-east of the basilica.[104] Knowledge of this part of the city is not helped by the existence here of the modern Termini station, but a general picture of the ancient roads in the area can be discerned. These roads were: a road from the north (that was an extension of the *via Salaria* (*nova*) from its intersection with the *Alta Semita*), the *via Labicana-Praenestina* from the south-east and the *via Tiburtina* from the north-east, the latter two merging and becoming the *clivus Suburanus*. This in turn became the *Argiletum*, which led into the *Forum Romanum*. The *Forum Esquilinum* was, as a result, a hub for human and wheeled traffic into the city, this area also being the focus for the water and food supply for Rome.[105] The *vicus Patricius*, a major internal road, also ran just to the west of the basilica and minor roads immediately around the basilica run towards it or are parallel to it.[106] (fig.28) As such, the basilica seems to have been oriented for maximum visibility from major thoroughfares, and from other hills and regions in the city. Most people coming into the city from the north or east would have found themselves by the basilica, and all would have seen it. The statement was clear to them: Rome was now a Christian city.

3.6.3 Titulus Sabinae/S. Sabina on the Aventine Hill

At about the same time another Christian building was built on a high point in the city: a basilica dedicated to a martyr or donor named Sabina, which survives intact today. Although this basilica is not on the summit of the hill—that area was occupied in all probability by the temples of Diana and Minerva—it is at its western edge, on a ridge dominating the view from the Tiber. This part of the hill drops very sharply down to the river, so any view of the basilica from the west would have been unencumbered to those coming up the river in either direction, and to those looking from the *Transtiberim* region of the city. As a result, this basilica would have provided another obvious sign of the Christianisation of the city to those areas in particular, and especially to sea trade to Rome. (fig.29) A similarity with the possible site of the Temple of Castor and Pollux at Ostia may be apparent here, both examples being a major religious landmark highly visible from a particular direction coming into the port, and as such providing a mental representation and landmark for that place for the viewer.[107] No expense was spared on this basilica either, the columns for example were specially commissioned or all bought from the same building, and rich furnishings were provided.[108] This further emphasises the deliberate attempt to make this an impressive and imposing structure both inside and out.

The basilica was begun by a priest or bishop named Peter of Illyria during the pontificate of Celestine I (422-32), but not completed or dedicated it seems until that of Sixtus III (432-40).[109] The building was bounded by the *vicus altus* and *vicus Armilustri*, now the Via di Sancta Sabina, on its eastern and western sides, which determined its orientation. The *vicus Armilustri* also led to the *Porta Ostiensis*. The list of presbyters for the synod of 499 separates two representatives of a *titulus sabinae* and one for a *titulus sanctae sabinae*. This may indicate a confusion about the origin of its name—whether a saint or a lay donor of the same name—an official and unofficial nomenclature, or two separate foundations with only our example surviving.

---

[101] Frischer B. *et al.* 'Virtual reality and ancient Rome: the UCLA cultural VR Lab's Santa Maria Maggiore project', in *Virtual Reality in Archaeology: Computer Applications and Quantitative Methods in Archaeology (CAA)*, edd. J. A. Barceló, M. Forte, and D. H. Sanders (2000) 155-62. Sadly we lack any firm evidence for the original external decoration of Sixtus' basilica, but we can be sure it was impressive.
[102] See chapter 1: n.103.
[103] Noted by Frischer *et al.* 'Virtual reality and ancient Rome' (2000) 161.
[104] The precise location of the forum is unknown but it lay in the vicinity of the Arch of Gallienus (*Porta Esquilina*) and S. Vitus, confirmed by the discovery of two inscriptions describing a late restoration of the forum in A.D. 450, found in this area (CIL 6.1662, 31888): LTUR 2.298. The *Campus Esquilinus*, a place of execution, lay just outside the arch: LTUR 1.218-19 with refs.
[105] LTUR 5.138-39, 144-47.
[106] CBCR 3.12-13.
[107] Heinzelmann M. and Martin A. 'River port, *navalia* and harbour temple at Ostia: new results of a DAI-AAR project', *JRA* 15 (2002) 5-19, esp.14-18; Amm. Marc. 19.10.4 shows the continuing importance and existence of this temple in late antiquity.
[108] Brandenburg H. *Ancient Churches* (2005) 169.
[109] A large mosaic inscription in the church describes its foundation: ILCV 1.1778a; LP 1.235.

FIGURE 29: DETAIL OF PLATE 33 SHOWING S. SABINA AND LOCAL TOPOGRAPHY, IN LANCIANI R. *FORMA URBIS ROMAE* (MILAN 1893-1901).

This is resolved by the 6th century synod in 595, when only the latter name appears.[110]

There have been numerous remains found, within and under the basilica, of earlier buildings, all of which were still standing in the 4th century. This implies that these structures, of which the majority seem to have been residential, were destroyed partly or totally to make way for the basilica's construction in the 5th. The basilica both uses and overlies the walls of these buildings. (fig.30) The suggestion that one of these earlier structures, the so-called *dromos* building, was the original *titulus* cannot be proven and is more likely to have been a rich *domus*.[111] What does seem clear is that a wealthy priest or bishop wanted his investment in Rome to become a city landmark. Our ignorance as to the nature of the external decoration of the 5th century *titulus* means we cannot know how eye-catching the building was, but its location in the city provided it with a dominating position and meant it could be widely seen, from the western neighbourhoods at least.

3.6.4 Sanctus Stephanus/Santo Stefano Rotondo on the Caelian Hill

Again in the mid 5th century, we see an unusual round Christian building dedicated to the martyr Stephen built on the summit of the Caelian Hill. This structure was completed under Simplicius (468-83),[112] and was a new build of the era. It used specially commissioned columns, and was not a reuse of a pagan structure, as was first thought. Part of the demolished barracks of the *peregrini* lay beneath it, and extended east and west of it. (see fig.31) They were still in use in the mid 4th century. We cannot say whether the barracks were demolished to build the Christian structure, but a structure found beneath the ancient floor of the church and above the demolished barracks, may represent this intermediate phase. This may be a house or an earlier Christian building. The land on which the barracks lay must have been owned by the imperial fisc and so this Christian foundation may well have been imperially funded, perhaps by Valentinian III and Galla Placidia, with the bishop then dedicating it on its completion. The area was characterised by several relic chapels and those dedicated to saints by the 5th and 6th century. This was also an aristocratic area, with several large *domus* in the vicinity, notably that of the rich *Valerii*, who could have bought the land from the emperor themselves.[113]

---

[110] MGH.AA 12. 411, 412, 414; MGH. Ep. 1.367.
[111] Darsy F. M. D. *Recherches archéologiques à Sainte-Sabine sur l'Aventin: géologie, topographie, sanctuaires archaïques, culte isiaque, ensemble architectural paléochrétien* (1968); CBCR 4.78-98; LTUR 4. 221-22.
[112] LP 1.249. Perhaps it was meant as a martyr shrine, although without a relic of the protomartyr himself, the only known relics here being those of Primus and Felicianus, from the 7th century: CBCR 4. 236-37; LP 1.332-33.
[113] Barracks still in use in mid 4th century: Amm. Marc. 16.12.65. Archaeology and structural analysis: CBCR 4.199-240; LTUR 4. 373-75; Brandenburg H. *Die Kirche S. Stefano Rotondo in Rom: Bautypologie und Architektursymbolik in der spätantiken und frühchristlichen Architektur* (1998); Brandenburg H. 'Santo Stefano Rotondo in Roma: funzione urbanistica, tipologia architettonica, liturgia ed allestimento liturgico', *Meded* 59 (2000) 27-54. The surrounding area in late antiquity: Pavolini C. 'La sommità del Celio in età imperiale: dai culti pagani orientali al culto cristiano', in *Santo Stefano Rotondo in Roma: archeologia, storia*

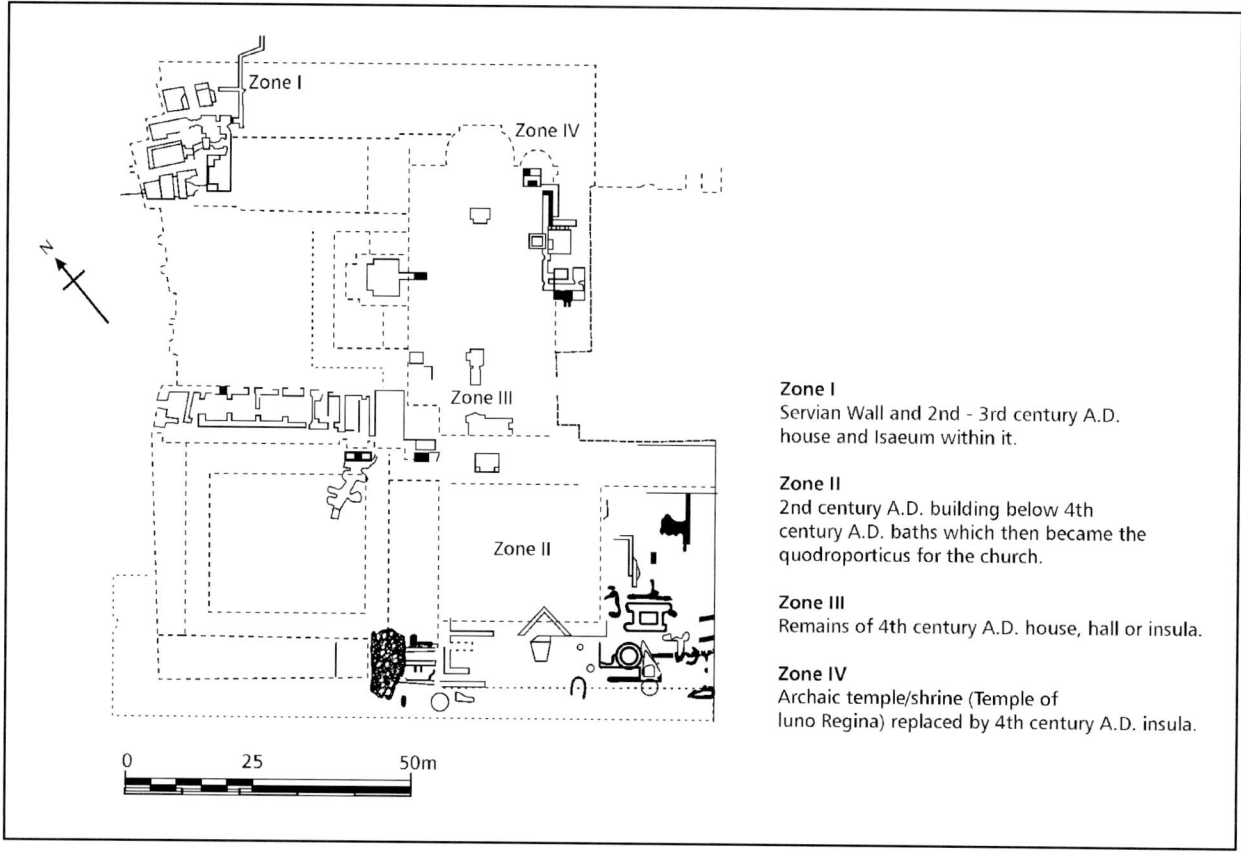

FIGURE 30: PLAN OF S. SABINA AND SURROUNDING ARCHAEOLOGY. DRAWN BY ABBY GEORGE FROM A BASE PLAN IN DARSY F. M. D. *RECHERCHES ARCHÉOLOGIQUES À SAINTE-SABINE SUR L'AVENTIN: GÉOLOGIE, TOPOGRAPHIE, SANCTUAIRES ARCHAÏQUES, CULTE ISIAQUE, ENSEMBLE ARCHITECTURAL PALÉOCHRÉTIEN* (VATICAN CITY 1968) 52, FIG.2.

Either way, this was meant to be an aristocratic statement to be compared favourably with the Lateran basilica constructed by Constantine, it being only about 750 metres to the east. It speaks of a now confident Christianity with an influential aristocratic following, through the imperial house or otherwise. Topographically speaking it was at the same height as the nearby Lateran, but on all the other three sides here the land descends, abruptly to the south and west. As such, from those directions this new Christian building of unusual design, stood as a new, highly visible and eye-catching landmark in the landscape, the clear intention of the donor.[114]

3.6.5 The Palatine

It is worth noting briefly that several Christian buildings were built at the base of the Palatine Hill, from the 4th century with S. Anastasia, and then, in the 6th to 8th century, with S. Teodoro and S. Maria Antiqua on its eastern side. This is likely to have been as a result of the increasing importance of the area during the Byzantine administration of the city. Only two Christian foundations that we know about were actually built on the summit of the hill however: an oratory to St. Caesarius within the Imperial Palace and a bishop's palace in the early 8th century.[115] As a result, the only foundation that may be of interest to us here is S. Caesario, which was inserted into the upper peristyle of the *Domus Augustana*, perhaps in the mid 4th to early 5th century, as some sort of imperial private chapel.[116] As such, it would not have been visible from beyond the palace walls, and so lies beyond the scope of this chapter.

---

dell'arte, restauro: atti del convegno internazionale, Roma 10-13 ottobre 1996, edd. H. Brandenburg and J. Pál (2000) 17-27; Pavolini C. 'Le *domus* del Celio', in *Aurea Roma* (2000) 147-48; Brenk B. 'La cristianizzazione della Domus dei Valerii sul Celio', in *The Transformations of Urbs Roma* (1999) 69-84; LTUR 2.207; Pavolini C. 'L'area del Celio tra l'antichità ed il medioevo alla luce delle recenti indagini archeologiche', in *La storia economica di Roma nell'alto Medioevo alla luce dei recenti scavi archeologici: atti del seminario, Roma, 2-3 aprile 1992*, edd. L. Paroli and P. Delogu (1993) 53-70 with the gradual abandonment of the area from this 5th century period. The existence of a mithraeum here, as part of the barracks, can be seen as incidental to the placement of the church, as the cult centre went out of use around the end of the 4th century, some sixty years before the construction of the Christian building: Lissi-Caronna E. *Il mitreo dei Castra Peregrinorum (S. Stefano Rotondo)* (1986).

[114] For the influences on and importance of the design and layout of the church see: Brandenburg H. 'S. Stefano Rotondo, der letzte Großbau der Antike in Rom. Die Typologie des Baues, die Ausstattung der Kirche, die kunstgeschichtliche Stellung des Kirchenbaues und seiner Ausstattung', in *Santo Stefano Rotondo in Roma* (2000) 35-65.

[115] For S. Anastasia see within chapter 5 below. For the other churches and for the development of the Palatine from the late antique to the medieval period, see Augenti A. *Il palatino nel Medioevo* (1996) esp. 37-45 and 50-60 with refs.; Augenti A. 'Continuity and discontinuity of a seat of power: the Palatine hill from the fifth to the tenth century', in *Early Medieval Rome and the Christian West: Essays in Honour of Donald A. Bullough*, ed. J. M. H. Smith (2000) 43-57 and refs.

[116] Greg. *Ep.* Appendix 8; Ungaro L. 'Note sulle strutture tarde del palazzo imperiale sul Palatino', *RdA* 3 (1979) 106-13 esp. 109-10 with refs.; LTUR 1.231.

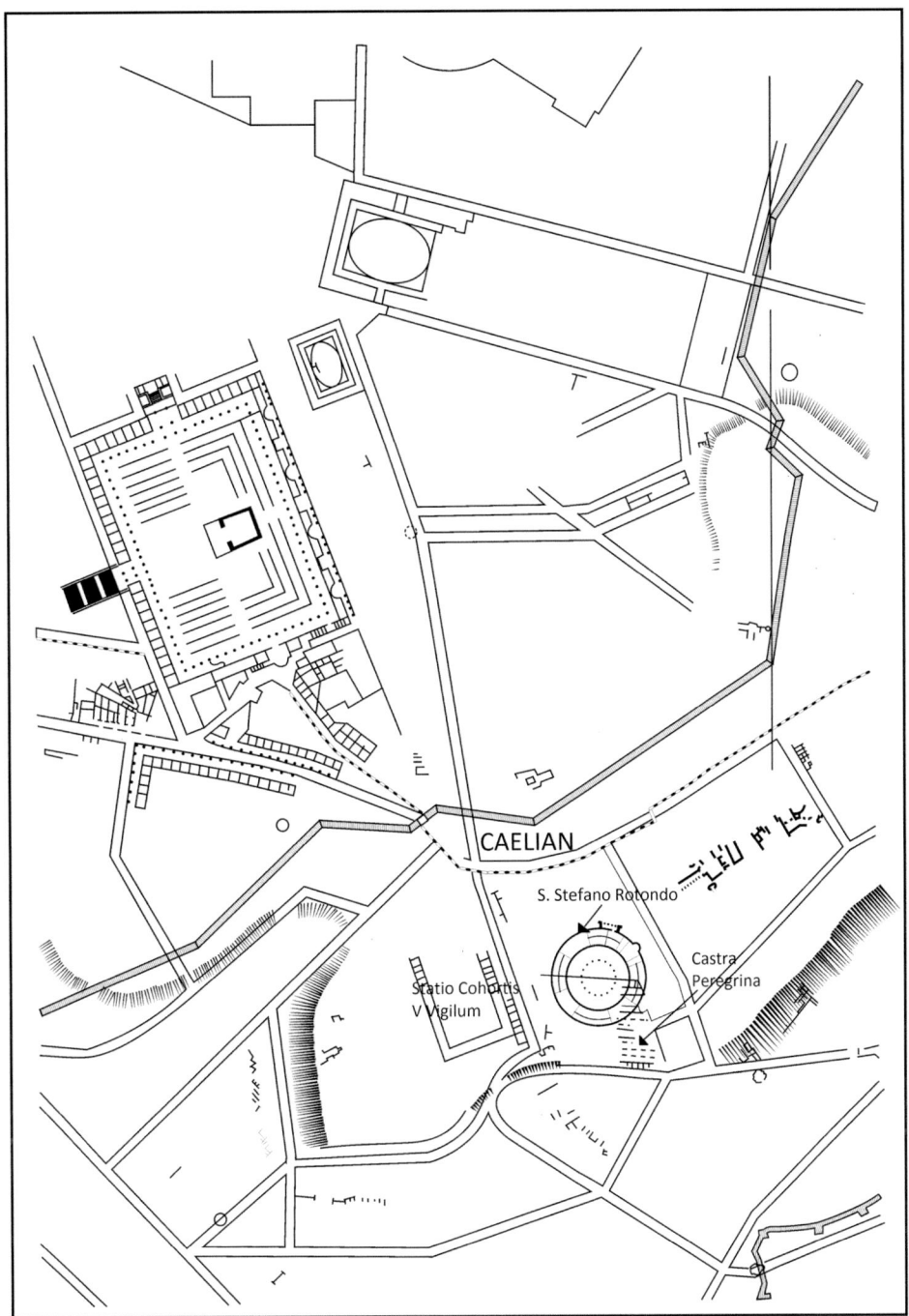

FIGURE 31: PLAN OF S. STEFANO ROTONDO AND SURROUNDING ANCIENT STRUCTURES. DRAWN BY ABBY GEORGE FROM THE BASE PLANS IN PLATE 36 IN LANCIANI R. *FORMA URBIS ROMAE* (MILAN 1893-1901) AND BRANDENBURG H. AND PÁL J. EDD. *SANTO STEFANO ROTONDO IN ROMA: ARCHEOLOGIA, STORIA DELL'ARTE, RESTAURO; ATTI DEL CONVEGNO INTERNAZIONALE, ROMA 10-13 OTTOBRE 1996*, (WIESBADEN 2000) FIG. 33, TAFEL. 13.

A basilica of some description also lay on the Pincian hill at the northern edge of the city, dedicated to St. Felix. It is first mentioned in the 8th century, however, as ruinous, was destroyed in the 16th century and its location is also unclear.[117] As a result we cannot judge whether it could be seen widely in the city, so we will not discuss it further.

---

[117] LP 1.500, 517 n.41; Sotinel C. 'Chronologie, topographie, histoire: quelques hypothèses sur *S. Felix in Pincis*, église disparue', in *Ecclesiae Urbis* (2002) 449-71 and refs.

3.7 Conclusion

It is clear then, despite there often (but not always) diminutive size, several of the intra-urban Christian centres of this period made a visual and/or spatial impact on the Roman landscape. It is difficult to argue that this was all entirely coincidental or accidental, especially considering that the prestige of the donor-builders of these structures would have been greatly enhanced by such visual and spatial prominence. While these mainly small structures would have clearly had less of a macro impact on the urban environment than the larger, central, public 'pagan' cult centres, founded in the Republican and early Imperial eras, on a micro street level scale the Christian buildings cited here were a prominent addition to the built environment. The incidences of their clustering off major arterial roads and their deliberate encroachment of public spaces would have made them noteworthy and prominent investments for their donors. Equally, those foundations built with entrances directly off main roads and within prestige buildings would also have benefitted from their locations. At the same time, there were three larger Christian basilicas built at the summit of hills in the city, a strategy seen in the temple builders of old. This seems to suggest that where budget allowed, the ambition of Christian builders was no less great than the donors of religious buildings in previous centuries, with their motivations of the same hue.

4. The Tituli of Equitius and Sylvester in the Subura

Ahaz gathered together the furnishings from the temple of God and cut them in pieces. He shut the doors of the Lord's temple and set up altars at every street corner in Jerusalem (2 Chronicles 28:24).[1]

All previous studies of Roman topography have looked at the subject in a macro top-down way, a result of limited micro evidence and a scholarly habit of wanting to produce grand general statements on the subject. Yet, to fully appreciate the Christianisation of the urban landscape we need to examine it in a micro street-level perspective, which, in the above chapters, we have as far as possible been trying to do. The example that allows us to do this best, though, is the *titulus Equitii/Silvestri* complex, which is now below or near the 9th century S. Martino ai Monti basilica in the ancient Subura area. There are a series of slabs of the Severan Marble Plan, created between A.D. 203-11, that show the area immediately around the current church, that is, approximately a century or so before the apparent creation of this Christian foundation(s).

We know from other Roman cities with continued early medieval occupation, that the central urban configuration remained largely the same, with changes largely occurring in function within existing buildings. So we can be fairly confident that the layout of this part of the Subura represented in the Plan broadly shows the situation into the 6th/7th centuries. The detail that the Plan provides allows us to tentatively recreate the neighbourhood into which the *titulus/tituli* were inserted, and see the sort of impact this intervention would have made on that landscape and the people living in it. The following analysis will, I hope, help elucidate more clearly the practical processes involved in the initial phase of spatial Christianisation in Rome, and its results.

4.1 What, Where and How Many?

4.1.1 The Written Evidence

Unfortunately there is a great deal of confusion as to the number, identity and, most importantly for us, location of the various Christian foundations relating to the current 9th century church on the site. We lack firm pre-6th century archaeological evidence for Christian activity here, so although the area existing around the (as yet) undetectable 4th c. *titulus* is well-documented, conversely the first Christian structure on the site is little understood. A brief survey of the scholarship looking at the problem is therefore worth examining here, which will allow us to come to some conclusions as well.

A major problem featured in the discussion is the question as to whether we are looking at one or two Christian foundations here: a *titulus Equitii et Silvestri*, or one whose name is interchangeable between the two; or a *titulus Equitii* and a separate *titulus Silvestri* nearby. Our main source, the LP, is the source for the confusion. The issue is, what are the nature of the sources the mid 6th century author(s) of the lives of the 4th-6th century bishops drawing on? The life of Sylvester (314-35) describes him creating an *ecclesia* on the land or estate of a priest named Equitius near Domitian's baths (the Baths of Trajan[2]), and establishing it as a *titulus*, where it is still to this day (that is, the mid 6th century) known by that name.[3] This rather detailed description of the land grant and its 6th century name seems quite definitive in proving that this *titulus* existed in this area from the early 4th century, and that the life's author had access to a reliable archive. Later in the same *vita*, we hear of an apparently separate episcopal foundation of a *titulus Silvestri* next to Trajan's baths, although in other variant manuscripts it is also called the *Equiti(i)/Aequicii*. Even in the manuscript used by Duchesne the *titulus Equitii* is mentioned again at the end of the donation list, this time donated by the emperor, not the bishop.[4] Duchesne believes the similarities in the donations to each may suggest that this is a case of differing manuscripts, or part of the same archive record, describing a single foundation.[5]

The synod attendee lists of 499 and 595 seem to back up the idea that this was a single foundation with an interchangeable name, with priests of the *titulus Equitii* appearing in 499 and those of a *titulus Silvestri* in 595, but never clergy from both.[6] Equally, the LP's life of Symmachus (498-514) simply describes him constructing from the ground up (*a fundamento*) a basilica of Saints Sylvester and Martin, that is an entirely new construction dedicated also to the 4th century bishop, as well as Martin of Tours.[7] Yet, a document written almost at the same time as the creation of this official life, the so-called Laurentian Fragment, and all subsequent references to this foundation—that is those describing the contemporary situation—expressly describe two separate buildings. The Laurentian Fragment, a small surviving part of an alternative set of papal biographies, clearly describes

---

[1] Translation: *New International Version* (1984).
[2] These baths were erroneously believed to have been built under Domitian by the Middle Ages, an idea which may stem from the work of Jerome (*Chron.* 2105=AD 89), itself deriving from the writings of Eusebius.
[3] LP 1.170.
[4] For the debate surrounding these donations see Hillner J. 'Families, patronage' (2007) 225-61, esp. 230.
[5] LP 1.187 n.119.
[6] MGH. AA.12. 411, 413; MGH.Ep. 1.366-67.
[7] LP 1.262.

a structure dedicated to St. Martin and another separate foundation to St. Sylvester nearby, not one single building.[8] Equally, the far more numerous differences in the donation lists of the *titulus Equitii* and the *titulus Silvestri* in the *LP* cannot easily be explained away.

Furthermore, the life of Hadrian I (772-95) describes the *ecclesiam beati Martini* as near to the *titulus* of St. Sylvester.[9] Also, the Einsiedeln Itinerary, which dates to the late 8th to early 9th century, and seemingly an eye-witness guide, describes two structures, one to St. Sylvester and the other to St. Martin, as in the Subura on the same side of the road going south.[10] In the same period we hear for the first time about a *diaconia Sancti Silvestri et Sancti Martini*,[11] which may be, judging by the name, the institution that served both foundations. It was under Sergius II (844-47) that the older S. Martino basilica, presumably that built by Symmachus, was found ruinous or demolished, and built entirely anew in, according to one manuscript, 'a place not very different'.[12] This recalls the description of the rebuilding of S. Prassede by Pascal I (817-24), where this exact phrase is used and where the work involved a reorientation and redecoration on the same site as the older basilica.[13] This would suggest that the remains of Symmachus' basilica lie somewhere below the current Sergian church, which follows the pattern of most church rebuilds.

4.1.2 The Archaeology

The archaeology immediately around the existing 9th century building can also help us here in trying to identify and locate the 4th and 5th/6th century foundations. This in turn will allow us to fit them in quite accurately into the immediate neighbourhood, known largely through the Severan Plan, but also through archaeological discoveries in the region of the current S. Martino ai Monti, which we will now discuss.

Unfortunately, there have been no formal investigations below the church itself, although as a result of some seemingly damaging work on the current church's floor in 1901, it was reported that subterranean painted rooms were seen below it, as well as funerary reliefs or inscriptions.[14] This may suggest a Christian building, but, as we have said, it is more the fact that an existing early medieval church is above it that makes it very likely that its palaeo-Christian predecessor, described as in this area, lies partially or completely beneath it. The high podium below the 9th century church, created with the use of large tufa blocks in four courses, also implies the remains of a structure beneath it.[15]

4.1.2.1 The Roman Hall

Other discoveries that point to earlier 4th-6th century buildings on this site have been found to the north and south of the current church. Before tackling these we need to first examine the vexed question of the identity and purpose of the Roman hall approximately 11 metres to the west of the 9th century church, and located about 10 metres below it, as well as the vaulted chamber and wall of another building that lies in the space between the hall and the church's west wall. To describe it we will use the labels and terms utilised by Krautheimer in his detailed analysis of the structures in 1967. (fig. 32) Many of his conclusions will be followed as well.[16]

The whole area consists of a six roomed hall, divided up by vaults and piers (bays D-K) whose wall typology implies an early 3rd century date.[17] To the west of F, another room (C) was added slightly later, to the north of which was an open space, possibly a courtyard or garden surrounded by a low wall of ancient date. Above the hall was an upper floor(s), but the Carolingian and Romanesque monasteries built above it meant their traces were lost. The medieval monastery itself was destroyed in the 20th century when some analysis was possible.[18] Beyond the east wall of the hall lies a long rectangular courtyard, about 6 metres wide, framed by the west wall of a structure known as 'Building P'. This wall dates to the late 3rd century. Sometime in the 4th century this courtyard was vaulted over and the entrance to 'Building P' in this wall was enlarged and rooms were created above this new vaulting. Around the turn of the 6th century a series of further modifications were made, which are certainly of a Christian character.

The two central piers of the hall were enclosed by a thick wall, with a small niche created on their west side, and walls of the same type were built around the piers between the bays G-K and the now vaulted corridor L-N, the dividing wall of which was now pierced with openings. This joined the hall, the corridor and in turn 'Building P' definitively into one complex. In this corridor and on the walls elsewhere, including on the thick walls around the central hall piers, there were now paintings of a Christian character, and at the same time a niche was created in the

---

[8] LP 1.46, 262 n.35.
[9] LP 1.507.
[10] Val. Zucc. 2.192.
[11] LP 2.12, 41 n.64.
[12] LP 2.93-94, 98.
[13] LP 2.54; LTUR 4.326; Affanni A. M. *La Chiesa di Santa Prassede: la storia, il rilievo, il restauro* (2006); Roccoli A. *Santa Prassede, San Martino ai Monti, Santi Quattro Coronati: tre esempi di rinascenza carolingia* (2004).
[14] Accorsi M. L. 'Il complesso dei SS. Silvestro e Martino ai Monti dal III al IX secolo. Appunti di studio', in *Ecclesiae Urbis* (2002) 562 with ref. (533-63).

[15] CBCR 3.108.
[16] CBCR 3.97-108, 115-118.
[17] It has been argued that the hall, or at least part of it, may in fact date from AD 131, on the basis of a brickstamp said to have been found in the area of the building: Boaga E. 'Il complesso titolare di S. Martino ai Monti in Roma', in *Dalla Chiesa antica alla Chiesa moderna. Miscellanea per il cinquantesimo della Facoltà di storia ecclesiastica della Pontificia università gregoriana*, edd. M. Fois, V. Monachino and F. Litva (1983) 6-7 (1-17). This provenance is uncertain however. Silvagni, in the early 20th century, thought that the structure was in fact a (3rd century) house, before it was the *titulus* of Equitius-Silvestri: Silvagni A. 'La basilica di S. Martino ai Monti' (1912).
[18] What there is can be found in Vielliard R. *Les origines du titre de Saint-Martin aux Monts à Rome* (1931).

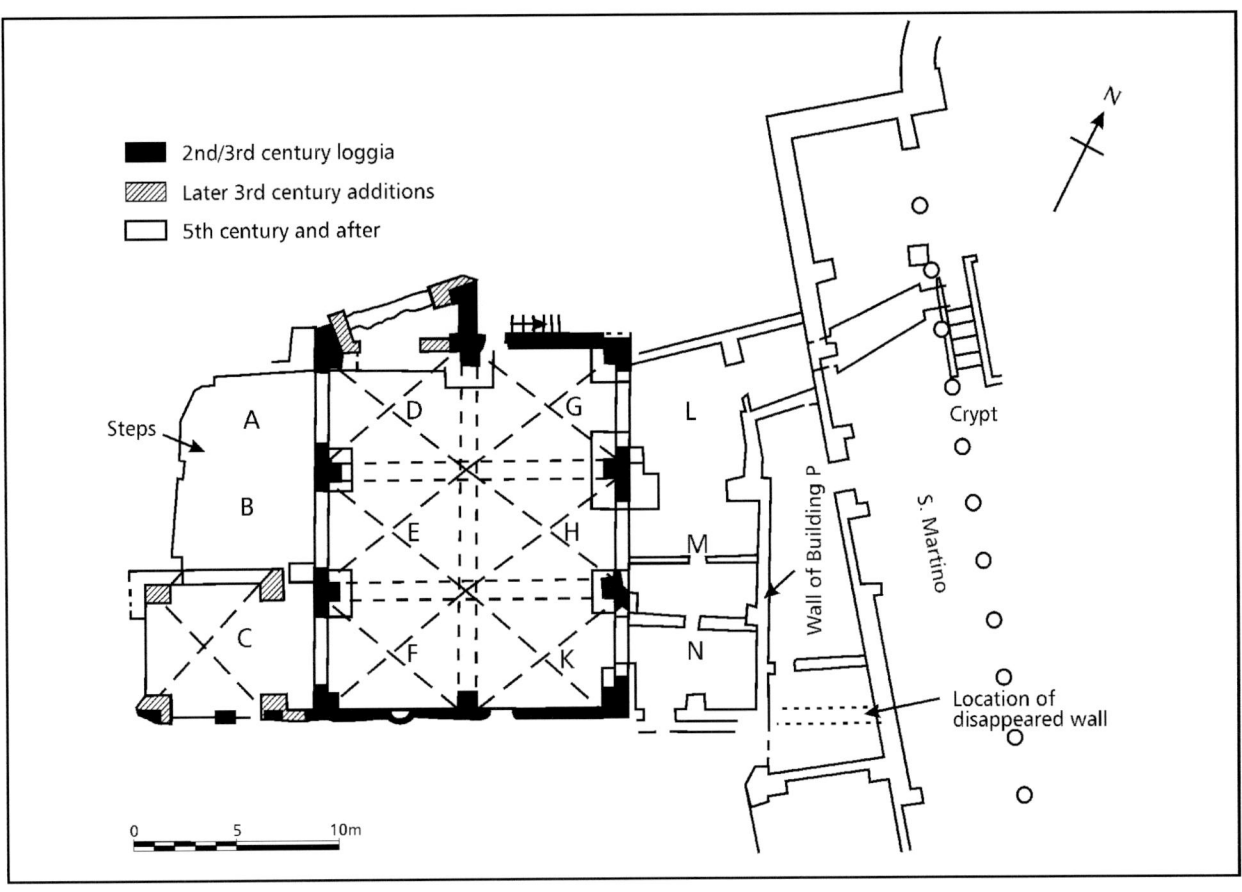

FIGURE 32: PLAN OF THE HALL NEXT TO THE CURRENT S. MARTINO AI MONTI. DRAWN BY ABBY GEORGE FROM A BASE PLAN IN CLARIDGE A. *ROME: AN OXFORD ARCHAEOLOGICAL GUIDE* (OXFORD 1998) 301, FIG. 147.

south wall of room F with a mosaic depiction of a saint or martyr, possibly Saint Sylvester.[19]

The interpretation of these modifications is crucial in positioning and identifying the pre-Sergian Christian buildings in the area and here we largely, but not completely, follow Krautheimer's conclusions.[20] The hall seems to be a commercial structure judging by its layout and utilitarian architecture and floor, and was originally perhaps a market or series of storerooms, an idea reinforced by the possible presence of masonry counters within it in some areas. The idea that the hall was a 3rd century Christian meeting-place cannot be sustained.[21] The 4th century changes, within the rectangular courtyard to its east and the enlargement of the entrance into 'Building P', could be interpreted as the first Christian interventions here, in other words to provide a covered vestibule with an impressive entrance from the street, presumably lying to the north of room L, leading into a now equally embellished entrance into 'Building P'. It is tempting to see the west wall of this building as that of the *titulus Equitii* or *Silvestri*, but without further investigations of it we must be cautious. This building clearly changed in use and increased in importance in the 4th century, but we cannot positively identify its purpose.

It is certain that a 4th century Christian structure lies in this area and most probably under the existing Sergian church, but that structure may well not be 'Building P'. However, the late 5th to early 6th century Christian modifications of the hall and the now vaulted L-N corridor, as well as the wall that separates them, does indicate that by this time at least the hall, and in turn 'Building P', with the corridor linking them, was also put to Christian use. Krautheimer's idea that the hall now acted as an extended vestibule to 'Building P' rightly connects the two structures in a Christian use, but it seems more likely that the hall had now become the *diaconia Sancti Silvestri et Sancti Martini* mentioned for the first time in the late 8th to early 9th century,[22] but very likely existing from the 6th like many others elsewhere. Its insertion in a commercial storage building fits into the pattern observed with many other diaconia found elsewhere in the city, a pragmatic, utilitarian decision made for practical reasons.[23] A large gem encrusted cross was painted above the vault of bay E orientated to be viewed looking east towards H and the corridor that led to 'Building P'. This, coupled with the

---

[19] Davis-Weyer C. and Emerick J. J. 'The early sixth century frescoes at S. Martino ai Monti in Rome', in *Römisches Jahrbuch für Kunstgeschichte* 21 (1984) 1-60.
[20] See this chapter: n.16.
[21] Vielliard R. *Les origines du titre de Saint-Martin aux Monts à Rome* (1931).
[22] LP 2.12, 41 n.64. See above.
[23] This idea is shared by M. Cecchelli: Cecchelli M. 'Dati da scavi recenti' (1999) 228 n.4.

location of the niches in the central hall piers—created with the construction of the thick walls around them—suggested to Krautheimer an entrance via a triangular vestibule north of room D, which led the visitor along the axis E-H from the entrance. (fig. 32)

Rather than a vestibule, for me the cross informs the attendee in the diaconia the location of another Christian building or another part of the diaconia which 'Building P' may have now been. This, interestingly, diverts them away from the oratory niche with the mosaic of a saint, situated in the south wall of room F. We also need to factor in the possible use of the now disappeared floor(s) above the surviving hall and those that were located above the vaulted corridor L-N. Was one being led upstairs? Did these rooms have a much earlier Christian function with the ground floor only being converted later? The date of these modifications ties in chronologically with the work ascribed in the *LP* to Symmachus (498-514) who builds anew a basilica to Saints Sylvester and Martin near the Baths of Trajan, or a basilica to Saint Martin close to Saint Sylvester's with the money of a Palatinus.[24] The list of the attendees of the Roman synod of 499 convened by Symmachus, according to Krautheimer, describes a *presb. sci. Martini tit. Aequitii* rather than just the Equitian *titulus*,[25] which both indicates that Symmachus must have completed his basilica within a year of the beginning of his pontificate and that it superseded the earlier *titulus* of Equitius or both were administered jointly.

Yet, this variant name does not in fact appear in any of the published versions of the list. However, this is the last reference to the *titulus Equitii* in the ancient and early medieval sources, with only the *Silvestri* and *Martini* appearing after this, as separate buildings.[26] This suggests that the Symmachan basilica to Saint Martin of Tours replaced, and was therefore most likely built over or within, the 4th century *titulus* of Equitius, and that a foundation dedicated to Sylvester was a different building next to it. The absence of presbyters of a *titulus Silvestri* in the 499 list also does not mean that one did not exist at this time. There are no priests from much larger basilicas that we know existed, for example S. Maria Maggiore, and it could be that the same presbyters of the Equitian foundation also administered the neighbouring centre dedicated to Sylvester. The earlier joint dedications of one building must therefore be a result of the confusion by the papal archivists over the centuries. The reuse of several architectural pieces of 6th to 8th century date in the later current church, also points to a monumental building from that period on this site.[27]

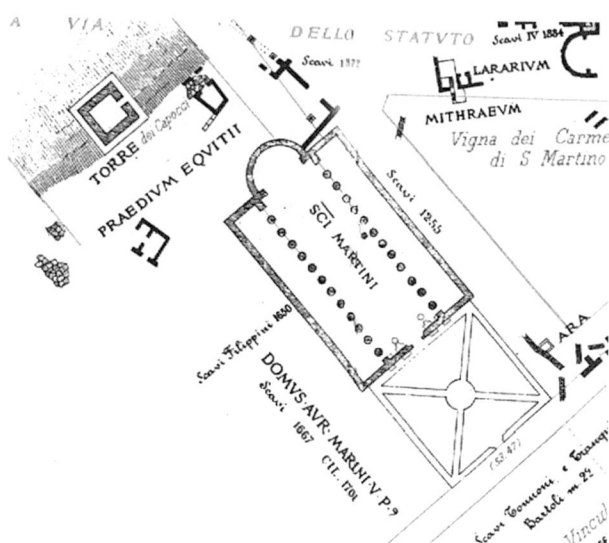

FIGURE 33: DETAIL OF PLATE 23 SHOWING S. MARTINO AI MONTI AND SURROUNDING ARCHAEOLOGY, IN LANCIANI R. *FORMA URBIS ROMAE* (MILAN 1893-1901).

If a building under the Sergian church was the *titulus* of Equitius, perhaps 'Building P', and another or the same structure was later the Symmachan basilica, where was the Silvestrian foundation? The hall I contend was the diaconia, also likely founded by Symmachus at some other time in the early 6th century, so we must look elsewhere for this other Christian building. It is now a good time then to analyse the other archaeological discoveries immediately around the current church of Saint Martin.

4.1.2.2 Discoveries Elsewhere: the Titulus Silvestri?

North-east of the apse a series of walls and columns were discovered in the late 19th century. During the reconstruction of the 17th century staircase by the apse, two rectangular rooms were found, one of which had a row of columns of various marbles within it, which were discovered around 2 metres below ground level. (see fig. 33) Lanciani saw this as a house and where the palaeo-Christian *titulus* was situated. The walls were poorly faced and of 3rd century type, surviving to a height of 1.6m, while above them were layers of tufa and tile fragments datable to the late 4th century. On the walls there survived some plaster from the 5th and 6th c. The bases of the columns had rounded top corners of a Lombardic type (mid 6th-mid 8th century) and there were mosaic and terracotta slab floors. (see fig.34) The almost complete destruction of this building was linked with the construction of the Symmachan building here.[28]

During the demolition of the medieval monastery to the south and west of the church in the mid 20th century, and also during the church's redecoration in the 17th, more discoveries were made in these areas. In the area that now corresponds to the sacristy, during the demolition of

---

[24] See above.
[25] CBCR 3.122.
[26] They are mentioned together as the name of the diaconia in the late 8th-early 9th century however, but, as suggested above, this may simply mean it was the diaconia of both the foundations here. The description of two separate foundations in the Einsiedeln Itinerary, written around the same time, shows this to be the case.
[27] Boaga E. 'Il complesso titolare di S. Martino ai Monti in Roma', in *Dalla Chiesa antica alla Chiesa moderna* (1983) 11.

[28] *NSc* (1892) 342; Lanciani R. 'Scoperte presso s. Martino ai Monti', *BullCom* 21 (1893) 26-29; Accorsi M. L. 'Il complesso', in *Ecclesiae Urbis* (2002) 553-56 (533-63).

FIGURE 34: PHOTO OF TRENCH, WITH FINDS, JUST EAST OF APSE OF S. MARTINO AI MONTI. COURTESY OF THE BRITISH SCHOOL AT ROME: THE BSR PHOTOGRAPHIC ARCHIVE, BULWER COLLECTION, MISC.33.

several of the walls here, on the eastern wall was seen part of a brick arch and a few blocks of tufa similar to that still visible in the cellar beneath the atrium of the church. In this area a column and a jewelled cross was also found. Walls brought to light to the south-east of the church also point to evidence for a colonnaded peristyle situated in front of its façade. These all appear to be 9th century features, however, and part of ancillary buildings of the Sergian rebuild.

Nevertheless, a plan of the monastery and gardens in the 19th century shows a now disappeared wall (see fig.32) that is the same thickness and alignment as the south wall of the 3rd century hall, and so is likely to be a contemporary continuation of 'Building P' under the church. Other discoveries of walls in the monastery garden have now disappeared, but many of these features were believed to be part of the Symmachan basilica by the Carmelite monks who researched it, with a relic well, and its subsequent embellishment, found in the current sacristy area believed to mark the apex of the Symmachan apse.[29] As these features are now lost or ambiguous (notably the columns, now lying in rooms M and N) we cannot be certain as to their date, but the photos of the last century seem to show that they are 9th century and part of the Sergian monastery complex.[30]

---
[29] Boaga E. 'Il complesso titolare di S. Martino ai Monti in Roma', in *Dalla Chiesa antica alla Chiesa moderna* (1983) 13, 15; Accorsi M. L. 'Il complesso', in *Ecclesiae Urbis* (2002) 542-43, 559-62.
[30] LP 2.96.

The most interesting remains for identifying the *titulus Silvestri*, therefore, are those found to the north-east of the existing church. The remains of colonnaded rooms with evidence for occupation into the early medieval period here, point to a building that could still have been in use on the eve of the construction of the Sergian basilica in the 9th century. The medieval column base implies it was still in use beyond the 6th century, and therefore intact after the construction of Symmachus' basilica to St. Martin. The description we have of the building of S. Lucia in Orfea/Selci under Honorius (625-38) on the Clivus Suburanus, just to the north-west, as *iuxta sanctum Sylvestrum* implies this structure lay nearer to it than the Symmachan basilica of St. Martin.[31] (fig. 35) The Einsiedeln Itinerary, written not long before the Sergian rebuild (and the demolition of both these earlier buildings), also shows that the two foundations to Sylvester and Martin were next to each other, further east than S. Lucia, with S. Silvestri perhaps nearer to it, and on the same side of the road as the Honorian foundation.[32]

Remains of further rectangular rooms, just west of our colonnaded early medieval room—visible in Lanciani's plan of the city, and labelled '*praedium Equitii*' by him —between the current church apse and the medieval Torre dei Capocci, may be evidence for the extension of this building around 35m, running south-west.[33] (see fig.33) Lanciani dates the walls to the 2nd century but with 4th century occupation evident, and argues for all the rooms together to be a house.[34] This I believe, is an excellent candidate for the *titulus* of Sylvester, a house or secular basilica that was converted into a Christian building in the 4th century and continued to be so, alongside the basilica to St. Martin built by Symmachus in the 6th century, just to the south. The *titulus Silvestri* still existed in the late 6th century, with its priests attending the synod of that year, and was probably only demolished by the 9th century builders of the current basilica to both Sylvester and Martin. The colonnaded room found just east of the 9th century apse shows evidence for 'Lombardic' or early medieval use and redecoration, and thus its survival beyond the early 6th century and into the 9th is very possible.

The apse and reliquary of the current church lie over the middle of this earlier building, which may be an attempt by the 9th century architects to respect an older relic well or sacred spot and place it at the apex of the new basilica. This may explain the excessively high tufa podium on which the Sergian church sits, and its completely different alignment to any earlier structures in the immediate area.

---
[31] LP 1.324
[32] Val. Zucc. 2.192. The idea that the *titulus* of Equitius, and subsequently the Symmachan S. Martino, should be identified with the late Roman hall building above the Roman arcades just east of the current S. Lucia (and now the convent attached to the church), is unconvincing: Apollonj-Ghetti B. 'Le chiese titolari di S. Silvestro e S. Martino ai Monti', in *RACrist* 37 (1961) 271-302. The hall is in fact more likely to be the Honorian S. Lucia (CBCR 3.123-24), converted from an aristocratic basilica.
[33] FUR plate 23 (detail).
[34] Lanciani R. 'Scoperte presso s. Martino ai Monti', *BullCom* 21 (1893) 26-27.

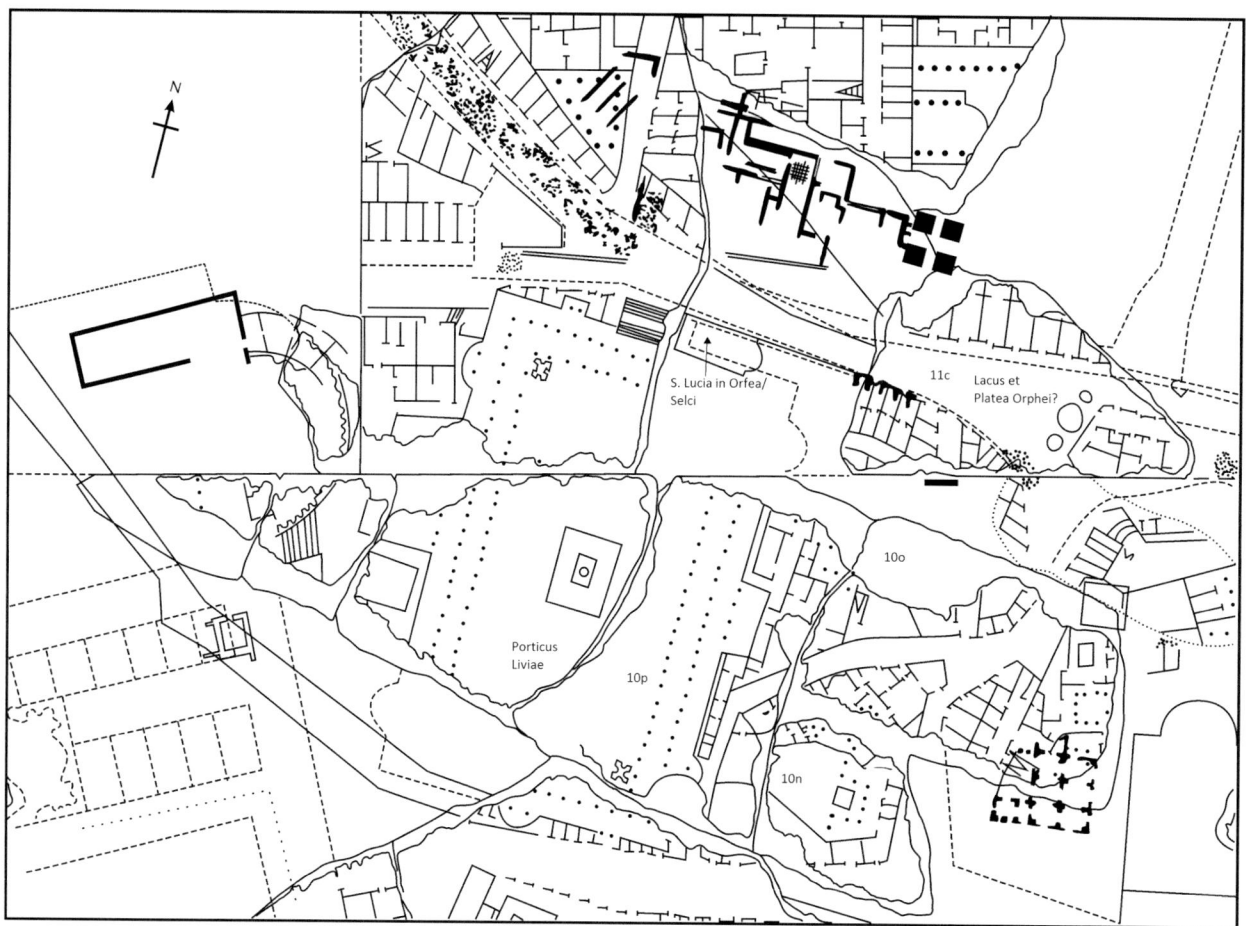

FIGURE 35: SECTIONS OF THE SEVERAN PLAN WEST OF S. MARTINO AI MONTI. DRAWN BY ABBY GEORGE FROM A BASE ILLUSTRATION IN RODRÍGUEZ ALMEIDA A. 'AGGIORNAMENTO TOPOGRAFICO DEI COLLI OPPIO, CISPIO E VIMINALE SECONDA LA *FORMA URBIS MARMOREA*', RENDPONTACC 48 (1975-76) 263-78.

4.1.3 The Severan Plan Evidence

Now is a good point in which to examine the Severan Plan slabs and reconstruct the immediate area where these two Christian foundations were situated, either partly or completely under the existing church. With our 4th century house/building just to the north and below the Sergian basilica that we have just discussed, a part of the surviving Severan Plan can in fact inform us some more about its layout.

The generally accepted reconstruction of the location of the plan's slabs is the magisterial work of A. Rodriguez Almeida.[35] The reconstruction of our study area in the Subura does however make no allowance for the known 3rd century and earlier archaeology in the area.[36] (see figs.35-36) That is to say, the outlines of the structures of the Plan are not aligned with the known archaeological remains discovered around the church and described above. Yet, this is the correct approach, that is to fit the pieces together following a scientific method, but because the Plan is the result of the piecing together of a series of earlier, smaller, land survey maps, and with a differing scale used for monumental and non-monumental buildings, while the details are very precise it does mean the angle of structures and whole areas are sometimes skewed, and do not fit and align with a topographical plan. This means we can identify with some certainty, in spite of the plan not fitting exactly over the archaeology, the 3rd century hall to the west of S. Martino ai Monti as the *domus* and peristyle in the Severan Plan in fragment 10o (see figs.35 and 36).[37] Equally, the colonnaded halls or peristyles seen in the Plan situated just to the north of where the current church lies (within the large frag. 10g: see fig.36)—of which we now have more detail thanks to the drawing of a lost fragment fitting in next to it[38] (frag. 10aa/frag. 706: see fig.36)— can be associated with the rectangular colonnaded rooms excavated just east of the apse described above, which are an excellent candidate for the *titulus Silvestri*. It is to these features that we will first turn now.

---

[35] Rodríguez Almeida A. *Forma urbis marmorea: aggiornamento generale 1980*, 2 vols. (1981) with later work (see below).
[36] Rodríguez Almeida A. 'Aggiornamento topografico dei colli Oppio, Cispio e Viminale seconda la *Forma urbis marmorea*', *RendPontAcc* 48 (1975-76) 263-78.
[37] Rodríguez Almeida A. 'Aggiornamento topografico' (1975-76) 270-71; Rodríguez-Almeida E. 'I confini interni della "regio V", Esquiliae, nella *Forma Urbis Marmorea*', in *L'archeologia in Roma capitale tra sterro e scavo* (1983) 113 (106-15).
[38] Rodríguez Almeida A. 'Aggiornamento topografico' (1975-76) 270.

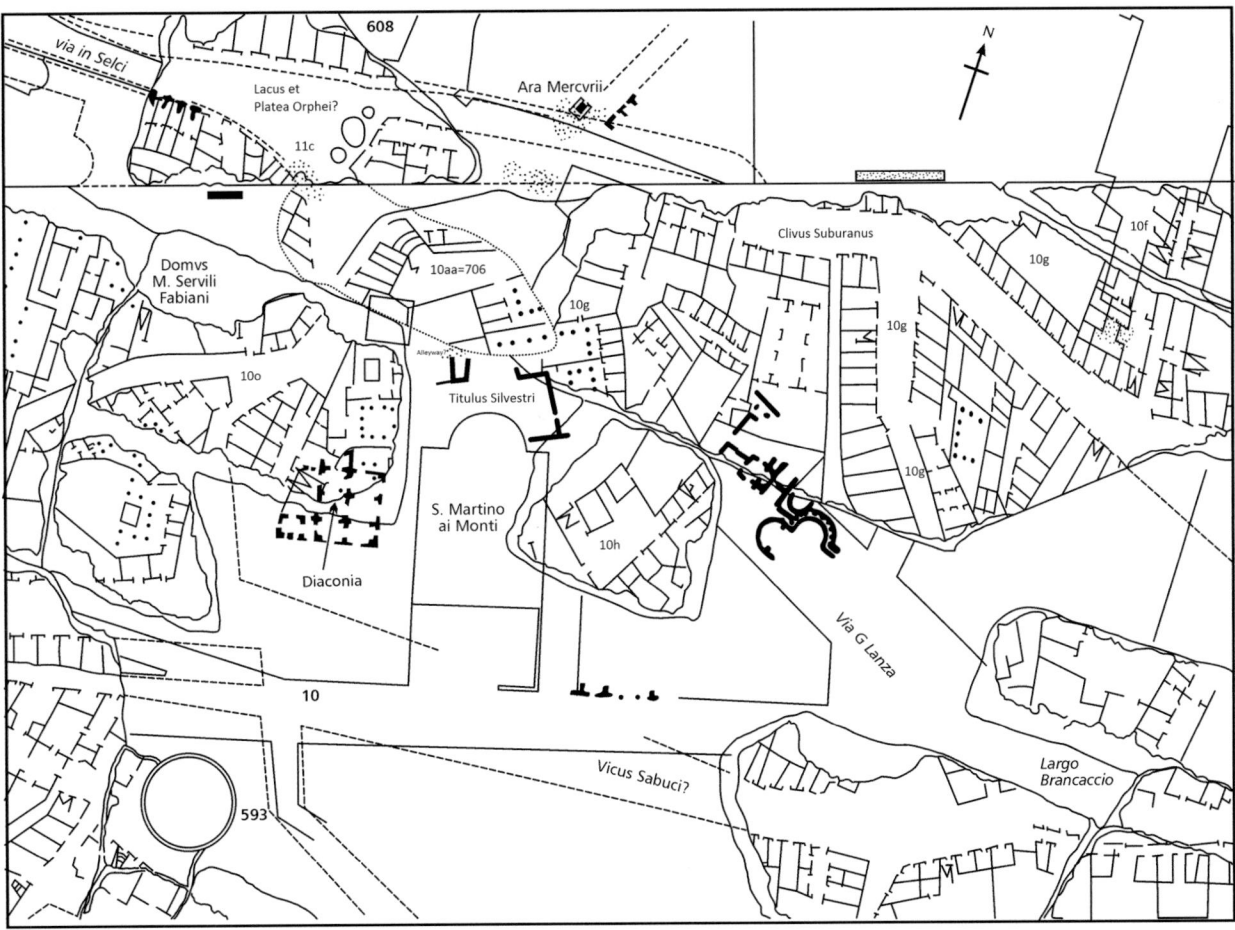

FIGURE 36: SECTIONS OF THE SEVERAN PLAN AROUND AND TO THE EAST OF S. MARTINO AI MONTI. DRAWN BY ABBY GEORGE FROM A BASE ILLUSTRATION IN RODRÍGUEZ ALMEIDA A. 'AGGIORNAMENTO TOPOGRAFICO DEI COLLI OPPIO, CISPIO E VIMINALE SECONDA LA *FORMA URBIS MARMOREA*', RENDPONTACC 48 (1975-76) 263-78.

4.1.3.1 The Titulus Silvestri on the Severan Plan?

These features now below and just to the north of the 9th century church, discovered in the late 19th century, have, as we have described above, characteristics of a colonnaded space, whose columns were still standing in the early middle ages. Two features in the Severan Plan in this area show the same features, that is colonnaded spaces. The one furthest to the south, that may in fact run directly below the 9th century apse, has a set of dashed lines that separate off a square or rectangular area of columns from another space to the west of it. This suggests a structure with a colonnaded portico leading onto a separated but connected space (see fig.36) This portico is very likely to be the colonnaded space found by Lanciani, that had since been restored, with new column bases and wall plaster in late antiquity and the early middle ages, from the early 3rd century incarnation shown on the plan.

The three rooms visible along the eastern edge of this portico are connected to it and appear only accessible from it, suggesting private rooms rather than shops. A colonnaded space lies next to it to the north of our portico with three connected rooms also on its eastern edge. However, there appears to be a wall separating them, with a doorway visible on the opposite northernmost wall giving access from a space to the north of that. This northernmost colonnaded space lacks columns (or perhaps they are simply piers) on its southern edge. This may imply that the two spaces are connected on an upper floor not represented on the Plan. Indeed, the lack of street accessibility seen here and in much of the surrounding buildings implies either private structures, or, due to the hilly and undulating nature of the natural topography in this region of the city, that access was granted from upper or lower floors that are not visible.[39] Stairs appear as 'V' shaped features on the plan and are frequent in this part of it, so this is a reasonable assumption.

It is not clear from the plan what this building(s) was in the early 3rd century, but the rooms running along the eastern edge of the colonnaded/piered rooms and accessible from them is not typical of a private *domus* (although this cannot be ruled out) but rather it may be a storage or utilitarian structure. However, the southernmost square portico

---

[39] Najbjerg T. and Trimble J. 'Large section of the Subura neighborhood (*Subura*) on the Oppian Hill, including the Clivus Suburanus (*clivus Suburanus*) and a small bath (*balneum*)', *Stanford Digital Forma Urbis Romae Project*, http://formaurbis.stanford.edu/fragment.php?record=43 (accessed 2/08/12).

here, if indeed it is square, is suggestive of a private rich residence. Whatever the case, we can be fairly confident that this portico is the structure discovered by Lanciani and that it remained in use, and largely retaining the same form, as late as the 8th century perhaps, judging from the 'Lombardic' column bases described by the 19th century excavators. This does imply a continued high status use, and such an elaborate newly renovated structure in early medieval Rome is most likely to be either a 'palace', a monastery or a church.

For a 9th century church to destroy part of it, by its apse being built over it, indicates an ecclesiastical use, as it is unlikely at this time that an aristocratic residence would have been deliberately destroyed for this purpose, with this area being far less densely populated at the time, so the home to many other available building plots. More likely is that the alignment and position of the apse is respecting an earlier ecclesiastical structure or reliquary (or believed martyrdom?) site and therefore superseding it, yet preserving an earlier Christian structure. The unnecessary height of the 9th century tufa podium, as we have mentioned, also implies that important, yet now superfluous, Christian buildings lie partially or completely underneath it. This is what makes me think that this colonnaded portico here led to a Christian *titulus*, the *titulus Silvestri*, from the 4th century, a building that was embellished in the 6th century or later, but then ultimately demolished in order to build the larger and more impressive current S. Martino ai Monti in the 9th century.

The placement of a now lost fragment next to the above slab, by Rodríguez Almeida, provides us with further information as to the structure of the northernmost colonnaded or piered space. This fragment, labelled as 10aa/frag.706 by Rodríguez Almeida, survives as a drawing in a 17th century publication of the Plan, and seems to fit on the eastern edge of 10g.[40] (see fig.36) This may in fact also show what was the house of Pliny the Younger.[41] If we accept this fragment's placement it shows that our northernmost colonnaded/piered space continued several metres more to the west with the line of columns or piers by its northern wall also continuing, indicating that this was a rather impressive structure and space, whatever its use. This fragment also shows that another structure lay to the north of it that also contained columns or piers, with three rooms leading off it on its western side. This repeats the pattern seen with our southernmost structure, found in the 19th century, and so they may have had similar uses. The former has been described as a peristyle that was part of a *domus*.[42]

---

[40] Rodríguez Almeida A. 'Aggiornamento topografico' (1975-76) 270; Rodríguez Almeida, E. *Forma Urbis Marmorea* (1981) 171 pl.7. Drawing of fragment survives in Bellori G. P. *Fragmenta vestigii veteris Romae ex lapidibus Farnesianis nunc primum in lucem edita cum notis* (1673) pl.7.
[41] Described in Martial: 10.20.4-11. Rodríguez-Almeida E. 'I confini interni' (1983) 113; LTUR 2.158-59, cf. LTUR 4.380.
[42] Najbjerg T. 'Renaissance drawing: a section of the Subura neighborhood (*Subura*) including a large residential unit (domus)?', *Stanford Digital Forma Urbis Romae Project*, http://formaurbis.stanford. edu/fragment.php?record=39 (accessed 3/08/12).

Yet this space had a large doorway that led to an irregular space north of it that was directly accessible from a public road via a set of curved stairs. That would suggest the irregular space was both on a height and was a public square. This does not exclude the possibility that this 'peristyle' was part of a *domus*, but such a large doorway directly off a public square may also suggest another utilitarian structure. A small room with a narrow alleyway off it was discovered where the western extension of the northernmost hall/courtyard is meant to be (see fig.36) so this may put the placement of this fragment here into question. However, such an alleyway may have existed at an earlier or later phase than the Plan, and the distortion inherent within it also comes into play, so we must reserve judgement.

Whatever the original purpose of these three spaces, they do all lend themselves to be meeting places for large groups of people, and so any Christian adaptations would have needed to be only minor. Their likely continued use and monumental nature, at least with the southernmost atrium/portico, into the 6th century and beyond also increases the likelihood of a Christian building here. This is to say there are several compelling reasons why the *titulus Silvestri* was here, the *titulus Equitii*/Symmachan basilica being located under the current church, and thus still unexplored.

4.1.3.2 The diaconia Sancti Silvestri et Sancti Martini

With the *titulus Equitii* and later Symmachan basilica most likely under the Sergian basilica, and thus only a subject for future excavators, we must now turn to the identity of the Roman hall just to the west of, and 10 metres below, the existing S. Martino ai Monti. The structure has been discussed above, and is I believe the diaconia for both the pre-Sergian Christian centres here. As such, we will now see what the Severan Plan can tell us about this building and the implications of that.

Accepting the clear distortion that the Plan displays in relation to the physical topography, the early 3rd century hall can be identified on the Plan. It was a new building when the Plan was drawn and appears as the western half of a semi-rectangular structure with a curved north-western corner. (see fig.36) There is now a curved medieval wall at this corner, built atop an earlier Roman low wall that marked out an open air space here, but this is perhaps represented by the square feature that protrudes from this side and which connects the hall to a narrow alley that runs north-south. The wall that marks out this square feature is likely to be the low wall found in the archaeology. South of this is a set of stairs (marked as 'V's on the Plan) indicating access to an upper level of the hall from the alleyway.[43] The angle of the north wall matches the angle of the north entrance of the hall, with its triangular vestibule, found in the archaeology. It does not seem to lead to a street though,

---

[43] Noted also by Claridge, but who argues that the stairs on the Plan correspond to rooms A-B: Claridge A. *Rome: an Oxford Archaeological Guide* (1998) 301-302. Stairs were indeed found here, but lead downwards to an unexplored cellar area (CBCR 3.101).

as has been argued,[44] but to another piered or colonnaded area which in turn led to a rectangular space with a square feature in the centre of it.

The hall itself is marked with the same holes thought to be columns by many commentators, but this hall never had these and thus the dots are likely generic markers of elements holding up a roof, whether piers or columns. The two spaces to the north of our hall have been interpreted as part of a *domus*. It has been suggested that the northernmost rectangular room with the square feature in the middle was the entrance courtyard with the square feature marking the *compluvium* in the roof; this then led to a peristyle courtyard which may have contained a vegetable or flower garden. The rooms west of this could have been slave quarters and/or a cooking area.[45] Whatever the veracity of this, this courtyard does seem connected to our hall to the south of it, with the hint of a doorway visible, and directly abutted it. The hall, as we have said, was also accessible from the alleyway via an open air courtyard and via a flight of stairs to the upper floor.

This leads us to the question as to the northern entrance of the hall with the triangular vestibule, which may just be visible on the Plan. Would there be direct access from a warehouse type building to a private aristocratic garden? Although this entrance is perhaps apparent on the Plan, evidence for a set of stairs was found on the outside of the hall, just east of it, which led to an upper storey.[46] Perhaps this was the level represented on the Plan for the 'garden', but where there was no access between it and the hall on the ground? According to the Plan the north wall of the hall continues on the same angle as this northern entrance, but this does not seem apparent from the archaeology. However, the Roman remains found just east of the 9th century apse, described above, and the two rooms found just to the north of the hall are on this same angled alignment (see fig.33), which also fit with the Plan in the immediate surroundings of the site of the 9th century basilica.

In any case, there does not appear to have been a street or alley north of the hall, but rather another pillared or colonnaded space which itself led onto the rectangular room with an *impluvium* or square structure in its centre. There were two rooms found in this area of 2nd century date with 4th century occupation, which seem to align well with the rooms off this space (see figs.33 and 36).[47] Perhaps this room and complex are rather, instead, part of baths, with the space with the possible central pool in fact being a *frigidarium*? The discovery of a 5th century inscription warning of the moral dangers of bathing, reused in the pavement of the 9th century church, suggests a bathhouse used by Christians was nearby.[48] Perhaps this building was instead the *domum in regione Orfea* (a reference to the *lacus Orphei* just to the north: see below), a donation to the *titulus* of Equitius described in the LP?[49]

This is all speculation, but it does make clear the proximity of buildings with very varied uses—both public and private, utilitarian and elite—in a relatively small area. Any idea of zoning needs to be dismissed for this part of the city at least. Equally, the purpose of the hall building could also be multifarious. The characteristics of the surviving floor of the hall we have examined does seem utilitarian, either storage or mercantile. However, the floors above may have had residential uses for example, just as *insulae* often had shops on the ground floor and flats above.[50] Indeed, this hall may represent the ground floor of an *insula*. A market, with storage areas, that led to a pillared or colonnaded *apodyterium* which then led, as it often did, to a *frigidarium* to the north, would seem like an ideal place for such a commercial structure. The bath's customers were also theirs. The stairs from this pillared room to the north and from the alleyway to the west gave access to upper floors.

The likely creation of the *diaconia* here in the late 5th to early 6th century, at the same time as a new Christian basilica just to the east or perhaps above it, marks an evolution of this type of space typical of many early diaconia in the city. The continued use of the northern vestibule entrance suggests that the room to the north of it was still utilised for some purpose as well, so this neighbourhood had not drastically altered yet by this time. This entrance had become superfluous though, or perhaps inaccessible, by the 9th century when it was blocked.[51] By this period then the Subura had certainly changed in character, which the differing alignment of the Sergian basilica also demonstrates.

4.1.4 Conclusion

What needs to be appreciated is that the early Christian buildings under and around the current S. Martino ai Monti were created or built anew in a vibrant, densely populated neighbourhood. This might seem at odds to us with our idea of Christian religious observance, but it gives us a clear image of the reality for Christians in this area in late antiquity. The city worked busily and noisily around a place of early Christian worship, but it is not until the late 5th to early 6th century that Christianity became a more visible feature on the landscape here, with the *ex novo* construction of the Symmachan basilica.

---

[44] CBCR 3.115.
[45] Najbjerg T. and Trimble J. 'Section of the Subura neighborhood (Subura) including the Porticus of Livia (porticus Liviae) and the Baths of Trajan (thermae Traiani)', *Stanford Digital Forma Urbis Romae Project*, http://formaurbis.stanford.edu/fragment.php?record=48 (accessed 3/08/12).
[46] CBCR 3.99.
[47] Lanciani R. 'Scoperte presso s. Martino ai Monti', *BullCom* 21 (1893) 26-27.
[48] Silvagni A. 'La basilica di S. Martino ai Monti' (1912) 408-10.
[49] LP 1.171.
[50] Religious uses cannot be ruled out either. A 3rd century mithraeum was found in the ground floor of an insula just south of the exedra of the Crypta Balbi. It was not put out of use until the mid 5th century: Ricci M. 'Crypta Balbi: l'area del mitreo', in *Roma dall'antichtà al medioevo* (2004) 231-41.
[51] CBCR 3.117 with fig.105.

This neighbourhood's public religious observance was not limited to Christianity of course, certainly up to the late 4th century a series of shrines and mithraea were located in the immediate vicinity. It is this religious as well as secular topography that I will now turn in order to understand how the area immediately around the *tituli* and the diaconia 'worked' from the 4th to the 7th century, and how these Christian institutions fitted into this. Movement, navigation, nodes and viewsheds will be discussed where possible in order to elucidate this. The effect of the gradual abandonment of the area from the mid 6th century also needs to be appreciated of course.

4.2 The Surrounding Neighbourhood

When discussing the church's immediate surroundings we will confine ourselves to the area covered by the Severan Plan slabs labelled 10n-p to the west of S. Martino ai Monti and the slabs 10g-h east of it. (see figs. 35-36) This will give us an accurate idea as to the urban landscape into which the Christian buildings were created a hundred years or so later. This difference in time is significant, but the picture we get from Mediterranean Roman cities where we have continued occupation through to the 7th century, such as at Ostia in the West and Aphrodisias in the East, is structural continuity. Although parts of the city were abandoned, the structures and buildings in the central part of town retained their earlier 1st to 3rd century configuration, with modifications and changes in use taking place within them. Some minor roads were blocked but important thoroughfares continued to be used.[52]

In other words, we can be fairly confident that the street and building layout in the Subura in Rome remained largely the same until the mid to late 6th century, with only changes in use affecting the buildings. After this we know a gradual abandonment then took place following the Gothic Wars. In this way, our discussion here only informs us of the spatial topography up to the time of the building of the Symmachan basilica and for a generation or so beyond this. For the late 6th into the 7th century we can make few certain statements, save that this part of the city was undergoing a state of radical change that altered forever the pattern of the lives of the people who continued to live here. What we can say though, is that the essential ancient road pattern in this part of Rome remained the same up to the late 19th century, as many roads that still exist today run along the same path as their ancient predecessors. The Via della Madonna dei Monti-Via Leonina-Via in Selci-Via di San Martino ai Monti-Via di San Vito roads follow the ancient *Clivus Suburanus* and the Via Urbana follows the *Vicus Patricius*, to name but two.

4.2.1 West of the Tituli

To the west of the Sergian basilica we have already examined the buildings depicted on the Plan that represent the Roman hall that still survives, that became a diaconia, and the spaces to the north of it. This may be a *domus* or a bath complex (see figs.35 and 36). To the west of this series of buildings, and accessible only from the colonnaded/piered space just to the north of our hall, is an irregular space of uncertain function. West of this is what looks like a narrow alleyway running north-south which on its other side has a set of shops. Another set of shops back onto them and face onto the crossroads of a major thoroughfare.[53] At its northern end a line dividing the alleyway into two may represent a ramp. The fork in the road here has a road running north-south along the set of shops just described and another fork running towards the east wall of the *Porticus Liviae*, which we will discuss shortly.

The island created by these two roads contains a series of interesting features (fig.35). A number of rooms that are connected to each other and accessible from the roads either side of the island, are apparent in the northernmost part of this area closest to the crossroads. Below these is a colonnaded or piered space that leads directly onto an apsed area with only a short wall separating them. The lower edge of this structure is unfortunately lost but this does appear to be a basilica.

A slab that fits just to the south of this (10n) has been argued to show a meeting hall for a *collegium*, a religious or professional group. On the basis of two dedicatory inscriptions found on this site to Vulcan, it has been suggested that he was the patron deity of this building and that the building acted as the headquarters of the *magistri vici Sabuci*, the dedication by them to the god found virtually on the very spot the building would have occupied.[54] Perhaps this patronage was because of the frequent fires in the area. The space itself has a series of small rooms along its eastern side that lead into a large irregularly shaped space with a square feature towards its eastern side surrounded by columns or piers on three sides with the side facing west fully visible. This suggests the framing of a feature to be viewed from the west, either an altar or a statue (of Vulcan?) most likely.

A room that abuts this space to the south is only accessible from an open area visible at the edge of this fragment, which must be the *vicus Sabuci* road.[55] Another room, that forms the south-east corner of this possible *collegium*,

---

[52] For Ostia, again see: Gering A. 'Plätze und Staßensperren' (2004) 299-382; Lavan L. 'Public space in late antique Ostia' (2012) 649-91. For Aprodisias see: Roueché C. *Aphrodisias in Late Antiquity: the Late Roman and Byzantine Inscriptions Including Texts from the Excavations at Aphrodisias Conducted by Kenan T. Erim* (1989); Erim K. T. *Aphrodisias: City of Venus Aphrodite* (1986); and the series *Aphrodisias Papers* edited by R. R. R. Smith *et al.* (1990-present).

[53] Najbjerg T. and Trimble J. 'Section of the Subura neighborhood', *Stanford Digital Forma Urbis Romae Project*, http://formaurbis.stanford.edu/fragment.php?record=48 (accessed 8/08/12).

[54] Najbjerg T. 'Possible headquarters (*schola*) of a professional organization (*collegium*) off the Vicus Sabuci (*vicus Sabuci*) in the Subura neighborhood (*Subura*)', *Stanford Digital Forma Urbis Romae Project*, http://formaurbis.stanford.edu/fragment.php?record=47 with refs. (accessed 10/08/12).

[55] Clear from the Vulcan dedication by the *magistri*, described above (CIL 6.801), and also that all the other road names in the area are known: see this chapter: n.54.

connects the road to the central hall just described, and as such may have acted as a vestibule to it. There is a piered or colonnaded space to the north of this building, which may or may not be associated with the basilica described above.

The slab adjoining this, 10p (see fig.35) shows the rest of the *collegium* building, which abuts an alleyway that runs along the eastern wall of the *Porticus Liviae*, a structure that dominates this slab and would have this part of Rome. The *collegium* building does not seem to be accessible from this direction, with the only entrance being the south-eastern one already described. 10p also shows the rest of the road that runs south-west from the crossroads to the wall of the *Porticus Liviae* and connects to the narrower alley that runs along it.

The narrow, long, rectangular structure that abuts this wall of the *Porticus* here between two of its exedrae, is said to be reminiscent of subterranean *Mithraea*.[56] This again brings to mind the Mithraeum that lay just outside the exedra of the Crypta Balbi, another public area from which it was obliquely connected.[57] It is likely the same arrangement occurred here, and this was therefore the Mithraeum for initiates visiting the *Porticus*. There does not seem to be any access from the street outside to the Mithraeum.

The *Porticus* itself, completed in 7 B.C. by Augustus for his wife Livia, was essentially a colonnaded garden housing a collection of paintings and dedicated to the goddess Concordia.[58] It was accessed via a set of stairs on its northern side, so from the *clivus Suburanus*. This structure acted therefore like a park in a British Victorian age city, a place to walk and relax in cultured surroundings. Consequently, this space served as a hub for the area for the people who lived here, especially the educated wealthy, and visually dominated it. In this way it also functioned as a navigational landmark for residents and non-residents, as well as a meeting place. It may also have had a more openly religious function—away from the possible Mithraeum off the eastern exedra—as well as a social and cultural one. The square feature in the centre of the portico has been argued to be a fountain or a small temple, possibly to Concordia.[59]

As such, the *Porticus* fundamentally affected the movement patterns of the immediate region. It was clearly still in use in the 3rd century when the Plan was drawn, and archaeology has confirmed that it continued to be so into the 5th century, with a fountain basin and a series of floors found in the central part of the *Porticus* which date to that period. By the mid 6th century, however, the area had become a graveyard.[60] In this way, as suggested above, this period marks the definitive transition from one type of movement pattern in this area, where people regularly moved to the *Porticus*, to one where this was reserved for funerals.

The *tituli* and diaconia here were situated on or just off the roads that led to it, so it may be the case that Christians and the poor who used those buildings from the 4th to the 7th centuries would have moved from those institutions, on feast days and Sundays in particular, to the *Porticus* after a service, with the poor going there to beg perhaps. For non-locals, the proximity of the *Porticus Liviae* to these Christian buildings would have aided a stranger in finding them in the streets; it provided a clear landmark to aim for. So for them movement ran from the *Porticus* to these Christian structures. From the 6th century with the construction of the Symmachan basilica, the Christian presence in the area was more obvious and also may have coincided with the beginning of the abandonment of the *Porticus*, it soon acting as a graveyard. The building of S. Lucia in Selci by the northern entrance to the *Porticus*, which could also be a 6th century foundation, may be connected to this transformation in function. (fig. 35)

Another nodal point here, at least before the 6th century, was the *lacus Orphei* as well as the open square that lay in front of it. Fragment 11c in the Severan Plan has been identified as showing this large fountain feature, which may be Augustan in origin (see figs.35 and 36).[61] It lay at the junction of the *clivus suburanus* and a road that ran south to the *vicus Sabuci* and the east wall of the *Porticus Liviae*. A series of features at the edge of the fragment, to the south of the *clivus* as it leads into the junction (probably shops), correspond to the travertine arcades still visible below the convent of S. Lucia.[62]

The structures described above from the drawn fragment 10aa fit into this area just below the fountain. Here the street widens and a set of curved stairs lead down from it to an open area next to the *domus* identified in this area as once of Pliny the Younger (see fig.36) and just north of where I situate the *titulus* of Sylvester.[63] We know from Martial that the street rose on the Clivus Suburanus leading up to the *Lacus Orphei* from the west, as it still does today to what is now the Piazza San Martino ai Monti. That is to say the fountain—which was in the 1st century A.D., according to Martial, surrounded by a theatre-type frieze and sculptures, including one of Orpheus, and seems to have consisted of three large circular basins—

---

[56] Najbjerg T. and Trimble J. 'Section of the Subura neighborhood', *Stanford Digital Forma Urbis Romae Project*, http://formaurbis.stanford.edu/fragment.php?record=48 (accessed 10/08/12).
[57] See this chapter: n.50.
[58] Completion: Ov. *Fast.* 6.637-48; Suet. *Aug.* 29.4; Dio Cass. 54.23.1-6, 55.8.2. Character: Ov. *Ars am.* 1.71; Plin. *HN* 14.11; Plin. *Ep.* 1.5.9; Strabo 5.236.
[59] Fountain: Platner S. B. and Ashby T. *Dictionary* (1929) 423; Carettoni G. *et al* edd. *La pianta marmorea di Roma antica: Forma Urbis Romae*, vol. 1 (1960) 69. Temple: Coarelli F. *Guida archeologica di Roma* (1975) 206; Boudreau Flory M. 'Sic exempla parantur: Livia's shrine to Concordia and the Porticus Liviae', *Historia* 33.3 (1984) 310 (309-30).
[60] De Fine Licht K., Cozza L., Panella C., Motta R. 'Colle Oppio', in *Roma: archeologia nel centro*, vol. 2: *La "città murata"*, edd. A. M. Bietti Sestieri *et al.* (1985) 468 (467-86); LTUR 4.127-29.
[61] Identification: Rodríguez-Almeida E. 'Aggiornamento topografico' (1975-76) 275-78. Augustan: Rodríguez-Almeida E. 'I confini interni' (1983) 112-13.
[62] Rodríguez-Almeida E. 'Aggiornamento topografico' (1975-76) 271.
[63] See this chapter: nn.40-42.

was situated on a ridge with the road sloping on either side.[64] The fountain still existed in the 4th century, and we have no reason to think its pagan mythological character endangered it in any way well beyond this time.[65]

This fountain and the open spaces around it were thus meeting places, a nodal point for much of the surrounding area, and the fountain itself an important local landmark.[66] The *tituli* of Sylvester and Equitius, the diaconia for both and later the Symmachan basilica were all located just south of this via the curved stairs. This, coupled with their proximity to the visually prominent social hub of the *Porticus Liviae*, meant these Christian buildings were ideally placed to be easily locatable, and from the time of the construction of the Symmachan basilica, were perhaps visually arresting as well to the large number of people who would have passed through along this route. We cannot say whether this was the intention of the builders or a happy coincidence, but it did mean that what may have been modest or outwardly invisible Christian buildings were quickly able to become well-utilised and locatable structures from the 4th century. Beyond the mid 6th century many of the ancient road paths continued to be used, but with less frequency and the ancient character of the area had been lost.[67] As such any comments on the movements of people from this period are more speculative.

4.2.2 East of the Tituli

To the east of the site of our Christian buildings a series of structures have come to light through archaeological investigations during the redevelopment of the area in the late 19th century. These enhance our view of this area from the Severan Plan evidence, available from fragments 10f-h. (see fig.36)

Fragment 10h, which corresponds to structures that existed in an area now partially below the Sergian basilica, on its eastern side, show a series of buildings. These are therefore located just to the south of the colonnaded space that may well be the *titulus* of Sylvester. A square open hall with two rooms on its westernmost wall is apparent in the centre of the fragment, with a set of stairs in its south-west corner. The two rooms are not accessible, at least from the floor shown (probably the ground floor) from the hall, but the northernmost room has an entrance that leads to another rectangular open hall to the north. This hall has a series of rooms abutting its southern wall but which are not connected to it. These in turn lead to a series of spaces than run south-west to north-east along the southern wall of the neighbouring open hall. Two of these are connected to it. One of these has a strange curved feature like a Greek 'alpha' within it. This has been interpreted as an arch or barrel vault for an elaborate entrance perhaps. The central hall has been argued to be the meeting hall of a *collegia* because of the limited access to it, with the space to the north of it possibly being a work area or extra living space for the shop owners of the 'shops' south of it, even though they are not connected with it.[68] A small alleyway to the south of the 'shops' and a road west of the central hall are also apparent.

The difficulty here is the assumption that the Subura was a mainly commercial area, and thus our interpretation of the spaces here tends to veer towards them being of this type. Although Martial characterises the area in this way in the 1st century, it may have evolved into a more mixed neighbourhood by the 3rd century and into the 4th. Indeed, there are many spaces on the Plan here that can be seen simply as *domus* and *insulae* as well as shops. So the Subura may have been little different from most regions of the city by this time and not particularly commercial, or indeed as sordid and crime-ridden as Martial implies a few hundred years earlier.

Interestingly, these structures just to the east of the current church, which are unlikely to have survived in the same form on the eve of the construction of the Sergian basilica in the 9th century over them, may in fact still be apparent in some form from the series of Roman walls still visible in the south-east corner of the basilica today. (see fig.37) Their alignment seems to mirror the south-west to north-east alignment of the buildings represented on the Plan here. We can say then that these structures survived to some extent here, even if only in ruins, up to the 9th century, which repeats the pattern seen with the late occupation of the colonnaded space found to the north that represents the *titulus Sylvestri*. Perhaps this part of the Subura was not totally abandoned, with a series of buildings of Roman origin still being used for a variety of purposes.

Fragment 10g, a large piece that has been placed to the north of 10h, is extremely valuable in reconstructing more of this area, as it also overlaps an area where there was a series of important archaeological discoveries made in the late 19th century. (see fig.36) We have already discussed part of this slab in detail as it includes the colonnaded space found just east of the Sergian apse, as well as the colonnaded/piered space to the north of it. The space above that seems to be another piered or colonnaded space, if the placement of the drawn fragment 10aa is to be believed. There was also the excavation of a room and part of a road in this area as discussed above.[69] (fig. 33)

---

[64] Mart. *Epigram* 10.20.4-11.
[65] *Not. Rom.* V: Nordh ed. *Libellus* (1949) 79.16.
[66] The area immediately around the Trevi Fountain in modern Rome springs immediately to mind as an analogy.
[67] The appearance of churches and monuments along the ancient roads in medieval *itineraria* attest to their continued use. Yet, the description of the Sessorian Palace (*Palatium iuxta Iherusalem*) in the south-east corner of the city as visible from the left side of the road, from what is probably the *clivus Suburanus*, after passing our two *tituli* going east, in the late 8th/early 9th century (in the Einsiedeln Itinerary: Val. Zucc. 2.192-93), is also indicative of the ruination by this time of most of the buildings that once occupied the land in between.

[68] Najbjerg T. 'A section of the Subura neighborhood (*Subura*)', *Stanford Digital Forma Urbis Romae Project*, http://formaurbis.stanford.edu/fragment.php?record=44 (accessed 19/08/12).
[69] Lanciani R. 'Scoperte presso s. Martino ai Monti', *BullCom* 21 (1893) 26-27; *NSc* (1895) 245: this particular room is not discussed in detail, however.

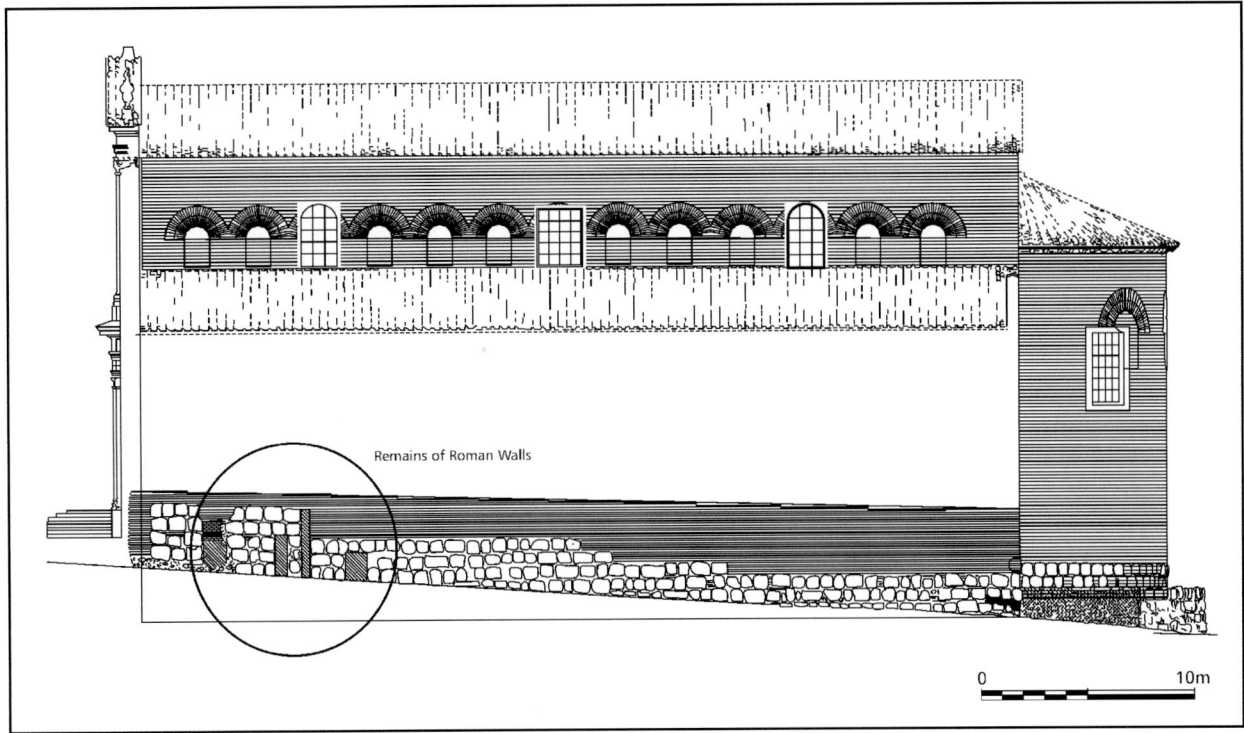

FIGURE 37: SECTION OF EAST WALL OF S. MARTINO AI MONTI SHOWING ROMAN WALLS. DRAWN BY ABBY GEORGE FROM A BASE SECTION BY SPENCER CORBETT (USING A SURVEY BY WOLFGANG FRANKL), IN CBCR 3.

Further east the area is dominated by two streets running broadly east-west and north-south (fig.36). Both are lined with what look like shops of roughly equal size, apart from a few larger examples on the western side of the north-south road. A few have stairs which probably lead to the upper floor(s) of the whole block. A narrow alleyway runs parallel to the north-south road, behind the shops, it widening at the southern end. The wide east-west street has been identified as the *clivus Suburanus*, the major artery through this part of the city.[70] The implication here is that this section of the street at least was a commercial, retail area.

The remainder of the structures here are difficult to identify, but the enclosed building with a colonnaded/piered space in the middle of it, situated behind (east of) the shops south of the *clivus*, has been argued to be a *balnea*, the central space being the *palaestra* (fig.36). The rooms east of it may be a brothel. The fact that access seems to be limited between the spaces shown on the plan here may be explained as carver errors, a multiplicity of private spaces or the undulating nature of the topography here, meaning access was achieved at higher or lower levels not shown on the Plan.[71]

This *balnea* area corresponds approximately to where a series of interesting archaeological discoveries were made in the late 19th century when a series of new roads and sewers were laid in this part of the city (see fig.36: features marked in bold). The fact that these discoveries do not seem to match up in any way with the features seen on the Plan may be a sign of the distortion of the Severan survey here, which has been argued to explain the unusually trapezoid shape of the insula as a whole where the bath house lies.[72] It is better then to see this group of buildings drawn on the Plan as an accurate representation of what was here, but not an accurate representation of where they were in relation to the buildings around them. Also, the structure discovered here in the 19th century dates to the early 4th century, so we may deduce that some of the shops and the bath house in this insula were lost or modified with its creation.

This apsed structure with adjoining rooms (fig. 36: in bold) has been identified as part of a large Constantinian era house, and was excavated from 1883-86 just to the east of S. Martino ai Monti. According to the excavators it contained a library, a nymphaeum, baths, a 2nd century A.D. street shrine to Isis-Fortuna—which became the house *lararium* in the 4th century—and below this a Mithraeum, accessible via a set of stairs. A series of other

---

[70] The idea that this part of the city, east beyond the *lacus Orphei*, was no longer the Subura, and so the street was therefore named something else, is unsustainable: Jewish synagogue by Esquiline gate described as in the Subura: LTUR 4.379. Cf. Rodríguez-Almeida E. 'Aggiornamento topografico' (1975-76) 278. This area was probably know as the lesser Subura: CIL 6.9526 (LTUR 4.380).
[71] Najbjerg T. and Trimble J. 'Large section of the Subura neighborhood (*Subura*)', *Stanford Digital Forma Urbis Romae Project*, http://formaurbis.stanford.edu/fragment.php?record=43 (accessed 20/08/12)

with Reynolds D. W. *Forma Urbis Romae: the Severan Marble Plan and the Urban Form of Ancient Rome* (Ph.D. diss., Univ. of Michigan 1996) fig.3.41.
[72] Carettoni G. *et al* edd. *La pianta marmorea di Roma antica*, vol.1 (1960) 69 n.3; Reynolds D. *Forma Urbis Romae* (1996) 98-99.

cult sculptures, of eastern and Roman deities, was also found in the Isis shrine.[73]

A compital shrine of Republican date with an Augustan rededication was found in 1888 at the crossroads of the modern Via S. Martino ai Monti and Via Lanza (fig.36: 'Ara Mercurii'), so just to the north of the existing church apse, as well as architectural and decorative floors and marble pieces in later years.[74] This all portrays a neighbourhood that is a potent mixture of religious activity (both 'pagan' and Christian) and rich housing in late antiquity. This area, just to the east and north of the Sergian basilica, we know, thanks to the Plan, was commercial in nature as well, but the frequency with which rich decoration and remains of rich late antique *domus* appear in the archaeological record here, suggests that the area changed to a more elite neighbourhood in the century after the Plan's creation.[75] This may have meant the shops we see in the area, and the small apartments above them, disappeared or were greatly modified.

It is also clear that 'pagan' religious activity, even though the area lacked a significant temple—the possible small Temple of Concordia within the Porticus of Livia notwithstanding—was widely taking place within the streets at small shrines and also within rich houses in late antiquity. This reflects the more widespread trend of cultic activity by this time to move away from public practice at temples to semi-private worship and secretive mystery cults, seen here with the subterranean mithraeum (with another existing perhaps along the east wall of the *Porticus Liviae*) and the Isaeum.

The proximity of the Mithraeum below the house (as well as the Isaeum) to the site of the Christian *tituli* has caused B. Apollonj-Ghetti to suspect this is part of the pattern seen elsewhere with Christian buildings and Mithraea being approximate, and part of a deliberate confrontation with the mystery cults.[76] However, both the Mithraeum and Isaeum *lararium* were both invisible from the street and so, as with the other cases where mithraea and *tituli* are close to each other, the proximity is purely coincidental.[77]

The other evidence from the Plan for the area east of S. Martino suggests the series of open spaces behind the shops fronting onto the streets were storage areas or stables perhaps for the transport of goods. The trapezoid building in the middle of fragment 10g (see fig.36), with dashed north-south lines, suggests this may have been an arcaded structure. It had access to open spaces to its north and south and, if storage areas, would imply the arcades held some sort of market, appropriate for this commercial district.

4.3 Conclusion

This part of the Subura was therefore, in the early 3rd century, a more commercial and domestic area, which then became more gentrified in places with rich *domus* appearing. Domestic and street shrines were also a feature. Here the movement patterns were focused along the *clivus Suburanus* and north-south road here that were lined with shops with a possible bath house behind them. These patterns changed with the introduction of the large Constantinian house—which may be on the site of the porticoed courtyard/bath complex in fragment 10g— creating a more private access route, with the *clivus* now being the sole focus for the majority of human traffic, there now being a largely east-west flow, with the *vicus Sabuci* running this way to the south. Further west the area had a more social and recreational focus with the *Porticus Liviae*.

The baths, *collegia*, the porticus of Livia, the shops, markets, houses, *insulae*, squares, halls, street shrines, *mithraea*, Christian *tituli* and the *lararium* show the intrinsic nature that leisure and religious activity played within the streets alongside the commercial and residential. There was no zoning here. More importantly for our purposes we can see that the newly favoured Christian religion fitted into the neighbourhood of the Subura architecturally in the same unobtrusive way as the pre-existing pagan shrines at first. Only with the construction of the Symmachan basilica here did Christianity begin to be the visually dominant religious feature of the area; there was no temple in the immediate vicinity, the possible example in the Porticus being small and invisible from the outside.

From the time of Pope Symmachus in the late 5th to early 6th century, Christianity was therefore a visible feature of the neighbourhood. His purpose-built basilica provided another focus for movement in the area, alongside the porticus of Livia and the shops, collegia and baths here. With the abandonment of the Porticus in the mid 6th century, seen by the appearance of burials within it, and the gradual depopulation and relative abandonment of the area in general, the basilica was now perhaps the sole focus for social gathering in the central Subura, with the Porticus

---

[73] *NSc* (1883) 370, (1884) 153-54, 189-90, (1885) 67-68, 154-55, (1886) 207; Visconti C. L. 'Del larario e del mitreo scoperti nell'Esquilino presso la chiesa di S. Martino ai Monti', *BullCom* 13 (1885) 27-38; Ensoli Vittozzi S. 'Le sculture del 'larario' di S. Martino ai Monti. Un contesto recuperato', *BullCom* 95 (1993) 221-43; Ensoli S. 'I sanctuari di Iside e Serapide a Roma e la resistenza pagana in età tardoantica', in *Aurea Roma* (2000) 280 (267-87); LTUR 3.260 for other mithraic finds in the area.
[74] Crossroads shrine: *NSc* (1888) 224-25; Gatti G. 'Di un sacello compitale dell'antichissima regione esquilina', *BullCom* 16 (1888) 221-22 (221-39). The shrine may be to Mercury *Sobrius*: Lanciani R. 'Scoperte presso s. Martino ai Monti', *BullCom* 21 (1893) 28; LTUR 5. 190. Architectural and decorative finds: *NSc* (1892) 475, (1893) 116; (1895) 319, 359, (1906) 400-401.
[75] Two inscriptions, found just west of S. Martino, below the monastery and just east of the *Porticus Liviae* area, has suggested two more *domus* in the area, of late 3rd and 2nd century date, respectively: Lanciani R. *Forma* (1893-1901) pl. 23; CIL 6.1701b, 1517; LTUR 2.66, 178.
[76] Apollonj-Ghetti B. 'Le chiese titolari' (1961) 271-72.
[77] Mithraea were located in large numbers throughout the city, as many as seven hundred existed perhaps (based on their frequency at Ostia: Coarelli F. 'Topografia mitriaca di Roma', in *Mysteria Mithrae*, ed. U. Bianci (1979) 76-77 (69-79)), so the likelihood of coming across one by chance, or being near one, was high. When discovered by Christian builders the mithraea were deliberately destroyed however, eg. that beneath S. Clemente, but here at least there is also some evidence for coexistence: LTUR 3.258 with refs.

now possibly providing the basilica with a graveyard for local Christians.

This pattern of Christian intervention in the urban fabric of Rome is not repeated everywhere, as we have seen above, some *tituli* were meant to make a mark straight away, but the story here shows that many earlier Christian donors and builders did not look for such notoriety. Yet, the *tituli* of Sylvester and Equitius and the later diaconia were all easy to locate within the dense urban sprawl of the Subura, located as they were next to two major landmarks and social hubs: the Fountain of Orpheus and the Porticus of Livia. They worked with the movement patterns of the people in the area, even if they were largely anonymous from the outside. This changed by the early 6th century with Symmachus' basilica, but soon after the whole Subura also changed forever.

5. Some Other 4th-7th Century Intramural Christian Basilicas in their Urban Context

And on the twentieth day of the ninth month, all the people were sitting in the square before the house of God, greatly distressed by the occasion and because of the rain (Ezra 10:9).[1]

This final chapter will examine a few more Christian basilicas where we can deduce an interesting primary topographical context. This completes a picture of early Christian building in Rome; that is to say occasionally practically minded and at times with an eye on becoming a prominent feature of that part of the urban landscape. Several of the examples below display the same features but now through proximity to major ancient monuments that drew crowds. We cannot say with any confidence whether these Christian centres were constructed in these places entirely for that reason, but what we can say with some assurance is that the Christian authorities were not blind to the importance of these prominent structures to the population of the city. We need to understand how the Christian centres close to them 'worked' in order to fully comprehend the early Christian topography of Rome.

In an earlier chapter we have seen that two *tituli* were constructed within or just outside the entrance to the large imperial *thermae* in Rome. This had a practical benefit for these Christian institutions, as we have argued, but also the sheer number of people that would regularly congregate here, up to the mid 6th century at least, would also provide the *tituli* in question with regular attendees and potentially Christianise bathing activity here, a practice which many Church leaders were suspicious of. Below we will briefly examine those other early Christian buildings which were built within or next to buildings such as circuses, theatres and stadia where large groups of Rome's population regularly gathered. We will also look at one special example where a *titulus* was created right next to a large and important 'pagan' shrine.

The criterion I will be using is that the Christian structure in question must be visually and spatially linked, through close proximity (up to 150 metres) to the other building. In the warren of small streets and alleys, where our precise topographical knowledge is very patchy, visibility is an unknown quantity most of the time, but the size and precise location of an early *titulus* coupled with our knowledge of road layout and movement patterns, does allow us to deduce that there was a spatial association at least. All these locations may suggest they were actively sought sites. Whether some were and others not, for the contemporary inhabitant these associations existed and played into the wider picture of spatial Christianisation of the city and the new religion's integration into city life.

Our first example is a slightly different case, however. The *titulus Damasi*, also known as the *titulus Laurenti in Damaso*, or *in prasino*, presents us with a few topographical and archaeological problems which are worth discussing with regards the question of strategic intramural Christian building. This foundation, from its various names, conjures up three important elements relating to it: bishop Damasus (366-84); the martyr St. Lawrence; and the stables for the circus factions. It is the possible relationship between all three, and how that relates to the archaeological and topographical evidence, that will be tackled here.

5.1 Damasus and the Circus

5.1.1 Titulus Damasi

The first formal Christian basilica on this site near the Theatre of Pompey is Damasian, but there is a strong argument to suggest some sort of Christian centre was founded here a generation earlier.[2] An inscription read at the church in the 9th century, but now lost, tells us that Damasus' father, Antonius, rose from *exceptor* to priest, and Damasus himself was a priest 'in this place', which implies a previous Christian place of worship on this spot, as opposed to it just being his house, as has been suggested. Another inscription, also now lost, again implies a pre-existing Christian centre, with it describing Damasus embellishing the building with columns and possibly an archive, rather than creating a new *titulus*.[3]

Recent excavations from 1988-93 and 1998-2000 have conclusively found Damasus' foundation, running east-west under what is now the courtyard of the Palazzo della Cancelleria, as well as evidence of earlier buildings, which included a large colonnaded portico which was incorporated into the Damasian structure. (figs.38 and 39) It has also been established that another structure, to the east of the possible courtyard, is likely to be a stable building, in use from the Flavian period to the mid 4th century and demolished to build the remainder of the Christian basilica. This basilica had its entrance to the east and lay parallel with an ancient road to its south, with another medieval one possibly to its north. The side walls of the basilica and part of the nave floor have been found, but the apse has been lost. The date of the construction of the basilica, assigned to Damasus in the LP, has been

---

[1] Translation: *New International Version* (1984).

[2] For the arguments and the possible significance of the Laurentian dedication, see: Blair-Dixon K. 'Damasus and the fiction of unity: the urban shrines of Saint Laurence', in *Ecclesiae Urbis* (2002) 331-52.

[3] ICUR 2. 135 n. 7, 151 n. 23; LP 1. 212.

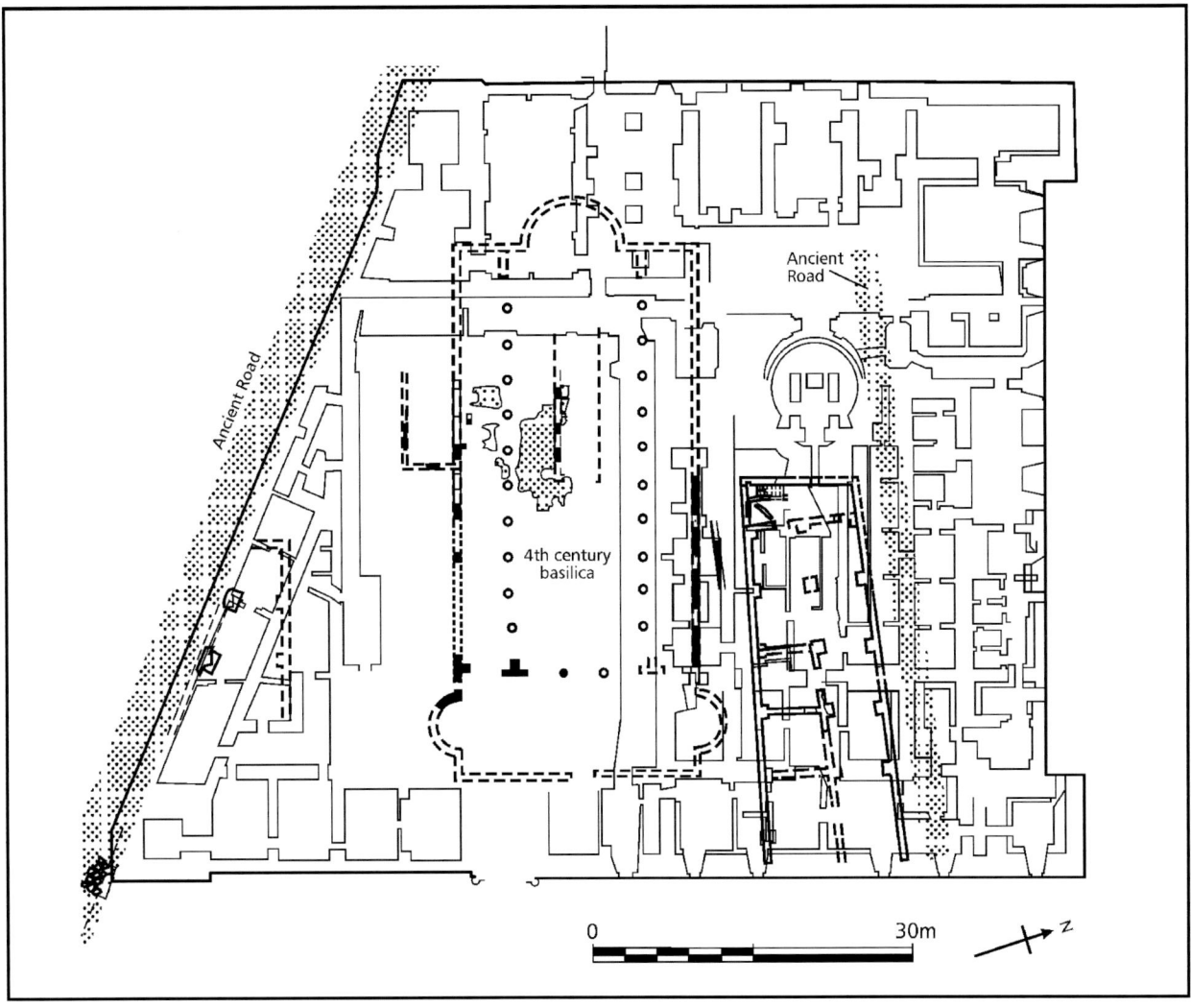

FIGURE 38: RECONSTRUCTED PLAN OF THE 4TH CENTURY S. LORENZO IN DAMASO WITH SURROUNDING STRUCTURES AND ROADS. DRAWN BY ABBY GEORGE FROM A BASE ILLUSTRATION BY G. SCHINGO, IN FROMMEL C. L. AND PENTIRICCI M. EDD. *L'ANTICA BASILICA DI SAN LORENZO IN DAMASO: INDAGINI ARCHEOLOGICHE NEL PALAZZO DELLA CANCELLERIA (1988-1993)*, 2 VOLS. (ROME 2009) 270, FIG. 4.

confirmed as such by finds of coins and ceramics within the structure. The basilica was completely destroyed in the late 15th century when the Palazzo della Cancelleria was built and a new church was constructed just to the north.[4]

Remains of what might be a small subterranean mithraeum were discovered just to the south of the 'stable' building, so beneath the area just by the entrance to the Damasian basilica. (see fig. 39) A cylindrical altar with a mithraic dedication and another inscription dedicated by the same priest, reused in the basilica, came to light here, as well as a niche for a possible tauroctony relief. The *speleum* seems to have had a brief life, however, it being out of use by the second half of the 3rd century, so any connection to later Christian activity can be said to be purely coincidental. However, the records of the excavation and the context of the finds are questionable, so we cannot be certain as to its date or structure.[5]

More importantly for us is the existence of stables beneath the Damasian basilica. As has already been noted by

---

[4] For the lastest synthesis and discussion of the excavations see: Frommel C. L. and Pentiricci M. edd. *L'antica basilica di San Lorenzo in Damaso: indagini archeologiche nel Palazzo della Cancelleria (1988-1993)*, vol. 1: *Gli scavi* (2009) passim (but esp. p.233 for diagnostic finds within basilica context and see vol. 2). Construction assigned to Damasus and gifts to it: LP 1.212-13. Presbyters of foundation at synods of 499 and 595: MGH.AA.12.411; MGH.Ep. 1.367. The statement by Blair-Dixon (via Federico?) Guidobaldi) that there is no evidence for stables here, is therefore misleading (Blair-Dixon K. 'Damasus and the fiction of unity', in *Ecclesiae Urbis* (2000) 338-40 (331-52)) whatever one's interpretation of those remains might be. For the idea of a medieval road to the north of the paleochristian building see Prandi A. 'Il luogo dell'antica basilica di San Lorenzo in Damaso e l'Itinerario Einsiedeln', in *Archivio della Società Romana* 74 (1951) 161-67 esp.166-67. The contemporary construction, or extensive reconstruction, of a porticoed road just to the south of the church (the Porticus Maximae), that ran to the pons Aelius, can only have helped the notoriety of Damasus' new foundation: CIL 6.1184; Platner S. B. and Ashby T. *Dictionary* (1929) 423-24 with references.

[5] Pentiricci M. 'Lo scavo periodi 1-7', in *L'antica basilica di San Lorenzo in Damaso* (2009) 1.171-74, with Nogara B. and Magi E. F. 'Un Mitreo nell'area del Palazzo della Cancelleria Apostolica', in *Hommages à Joseph Bidez et à Franz Cumont* (1949) 229-44.

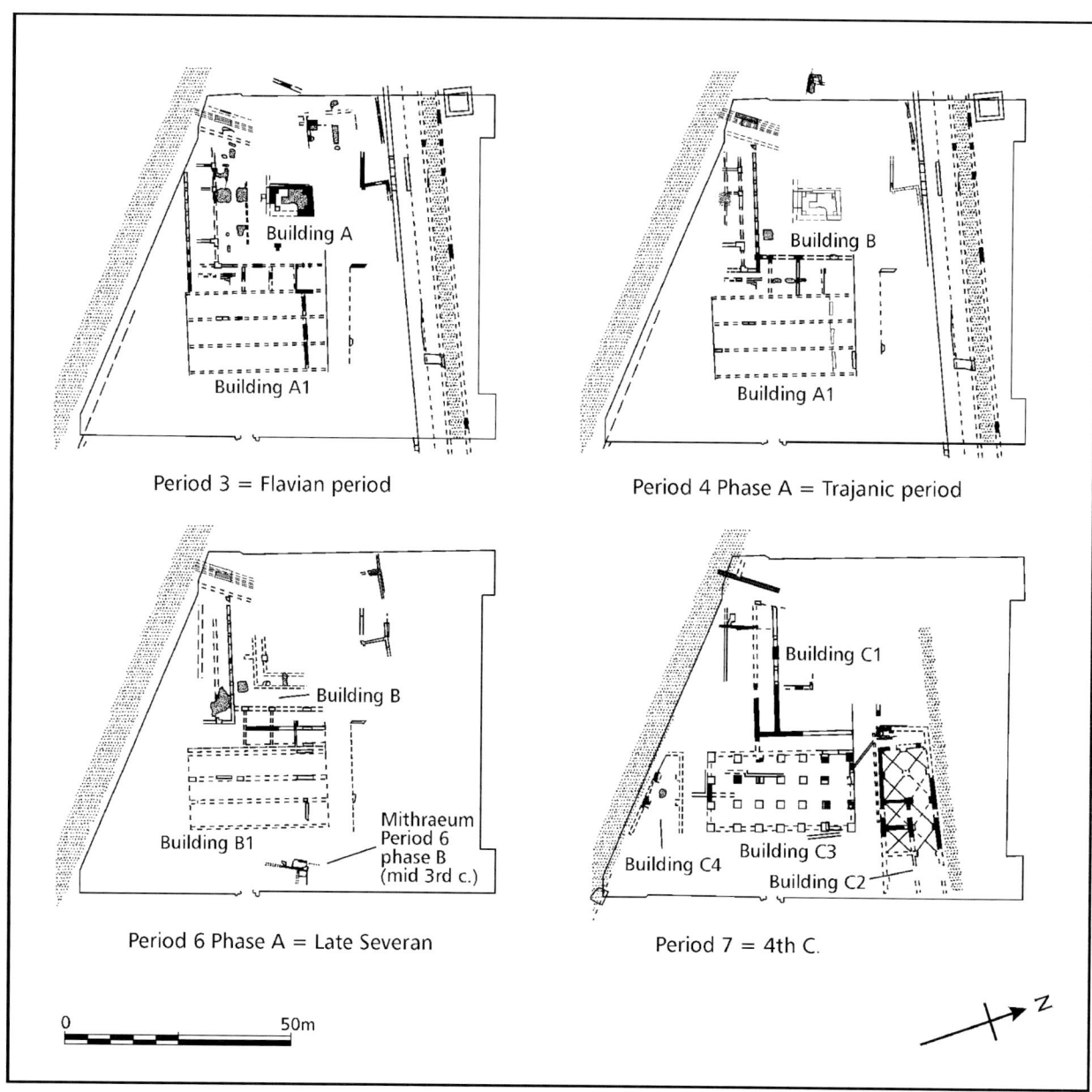

FIGURE 39: PLANS OF THE DIFFERENT PHASES OF THE ANCIENT STRUCTURES ON THE SITE OF S. LORENZO IN DAMASO. DRAWN BY ABBY GEORGE FROM BASE PLANS BY G. SCHINGO, IN FROMMEL C. L. AND PENTIRICCI M. EDD. *L'ANTICA BASILICA DI SAN LORENZO IN DAMASO: INDAGINI ARCHEOLOGICHE NEL PALAZZO DELLA CANCELLERIA (1988-1993)*, 2 VOLS. (ROME 2009) 171, FIG. 92 AND 207, FIG. 4.

Pentiricci recently, the archaeological and written evidence both point to a connection between Damasus, the political use of the charioteers in the circus, and this foundation.[6] The epigraphic evidence also plays into this, and also supports the idea that the stables of the green circus faction lie below the 4th century Christian basilica.

An inscription read in this basilica in the early middle ages makes it clear that the building was also known as *in prasino*, and an inscription preserved in the 16th century Palazzo della Cancelleria describes a *M. Aurelius Liber* who is an *agitator factionis Prasinae*, and which seems to have been found during the construction of the palace at that time.[7] The 4th century Regionary Catalogues also confirm the stables' presence in this region of the city.[8] Furthermore, Ligorio in the 16th century describes the site of the palace as that of the headquarters of the circus factions, but his descriptions of finds must be treated with caution.[9] The flooring patterns seen in the pre-Damasian

---

[6] Pentiricci M. 'Damaso, protagonista dello scenario politico dell'Urbe della seconda metà del IV secolo', in *L'antica basilica di San Lorenzo in Damaso* (2009) 1.291-312.

[7] ICUR 2. 134 n.5; CIL 6.10058=ILS 5296.

[8] *Not. Rom.* VIIII: Nordh ed. *Libellus* (1949) 86.14.

[9] See Pentiricci M. 'Il settore occidentale del campo marzio tra l'età antica e l'altomedioevo', in *L'antica basilica di San Lorenzo in Damaso* (2009) 1.52-53

structure under his basilica has also been linked to the circus factions.[10]

Despite numerous alterations through the centuries, the building labelled A1 and C3 by the archaeologists, can be compared with known stable buildings elsewhere in the empire and it is apparent that this building had the same function from the mid 1st century A.D. to the mid 4th. (see fig.39) In its final phase it consisted of a rectangular space divided by a series of travertine pillars. The buildings to the north and south of it may have been shops (C2 and C4). The colonnaded portico to the west of C3, building C1, may have been part of a private residence.[11] This could have been the property of Damasus' family judging by the inscription read on the outside of the Damasian basilica in the early medieval period, which suggests that either Damasus or his father had become a priest here, and Damasus was either 'parish priest' at the basilica or was living there before he became bishop.[12] This suggests that there was already some sort of Christian structure in place before Damasus' pontificate, perhaps just a hall or converted house, in this proximity to the stables. In this way, the colonnaded portico (C1) just west of the stables may relate to this house or pre-existing family structure, with this being incorporated into the new purpose-built basilica for Christian worship, and the stables of the Green faction being demolished for the purpose.

The written evidence seems to point to another more practical relationship between Damasus and the circus charioteers. This can be found in a petition concerning the dispute surrounding the election of the pope in 366, between Damasus and his rival Ursinus. It is clearly pro-Ursinian in its description of Damasus, but at the same time we cannot dismiss all that is says, in spite of some undoubted exaggeration on the part of the authors. It reports that Damasus, *cum perfidis*, employed men from the arena, chariot racers, as well as workmen, all armed with swords and clubs, to take the basilica that Ursinus and his supporters held in Rome.[13] This need not be untrue; indeed it is likely that Ursinus employed similar people, somewhat of a Roman tradition in times of conflict in the city. What is more important from our point of view is the possible link between Damasus and those chariot racers. It shows that he relied heavily on these people during the time of his disputed election, and had them to thank in effect for his eventual acceptance and official approval as bishop of Rome. Perhaps he and his aristocratic family partly owned the faction? Because of this controversial rise to power he also needed to gain the goodwill and approval of the Christians of the city. We can see both motivations behind this foundation.[14]

As K. Blair-Dixon has argued, to dedicate this basilica to Saint Lawrence is an attempt to unify the fractious Christian population of the city behind a popular martyr,[15] but also its location in the city shows he and his family had an association with the Green faction charioteers, the basilica being built over their stables, which they owned or acquired next to their family property. Perhaps this was a sign to the city's population that now he and his family had turned their back on this group, and any violent association with them, by demolishing their stables and building on top of it a new, unifying, purpose-built Christian place of worship? This construction, demolishing the main part of an important building for the city, would have required special permission, by the Urban Prefect perhaps, as noted by Pentiricci.[16]

Such a move cannot have been anything other than symbolic, highly ambitious, as well as controversial: the Greens were the main circus faction, and a favourite of many emperors.[17] This link between Damasus and the charioteers is all in spite of the apparently orthodox Christian view of the Circus games as problematic, but does chime with the occasionally violent nature of Roman politics, something also reflected in earlier disputed papal elections.[18]

5.1.2 Titulus Anastasiae

A foundation not described in the context of Damasus and the circus factions is his likely construction of the basilica of S. Anastasia. This structure is situated at the foot of the south-west corner of the Palatine hill, less than 40m from the Circus Maximus. (fig.40) There has been some doubt as to whether Damasus did found this basilica, as a 5th century inscription by Pope Hilarius (461-67)—which was read in the basilica in the 9th century, and is now lost—only says he decorated the apse, and there is no mention of the foundation in Damasus' *vita* in the LP.[19] It is, however, very likely to be his foundation due to his role in the decoration, likely to be the first, combined with the remains of a 4th century apse and altar that have been found under the current church, and other late antique

---

[10] Krautheimer R. 'Die Kirche San Lorenzo in Damaso in Rom. Vorläufiger Grabungsbericht', in *Akten des XII. Internationalen Kongresses für Christliche Archäologie* (1995) 958-63.
[11] Frommel C. L. and Pentiricci M. edd. *L'antica basilica di San Lorenzo in Damaso*, vol. 1: *Gli scavi* (2009) passim.
[12] ICUR 2. 135, n.7 and see above.
[13] *Coll. Avell.* (ed Guenther) 1.7.
[14] The church's proximity to the Theatre of Pompey, and the 'Greens' becoming a theatrical group as well, may provide another, albeit more tenous, association with Damasus' foundation. However, the evidence for this development of the circus factions only begins in the mid 5th century, and comes from the East: Roueché C. *Performers and Partisans at Aphrodisias in the Roman and Late Roman Periods* (1993) 45.
[15] Blair-Dixon K. 'Damasus and the fiction of unity' (2000) 331-52. This unifying policy is argued to have been the motive behind Damasus' famous martyr epigrams: Sághy M. 'Scinditur in partes populus: Pope Damasus and the martyrs of Rome', *Early Medieval Europe* 9.3 (2000) 273–87.
[16] Pentiricci M. 'Damaso, protagonista dello scenario politico dell'Urbe della seconda metà del IV secolo', in *L'antica basilica di San Lorenzo in Damaso* (2009) 1.311-12 (291-312).
[17] Suet. *Calig.* 55.
[18] Notably between Liberius and Felix: for a summary of Christian views on the games and the violence surrounding several disputed elections to the Roman bishopric, and late Roman urban violence in general, see: Pentiricci M. 'Damaso, protagonista', in *L'antica basilica di San Lorenzo in Damaso* (2009) 300-309 and for its topographical dimension see Curran J. R. *Pagan City and Christian Capital* (2000) 137-42.
[19] ICUR 2. 24, n.25 and 150, n.18; ILCV 1.1782.

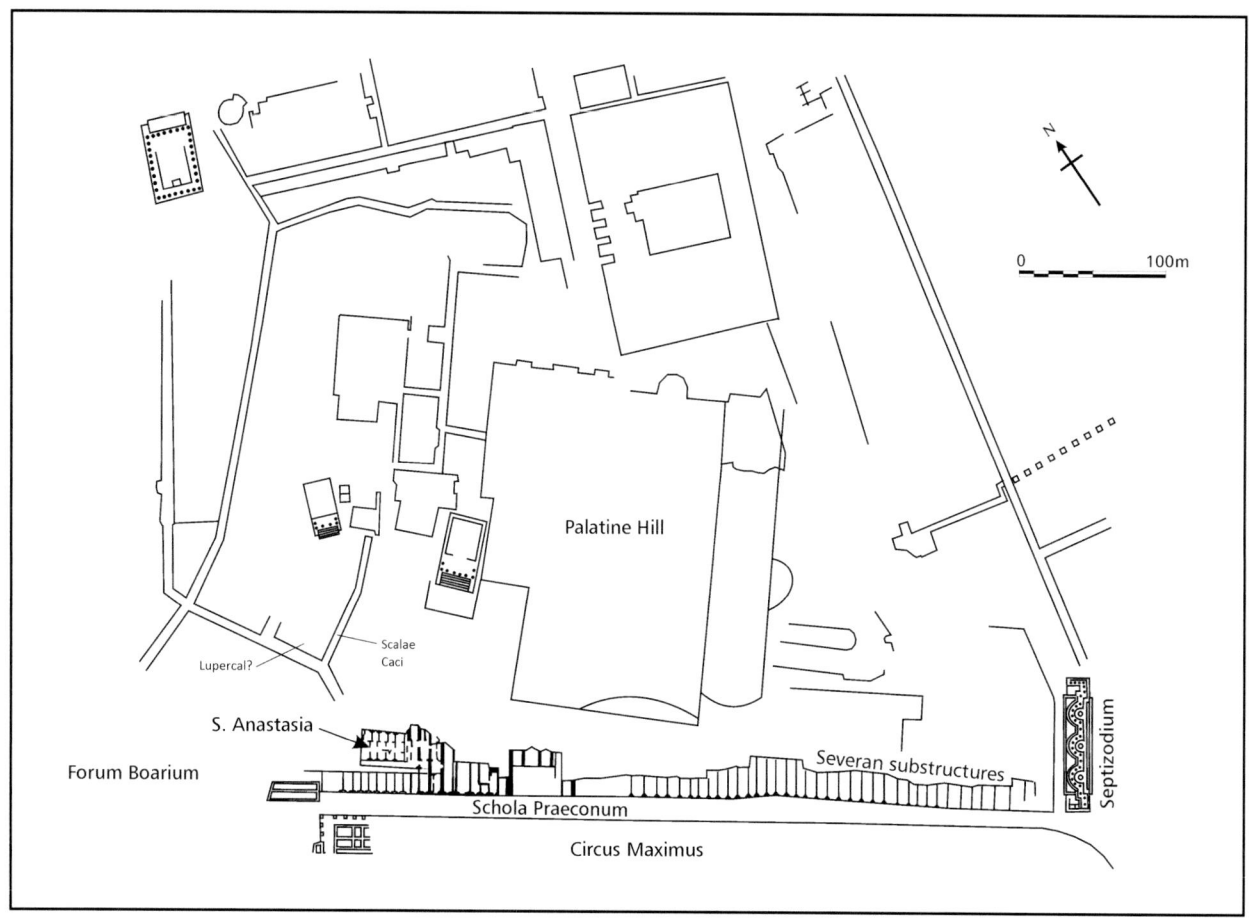

FIGURE 40: OUTLINE PLAN OF CAPITOLINE HILL SHOWING S. ANASTASIA AND SURROUNDING STRUCTURES. DRAWN BY ABBY GEORGE FROM BASE PLAN IN COARELLI F. *GUIDA ARCHEOLOGICA DI ROMA* (MILAN 1974) 136.

decorative features reused in the existing church.[20] Also, S. Anastasia is not mentioned in any other 4th century life in the LP, or indeed within Hilarius'.

Archaeology points to a mid 4th century basilica being built on Antonine and Severan substructures. The basilica itself was built into an *insula*, which formerly contained a shop/apartment complex. It was built on top of, and perpendicular to, the ground floor rooms of the *insula* and was bounded by two narrow Roman streets, one to its north and the other to the south. These determined the basilica's axis and closed it in from the Palatine buildings above and the road by the Circus respectively. (fig.41) There is no evidence to suggest that this site was already a place in which Christians congregated. More recent analysis has shown that the 4th century apse—of a different phase to the rest of the surviving basilica, which is from the time of Theodoric—was built into the first floor of the imperial balcony structure that overlooked the circus.[21] (fig. 41) A baptistery may have been added by the prefect Longinianus in the early 5th century, although the inscription could refer to the example at S. Pietro in Vaticano.[22]

Building on the first floor of an *insula*, perhaps across the rooms rather than creating a naved building within one space, meant the pre-existing Roman structure must have been largely out of use, was extensively modified or partly destroyed by the Christian builders in order to use this site. It also used and denuded imperial property in its construction. This is more suggestive of a deliberately acquired site, than a donated one. Curran stresses the *titulus*' proximity to the pagan temples and imperial palaces of the Palatine, but its closeness to the Circus is

---

[20] See the following footnote. For the theory that the church existed in AD 351 see: Matthews J. F. 'The poetess Proba and fourth-century Rome', in *Institutions, société et vie politique dans l'Empire romain au IVe siècle ap. J-C*, edd. M. Cristol, Y. Duval, C. Lepelley and L. Piétri (1992) 299-303.
[21] Whitehead P. B. 'The church of S. Anastasia in Rome', *AJA* 31.4 (1927) 405-20 (with the theory, to explain the location of the church, that it was the palace church, named after Constantine's half sister (pp.413-

14). But why build a palace church outside the palace?); Montini R. U. *S. Anastasia* (1958); CBCR 1.47-61; LTUR 1.37-38; Carandini A. with Bruno D. *La casa di Augusto dai Lupercalia al Natale* (2008) 259-60, 262-63; Cerrito A. 'Contributo allo studio del *titulus Anastasiae*', in *Marmoribus vestita* (2011) 345-54, 366-71. The church may have been partially founded by the Anici family: Lizzi Testa R. *Senatori, popolo, papi* (2004) 116-17. The church was once thought to be completely independent of the circus: Platner S. B. and Ashby T. *Dictionary* (1929) 118. The church may also have had a funerary role, but probably only from about the 6th century, as well as an early chapel to St. Christopher: Cerrito A. 'Note a margine di un precedente contributo per lo studio della basilica di S. Anastasia al Palatino (Roma): approfondimenti e nuove osservazioni', *RACrist* 87-88 (2011-12) 328-43 (317-56).
[22] ICUR 2.150 n.19. Whitehead P. B. 'The church of S. Anastasia' (1927) 412-13; CBCR 1.43-48; LTUR 1.38.

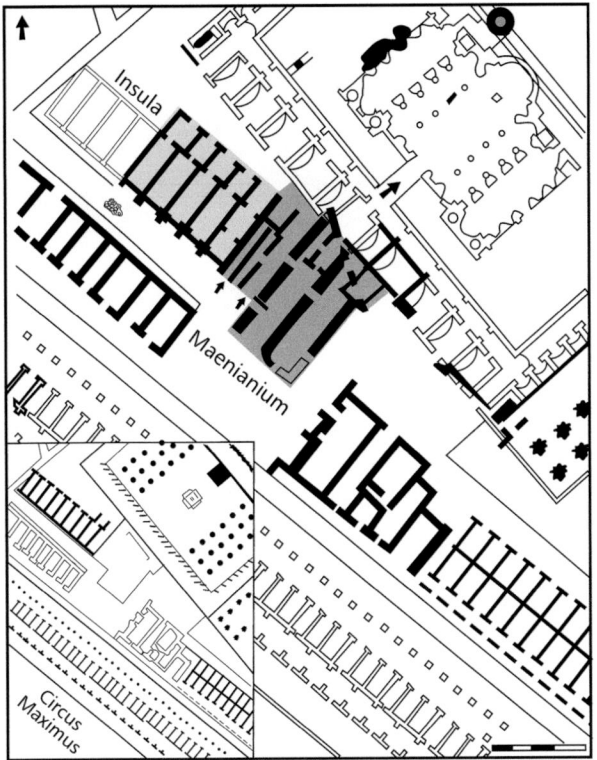 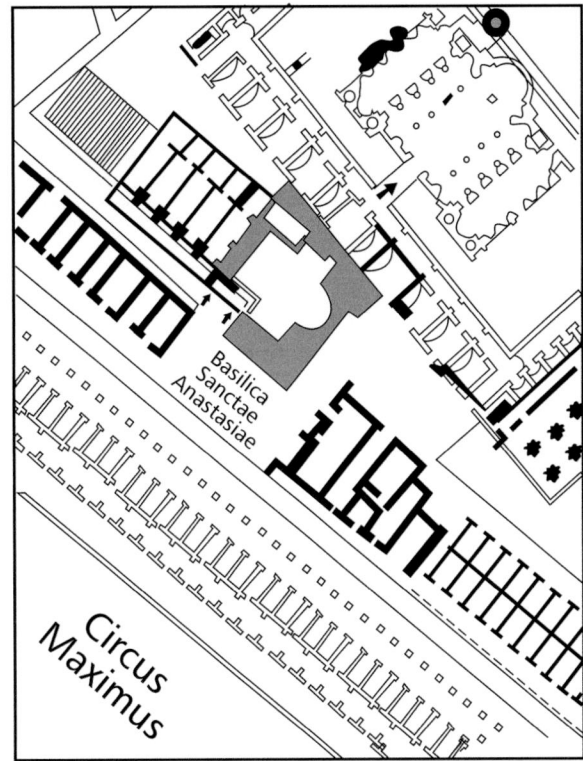

FIGURE 41: PLAN OF S. ANASTASIA WITH PRECEDING PHASES AND IMMEDIATELY SURROUNDING SUBSTRUCTURES. DRAWN BY ABBY GEORGE FROM BASE PLANS IN CERRITO A. 'CONTRIBUTO ALLO STUDIO DEL *TITULUS ANASTASIAE*', IN *MARMORIBUS VESTITA: MISCELLANEA IN ONORE DI FEDERICO GUIDOBALDI*, EDD. O. BRANDT AND P. PERGOLA (VATICAN CITY 2011) 358, A AND B.

equally or more significant.[23] Such an unusual, awkward, location for a Christian place of worship, in a largely non-residential area, seems likely to be a statement of some sort. Damasus' reliance on charioteers from his election dispute may be a clue to its placement, as a Christian basilica being squeezed between two streets, requiring the partial demolition of an *insula* perhaps, less than 40 metres from the Circus Maximus and built into the imperial balcony that overlooked it, does imply a will to find a spot in such proximity. Was this to acknowledge the support of the Greens, or to provide a power base for himself near to where they plied their trade?

The basilica may also have been an opportunity for the ecclesiastical authorities to link themselves physically with such popular entertainment, and be associated with it, or at least be in a position to influence it. Indeed, the *titulus* may have been deliberately placed here to provide somewhere for the charioteers to give thanks to the Christian God after a victory, as part of the Christianisation of the games the emperors were now keen to promote.[24] The fact that it has three presbyters in 499 indicates the foundation's importance.[25] All these other theories that have been proposed to explain this early foundation's location, have,

however, overlooked this Damasian connection with the charioteers.

5.1.3 Conclusion

We can see, therefore, that the Damasian foundations of the *titulus Damasi*, built over the Green Faction stables, and the *titulus Anastasiae*, built next to the Circus Maximus, could be connected. Damasus may be acknowledging the role played by charioteers in his election as bishop, by attempting to Christianise them and the races. This is also a bishop desperate to unify the Roman Christian community, and to increase his own popularity by associating himself with the circus games.

5.2 Christian Basilicas and Important Cultic Sites

There are two early Christian basilicas in Rome that seem to have had some sort of relationship with a pagan centre. Both of them were very close to major cult sites in the city, and as such a spatial, and possibly visual, link can be argued. There is no reason to think this was an aggressive move however, but rather indicative of a Roman Christian elite who were not intimidated or keen to avoid important 'pagan' shrines in their building activity. These foundations below indicate a harmonious and integrative religious topography in late antique Rome on a micro level. The old orthodoxy of Christian building sponsors avoiding pagan

---
[23] Curran J. R. *Pagan City* (2000) 142-44. For more on the church and its 'pagan' cultic surroundings, see below.
[24] Cameron Al. *Circus Factions: Blues and Greens at Rome and Byzantium* (1976) 152.
[25] MGH.AA.12.413, 414.

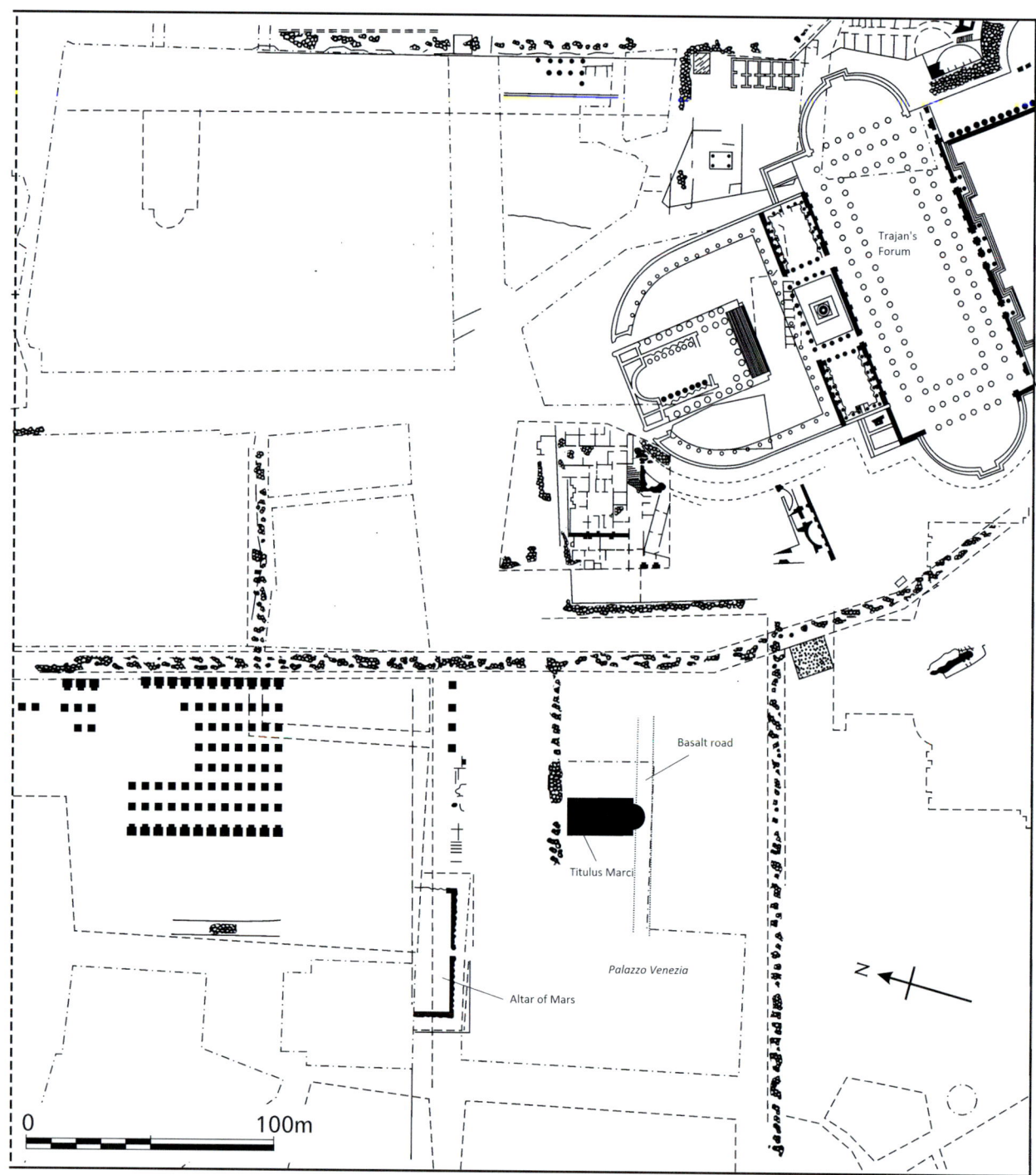

FIGURE 42: PLAN OF AREA OF S. MARCO AND SURROUNDING ARCHAEOLOGY. DRAWN BY ABBY GEORGE, WITH ADDITIONS BY AUTHOR, FROM A BASE PLAN IN GATTI G."SAEPTA IULIA' E 'PORTICUS AEMILIA' NELLA 'FORMA' SEVERIANA', IN *BULLCOM* 62 (1934) 123-49, FIG. 1.

sites in the city needs to be overturned.[26] It is difficult to say whether these two building programs were deliberately placed to be near these pagan cult centres, and so were not, perhaps, examples of 'strategic' building as such, but the clear spatial and potentially visual, relationship between a Christian and pagan cult centre that undoubtedly resulted from these projects, is worth commenting on.

---

[26] The main concern of the Roman Church was just as much heretics and dissenters than 'pagans': Maier H. O. 'The topography of heresy' (1995) 232-49.

5.2.1 Titulus Marci

This foundation has been described above in relation to its apse encroaching onto a road.[27] For our purposes here, what is also important is that the 4th century entrance to the *titulus* faced north towards the Campus Martius, rather than south as previously believed. In the immediate area just to the north of the basilica there is good evidence to think

---

[27] See above chapter 3: Apsidal Road Encroachment.

that there stood the very large and well-known Altar of Mars, and just to the north of this the god's temple. (fig.42) The importance of the altar is clear from its antiquity and its centrality to the military affairs of the Roman state, particularly in the Republic, the campus being originally the Roman army's training ground. The altar certainly existed in 435 B.C., and may even date to the regal period.[28] A passage of Livy points to its existence in the campus near the *porta Fontinalis*, in other words the area just beyond the Republican *pomerium*, that is, the Servian boundary of the city.[29] Such a location was customary for monuments or temples associated with military matters and their gods. The location of a possible temple of Mars connected to the altar and the archaeological evidence can narrow down its location.

These sources point to a site for the altar within the area bounded by the *Divorum* and *Iseum* in the west, the *via Lata* to the east, and the *vicus Pallacinae* and Temple of Hadrian to the south and north respectively.[30] A large south wall, more than sixty metres long, of a square or rectangular structure of imperial date, with evidence of a much older smaller construction beneath it, was found on the Via del Plebiscito in 1925. (fig.42) The monument seems to have had a massive perimeter wall within which were niches, probably for statues, as well as a larger one possibly for sacrifices. The design of the structure implies some sort of procession took place within it, consistent with that carried out before a lustral sacrifice, something that was associated with Mars. The remains of a large elaborately decorated travertine wall, found during the construction of the Pamphili palace further north in the 17th century, may be the remains of the Mars temple *in campo*.[31]

This location for the altar would mean that the distance between its southern wall and the entrance door of Marcus' basilica was about 30 metres. (fig.42) Whether Bishop Marcus intended to build the basilica on this spot for that reason is impossible to say, but he cannot have been unaware of the altars existence, it being so close. The discovery, also in the 1920s excavation, of several richly decorated rooms of 4th or 5th century date not far from what we now know is the entrance of the *titulus*, may also be significant for understanding the spatial relationship between the altar and the Christian centre in this first phase. The altar seems to have still been in use in the mid 4th century as the *Natalis Martis* of the 1st March appears in the Calendar of A.D. 354, and the altar would have been central to the celebrations.[32]

There was a period then when both centres were active, and even when not in use the altar was still an imposing, profoundly pagan, monument bristling with statuary. It was also an historic monument to Rome's proud military history, and as such was certainly a powerful feature of the urban landscape. The association of 'paganism' with Rome's past successes always sat uneasily with many Christians, with many writers dedicating whole works to dispel this view.[33] Was this Marcus' way of confronting such an issue, or was he trying to associate Christianity with that success, with his basilica being a tentative statement of the religion's movement towards being the new guardian of the state? Was this just a coincidental relationship? The prospect of one of the first purpose-built Christian buildings inside the city being so near to such an important pagan shrine was clearly not a concern for Marcus in any case, and nor perhaps for the *titulus'* congregation.

It is examples such as this that require us to rethink our image of pagan and Christian topography and its relationship in late antique Rome. We need to move away from the confrontational or avoidance model, to one where both sorts of cult place sat harmoniously in the urban landscape, often in very close proximity to each other. Certainly, bishops or Christian aristocrats had no issues with building next to or near pagan spaces, whether or not an underlying agenda lay behind such moves. Whether some pagans objected to such foundations we cannot say. Whatever the case, the altar and Marcus' *titulus*, significantly one of the first formal Christian centres inside the city, were visually and mentally linked in the minds of passers-by. Christians from the north attending services would have to walk past it, and it may even have been visible from the basilica doors. Whether such a relationship was intended or not, for the worshippers at the basilica in its early life and for local residents, some sort of association existed.

Our second example of a spatial link between a Christian and pagan space in Rome reinforces the picture of a non-segregated and integrated religious topography between pagans and Christians. In this case, a foundation we have already encountered, it is one where a pagan procession route, as well as its focus, had an association with an early Christian basilica.

5.2.2 Titulus Anastasiae

We have just discussed this *titulus* in relation to its proximity to the circus, but, coincidentally, it also lay on the procession route of a notably popular and persistent pagan festival, the *Lupercalia*, and was also near the Lupercal shrine itself.[34] Both the Circus and the Palatine were full of pagan temples and shrines, the closest to the basilica was

---

[28] The altar was associated with the census, and the Villa Publica (the censor's office) was built in 435 BC: Livy, 4.22.7 and 40.45.8. It may be older: Festus, 204 L.
[29] Livy, 35.10.12.
[30] Livy, 56.24.3; Dio Cass. 56.24.3; Ov. *Fast*. 2.859-60; LTUR 3.223-25. For an alternative location for the altar further north on the campus, see Welin E. 'Ara Martis in campo. Zur Frage der Bedeutung und des Umfanges des Campus Martius', *OpRom* 1 (1954) 166-90.
[31] Mancini G. 'Roma', *NSc* (1925) 239-42 (225-43); LTUR 3.225.
[32] 1920s excavation: Mancini G. 'Roma', *NSc* (1925) 243 (225-43). Calendar of 354: Degrassi A. ed. *Fasti anni numani et iuliani: accedunt ferialia, menologia rustica, parapegmata* (Inscriptiones Italiae 13.2)

(1963) 242-43. The day has disappeared less than a century later though: Calendar of Polemius Silvius: Degrassi A. ed. *Fasti* (1963) 266.
[33] Eg. August. *De civ. D.* and Orosius' *Historiarum adversus paganos libri VII*.
[34] Features that have long been noted: Cecchelli C. 'Una nuova ipotesi sul sito del 'Lupercal' (S. Anastasia in Palatio e il Lupercale)', *Roma* 21 (1943) 313-17.

the Lupercal however, its most likely location being the area of a steeply stepped street, the *scalae caci*, about 100 metres from the *titulus*.[35] (see fig.40) The precise location of the shrine or the form it took is unknown. The fact that it may have simply been the embellishment of a natural cave feature—representing the place where Faustulus discovered Romulus and Remus being suckled by the she-wolf—is the likely reason for the lack of remains. Christian destruction should not be ruled out either.

We know that this shrine and its associated festival, the *Lupercalia*, were still active in the late 5th century, at least a hundred years after the foundation of S. Anastasia. Pope Gelasius' letter, the *Contra Lupercalia*, written in 494, shows both the particular persistence of this festival and its long-standing popularity, which clearly exercised the Christian authorities in the city.[36] The festival took place on the 15th February, and involved the sacrifice of a goat and a dog at the Lupercal. This was followed by a group of young men of high social class dressed only in goat skins running around the base of the Palatine—or between the Lupercal and the *via Sacra*, or perhaps all over the Palatine with no specific route—whipping people with branches or goat skin thongs. Another route may have consisted of only a part of the Palatine and a procession up and down the *via Sacra* from Caesar's time, but none of these routes could have avoided the Christian basilica.

Late Republican and early imperial sources are unclear as to the festival's religious meaning and significance; was it a fertility or purification rite? Certainly by Gelasius' time in the late 5th century A.D. such obscurity can only have been amplified. As such, modern scholars still find the Lupercalia a puzzle. Some believe the rite to be magical, religious, associated with kingship, connected to the dead, fertility or to the early agricultural life of Rome.[37] Whatever the case, on the 15th February at least, there would have been some spatial interaction between S. Anastasia and the Lupercal, with its associated procession, although any tension seems to have been only felt amongst the Christian authorities, as Gelasius' letter implies popular Christian participation.

Other descriptions of traditional processions going past Christian basilicas show a similar dichotomy between Christian congregation and clergy, and can give us a clearer idea as to the likely situation on the Palatine. In the East, in Antioch in the mid 4th c. (although the source is probably 6th century) an exotic dancer and her entourage annoy the clerics of a Christian basilica outside which she passes, but excited all the people around them.[38] At Caesarea in Cappadocia in the 4th century, a group of drunken women taking part in a Dionysiac festival offended a group of Christian men, outside a Christian basilica, by their lewdness.[39] This seems to be a dislike for female drunkenness, rather than a wider disagreement with the festival in general though. Elsewhere in the West, at Arles at the end of the 5th century, a bishop is offended by lewd behaviour within a Kalends festival going past a Christian basilica in the city, but there is no sense of general Christian disapproval. Indeed, participation by Christians is described.[40] In Calama in Numidia in 408, there is, however, obvious pagan and Christian tension surrounding that town's continued observance of the Kalends festival in June. The festival halted outside a Christian basilica and its participants proceeded to 'mockingly' dance in front of it, which led to the clergy complaining. Interestingly the civil authorities would not act and a riot ensued with the burning of the basilica.[41] We get the sense, though, that this was a deliberately provocative gesture by a group of hardline 'pagans', rather than the usual activity of a popular civic festival. Indeed, such an incident is very unlikely to have occurred in Rome, where more tension was felt between Christian groups it seems. The scenarios at Antioch and Arles present the likely model for the situation around S. Anastasia during the *Lupercalia*.

In Rome, many of the Christian, as well as many of the pagan participants by this period, probably saw the *Lupercalia* festival as simply an archaic rite that signified Roman identity and history more than a religious ceremony.[42] However, there was certainly an association between the festival and the Christian basilica on the 15th February, and with the Lupercal shrine on the other days of the year simply because of the short distance between the two. S. Anastasia was the most central Christian building in Rome until the 6th century, so its mere presence is symbolic in any case. Any association, whether planned or not, with one of, if not the most persistent pagan festival and its shrine may not be a coincidence. Perhaps the existence of an important Christian centre here made the festival and its shrine acceptable and contributed to its longevity? Was Damasus, by constructing the basilica on this particular spot by the circus also hoping to counter

---

[35] The various shrines within and around the Circus were separated from the church by the Circus' outer wall, so visually and spatially the two buildings were entirely separate. Those shrines just outside the Circus, like the Temple of Flora and *Sol et Luna*, were on its Aventine side. Location of Lupercal: LTUR 3.198-99 with refs. Both the *Lupercal* and the 'House of Romulus' appear in the 4th century lists of the contents of Rome: *Not. Rom.* X: Nordh ed. *Libellus* (1949) 89.9, 90.7. The recent (January 2007) discovery of a richly decorated cave vault under the *Domus Augusti* is more likely to be a private nymphaeum than the *Lupercal* cave.
[36] Pornarès G. ed. and transl. *Lettre contre les Lupercales et dix-huit messes du Sacramentaire léonien* (1959) 162-89. For the idea that the letter was in fact written by Felix III, Gelasius predecessor, see Duval Y-M. 'Des lupercales de Constantinople aux lupercales de Rome', *REL* 55 (1977) 246-50; *Coll. Avell.* (ed. Guenther) 101; festival recorded in the Calendar of Polemius Silvius (AD 448-49): Degrassi A. ed. *Fasti* (1963) 265.
[37] Varro, *Ling.* 6.13.34; Plut. *Vit. Rom.* 21.3-8, *Vit. Caes.* 61.3-4; August. *De civ. D.* 18.12; Scullard H. H. *Festivals and Ceremonies of the Roman Republic* (1981) 76-78 and refs; Harmon D. P. 'The public festivals of Rome', *ANRW* 2.16.2 (1978) 1441-46 (1440-68); Wiseman T. P. *Remus. A Roman Myth* (1995) 82, 85-88.
[38] *Life of St. Pelagia the Harlot*, 4-5: Petitmengin P. *Pélagie la Pénitente. Métamorphoses d'une légende*, vol 1: *Les textes et leur histoire* (1981). The legend survives in several versions.
[39] Basil, *Homilia in Ebriosos*, 1 (Homily 14 in Migne, *PG* 31.445-46).
[40] Caesarius, *Serm.* 192 and 193.
[41] August. *Ep.* 91.8. I thank Luke Lavan for this and the previous three references.
[42] The original route may have been associated with the foundation of the city: see Rykwert J. *The Idea of a Town: the Anthropology of Urban Form in Rome, Italy and the Ancient World* (1976) 93-96.

this popular festival and the shrine's importance, which backfired, or perhaps trying to use that potency for the Church's own ends?[43] Was this foundation's location by the Lupercal also perhaps to link Christianity with one of the foundation myths of the city, in the same way as various bishops, especially Damasus, had tried to do with Peter and Paul as the new founders of a Christian Rome?

As we have seen, there is a compelling political reason why Damasus would want a foundation during his episcopate to be near the Circus, so any connection S. Anastasia had with the Lupercal and its festival could well have been coincidental and incidental. Yet Damasus, ever the man for an opportunity and a statement, may have also sought to confront or associate the Church with a popular and highly symbolic festival. In any case, a visual association is likely to have existed between the *titulus* of Anastasia and the Lupercal shrine throughout the year, and certainly spatially with the festival procession itself on the 15th February.[44]

5.3 Centres of Congregation

5.3.1 Sacellum Sanctae Agnetis Agonis/S. Agnese in Agone

This Christian structure, more accurately described as an oratory before the 17th century reconstruction, is located on the western side of the Piazza Navona, the ancient Stadium of Domitian. We first hear of it within two of the late 8th/early 9th century itineraries of the city for pilgrims as *Circus flamineus ibi sca. Agnes*. This becomes *sanctae Agneti Agonis, de cripta Agonis* or *de Agone* by the 12th, 13th and 14th centuries, respectively.[45] As such, its creation may date just beyond the chronological scope of this book, but is worth mentioning as a good example of a strategic foundation in the early medieval period. These, as we have seen in projects of the same period above, often pragmatically reused abandoned prestige Roman buildings.

The current baroque church greatly altered the earlier oratory's structure, although it is still accessible from the church today. As such, much of the information for its original appearance and structure comes from the 16th century sketches and writings of Ugonio.[46] (fig.43) From these it seems that the oratory consisted of a small narrow hall located between two sets of arches of decreasing size. These may therefore have supported the seats of the Stadium of Domitian. So the chapel was effectively

FIGURE 43: DETAIL OF SKETCH OF P. UGONIO OF S. AGNESE IN AGONE (BARB. LAT. 1994, P.362). SCANNED FROM A REPRODUCTION IN DE GREGORI L. *PIAZZA NAVONA PRIMA D'INNOCENZO X* (ROME 1926) 24.

created beneath them. Several altars also seem to have existed within the space.[47]

By tradition, it is held that this oratory was built on the site of the martyr Agnes' martyrdom, thus explaining its location in such an unusual place within the former stadium. Yet this tradition does not hold up to scrutiny, and a more pragmatic purpose behind its location is more likely.

Within all the versions of the *passio* of St. Agnes, it is interesting to note that no mention of the Stadium is made. Only a reference to a theatre is brought up during the story of Agnes' martyrdom in the 6th century, and Prudentius writing a hundred years or so earlier describes her being beheaded outside a brothel in the corner of a square (*in plateae*), or more likely a street.[48] Ambrose, writing in 377, only describes Agnes' youth and the fact that she was beheaded, and Damasus (366-84) similarly makes no mention of any place of martyrdom, only her youth once more and that she was burnt instead.[49] From this it seems apparent that the belief that Agnes was martyred in the Stadium of Domitian was a later one, and had more to do

---

[43] Also, the adjacent Circus Maximus itself was effectively dedicated to the equally popular cult of Sol: Tert. *De spect.* 8.1; Quinn Schofield W. 'Sol in the Circus Maximus', in *Hommages à Marcel Renard*, ed. J. Bibauw (1969) 639-49.
[44] See also Mulryan M. 'The Temple of Flora or Venus' (2011) 215-22.
[45] Einsiedeln Itinerary (8th/9th century): Val. Zucc. 2.180, 195; Mirabilia (12th-14th century): Val. Zucc. 3.255, 286, 299. Hülsen C. *Le chiese di Roma* (1927) 168.
[46] De Gregori L. *Piazza Navona prima d'Innocenzo X* (1926); Armellini M. (and Cecchelli C. ed.) *Le chiese di Roma* (new edn. 1942) 470.

[47] CBCR 1.39; Sciubba S. and Sabatini L. *Sant'Agnese in Agone* (1962) 5-24; LTUR 1. 27-28. A recent analysis of Ugonio's sketch and writings, alongside later plans of the medieval structures, has given us a more detailed idea of the contents, layout and external appearance of the building, and suggests that the medieval cult centre was larger than Ugonio suggests: Guidobaldi F. 'La chiesa medievale di S. Agnese in Agone', *RACrist* 87-88 (2011-12) 401-52.
[48] *AA.SS.* Ian. II. 353 (for this being early 6th century see: Lanéry C. *Ambroise de Milan hagiographe* (2008) 359-61); Prudent. *Perist.* 14.38-90. For *platea* meaning a street see: Spanu M. 'Considerazioni sulle plateae di Antiochia', in *Actes du Ier congrès international sur Antioche de Pisidie*, edd. T. Drew-Bear, M. Taşlıalan and C. M. Thomas (2002) 351 n.20 (349–58). But *platea* meaning forum is possible at Thubursicu Numidiarum in the mid 4th c., where there was a *forum novum* and *platea vetus*: CIL 8.4878; Conti S. 'Attività edilizia e restauri nei centri africani durante il regno dell'imperatore Giuliano', *Africa Romana* 15.3 (2004) 1687 (1681-92). I thank Luke Lavan for the references for *platea*.
[49] Amb. *De Virginibus* 1.2; Ferrua A. ed. *Epigrammata Damasiana* (1942) no.37.

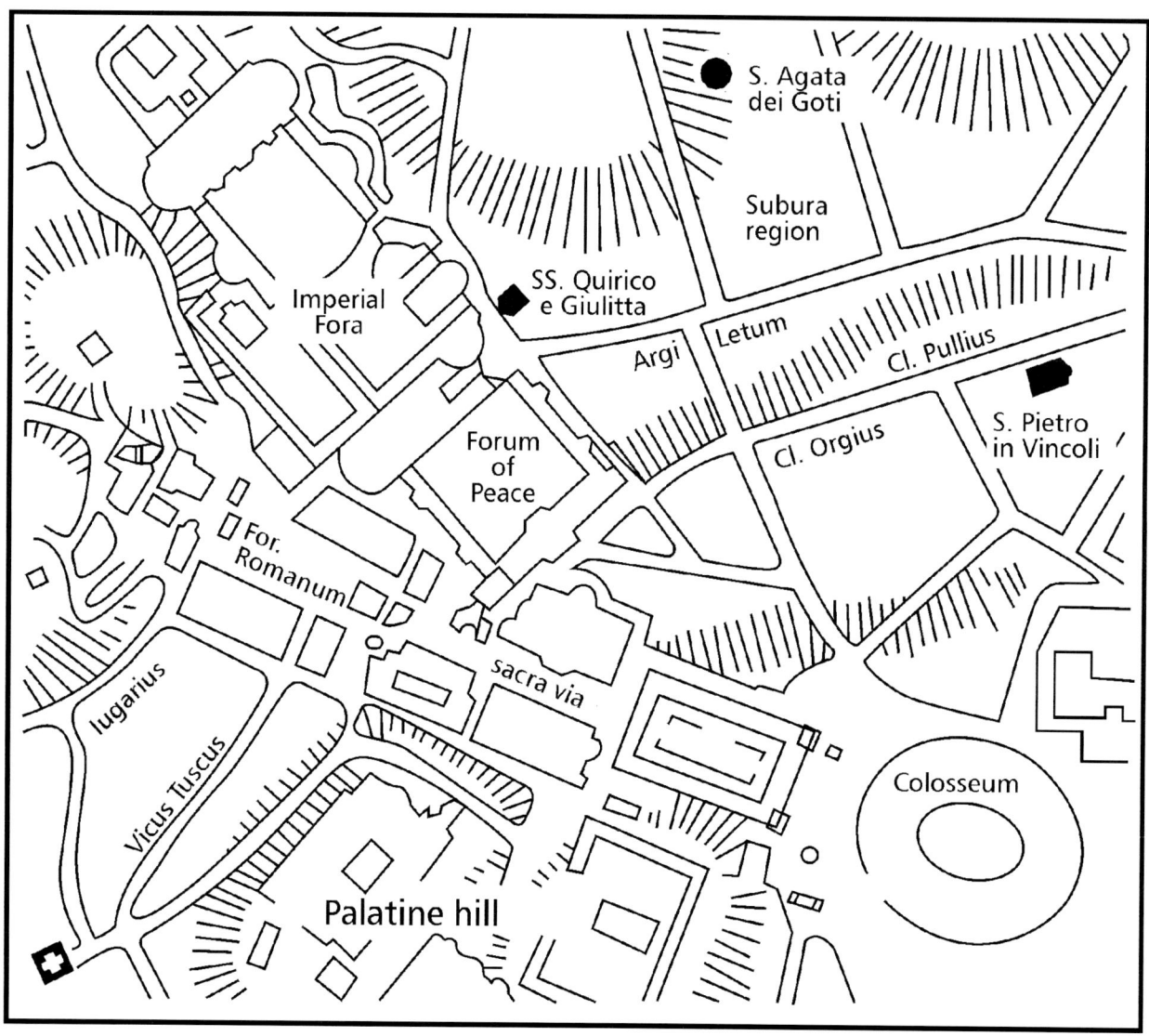

FIGURE 44: OUTLINE PLAN OF CENTRAL ROME SHOWING LOCATION OF SS. QUIRICO E GIULITTA AND SURROUNDING ANCIENT STRUCTURES. DRAWN BY ABBY GEORGE FROM A BASE PLAN IN REEKMANS L. 'L'IMPLANTATION MONUMENTALE CHRÉTIENNE DANS LE PAYSAGE URBAIN DE ROME DE 300 À 850', IN *ACTES DU IXE CONGRÈS INTERNATIONALE D'ARCHÉOLOGIE CHRÉTIENNE* (ROME 1989) 861-915.

with the reputation that place had for brothels than any older tradition. Further, the fact that we have no record of this oratory until the late 8th century, coupled with the lack of any reference to it in the 6th century *passio* of the saint, suggests the oratory's placement here took place somewhere between those two dates.[50]

In other words, the idea of Agnes' martyrdom in the Stadium is a suspiciously late addition to the martyrological landscape of Rome. This implies a 'best guess' scenario was used for its location, and that it was an opportunistic and pragmatic intervention that sought to take advantage of the martyr's popularity. Whether any connection to a brothel was a later interpolation in order to 'spice up'

the story we cannot say, however the inconsistencies surrounding her mode of death shows that rumour, and an unreliable oral tradition, played a significant part in its creation, including the place of her death as well no doubt. S. Agnese in Agone, then, seems to be representative of an opportunistic foundation to take advantage of the saint's popularity in the 7th and 8th centuries by building an oratory on a site that, albeit without any basis in tradition, was seen as a likely, or believable, place for Agnes' death.

Its placement within the ruins of the Stadium of Domitian needs to be explained in another way therefore. This was more likely due to this place still being a popular focal point for the people of this part of the city, now the centre of a less populous medieval Rome.[51] It was also not far from

---

[50] Which the only remaining early medieval part of the floor mosaic, dating presumably from the oratory's foundation, seems to confirm. It may date from as early as the 6th century, but is more likely from the 7th-8th century: Guidobaldi F. 'La chiesa medievale' (2011-12) 441-48 for the debate.

[51] There seems to have been a concentration of population inside the walls in this Tiber bend area, but that is not to say the rest of the city was abandoned. See for example: Spera L. 'Le forme della cristianizzazione nel quadro degli assetti topografico-funzionali di Roma tra V e IX

the main pilgrim route that led to S. Pietro in Vaticano, still known today as the Via del Pellegrino.

5.3.2 SS. Quirico e Giulitta

Another foundation in the Subura, initially dedicated to the martyrs Lawrence and Stephen it seems, is from the first half of the 6th century, and was situated just east and behind the Forum of Nerva, and built next to the large arch known as the Arco dei Pantani in the Middle Ages, itself by the *porticus absidata*.[52] These both led into Nerva's forum and the formal centre of the city from the Subura, so this area outside the basilica was a well-used route for locals, visitors and dignitaries. Architectural features that still survive within the current church and the discovery of a now lost ancient altar, attest to this early 6th century foundation.[53]

This is now the church of SS. Quirico e Giulitta and was, perhaps, a rare *ex novo* build of this era,[54] which, coupled with its prominent position in the city, suggests this was an important foundation to the popular martyrs. The original dedication, to the deacon martyrs Lawrence and Stephen, is suggested by the existence of an ancient mosaic depicting the two men in the first apse, described in the 16th century by Ugonio.[55] The church is also described in the 12th century *mirabilia* as at or near to the *basilica Iovis*, a structure mentioned in Lawrence's 6th century *passio* as where he was initially interrogated.[56] The basilica had lost this original Laurentian dedication by the late 8th-early 9th century,[57] but it is not clear why. Perhaps it had obtained the relics of Quiricus and Julietta by that time?

In any case, the basilica was built in a very prominent location just behind the imperial fora and on the important *Argiletum-Clivus Suburanus* road (fig.44). This route also led to the equally important *Vicus Patricius* street and the centre of the city from the populous Subura. It may, therefore, have been deliberately placed here to profit from this favourable location at a movement hub, to benefit the basilica itself and the donor who founded it.

This area of the city retained its importance through the early medieval period, with the Forum of Nerva now containing aristocratic houses and gardens.[58] This foundation would therefore have kept its prestige due to its location in the city, in spite of the diminishment of the urban area around it at that time.

5.4 Conclusion

These final few examples of Christian foundations also display the same spatial awareness from their donor-builders than those in earlier chapters. The location of two of Damasus' intramural foundations, one by the Circus Maximus the other on the site of the stables of the Green circus faction, can be argued to have been politically motivated, in terms of his use of the Greens to gain the episcopate and the popularity of the circus games. Equally, two centres dedicated to popular Roman martyrs, Agnes and Lawrence, were built in popular hubs or urban nodes, where people would frequently be. At the same time, two 4th century basilicas were constructed in close proximity to major 'pagan' shrines. This should dispel the myth of Christian avoidance of such places and that a binary topography existed. The Christian donor-builders here cannot have unaware of these cultic centres' existence before any building work was carried out, but we cannot say whether it was meant as a provocative gesture or not.

---

secolo', *Postclassical Archaeologies* 1 (2011) 309-47; Costambeys M. 'Burial topography' (2001) 169-89.
[52] *Not. Rom.* IIII: Nordh ed. *Libellus* (1949) 77.15.
[53] Armellini M. *Le chiese di Roma* (1891) 172-75; CBCR 4.37-50; Bosi M. *SS. Quirico e Giulitta* (Rome 1961); LTUR 4.179-80.
[54] However, it may have been built into a pre-existing late antique house: Guidobaldi F. 'Una domus tardoantica e la sua trasformazione in chiesa dei SS. Quirico e Giulitta', in *Res Bene Gestae. Ricerche di storia urbana su Roma antica in onore di Eva Margareta Steinby*, edd. A. Leone, D. Palombi, S. Walker (2007) 55-78.
[55] Ugonio P. *Historia delle stationi che si celebrano la Quadragesima* (1588) c.277, cited in CBCR 4.41 n.5. The two deacons are still buried within San Lorenzo fuori le Mura today, with the 13th century apse mosaic there also depicting them both. SS. Quirico e Giulitta also housed some of the relics of Lawrence in the 16th century: Ugonio P. *Historia* (1588) c.277.
[56] Several other buildings in the legend are also referred to in the same passage: Mirabilia (12th century): Val. Zucc. 3.26. Buildings in Lawrence's passio: *AA.SS.* Aug. 2.519; Follieri E. 'Antiche chiese romane nella passio greca di Sisto, Lorenzo ed Ippolito', *Rivista di Studi Bizantini e Neoellenici* 17-19 (new series) (1980-82) 55-56 (43-71). For the possible creation of a Laurentian pilgrimage route at this time, and the implications of that, see: Mulryan M. 'Movement and the hero: following St. Lawrence in late antique Rome', in *The Moving City. Proceedings of the Colloquia Held at the Swedish and Dutch Institutes in Rome (2nd-4th May 2011 and June 13-15th 2012)*, edd. S. Malmberg and J. Bjørnebye (forthcoming 2014), contra Behrwald R. 'Heilsgeschichte in heidnischer Szenerie: die Denkmaltopographie Roms in der christlichen Legendenbildung', in *Rom in der Spätantike* (2012) 267-92.
[57] Einsiedeln Itinerary: Val. Zucc. 2.177, 192.

[58] Santangeli Valenzani R. 'Strade, case e orti nell'altomedioevo nell'area del Foro di Nerva', *MEFRM* 111 (1999) 163-69.

6. Conclusion

I have attempted here to establish that there were several examples of Christian foundations in Rome, from the 4th to the 7th centuries, that show evidence for having been strategically placed. Certain Christian donors, like all building donors in earlier centuries, wanted their investment to be as prominent as possible in the urban landscape. Whether these individuals were lay or clerical, the motivation was the same. Another feature of several foundations was a practical and utilitarian motivation, evident in the many examples of Christian basilicas created within or next to baths before the advent of purpose-built baptisteries, which meant easy access to water for the essential liturgical and baptismal needs of the centre were already in place. Several early examples were provided with small bath houses in their property donations. There are also some basilicas that were created next to or within popular places of congregation, with one early example that was situated next to one of the most important 'pagan' shrines in the city. There is also evidence to suggest the 4th century bishop Damasus wished to be associated, and align himself, with the circus games and its factions. In the Subura area of the city, two Christian centres were created within the streets by two major places of congregation, and so worked with the movement patterns of the area. This meant they were easily discoverable for those wanting to find them, with a warehouse/hall between them reused as a welfare centre. Until the early 6th century the Christian presence here was largely invisible, although not hidden.

In these early centuries of Christianity in the city it has been established that lay donors in most cases just gave money to the Church or founded benevolent establishments (*diaconia*, *xenodochia*, sick-houses), rather than donating a building to convert into a Christian basilica. The evidence we have points to a clerical building bureaucracy using that donated money, and so the ability to acquire sites in the city to build/convert was possible. This is the situation we see with the *titulus Vestinae*, with Vestina's money (obtained from the selling of her jewellery) being used by several clerics to create the basilica, who then named the foundation after her, in her honour. This is likely to have been the most common arrangement into the 5th century at least. In later centuries bishop-led projects become more common, but are likely to have occurred earlier as well. Most Roman bishops were aristocrats, and their own personal wealth, plus that provided by state donations, also made site/building purchase both possible and politically expedient.

The location of temples in the 'Classical City' model shows that they were intended to be widely seen throughout, and act as markers and landmarks in a macro way. Their visual domination of the ancient city landscape was one of the defining features of it, a result of their appearance on hills and high points. They were also an integral part of the day-to-day 'working' of the *polis/urbs*, thus their appearance in *agorai/fora* and other places of mass congregation, such as circuses and theatres, as part of the religious function of the activities there.[1] In the Roman city we see that every neighbourhood had its own shrine. This is the fundamentally 'pagan' urban landscape into which purpose-built Christian buildings had to fit into. Thus, it is unhelpful and inaccurate to speak of these foundations in Rome as avoiding 'pagan' places, as this was impossible.

From the 5th century it is clear that Christian building donors also increasingly aimed for their foundations to impact on the city in a macro way on hills. However, before this many basilicas do aim to make an impact as well, if only at a street-level, micro way, because of the limited land and funds available for many of those lay and clerical projects. Such micro-impact was done by having an active relationship with the main road that lay next to them: by facing directly onto it or partially blocking it with its apse. When more money and space was available, and when central prestige buildings were no longer actively used—as with the imperial extramural, and 6th and 7th century intramural, examples—the Christian builders were no less ambitious than their 'pagan' forebears. By the 6th and 7th centuries we begin to increasingly see (albeit modest) Christian basilicas appearing in centres of congregation, like the temples of old, such as in the Roman Forum, at the entrance to the Forum of Nerva, and the Stadium of Domitian. Yet, this practice also begins to an extent in earlier centuries, with examples just beyond the walls of the Circus Maximus and the Baths of Caracalla and within the Baths of Diocletian.

We need to see the early Christian building programme in Rome not entirely as a series of random events—which it would appear to be if viewed from a macro top-down map—or perceive Christian builders as somehow differently motivated compared to their earlier 'pagan' counterparts. With many early examples it is true that there is no reason to think they were built where they were with any particular purpose in mind, but with the examples we have discussed here, many others seem to have actively sought to use useful and available water facilities and at least attempted to make a visual impact on the surrounding landscape in either a micro or macro way. A few were also constructed in places where people gathered. A particular case study of two early Christian foundations in the Subura shows that even these were located by two major places of

---

[1] Vitr. *De arch.* 1.7.1-2, 4.5.2.

congregation, and so could be easily found in the warren of shops, warehouses, baths, *insulae* and *domus* that characterised the area.

Many of the early Christian basilicas of Rome were neither invisible nor hidden. Some very quickly became integral features of the Roman landscape.

Bibliography

Ancient Sources

Standard editions have been used throughout. For those authors without these, the editions used are given below.

AA.SS. = Bollandists edd. *Acta Sanctorum*, 67 vols. (Brussels 1902-70, repr. of orig. Antwerp 1643-1883).

Acta Vercellenses 35 (in Lipsius R. A. ed. *Acta Apostolorum Apocrypha*, vol.1 (Leipzig 1891) 7-8, 171, 233).

Ambrose, *De Virginibus*.

Ambrose, *Epistulae*.

Ambrose, *Contra Auxentium*.

Ambrose, *In Psalmum David CXVIII Expositio* 8.22,

Ambrose, *De Officiis*.

Ambrose, *De Viduis*.

Ammianus Marcellinus, *Res Gestae*.

Appian, *Bella Civilia*.

Apuleius, *Metamorphoses*.

Athanasius, *Apologia contra Arianos*.

Augustine, *De civitate Dei*.

Augustine, *Epistulae*.

Aurelius Victor, *Caesares*.

Aurelius Victor, *Epitome de Caesaribus* (authorship disputed).

Basil, *Homiliae*.

Caesarius of Arles, *Sermones*.

Calendar of 354 (in Degrassi A. ed. *Fasti anni numani et iuliani: accedunt ferialia, menologia rustica, parapegmata* (Inscriptiones Italiae 13.2) (Rome 1963)).

Calendar of Polemius Silvius (in Degrassi A. ed. *Fasti anni numani et iuliani: accedunt ferialia, menologia rustica, parapegmata* (Inscriptiones Italiae 13.2) (Rome 1963)).

Cassiodorus, *Variae*.

Chronicle of the City of Rome (in *The Chronography of 354*: MGH.AA.(see below) 9: *Chronica Minora*, ed. T. Mommsen, vol. 1 (Berlin 1892)).

Cicero, *Epistulae ad Atticum*.

Cicero, *Pro Sexto Roscio Amerino*.

Cicero, *In Verrem* 2.3.16.

Cicero, *De Legibus*.

CIL = *Corpus inscriptionum Latinarum*, 17 vols. (to date) (Berlin 1853-   ).

Claudian, *de sexto consulatu Honorii* (Platnauer M. transl. *Claudian*, vol. 2 (London 1922) 70-122.

Cod. Theod. = *Codex Theodosianus* (in Mommsen T. and Meyer P. M. edd. *Theodosiani libri XVI cvm Constitvtionibvs Sirmondianis et Leges novellae ad Theodosianvm pertinentes*, 2 vols. (Berlin 1905)).

Coll. Avell = Guenther O. ed. *Epistvlae imperatorvm pontificvm aliorvm inde ab a. CCCLXVII vsqve ad a. DLIII datae Avellana qvae dicitvr collectio* (CSEL 35.1 and 2) (Vienna 1895).

Council of Chalcedon: Canons (in Price R. and Gaddis M. edd. and transl. *The Acts of the Council of Chalcedon*, 3 vols. (Liverpool 2005).

Cyprian, *Epistulae*.

Dio Cassius, *Romaika*.

Diodorus Siculus, *Bibliotheca historica*.

Festus = Sextus Pompeius Festus, *De Verborum significatu*.

Einsiedeln Itinerary (in Valentini R. and Zucchetti G. *Codice topografico della città di Roma*, vol. 2 (Rome 1942)).

Gerontius, *Vita S. Melaniae Junioris* (in Laurence P. ed. and transl. *La vie latine de sainte Mélanie* (Jerusalem 2002)).

Gregory, *Epistulae*.

ICUR = De Rossi G. B. ed. *Inscriptiones Christianae urbis Romae septimo saeculo antiquiores*, 3 vols. (Rome 1857-1915).

ICUR (NS) = De Rossi G. B. *et al* edd. *Inscriptiones Christianae urbis Romae septimo saeculo antiquiores. Nova series*, 10 vols. (Rome-Vatican City 1922-92).

ILCV = Diehl E. ed. *Inscriptiones Latinae Christianae veteres*, 4 vols. (Berlin, 2nd edn. 1961-67).

ILS = Dessau H. ed. *Inscriptiones latinae selectae*, 3 vols. (Berlin, 3rd edn. 1962).

Jerome, *Chronicon*.

Jerome, *Epistulae*.

Jerome, *Liber contra Joannem Hierosolymitanum*.

Lactantius, *De mortibus persecutorum*.

Life of St. Pelagia the Harlot (in Petitmengin P. *Pélagie la Pénitente. Métamorphoses d'une légende*, vol 1: *Les textes et leur histoire* (Paris 1981).

Livy, *Ab urbe condita libri*.

LP = *Liber Pontificalis*, ed. L. Duchesne, 2 vols. (Paris 1886-92).

Malalas (John), *Chronographia*.

Mark = St. Mark, *The Gospel According to Mark*.

Mark the Deacon, *Life of Porphyry* (in Hill G. F. transl. *The Life of Porphyry, Bishop of Gaza* (Oxford 1913)).

Martial, *Epigrams*.

Martyrologium Hieronymianum (in *AA.SS.* Nov. II.1).

Mirabilia (in Valentini R. and Zucchetti G. *Codice topografico della città di Roma*, vol. 3 (Rome 1946)).

Monumentum Ancyranum.

Notitia Regionum Urbis XIV (in Nordh A. ed. *Libellus de Regionibus Urbis Romae* (Lund 1949)).

Orosius, *Historiarum adversus paganos libri VII*.

Ovid, *Ars amatoria*.

Ovid, *Fasti*.

Palladius, *Historia Lausiaca* (in Wellhausen A. *Die lateinische Übersetzung der Historia Lausiaca des Palladius: Textausgabe mit Einleitung* (Berlin 2003)).

Passio SS. Donati et Advocati (in Tilley M. A. ed. and transl. *Donatist Martyr Stories: the Church in Conflict in Roman North Africa* (Translated Texts for Historians 24) (1996)).
Paulinus of Nola, *Epistulae.*
Paulinus of Nola, *Carmina.*
Plautus, *Captivi.*
Plautus, *Curculio.*
Pliny (the Younger), *Epistulae.*
Pliny (the Elder), *Naturalis historia.*
Plutarch, *Vitae Parallelae.*
Procopius, *De bello Gothico.*
Prudentius, *Contra Symmachum.*
Prudentius, *Peristephanon.*
Scriptores Historiae Augustae, *Alexander Severus, Marcus Aurelius Antoninus (Caracalla), Severus, Tyranni Triginta.*
Sidonius Apollinaris, *Carmina.*
Sidonius Apollinaris, *Epistulae.*
Strabo, *Geographica.*
Suetonius, *Divus Augustus.*
Suetonius, *Divus Iulius.*
Suetonius, *Gaius Caligula.*
Symmachus, *Epistulae.*
Symmachus, *Relationes.*
Tacitus, *Annales.*
Tertullian, *De spectaculis.*
Tertullian, *De baptismo.*
The Holy Bible: New International Version (London 1984).
Varro, *De lingua Latina.*
Vitruvius, *De architectura.*

Secondary Sources

Accorsi M. L. 'Il complesso dei SS. Silvestro e Martino ai Monti dal III al IX secolo. Appunti di studio', in *Ecclesiae Urbis: atti del congresso internazionale di studi sulle chiese di Roma (IV-X secolo): Roma 4-10 settembre 2000*, edd. F. and A. G. Guidobaldi (Vatican City 2002) 533-63.

Affanni A. M. *La Chiesa di Santa Prassede: la storia, il rilievo, il restauro* (Viterbo 2006).

Angelelli C. *La basilica titolare di S. Pudenziana: nuove ricerche* (Vatican City 2010).

Apollonj-Ghetti B. 'Le chiese titolari di S. Silvestro e S. Martino ai Monti', in *RACrist* 37 (1961) 271-302.

Armellini M. (and Cecchelli C. ed.) *Le chiese di Roma dal secolo IV al XIX* (new edn. Rome 1942).

Armellini M. *Le chiese di Roma dal secolo IV al XIX* (Rome 1891).

Augenti A. 'Continuity and discontinuity of a seat of power: the Palatine hill from the fifth to the tenth century', in *Early Medieval Rome and the Christian West: Essays in Honour of Donald A. Bullough*, ed. J. M. H. Smith (Leiden 2000) 43-57.

Augenti A. *Il palatino nel Medioevo: archeologia e topografia (secoli VI-XIII)* (Rome 1996).

Baldini Lippolis I. 'Private space in late antique cities: laws and building procedures', in *Housing in Late Antiquity: from Palaces to Shops*, edd. L. Lavan, L. Özgenel and A. Sarantis (Late Antique Archaeology 3.2) (Leiden-Boston 2007) 195-238.

Baldovin J. F. *The Urban Character of Christian Worship: the Origins, Development, and Meaning of Stational Liturgy* (Rome 1987).

Barkley Lloyd J. 'Krautheimer and S. Paolo fuori le mura. Architectural, urban and liturgical planning in late fourth century Rome', in *Ecclesiae Urbis: atti del congresso internazionale di studi sulle chiese di Roma (IV-X secolo): Roma 4-10 settembre 2000*, edd. F. and A. G. Guidobaldi (Vatican City 2002) 812-16.

Barrow R. H. *Prefect and Emperor: the Relationes of Symmachus, A.D. 384* (Oxford 1973).

Bartoli A. *I monumenti antichi di Roma nei disegni degli Uffizi di Firenze*, 5 vols. (Florence 1914-22).

Bartoli A. *Curia senatus: lo scavo e il restauro* (Rome 1963).

Bartolozzi Casti G. 'Battisteri presbiteriali in Roma: un nuovo intervento di Sisto III?', in *Studi Romani* 47.3-4 (1999) 270-88.

Bartolozzi Casti G. 'Nuove osservazioni sulle basiliche di San Pietro in Vincoli e dei Santi Giovanni e Paolo. Relazioni strutturali, proposte di cronologia', in *Ecclesiae Urbis: atti del congresso internazionale di studi sulle chiese di Roma (IV-X secolo): Roma 4-10 settembre 2000*, edd. F. and A. G. Guidobaldi (Vatican City 2002) 953-77.

Bartolozzi Casti G. 'Le trasformazioni di un complesso edilizio urbano: San Pietro in Vincoli', in *Roma dall'antichità al medioevo*, vol. 2: *Contesti tardoantichi e altomedievali*, edd. L. Paroli and L. Vendittelli (Milan 2004) 380-89.

Bartolozzi Casti G. and Zandri G. *San Pietro in Vincoli* (Rome 1999).

Behrwald R. 'Heilsgeschichte in heidnischer Szenerie: die Denkmaltopographie Roms in der christlichen Legendenbildung', in *Rom in der Spätantike: historische Erinnerung im städtischen Raum*, edd. R. Behrwald and C. Witschel (Stuttgart 2012) 267-91.

Bellori G. P. *Fragmenta vestigii veteris Romae ex lapidibus Farnesianis nunc primum in lucem edita cum notis* (Rome 1673).

Bertelli C. and Galassi Paluzzi C., *Santa Maria in via Lata*, vol. 1: *la chiesa inferiore e il problema paolino* (Rome 1971).

Bertoldi M. E. 'L'area archeologica di San Lorenzo in Lucina a Roma', *Bollettino di Archeologia* 13-15 (1992) 127-34;

Bertoldi M. E. *S. Lorenzo in Lucina* (Rome 1994).

Bjur H. and Santillo Frizell B. *Via Tiburtina: Space, Movement and Artefacts in the Urban Landscape* (Stockholm 2009).

Blair-Dixon K. 'Damasus and the fiction of unity: the urban shrines of Saint Laurence', in *Ecclesiae Urbis: atti del congresso internazionale di studi sulle chiese di Roma (IV-X secolo): Roma 4-10 settembre 2000*, edd. F. and A. G. Guidobaldi (Vatican City 2002) 331-52.

Boaga E. 'Il complesso titolare di S. Martino ai Monti in Roma', in *Dalla Chiesa antica alla Chiesa moderna. Miscellanea per il cinquantesimo della Facoltà di storia ecclesiastica della Pontificia università gregoriana*, edd. M. Fois, V. Monachino and F. Litva (Rome 1983) 1-17.

Bonanni A. 'La basilica di S. Susanna a Roma: indagni topografiche e nuove scoperte archeologiche', in *Akten des XII. Internationalen Kongresses für Christliche Archäologie*, edd. E. Dassmann and J. Engemann (Münster 1995) 586-89.

Bonanni A. 'Scavi e ricerche in S. Susanna a Roma. Le fasi paleocristiane e altomedievali', in *Atti del VII Congresso nazionale di archeologia cristiana, Cassino, 20-24 settembre 1993*, vol. 1, ed. E. Russo (Cassino 2003) 359-76.

Bonfioli M. 'La diaconia dei Ss. Sergio e Bacco nel Foro Romano. Fonti e problemi', *RACrist* 50 (1974) 55-85.

Bosi M. *SS. Quirico e Giulitta* (Rome 1961).

Boudreau Flory M. 'Sic exempla parantur: Livia's shrine to Concordia and the Porticus Liviae', *Historia* 33.3 (1984) 309-30.

Bowes K. *Private Worship, Public Values, and Religious Change in Late Antiquity* (Cambridge-New York 2008)

Brandenburg H. *Die Kirche S. Stefano Rotondo in Rom: Bautypologie und Architektursymbolik in der spätantiken und frühchristlichen Architektur* (Berlin 1998).

Brandenburg H. 'S. Stefano Rotondo, der letzte Großbau der Antike in Rom. Die Typologie des Baues, die Ausstattung der Kirche, die kunstgeschichtliche Stellung des Kirchenbaues und seiner Ausstattung', in *Santo Stefano Rotondo in Roma: archeologia, storia dell'arte, restauro; atti del convegno internazionale, Roma 10-13 ottobre 1996*, edd. H. Brandenburg and J. Pál (Wiesbaden 2000) 35-65.

Brandenburg H. 'Santo Stefano Rotondo in Roma: funzione urbanistica, tipologia architettonica, liturgia ed allestimento liturgico', *Meded* 59 (2000) 27-54.

Brandenburg H. *Ancient Churches of Rome from the Fourth to the Seventh Century: the Dawn of Christian Architecture in the West* (transl. from orig, German by A. Kropp) (Turnhout 2005).

Brandt O. 'Passiones e battisteri', in *Domum tuam dilexi. Miscellanea in onore di Aldo Nestori* (Vatican City 1998) 109-12.

Brandt O. 'Constantine, the Lateran, and early church building policy', in *Imperial Art as Christian Art, Christian Art as Imperial Art: Expression and Meaning in Art and Architecture from Constantine to Justinian*, edd. J. Rasmus Brandt and O. Steen (Rome 2001) 109-14.

Brandt O. 'Jews and Christians in late antique Rome and Ostia', *Opuscula Romana* 29 (2004) 7-27.

Brandt O. 'The archaeology of Roman ecclesial architecture and the study of early Christian liturgy', *Studia Patristica* 71 (2014) 21-52.

Brandt O. 'The early Christian basilica of San Lorenzo in Lucina', in *San Lorenzo in Lucina. The Transformations of a Roman Quarter*, ed. O. Brandt (Stockholm 2012) 123-154.

Brandt O. 'The excavations in the baptistery of San Lorenzo in Lucina in 1993, 1995 and 1998', in *San Lorenzo in Lucina. The Transformations of a Roman Quarter*, ed. O. Brandt (Stockholm 2012) 49-77.

Brandt O., 'La seconda campagna di scavo nel battisterio di S. Lorenzo in Lucina a Roma: rapporto preliminare', *OpRom* 20 (1996) 271-74.

Brandt O., 'Sul battistero paleocristiano di S. Lorenzo in Lucina', *Archeologia Laziale* 12.1 (1995) 145-50.

Brenk B. 'Kirche und Strasse im frühchristlichen Rom', in *Rom in der Spätantike: historische Erinnerung im städtischen Raum*, edd. R. Behrwald and C. Witschel (Stuttgart 2012) 171-91.

Brenk B. 'La cristianizzazione della Domus dei Valerii sul Celio', in *The Transformations of Urbs Roma in Late Antiquity*, ed. W. V. Harris (Portsmouth, Rhode Island 1999) 69-84.

Brenk B. 'Microstoria sotto la chiesa dei Ss. Giovanni e Paolo: la cristianizzazione di una casa privata', *RivIstArch* 18 (1995) 169-206.

Brown P. L. R. 'The rise and function of the holy man in late antiquity', *JRS* 61 (1971) 80-101.

Brown P. L. R. *Power and Persuasion in Late Antiquity: Towards a Christian Empire* (Madison, Wisconsin 1992).

Cabrol F. ed., *Dictionnaire d'archéologie chrétienne et de liturgie*, 15 vols. (Paris 1907-53).

Cameron A. 'The last pagans of Rome', in *The Transformations of Urbs Roma in Late Antiquity*, ed. W. V. Harris (Portsmouth, Rhode Island 1999) 109-21.

Cameron Al. *Circus Factions: Blues and Greens at Rome and Byzantium* (Oxford 1976).

Cameron Al. *The Last Pagans of Rome* (Oxford 2011).

Carandini A. with Bruno D. *La casa di Augusto dai Lupercalia al Natale* (Bari 2008).

Carboni F. "Scavi all'esedra nord-orientale delle Terme di Traiano, *BullCom* 104 (2003) 65-80.

Carettoni G. *et al* edd. *La pianta marmorea di Roma antica: Forma urbis Romae* (Rome 1960).

Carlà F. 'Milan, Ravenna, Rome: some reflections on the cult of the saints and on civic politics in late antique Italy', *Rivista di Storia e Letteratura Religiosa* 46.2 (2010) 197-272.

CBCR = Krautheimer R. *Corpus Basilicarum Christianarum Romae: the Early Christian Basilicas of Rome (IV-IX cent.)*, 5 vols. (Vatican City 1937-77).

Cecchelli C. 'Una nuova ipotesi sul sito del 'Lupercal' (S. Anastasia in Palatio e il Lupercale)', *Roma* 21 (1943) 313-17.

Cecchelli M. 'Note sui 'titoli' romani', *ArchCl* 37 (1985) 293-305.

Cecchelli M. 'Il sacello di S. Pietro e l'oratorio di S. Pastore in S. Pudenziana: una messa a punto', *Romano Barbarica* 9 (1986-87) 47-64.

Cecchelli M. 'Dalla Basilica Liberiana al complesso paleocristiano e altomedievale', in *Santa Maria Maggiore a Roma*, ed. C. Pietrangeli (Florence 1988) 71-84.

Cecchelli M. 'Valilae o valide? L'iscrizione di S. Andrea all'Esquilino', *Romano Barbarica* 11 (1991) 61-78.

Cecchelli M. 'S. Marco a Piazza Venezia: una basilica romana del periodo constantiniano', in *Costantino il Grande: dall' antichità all'umanesimo: colloquio sul Cristianesimo nel mondo antico: Macerata 18-20 Dicembre 1990*, 2 vols., edd. G. Bonamente and F. Fusco (Macerata 1992-93) 299-310.

Cecchelli M. 'La basilica di S. Marco a Piazza Venezia (Roma): nuove scoperte e indagni', in *Akten des XII. Internationalen Kongresses für Christliche Archäologie*, edd. E. Dassmann and J. Engemann (Münster 1995) 640-44.

Cecchelli M. 'Dati da scavi recenti di monumenti cristiani. Sintesi relativa a diverse indagini in corso', *MÉFRM* 111.1 (1999) 227-51.

Cecchelli M. 'S. Marco', in *Roma dall'antichità al medioevo*, vol. 1: *Archeologia e storia nel Museo Nazionale Romano Crypta*, edd. M. S. Arena *et al.* (Milan 2001) 635-36.

Cecchelli M. 'Santa Susanna', in *Roma dall'antichità al medioevo*, vol. 2: *Contesti tardoantichi e altomedievali*, edd. L. Paroli and L. Vendittelli (Milan 2004) 328-43.

Cecchini M. G. 'Terme di Caracalla. Campagna di scavo 1982/83 lungo il lato orientale', in *Roma: archeologia nel centro*, vol. 2, edd. A. M. Bietti Sestieri *et al* (Rome 1985) 583-93.

Cecchini M. G. 'Contributi sulla topografia della regione *duodecima piscina publica ubi dicitur Sancto Gregorio* in periodo altomedievale', *RACrist* 64 (1988) 89-107.

Cerrito A. 'Note a margine di un precedente contributo per lo studio della basilica di S. Anastasia al Palatino (Roma): approfondimenti e nuove osservazioni', *RACrist* 87-88 (2011-12) 317-56.

Cerrito A. 'Contributo allo studio del *titulus Anastasiae*', in *Marmoribus vestita: miscellanea in onore di Federico Guidobaldi*, edd. O. Brandt and P. Pergola (Vatican City 2011) 345-71.

Cerrito A. 'Sull'oratorio di S. Felicita presso di Terme di Traiano a Roma', in *Domum tuam dilexi: miscellanea in onore di Aldo Nestori* (Vatican City 1998) 155-84.

Chadwick H. 'Bishops and monks', *Studia Patristica* 24 (1993) 45-61.

Chastagnol A. *La préfecture urbaine à Rome sous le bas empire* (Paris 1960).

Chastagnol A. *Les fastes de la préfecture de Rome au bas-empire* (Paris 1962).

Christie N. *From Constantine to Charlemagne: An Archaeology of Italy AD. 300-800* (Aldershot 2006).

Cicerchia P. and Marinucci A. *Le Terme del Foro o di Gavio Massimo* (Scavi di Ostia 11) (Rome 1992).

Claridge A. *Rome: an Oxford Archaeological Guide* (Oxford 1998).

Clark E. A., *The Life of Melania, the Younger: Introduction, Translation, and Commentary* (New York 1984).

Coarelli F. *Guida archeologica di Roma* (Milan 1975).

Coarelli F. 'Topografia mitriaca di Roma', in *Mysteria Mithrae*, ed. U. Bianci (Leiden 1979) 69-79.

Coates-Stephens R. 'Dark-age architecture in Rome', *BSR* 65 (1997) 177-232.

Coates Stephens R. 'The walls and aqueducts of Rome in the early Middle Ages', *JRS* 88 (1998) 166-78.

Coates Stephens R. 'Gli acquedotti in epoca tardoantica nel suburbio', in *Suburbium. Il suburbio di Roma dalla crisi del sistema delle ville a Gregorio Magno*, edd. P. Pergola, R. Santangeli Valenzani and R. Volpe (Rome 2003) 415-36.

Coates-Stephens R. 'The water-supply of Rome from late antiquity to the early middle ages', in *Rome AD 300-800: Power and Symbol, Image and Reality*, edd. J. Rasmus Brandt, S. Sande, O. Steen and L. Hodne (Rome 2003) 165-86.

Coccia S. *et al.* 'Santa Maria in Trastevere: nuovi elementi sulla basilica paleocristiana e altomedievale', *Meded* 59 (2000) 161-74.

Coleman-Norton P. R. *Roman State and Christian Church. A Collection of Legal Documents to A.D. 535*, 3 vols. (London 1966).

Conti S. 'Attività edilizia e restauri nei centri africani durante il regno dell'imperatore Giuliano', *Africa Romana* 15.3 (2004) 1681-92.

Cooper K. 'The martyr, the *matrona* and the bishop: the matron Lucina and the politics of martyr cult in fifth- and sixth-century Rome', *Early Medieval Europe* 8.3 (1999) 297–317.

Cormack R. 'The visual arts', in *CAH* 14, *Late antiquity: Empire and Successors, AD 425-600*, edd. Av. Cameron, B. Ward-Perkins and M. Whitby (Cambridge 2000) 884-916.

Cosentino A. 'Il battesimo a Roma: edifici e liturgia', in *Ecclesiae Urbis: atti del congresso internazionale di studi sulle chiese di Roma (IV-X secolo): Roma 4-10 settembre 2000*, edd. F. and A. G. Guidobaldi (Vatican City 2002) 109-42.

Costambeys M. 'Burial topography and the power of the Church in fifth- and sixth-century Rome', *BSR* 69 (2001) 169-89.

Cozza L. 'I recenti scavi delle Sette Sale', *RendPontAcc* 47 (1974-75) 79-101.

Crippa M. A. 'L'urbanistica tardoantica e topografia cristiana, III-VII secolo', in *L'arte paleocristiana. Visione e spazio dalle origini a Bisanzio*, edd. M. A. Crippa and M. Zibawi (Milan 1998) 429-42.

Curran J. R. *Pagan City and Christian Capital: Rome in the Fourth Century* (Oxford 2000).

Dagron G. *Naissance d'une capitale: Constantinople et ses institutions de 330 à 451* (Paris 1974).

Dagron G. *Costantinopoli: nascita di una capitale (330-451)* (transl. A. Serafini) (Turin 1991).

Darsy F. M. D. *Recherches archéologiques à Sainte-Sabine sur l'Aventin: géologie, topographie, sanctuaires archaïques, culte isiaque, ensemble architectural paléochrétien* (Vatican City 1968).

Davis R. ed. and transl. *The Book of Pontiffs (Liber Pontificalis): the Ancient Biographies of the First Ninety Roman Bishops to AD 715* (2nd edn. Liverpool 2000).

Davis-Weyer C. and Emerick J. J. 'The early sixth century frescoes at S. Martino ai Monti in Rome', in *Römisches Jahrbuch für Kunstgeschichte* 21 (1984) 1-60.

De Fine Licht K., Cozza L., Panella C., Motta R. 'Colle Oppio', in *Roma: archeologia nel centro,* vol. 2: *La "città murata"'*, edd. A. M. Bietti Sestieri *et al.* (Rome 1985) 467-86.

De Gregori L. *Piazza Navona prima d'Innocenzo X* (Rome 1926).

De Rossi G. 'Dei musaici e d'altri monumenti fatti da Massimo prete', *BACrist* 1.5.4 (1867) 55-57.

De Rossi G. B. 'Oratorio privato del secolo quarto scoperto nel Monte della Giustizia presso le Terme Diocleziane', *BACrist* 3.1 (1876) 37-58.

De Rossi G. B. 'Pittura ritraente S. Felicita ed i sette figlinoli in un antico oratorio presso le terme di Tito', *BACrist* 4.3 (1884-85) 157-66.

De Spirito G. 'Ursino e Damaso - una nota', in *Peregrina curiositas: eine Reise durch den orbis antiquus: zu Ehren von Dirk van Damme,* edd. A. Kessler, T. Ricklin and G.Wurst (Freiburg 1994) 263-74.

Degrassi A. ed. *Fasti anni numani et iuliani: accedunt ferialia, menologia rustica, parapegmata* (Inscriptiones Italiae 13.2) (Rome 1963).

DeLaine J. 'Recent research on Roman baths', *JRA* 1 (1988) 11-32.

Delaine J. *The Baths of Caracalla: a Study in the Design, Construction, and Economics of Large-Scale Building Projects in Imperial Rome* (Portsmouth, Rhode Island 1997).

Delehaye H. 'L'amphithéatre flavien et ses environs dans les textes hagiographiques', *Analecta Bollandiana* 16 (1897) 235-52.

Delehaye H. *Étude sur le légendier romain: les saints de novembre et de décembre* (Brussels 1936).

Docci M. *San Paolo fuori le mura: dalle origini alla basilica delle "origini"* (Rome 2006).

Donker G. J. *The Text of the Apostolos in Athanasius of Alexandria* (Atlanta 2011).

Dufourcq A. *Étude sur les gesta martyrum romains* (Paris 1900).

Duval Y-M. 'Des lupercales de Constantinople aux lupercales de Rome', *REL* 55 (1977) 246-50.

Ensoli S. 'I sanctuari di Iside e Serapide a Roma e la resistenza pagana in età tardoantica', in *Aurea Roma. Dalla città pagana alla città cristiana,* edd. S. Ensoli and E. La Rocca (Rome 2000) 267-87.

Ensoli S. 'Le sculture del 'larario' di S. Martino ai Monti. Un contesto recuperato', *BullCom* 95 (1993) 221-43.

Episcopo S. 'La basilica di S. Marcello al Corso a Roma. Nuove scoperte', in *Akten des XII. Internationalen Kongresses für Christliche Archäologie,* edd. E. Dassmann and J. Engemann (Münster 1995) 734-40.

Episcopo S. *Il Titulus Marcelli sulla via Lata: nuovi studi e ricerche archeologiche (1990-2000)* (Rome 2003).

Erim K. T. *Aphrodisias: City of Venus Aphrodite* (London 1986).

Fagan G. G. *Bathing in Public in the Roman World* (Ann Arbor 1999).

Ferrua A. ed. *Epigrammata Damasiana* (Rome 1942).

Filippi G. and Barbera R. *Il Codice Epigrafico di Cornelio Margarini e le iscrizioni della Basilica di San Paolo fuori le Mura nel XVIII secolo: concordanze e inediti* (Vatican City 2011).

Fiocchi Nicolai V. 'Strutture funerarie ed edifici di culto paleocristiani di Roma dal III al VI secolo', in *Le iscrizioni dei cristiani in Vaticano. Materiali e contributi scientifici per una mostra epigrafica,* ed. I. Di Stefano Manzella (Vatican City 1997) 121-41.

Fiore P. 'Fortuna di un modello architettonico tardoantico: la chiesa dei santi Cosma e Damiano nel Foro Romano', *Quaderni dell'Istituto di storia dell'architettura* 39 (2002) 145-54.

Follieri E. 'Antiche chiese romane nella passio greca di Sisto, Lorenzo ed Ippolito', *Rivista di Studi Bizantini e Neoellenici* 17-19 (new series) (1980-82) 43-71.

Frischer B. *et al.* 'Virtual reality and ancient Rome: the UCLA cultural VR Lab's Santa Maria Maggiore project', in *Virtual Reality in Archaeology: Computer Applications and Quantitative Methods in Archaeology (CAA),* edd. J. A. Barceló, M. Forte, and D. H. Sanders (BAR-IS 843) (Oxford 2000) 155-62.

Frommel C. L. and Pentiricci M. edd. *L'antica basilica di San Lorenzo in Damaso: indagini archeologiche nel Palazzo della Cancelleria (1988-1993),* 2 vols. (Rome 2009).

Frutaz A. P. *Le piante di Roma,* 3 vols. (Rome 1962).

Frutaz A. P. 'La diaconia di S. Giorgio in Velabro', in *Collegium cultorum martyrum: primo exeunte saeculo 1879-1979* (Vatican City 1980) 159-87.

Gatti G. 'Di un sacello compitale dell'antichissima regione esquilina', *BullCom* 16 (1888) 221-39.

Gauthiez B. 'La transformation des rues à la fin de l'Antiquité romaine: contextes, processus', in *La rue dans l'Antiquité. Définition, aménagement et devenir de l'Orient méditerranéen à la Gaule: actes du colloque de Poitiers, 7-9 septembre 2006,* edd. P. Ballet, N. Dieudonné-Glad and C. Saliou (Rennes 2008) 141-48.

Geertman H. 'Ricerche sopra la prima fase di S. Sisto Vecchio in Roma', *RendPontAcc* 41 (1968-69) 219-28.

Geertman H. *More veterum. Il Liber pontificalis e gli edifici ecclesiastici di Roma nella tarda antichità e nell'alto Medioevo* (Groningen 1975).

Geertman H. 'The builders of the *Basilica Maior* in Rome', in *Hic fecit basilicam: studi sul "Liber Pontificalis" e gli edifici ecclesiastici di Roma da Silvestro a Silverio,* ed. S. de Blaauw (Leuven 2004) 1-16.

Geertman H. 'Forze centrifughe e centripete nella Roma cristiana: il Laterano, la basilica Iulia e la basilica Liberiana', in *Hic fecit basilicam: studi sul "Liber Pontificalis" e gli edifici ecclesiastici di Roma da Silvestro a Silverio,* ed. S. de Blaauw (Leuven 2004) 17-44.

Geertman H. 'La *Basilica maior* di San Lorenzo fuori le mura', in *Hic fecit basilicam: studi sul "Liber Pontificalis" e gli edifici ecclesiastici di Roma da Silvestro a Silverio,* ed. S. de Blaauw (Leuven 2004) 117-26.

Geertman H. 'Titulus sancti Sixti', in *Hic fecit basilicam: studi sul "Liber Pontificalis" e gli edifici ecclesiastici di Roma da Silvestro a Silverio,* ed. S. de Blaauw (Leuven 2004) 127-32.

Gerardi F. 'Note sulla topografia dell'Esquilino settentrionale nell'alto medioevo', in *Archeologia del medioevo a Roma: edilizia storica e territorio*, edd. L. Pani Ermini and E. de Minicis (Taranto 1988) 127-37.

Gering A. 'Plätze und Staßensperren an Promenaden. Zum Funktionswandel Ostias in der Spätantike', *RömMitt* 111 (2004) 299-382.

Ghilardi M. '"Com'essa sia fatta io, che l'ho vista, vengo a riferire". La città di Roma nel De Bello Gothico di Procopio di Cesarea', *Romanobarbarica* 19 (2006-2009) 109-35.

Ghilardi M. 'Iam vacua ardet Roma: la città di Roma al tempo di Gregorio Magno', in *Il tempo di natale nella Roma di Gregorio Magno*, M. Ghilardi and G. Pilara (Rome 2010) 1-105.

Goldschmidt R. C. *Paulinus' Churches at Nola* (Amsterdam 1940).

Goodson C. J. 'Material memory: rebuilding the basilica of S. Cecilia in Trastevere, Rome', *Early Medieval Europe* 15.1 (2007) 2–34.

Guenther O. ed. *Epistvlae imperatorvm pontificvm aliorvm inde ab a. CCCLXVII vsqve ad a. DLIII datae Avellana qvae dicitvr collectio* (=*Coll. Avell.*) (Vienna 1895).

Guidobaldi F. 'L'inserimento delle chiese titolari di Roma nel tessuto urbano preesistente: osservazioni ed implicazioni', in *Quaeritur inventus colitur: miscellanea in onore di padre Umberto Maria Fasola*, edd. P. Pergola and F. Bisconti, vol. 1 (Vatican City 1989) 383-96.

Guidobaldi F. 'L'organizzazione dei *tituli* nello spazio urbano', in *Christiana loca: lo spazio cristiano nella Roma del primo millennio*, ed. L. Pani Ermini (Rome 2000) 123-29.

Guidobaldi F. 'Osservazioni sugli edifici romani in cui si insediò l'ecclesia pudentiana', in *Ecclesiae Urbis: atti del congresso internazionale di studi sulle chiese di Roma (IV-X secolo): Roma 4-10 settembre 2000*, edd. F. and A. G. Guidobaldi (Vatican City 2002) 1033-71.

Guidobaldi F. 'La fondazione delle basiliche titolari di Roma nel IV e V secolo: assenze e presenze nel "Liber Pontificalis"', in *Atti del colloquio internazionale. Il Liber Pontificalis e la storia materiale: Roma, 21-22 febbraio 2002*, ed. H. Geertman (Rome 2003) 5-12.

Guidobaldi F. 'Una domus tardoantica e la sua trasformazione in chiesa dei SS. Quirico e Giulitta', in *Res Bene Gestae. Ricerche di storia urbana su Roma antica in onore di Eva Margareta Steinby*, edd. A. Leone, D. Palombi and S. Walker (Rome 2007) 55-78.

Guidobaldi F. 'La chiesa medievale di S. Agnese in Agone', *RACrist* 87-88 (2011-12) 401-52.

Harmon D. P. 'The public festivals of Rome', *ANRW* 2.16.2 (1978) 1440-68.

Heinzelmann M. and Martin A. 'River port, *navalia* and harbour temple at Ostia: new results of a DAI-AAR project', *JRA* 15 (2002) 5-19.

Henze C. 'San Matteo in Merulana', in *Miscellanea Francesco Ehrle*, vol. 2: *Per la storia di Roma e dei papi* (Rome 1924) 404-14.

Heslin P. 'Augustus, Domitian and the so-called Horologium Augusti', *JRS* 97 (2007) 1-20.

Hillner J. 'Le chiese paleocristiane di Roma e l'occupazione degli spazi pubblici', in *Ecclesiae Urbis: atti del congresso internazionale di studi sulle chiese di Roma (IV-X secolo): Roma 4-10 settembre 2000*, edd. F. and A. G. Guidobaldi (Vatican City 2002) 321-29.

Hillner J. 'Domus, family, and inheritance: the senatorial family house in late antique Rome', *JRS* 93 (2003) 129-45.

Hillner J. 'Clerics, property and patronage: the case of the Roman titular churches', *Antiquité Tardive* 14 (2006) 59-68.

Hillner J. 'Families, patronage and the titular churches of Rome, c.300-c.600', in *Religion, Dynasty and Patronage in Early Christian Rome, 300-900*, edd. K. Cooper and J. Hillner (Cambridge 2007) 225-61.

Hoare P. G. and Sweet C. S. 'The orientation of early medieval churches in England', *Journal of Historical Geography* 26.2 (2000) 162-73.

Hopkins K. *A World Full of Gods: Pagans, Jews and Christians in the Roman Empire* (London 1999).

Hubert E. *Espace urbain et habitat à Rome du Xe siècle à la fin du XIIIe siècle* (Rome 1990).

Hülsen C. *Le chiese di Roma nel medio evo: cataloghi ed appunti* (Florence 1927).

Johnson M. 'The fifth century oratory of the Holy Cross at the Lateran in Rome', *Architectura* 25.2 (1995) 128-55.

Johnston D. *Roman Law in Context* (Cambridge 1999).

Jones A. H. M. 'The date of the 'Apologia contra Arianos' of Athanasius', *JTS* 5 (1954) 224-27.

Junyent E. 'Le recenti scoperte nella chiesa titolare di S. Vitale', *RACrist* 16 (1939) 129-34.

Kaiser A. *Roman Urban Street Networks* (New York-London 2011).

Kirsch J. P. *Die römischen Titelkirchen im Altertum* (Paderborn 1918).

Klauser T. *Der Ursprung der bischöflichen Insignien und Ehrenrechte* (Krefeld 1949).

Krause J.-U. and Witschel C. edd. *Die Stadt in der Spätantike—Niedergang oder Wandel? Akten des internationalen Kolloquiums in München am 30. und 31. Mai 2003* (Stuttgart 2006).

Krautheimer R. 'Die Kirche San Lorenzo in Damaso in Rom. Vorläufiger Grabungsbericht', in *Akten des XII. Internationalen Kongresses für Christliche Archäologie*, edd. E. Dassmann and J. Engemann (Münster 1995) 958-63.

Krautheimer R. *Rome: Profile of a City, 312-1308* (Princeton 1980)

Krautheimer R. *Three Christian Capitals: Topography and Politics* (Berkeley 1983).

Künzle P. 'Zur basilica Liberiana: basilica Sicinini = basilica Liberii', *RömQSchr* 56 (1961) 1-61, 129-66.

La Regina A. dir. *Lexicon topographicum urbis Romae: Suburbium*, 5 vols. (2001-2008).

Lais G. *Memorie del titolo di Fasciola e discussione sul valore storico degli atti de' ss. mm. Flavia, Domitilla, Nereo, Achilleo* (Rome 1880).

Lampe P. *Christians at Rome in the First Two Centuries: From Paul to Valentinus* (transl. M. Steinhauser, ed. M. D. Johnson) (London 2003).

Lanciani R. 'Scoperte presso s. Martino ai Monti', *BullCom* 21 (1893) 26-29.

Lanciani R. *Forma Urbis Romae* (Milan 1893-1901).

Lanciani R. *The Ruins and Excavations of Ancient Rome: a Companion Book for Students and Travellers* (London 1897).

Lanciani R. *Storia degli scavi di Roma e notizie intorno le collezioni romane di antichità*, 4 vols. (Rome 1902-12).

Lanéry C. *Ambroise de Milan hagiographe* (Paris 2008).

Laubscher H. P. *Arcus Novus und Arcus Claudii, zwei Triumphbögen an der Vita Lata in Rom* (Göttingen 1976).

Lavan L. ed., *Recent Research in Late-Antique Urbanism* (JRS Supplementary Series 42) (Portsmouth, Rhode Island 2001).

Lavan L. 'Public space in late antique Ostia: excavation and survey in 2008-2011', *AJA* 116 (2012) 649-91.

Lavan L. *Visualising the Late Antique City: Secular Urban Space* (forthcoming 2014).

Lissi-Caronna E. *Il mitreo dei Castra Peregrinorum (S. Stefano Rotondo)* (Leiden 1986).

Liverani P. 'L'ambiente nell'antichità', in *Santa Maria Maggiore a Roma*, ed. C. Pietrangeli (Florence 1988) 45-53.

Liverani P. 'Progetto architettonico e percezione comune in età tardoantica', *BABesch* 78 (2003) 205-19.

Liverani P. 'L'episcopio lateranense dalle origini all'Alto Medioevo', in *Des 'domus ecclesiae' aux palais épiscopaux. Actes du colloque tenu à Autun du 26 au 28 novembre 2009*, edd. S. Balcon-Berry, F. Baratte, J.-P. Caillet and D. Sandron (Turnhout 2012) 119-32.

Lizzi Testa R. *Senatori, popolo, papi: il governo di Roma al tempo dei Valentiniani* (Bari 2004).

Llewellyn P. A. B. 'The Roman Church during the Laurentian Schism: priests and senators', *Church History* 45 (1976) 417-27.

Llewellyn P. A. B. 'The Roman clergy during the Laurentian Schism (498-506): a preliminary analysis', *Ancient Society* 8 (1977) 245-75.

Lo Cascio E. 'Il popolamento', in *Aurea Roma. Dalla città pagana alla città cristiana*, edd. S. Ensoli and E. La Rocca (Rome 2000) 52-54.

Lo Cascio E. 'La popolazione di Roma prima e dopo il 410', in *The Sack of Rome in 410 AD: the Event, its Context and its Impact: Proceedings of the Conference held at the German Archaeological Institute at Rome, 04-06 November 2010*, edd. J. Lipps, C. Machado and P. von Rummel (Palilia 28) (Wiesbaden 2013) 411-22.

LTUR = Steinby E. M. ed. *Lexicon topographicum urbis Romae*, 6 vols. (Rome 1993-2000).

Luciani R. and Settecasi S. *San Crisogono* (Rome 1996).

Magi F. *Il calendario dipinto sotto Santa Maria Maggiore* (Rome 1972).

Maier H. O. 'The topography of heresy and dissent in late fourth century Rome', *Historia* 44 (1995) 232-49.

Mancini A. 'La chiesa medioevale di S. Adriano nel Foro Romano', *RendPontAcc* 40 (1967-68) 191-245.

Mancini G. 'Roma', *NSc* (1925) 225-43.

Marcus L. (2007) "Spatial capital and how to measure it: an outline of an analytical theory of the social performativity of urban form", in *Proceedings to the 6th International Space Syntax Symposium, Istanbul, 2007*, edd. A. S. Kubat, Ö. Ertekin, Y. I. Güney and E. Eyüboðlou (Istanbul 2007) 005.1-005.12.

Marucchi O. 'Resoconto delle adunanze', *NuovB* 11 (1905) 274-75 (273-98).

Matthews J. F. 'The poetess Proba and fourth-century Rome', in *Institutions, société et vie politique dans l'Empire romain au IVe siècle ap. J-C*, edd. M. Cristol, Y. Duval, C. Lepelley and L. Piétri (Rome 1992) 299-303.

Matthiae G. 'Basiliche paleocristiane con ingresso a polifora', *BdA* 42 (1957) 107-20.

McLynn N. ''Two Romes, beacons of the whole world': canonizing Constantinople', in *Two Romes: Rome and Constantinople in Late Antiquity*, edd. L. Grig and G. Kelly (Oxford 2012) 345-63.

Meiggs R. *Roman Ostia* (2nd edn. Oxford 1973).

Meneghini R. 'Edilizia pubblica e privata nella Roma altomedievale. Due episodi di riuso', *MEFRM* 111 (1999) 172-82.

Meneghini R. and Santangeli Valenzani R. *Roma nell'altomedioevo: topografia e urbanistica della città dal V al X secolo* (Rome 2004).

MGH. AA. = *Monumenta Germaniae historica. Auctores antiquissimi*, 15 vols. (Berlin 1877-1919).

MGH. Ep. = *Monumenta Germaniae historica. Epistolae*, 8 vols. (Berlin 1891-1939).

Montini R. U. *S. Anastasia* (Rome 1958).

Montini R. U. *Santa Pudenziana* (Rome 1958).

Mulryan M. 'Movement and the hero: following St. Lawrence in late antique Rome', in *The Moving City. Proceedings of the Colloquia Held at the Swedish and Dutch Institutes in Rome (2nd-4th May 2011 and June 13-15th 2012)*, edd. S. Malmberg and J. Bjørnebye (forthcoming 2014).

Mulryan M. 'The establishment of urban movement networks: devotional pathways in late antique and early medieval Rome', in *TRAC 2011: Proceedings of the Twenty-First Annual Theoretical Roman Archaeology Conference*, edd. M. Duggan, F. McIntosh and D. J. Rohl (Oxford 2012) 123-34.

Mulryan M. 'The Temple of Flora or Venus by the Circus Maximus and the new Christian topography: the 'pagan revival' in action?', in *The Archaeology of Late Antique Paganism*, edd. L. Lavan and M. Mulryan (Late Antique Archaeology 7) (Leiden 2011) 209-27.

Najbjerg T. 'Renaissance drawing: a section of the Subura neighborhood (*Subura*) including a large residential unit (domus)?', *Stanford Digital Forma Urbis Romae Project*, http://formaurbis.stanford.edu/fragment.php?record=39.

Najbjerg T. and Trimble J. 'Large section of the Subura neighborhood (*Subura*) on the Oppian Hill, including the Clivus Suburanus (*clivus Suburanus*) and a small bath (*balneum*)', *Stanford Digital Forma Urbis Romae Project*, http://formaurbis.stanford.edu/fragment.php?record=43.

Najbjerg T. 'A section of the Subura neighborhood (*Subura*)', *Stanford Digital Forma Urbis Romae*

Najbjerg T. 'Possible headquarters (*schola*) of a professional organization (*collegium*) off the Vicus Sabuci (*vicus Sabuci*) in the Subura neighborhood (*Subura*)', *Stanford Digital Forma Urbis Romae Project*, http://formaurbis.stanford.edu/fragment.php?record=47.

Najbjerg T. and Trimble J. 'Section of the Subura neighborhood (Subura) including the Porticus of Livia (porticus Liviae) and the Baths of Trajan (thermae Traiani)', *Stanford Digital Forma Urbis Romae Project*, http://formaurbis.stanford.edu/fragment.php?record=48.

Nestori A. 'L'acqua nel fonte battesimale', in *Studi in memoria di Giuseppe Bovini*, vol. 2 (Ravenna 1989) 419-27.

Nogara B. and Magi E. F. 'Un Mitreo nell'area del Palazzo della Cancelleria Apostolica', in *Hommages à Joseph Bidez et à Franz Cumont* (Brussels 1949) 229-44.

Nordh A. ed. *Libellus de regionibus urbis Romae* (Lund 1949).

NSc = *Notizie degli Scavi di Antichità* (1876-present): section writers not given.

Orlandi S., Panciera S., Virgili P. 'Attività edilizia monumentale nel centro di Roma nel V sec. d.c. A proposito di una nuova iscrizione del prefetto urbano Rufius Valerius Messala', in *Les cités de l'Italie tardo-antique (IVe–VIe siècle)*, edd. M. Ghilardi, C. J. Goddard and P. Porena (Rome 2006) 123-36

Orlin E. M. *Temples, Religion and Politics in the Roman Republic* (Boston 2002)

Osborne J. 'The Jerusalem Temple treasure and the church of Santi Cosma e Damiano in Rome', *BSR* 76 (2008) 173-81.

Pardi R. *La diaconia di Santa Maria in Via Lata, Roma* (Rome 2006).

Parmegiani N. and Pronti A. *S. Cecilia in Trastevere: nuovi scavi e ricerche* (Vatican City 2004).

Pavolini C. 'L'area del Celio tra l'antichità ed il medioevo alla luce delle recenti indagini archeologiche', in *La storia economica di Roma nell'alto Medioevo alla luce dei recenti scavi archeologici: atti del seminario, Roma, 2-3 aprile 1992*, edd. L. Paroli and P. Delogu (Florence 1993) 53-70.

Pavolini C. 'I resti romani sotto la chiesa dei SS. Nereo e Achilleo a Roma. Una rilettura archeologica', *MEFRA* 111.1 (1999) 405-48.

Pavolini C. 'La sommità del Celio in età imperiale: dai culti pagani orientali al culto cristiano', in *Santo Stefano Rotondo in Roma: archeologia, storia dell'arte, restauro: atti del convegno internazionale, Roma 10-13 ottobre 1996*, edd. H. Brandenburg and J. Pál (Wiesbaden 2000) 17-27.

Pavolini C. 'Le *domus* del Celio', in *Aurea Roma. Dalla città pagana alla città cristiana*, edd. S. Ensoli and E. La Rocca (Rome 2000) 147-48.

Pazzelli R. *La Basilica dei Santi Cosma e Damiano in via Sacra* (Rome 2001).

Pelliccioni G. *Le nuove scoperte sulle origini del Battistero Lateranense* (Vatican City 1973).

Pentiricci M. 'Damaso, protagonista dello scenario politico dell'Urbe della seconda metà del IV secolo', in *L'antica basilica di San Lorenzo in Damaso: indagini archeologiche nel Palazzo della Cancelleria (1988-1993)*, edd. C. L. Frommel and M. Pentiricci, vol. 1 (Rome 2009) 291-312.

Pentiricci M. 'Il settore occidentale del campo marzio tra l'età antica e l'altomedioevo', in *L'antica basilica di San Lorenzo in Damaso: indagini archeologiche nel Palazzo della Cancelleria (1988-1993)*, edd. C. L. Frommel and M. Pentiricci, vol. 1 (Rome 2009) 52-53

Pentiricci M. 'Lo scavo periodi 1-7', in *L'antica basilica di San Lorenzo in Damaso: indagini archeologiche nel Palazzo della Cancelleria (1988-1993)*, edd. C. L. Frommel and M. Pentiricci, vol. 1 (Rome 2009) 171-74.

Pergoli Campanelli A. 'Nova construere sed amplius vetusta servare. Cassiodoro e la nascita della moderna idea di restauro', *StRom* 59 (2011) 3-40.

Petrignani A. *La basilica di S. Pudenziana in Roma secondo gli scavi recentemente eseguiti* (Vatican City 1934).

Pietri C. *Roma christiana: recherches sur l'Eglise de Rome, son organisation, sa politique, son idéologie de Miltiade à Sixte III (311-440)* (Rome 1976).

Pietri C. 'Recherches sur les domus ecclesiae', *Revue des études augustiniennes* 24 (1978) 3-21.

Pietri C. 'Donateurs et pieux etablissements d'après le légendier romain (Ve- VIIe s.)', in *Hagiographie, cultures et sociétés IV-XII siècle. Actes du colloque organisé à Nanterre et à Paris 2-5 mai 1979* (Paris 1981) 434-53.

Pietri C. 'Régions ecclésiastiques et paroisses romaines', in *Actes du XIe Congrès international d'archéologie chrétienne: Lyon, Vienne, Grenoble, Genève et Aoste, 21-28 septembre 1986*, ed. N. Duval (Vatican City-Rome 1989) 1035-62.

Pitts M. 'Roman pool may be for early Christian baptism', *British Archaeology* 91 (Nov.-Dec. 2006) 8.

Platner S. B. and Ashby T. *A Topographical Dictionary of Ancient Rome* (London 1929).

PLRE = *The Prosopography of the Later Roman Empire*, edd. A. H. M. Jones, J. R. Martindale and J. Morris (vol. 1: AD. 260-395) and J. R. Martindale (vols. 2 and 3: AD. 395-527, 527-641) (Cambridge 1971-92).

Pornarès G. ed. and transl. *Lettre contre les Lupercales et dix-hiut messes du Sacramentaire léonien* (Paris 1959).

Prandi A. 'Il luogo dell'antica basilica di San Lorenzo in Damaso e l'Itinerario Einsiedeln', in *Archivio della Società Romana* 74 (1951) 161-67.

Purcell N. 'The populace of Rome in late antiquity: problems of classification and historical description', in *The Transformations of Urbs Roma in Late Antiquity*, ed. W. V. Harris (Portsmouth, Rhode Island 1999) 135-62.

Quinn Schofield W. 'Sol in the Circus Maximus', in *Hommages à Marcel Renard*, ed. J. Bibauw (Brussels 1969) 639-49.

Rapp C. *Holy Bishops in Late Antiquity: the Nature of Christian Leadership in an Age of Transition* (Berkeley-London 2005).

Rava A. 'San Ciriaco in thermis', *Roma* 6 (1928) 160-68.

Reynolds D. W. *Forma Urbis Romae: the Severan Marble Plan and the Urban Form of Ancient Rome* (Ph.D. diss., Univ. of Michigan 1996).

Ricci M. 'Crypta Balbi: l'area del mitreo', in *Roma dall'antichità al medioevo*, vol. 2: *Contesti tardoantichi e altomedievali*, edd. L. Paroli and L. Vendittelli (Milan 2004) 231-41.

Richardson. L. *A New Topographical Dictionary of Ancient Rome* (Baltimore-London 1992).

Robinson O. F. *Ancient Rome: City Planning and Administration* (London-New York 1992).

Roccoli A. *Santa Prassede, San Martino ai Monti, Santi Quattro Coronati: tre esempi di rinascenza carolingia* (Rome 2004).

Rodríguez Almeida A. 'Aggiornamento topografico dei colli Oppio, Cispio e Viminale seconda la *Forma urbis marmorea*', *RendPontAcc* 48 (1975-76) 263-78.

Rodríguez Almeida A. *Forma urbis marmorea: aggiornamento generale 1980*, 2 vols. (Rome 1981).

Rodríguez-Almeida E. 'I confini interni della "regio V", Esquiliae, nella *Forma Urbis Marmorea*', in *L'archeologia in Roma capitale tra sterro e scavo* (Venice 1983) 106-15.

Roueché C. *Aphrodisias in Late Antiquity: the Late Roman and Byzantine Inscriptions Including Texts from the Excavations at Aphrodisias Conducted by Kenan T. Erim* (London 1989).

Roueché C. *Performers and Partisans at Aphrodisias in the Roman and Late Roman Periods* (London 1993).

RRC = Crawford M. H. *Roman Republican Coinage*, 2 vols. (London 1974).

Rykwert J. *The Idea of a Town: the Anthropology of Urban Form in Rome, Italy and the Ancient World* (London 1976).

Sághy M. '*Scinditur in partes populus*: Pope Damasus and the martyrs of Rome', *Early Medieval Europe* 9.3 (2000) 273–87.

Saliou C. 'Identité culturelle et paysage urbain: remarques sur les processus de transformation des rues à portiques dans l'antiquité tardive', *Syria* 82 (2005) 207-24.

Saliou C. 'La rue dans le droit romain classique', in *La rue dans l'Antiquité. Définition, aménagement et devenir de l'Orient méditerranéen à la Gaule: actes du colloque de Poitiers, 7-9 septembre 2006*, edd. P. Ballet, N. Dieudonné-Glad and C. Saliou (Rennes 2008) 63-68.

Salzman M. *On Roman Time: The Codex-Calendar of 354 and the Rhythms of Urban Life in Late Antiquity* (Berkeley 1990).

Salzman M. 'The christianisation of sacred time and space', in *The Transformations of Urbs Roma in Late Antiquity*, ed. W. V. Harris (Portsmouth, Rhode Island 1999) 123-34.

Salzman M. *The Making of a Christian Aristocracy: Social and Religious Change in the Western Roman Empire* (Cambridge, Mass.–London 2002).

Santangeli Valenzani R. 'Strade, case e orti nell'altomedioevo nell'area del Foro di Nerva', *MEFRM* 111 (1999) 163-69.

Sapelli M. 'La basilica di Giunio Basso', in *Aurea Roma. Dalla città pagana alla città cristiana*, edd. S. Ensoli and E. La Rocca (Rome 2000) 137-39.

Schaff P. and Wace H. edd and transl. *A Select Library of the Nicene and Post-Nicene Fathers of the Christian Church: Athanasius: Select Works and Letters* (New York-Oxford 1892 repr. Peabody, Mass. 1995).

Scharf R. 'Der Stadtprafekt Iulius Felix Campanianus', *ZPE* 94 (1992) 274–78.

Sciubba S. and Sabatini L. *Sant'Agnese in Agone* (Rome 1962).

Scullard H. H. *Festivals and Ceremonies of the Roman Republic* (London 1981).

Seeck O. ed. *Notitia dignitatum: accedunt Notitia urbis Constantinopolitanae et Laterculi provinciarum* (Berlin 1876).

Sessa K. 'Domestic conversions: households and bishops in late antique 'papal legends'', in *Religion, Dynasty and Patronage in Early Christian Rome, 300-900*, edd. K. Cooper and J. Hillner (Cambridge 2007) 79-114.

Shackleton Bailey D. R. ed. *Anthologia Latina. 1: Carmina in codicibus scripta* (Stuttgart 1982).

Silvagni A. 'La basilica di S. Martino ai Monti: l'oratorio di S. Silvestro e il titolo costantiniano di Equizio', in *Archivio della Reale Società romana di storia patria* 35 (1912) 329-437.

Sinnigen W. G. *The Officium of the Urban Prefecture during the Later Roman Empire* (Rome 1957).

Sjöqvist E. 'Studi archeologici e topografici intorno alla Piazza del Collegio Romano', *OpArch* 4 (1946) 47-98.

Smith J. Z. *Drudgery Divine. On the Comparison of Early Christianities and the Religions of Late Antiquity* (Chicago 1990).

Smith R. R. R. *et al.* edd. *Aphrodisias Papers*, vols. 1-4 (Ann Arbor-Portsmouth, Rhode Island 1990-2008).

Sotinel C. 'Chronologie, topographie, histoire: quelques hypothèses sur *S. Felix in Pincis*, église disparue', in *Ecclesiae Urbis: atti del congresso internazionale di studi sulle chiese di Roma (IV-X secolo): Roma 4-10 settembre 2000*, edd. F. and A. G. Guidobaldi (Vatican City 2002) 449-71.

Spanu M. 'Considerazioni sulle plateae di Antiochia', in *Actes du Ier congrès international sur Antioche de Pisidie*, edd. T. Drew-Bear, M. Taşlıalan and C. M. Thomas (Lyon 2002) 349–58.

Spera L. 'Le forme della cristianizzazione nel quadro degli assetti topografico-funzionali di Roma tra V e IX secolo', *Postclassical Archaeologies* 1 (2011) 309-47.

Spera L. 'Il vescovo di Roma e la città: regioni ecclesiastiche, tituli e cimiteri. Ridefinizione di un problema amministrativo e territoriale', in *Atti del XV Congreso Internacional de Arqueologia Cristiana (Toledo, 8-12 septiembre 2008)* (Vatican City 2013) 163-98.

Spera L. 'Characteristics of the christianisation of space in late antique Rome. New considerations a generation after Charles Pietri's 'Roma Christiana'', in *Cities and Gods. Religious Space in Transition*, edd. T. Kaizer, A. Leone, E. Thomas and R. Witcher (Leuven-Paris 2013) 121-42.

Spera L. and Mineo S. *Via Appia I. Da Roma a Bovillae* (Rome 2004).

Spinola G. 'La *domus* di Gaudentius', in *Aurea Roma. Dalla città pagana alla città cristiana*, edd. S. Ensoli and E. La Rocca (Rome 2000) 152-55.

Stasolla F. R. 'Balnea ed edifici di culto: relazioni e trasformazioni tra tarda antichità e alto medioevo', in *Ecclesiae Urbis: atti del congresso internazionale di studi sulle chiese di Roma (IV-X secolo): Roma 4-10 settembre 2000*, edd. F. and A. G. Guidobaldi (Vatican City 2002) 143-51.

Stasolla F. R. *Pro labandis curis: il balneum tra tarda antichità e medioevo* (Rome 2002).

Sterk A. *Renouncing the World Yet Leading the Church: The Monk-Bishop in Late Antiquity* (Cambridge, Mass. 2004).

Stöger H. *Rethinking Ostia: a Spatial Enquiry into the Urban Society of Rome's Imperial Port-Town* (Leiden 2011).

Swift L. J. 'Iustitia and Ius Privatum: Ambrose on private property', *AJP* 100 (1979) 176-87.

Testini P. 'L'oratorio scoperto al "Monte della Giustizia" presso la porta Viminale a Roma', in *Pasquale Testini: scritti di archeologia cristiana. Le immagini, i luoghi, i contesti*, vol.2, edd. F. Bisconti, P. Pergola, L. Ungaro (Vatican City 2009) 887-928 (orig. publ. in *RAC* 44 (1968) 219-60).

Testini P. 'Nota di topografia romana: gli edifici del prete Ilicio', in *Quaeritur inventus colitur: miscellanea in onore di padre Umberto Maria Fasola*, edd. P. Pergola and F. Bisconti (Vatican City 1989) 779-93.

Thacker A. 'Martyr cult within the walls: saints and relics in the Roman *tituli* of the fourth to seventh centuries', in *Text, Image, Interpretation: Studies in Anglo-Saxon Literature and its Insular Context in Honour of Éamonn Ó Carragáin*, edd. A. Minnis and J. Roberts (Turnhout-Abingdon 2007) 31-70.

Tucci P. L. 'Nuove acquisizioni sulla basilica dei Santi Cosma e Damiano', *StRom* 49 (2001) 275-93.

Tucci P. L. 'Nuove osservazioni sull'architettura del Templum Pacis', in *Divus Vespasianus. Il Bimillenario dei Flavi*, ed. F. Coarelli (Rome-Milan 2009) 158-67.

Turco M. G. 'Analisi delle apparecchiature murarie. Conferme e nuovi apporti', in *La chiesa di San Giorgio in Velabro a Roma. Storia, documenti, testimonianze del restauro dopo l'attentato del luglio 1993* (Rome 2002) 89-128.

Ugonio P. *Historia delle stationi che si celebrano la Quadragesima* (Rome 1588).

Ungaro L. 'Note sulle strutture tarde del palazzo imperiale sul Palatino', *RdA* 3 (1979) 106-13.

Val. Zucc. = Valentini R. and Zucchetti G. edd. *Codice topografico della città di Roma*, 4 vols. (Rome 1940-53).

Vermaseren M. J. and Van Essen C. C. *The Excavations in the Mithraeum of the Church of Santa Prisca in Rome* (Leiden 1965).

Vielliard R. *Les origines du titre de Saint-Martin aux Monts à Rome* (Rome 1931).

Vielliard R. *Recherches sur les origines de la Rome chrétienne* (1941).

Visconti C. L. 'Del larario e del mitreo scoperti nell'Esquilino presso la chiesa di S. Martino ai Monti', *BullCom* 13 (1885) 27-38.

Volpe R. 'La domus delle Sette Sale', in *Aurea Roma. Dalla città pagana alla città cristiana*, edd. S. Ensoli and E. La Rocca (Rome 2000) 159-60.

Von Harnack A. *Die Mission und Ausbreitung des Christentums in den ersten drei Jahrhunderten* (3rd edn. Leipzig 1915).

Von Schöenebeck H. *Beiträge zur Religionspolitik des Maxentius und Constantin* (2nd edn. 1962).

Ward-Perkins B. *From Classical Antiquity to the Middle Ages: Urban Public Building in Northern and Central Italy, AD 300-850* (Oxford 1984).

Welin E. 'Ara Martis in campo. Zur Frage der Bedeutung und des Umfanges des Campus Martius', *OpRom* 1 (1954) 166-90.

Wellhausen A. *Die lateinische Übersetzung der Historia Lausiaca des Palladius: Textausgabe mit Einleitung* (Berlin 2003).

Whitehead P. B. 'The church of SS. Cosma e Damiano in Rome', *AJA* 31.1 (1927) 1-18.

Whitehead P. B. 'The church of S. Anastasia in Rome', *AJA* 31.4 (1927) 405-20.

Wiseman T. P. *Remus. A Roman Myth* (Cambridge-New York 1995).

Yegül F. K. *Baths and Bathing in Classical Antiquity* (New York-Cambridge, Mass.-London 1992).